PERFIDIOUS ALBION

The Origins of Anglo-French Rivalry
in the Levant

By the same author

Rebellion in Palestine

Anglo-Egyptian Relations 1800-1953

The Puritan Tradition in English Life

The Seat of Pilate

Arab Nationalism and British Imperialism

The Persian Gulf in the Twentieth Century

Iran: A Short Political Guide

The Making of the Suez Canal

Four Aspects of Egypt

Late Victorian: The Life of Sir Arnold Talbot Wilson

Mission to Khartum: The Apotheosis of General Gordon

Cromer in Egypt

Fiction

Trouble in Muristan

PERFIDIOUS ALBION

The Origins of Anglo-French Rivalry
in the Levant

JOHN MARLOWE

ELEK BOOKS
LONDON

Acknowledgements

Transcripts of Crown copyright records in the Public Record Office appear by permission of the Controller of HM Stationery Office.

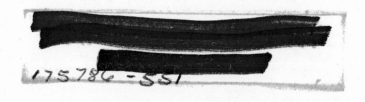

175786 -551

All rights reserved

Published in Great Britain by
ELEK BOOKS LIMITED
2 All Saints Street London N1

ISBN 0 236 15425 7

© 1971 John Marlowe

Printed in England by
Weatherby Woolnough Ltd.
Wellingborough

CONTENTS

The Levant during the first half of the nineteenth century.

INTRODUCTION

The epithet *perfide Albion* began to be applied by Frenchmen
to England after two centuries of endemic hostility between the
two countries, ending with the Napoleonic wars, had been
succeeded by the suspicious rivalry which characterized their
relations throughout the remainder of the nineteenth century.
It was occasionally, as in the Crimean War, muffled up into
a temporary alliance; rather more often it became embittered
up to, but never over, the verge of actual warfare, as over Syria
in 1840 and Fashoda in 1898. The Anglo-French Entente in
1904, which inaugurated a new and, as it proved, unexpectedly
permanent alignment in European affairs, by no means put a
term to it. As in an unhappy marriage, the enforced tyranny of
common interests made each party think the worst of the other.

This rivalry and suspicion, so much more corroding to mutual
appreciation and respect than the open hostility and continual
warfare of the seventeenth and eighteenth centuries, had its
origins in, and was mainly concentrated upon, the Levant.
Throughout all the political vicissitudes of their history, the
French have always regarded themselves as both the custodians
of European civilization and the heirs of the Crusaders. In this
light they have regarded the Levant—Constantinople, Asia
Minor, Syria and Egypt—as a Europa Irredenta, as the cradle
of Graeco-Roman civilization temporarily alienated to Islam.
This conception, almost grotesque as it may seem to-day, is
an identifiable thread in the tangled skein of French foreign
policy throughout the nineteenth and through much of the
twentieth century. It was a part of the motive behind French
policy over Bonaparte's invasion of Egypt in 1798, the subsequent French support for Mohamed Ali, the Crimean War, the
Suez Canal, the British occupation of Egypt, and the territorial
settlement of the Levant after the 1914-18 war.

In all, or nearly all, these matters, France found herself at
odds with England. Neither British policy nor British public
opinion attached any importance to the Europa Irredenta view

7

of the Levant. British policy showed a consistent preference for keeping the countries of the Levant under Moslem rule rather than for partitioning them out among the Christian Powers of Europe. In this preference, perhaps, may be discerned one of the roots of that widespread French suspicion, baldly enunciated by General de Gaulle, that the English were insufficiently European to be fit members of the Common Market.

It all began with the British acquisition of her Indian possessions at the Treaty of Paris in 1763. Thereafter, there grew up in England, being reflected in British policy and in British public opinion, a mystique about India analogous to the French mystique about the Europa Irredenta of the Levant. But, whereas the French saw their role in the Levant as one of re-introducing European culture to its peoples, the British saw their role in India rather differently. India was to become, not a number of Provinces assimilated to Europe, but an Eastern Empire ruled by Great Britain. The possession of India, like the possession of the rest of the British Empire, was seen as detaching England from, and not as assimilating the Empire to, Europe.

This Imperial mystique took some time to develop, but, well before the end of the Napoleonic wars, the security of India's frontiers, and the security of communications between England and India, had already begun to play an almost obsessive role in British foreign policy. In this context, the possibility of the occupation of the Levant by a European Great Power, or combination of Great Powers, was seen in much the same light as the possibility of a similar occupation of the Low Countries. The one threat was seen as 'a pistol pointed at the heart of England'; the other as a thumb pressed against England's jugular vein.

The latter threat was seen to be presented by both France and Russia. It was met by a policy of preserving the sovereign independence and territorial integrity of the Ottoman Empire and of so manipulating the Concert of Europe as to avoid a coalescence between France and Russia directed towards the break-up of the Ottoman Empire. The grand object of this policy was to keep the Russians out of Constantinople and Asia Minor, and the French out of Egypt and Syria, without going to war with either, and using the support of the one to frustrate the ambitions of the other.

The pursuit of this policy involved the necessity for a permanent and powerful British naval presence in the Mediterranean as a means of giving credibility to the exercise of British diplomatic pressure at Constantinople. It also led to a continual process of British interference in the internal affairs of various Ottoman Provinces. Given the reality of the threat, and the importance of the objective, the policy was pursued with great virtuosity and almost complete success until the rise of the German Empire, and the presence of a greater and more urgent threat to British security, led to its temporary abandonment at the end of the nineteenth century.

The legend of *perfide Albion* arose from a French conviction that this British policy, in so far as it was directed against France, was misdirected in that it attributed to France designs against Great Britain which she did not in fact harbour, and perfidious in that it was actuated by an unreasonable and unreasoning hostility, not only towards the French people, but towards the whole concept of the French civilizing mission in the Levant, which had the objects of preserving the Levant from Russian tyranny and of rescuing it from Turkish barbarism. When the first crunch came in 1839-41 Great Britain, in the person of Palmerston, was seen as allying herself, for entirely selfish and predatory ends, with barbarism and tyranny and against European civilization. Nothing that has happened since has erased this impression of British perfidy from the French mind, and much that has happened since, particularly in the Levant, has tended to confirm it.

This book, which traces British and French policy in the Levant from the British acquisition of India in 1763 to Palmerston's diplomatic victory over the French in 1840, leads to the conclusion that British suspicion of French designs in the Levant was chimerical. It was based on the real and intended threat to British communications with, and possession of, India posed by Bonaparte's invasion of Egypt. It was assumed, particularly by Palmerston, that post-Napoleonic French policy in the Levant continued to be directed against the British possessions in India. In fact, all the evidence goes to show that this was a complete misapprehension. The French, like the British, wished to keep the Russians out of Constantinople and Asia Minor; to that extent they, like the British, were interested in the territorial integrity and sovereign independence of the Ottoman Empire. But, unlike the British, they were prepared to envisage, without taking any active steps to bring about, a dissolution of that Empire. In such an event they looked forward to having a predominant influence in Egypt and Syria. But this anticipation was due quite genuinely to their ideas about Europa Irredenta and the French 'civilizing mission', and not at all to any hostile designs against England. (Although, obviously, in the event of France and England going to war over some other matter, a French presence in Egypt might have posed a threat to India.)

The British misapprehension arose from a total failure to appreciate the French concept of a 'civilizing mission', which they regarded as masking crude strategic and mercantile designs. For, from the British point of view, imperial policy was, at that time, only comprehensible in strategic or mercantile terms. It was not until some forty years later that the concept of the 'white man's burden' was evolved as the British equivalent of the 'civilizing mission' and as the ethical justification for imperial expansion. And it was not until over a hundred years later that the strategic and mercantile considerations which had dictated imperial expansion were seen to be illusory.

Palmerston's view of the Levant is illustrated by his well-known remark about a traveller between London and York not wanting to own all the inns on the road provided that he could be sure of getting his mutton chop at each of them. No more did he want to control the territories between England and India provided he could pass freely through them. But he had a grave suspicion of 'tied houses' and regarded the French 'civilizing mission' in the Levant as he would have regarded brewers' advertisements in justification of them. Like some modern travellers, he did not mind his inns being dirty so long as they were 'free houses'.

CHAPTER ONE

THE OVERLAND MAIL AND THE EASTERN TRADE

From the end of the fifteenth century onwards, the great discoveries by the navigators of Western Europe began to divert the main channel of world trade away from the Mediterranean and the overland routes from Asia and onto the high seas. Starting with Vasco da Gama's voyage round the Cape of Good Hope to India in 1497, much of the trade between Europe and the Indies which had previously passed along the overland caravan routes to the Mediterranean was diverted round the Cape of Good Hope, first by the Portuguese, the pioneers of this route, and later by the English and Dutch and, to a much lesser extent, the French. This trade was mostly in the hands of powerful monopolist national companies. The British East India Company, founded by Royal Charter in 1600, eventually became the agency by which the British possessions in India were conquered and administered and by which the maritime approaches to India were policed.

But the total expansion of the Eastern trade with Europe, which resulted from the influx of gold and silver into Europe from the Western Hemisphere, meant that a considerable volume of trade still continued to pass by the overland routes, although the bulk of it was diverted. Far more deleterious to the prosperity of the Levant than the diversion of part of the Eastern trade was the steady westerly movement of the centre of gravity of the world's material and cultural civilization, and the increasing isolation of Islam from the inventions and discoveries which were beginning to transform life in Western Europe. This isolation was self-imposed and largely due to Moslem consciousness of, and resentment at, the cultural and material superiority of the Christian West which was beginning to develop as a result of that quickening of the spirit in the West, known as the Renaissance, which set in train such a remarkable process of material discovery, scientific achievement and political enfranchisement. When the Crusaders had come to the Levant at the beginning of the twelfth century, the Saracens had been their superiors in all the arts of peace and war. The gradual shift of superiority to the West over the next six centuries confused and bewildered the Moslem world, which retreated into fanaticism and intolerance, thereby insulating itself from, and accentuating, Western superiority. Nowhere was this tendency more apparent than in Egypt where, by the end of the eighteenth century, largely as a result of the intolerance of the inhabitants for the peoples and customs of the West, contacts with Europe had become minimal. A characteristic example of this attitude was the prohibition of the main, or western, harbour of Alexandria to Christian vessels on the ground that its use by them would enable their crews to observe Moslem women unveiled on the roofs of houses overlooking the port. Instead, Christian vessels were compelled to use the new, or eastern, harbour, which was not overlooked by Moslem houses, but which had a sand bar, inadequate anchorages, and was very dangerous to enter or leave.[1]

This isolation, which became a matter of Ottoman policy throughout the Empire and which, acceptable as it was to all good Moslems, did much to commend Ottoman rule to its Moslem subjects, was accompanied by an Ottoman desire, for economic reasons, to benefit from the possibilities of trade with Christian Europe. The pattern of social 'apartheid' with commercial cooperation was set by the various 'capitulations' treaties between the Christian Powers and the Porte, the first of which was concluded between France and Turkey in 1535 and which, like all subsequent capitulations treaties, was applicable to all the dominions of the Ottoman Empire. The object of these treaties, which owed at least as much to Ottoman as to European initiatives, was, on the one hand, to enable Christian merchants to live in the Ottoman dominions with reasonable security for life and property and, on the other hand, to discourage any measure of social integration between Christians and Moslems. In any view of the complexion taken by the capitulations during the nineteenth century, when they were exploited as instruments of European privilege, it is worth remembering that they were, in their inception, at least as much a recognition of Moslem exclusiveness as they were a grant of privileges to Christians.

The pattern of life led by European communities in the Levant up to the end of the eighteenth century was conditioned by the capitulations treaties. The members of each European 'nation', which consisted entirely, or almost entirely, of merchants and their families, lived together in a particular quarter of the town under the leadership and protection of their Consul. Their place of residence, which was also a warehouse for their goods and a counting-house for their business, was known as a 'factory' in English and *échelle* in French. The merchants were members of the national monopoly company trading with the Ottoman dominions—in the case of the English the Levant (colloquially known as the Turkey) Company, and in the case of the French la Compagnie du Levant—and, by the terms of their membership, were subject to the rules and regulations of the Company and to the jurisdiction of their Consul who, in the case of the English, was appointed and paid by the Levant Company. The Ambassador in Constantinople, from whom the Consuls depended, was the head of the national community in the Ottoman Empire, the ultimate arbiter in all disputes, and the ultimate protector in all cases of difficulty and danger. The British Ambassador was appointed jointly by the Crown and the Levant Company.

The Levant Company had been founded by Royal Charter in 1581, some twenty years before the East India Company, and had a monopoly of all trade between England and the Ottoman Empire. Since this monopoly did not include trade between the Indies and the Ottoman Empire, the Levant Company had no incentive to encourage it and, so far as Eastern goods were concerned, preferred to purchase in England goods imported by the East India Company via the Cape, and re-export them to the Ottoman dominions. They also maintained that any trading in the Ottoman Empire by the East India Company was *ultra vires* the East India Company's Charter and an infringement of their own monopoly. The French monopoly arrangements with their Compagnie des Indes (founded in 1664) and Compagnie du Levant were less rigid. This helps to explain the different French attitude towards the development of the Eastern trade with Egypt which will be described later.

The 1535 capitulations treaty between France and the Ottoman Empire, which was successively renewed and expanded in 1569, 1581, 1597, 1604, 1673 and 1740, formed the basis of the capitulations regime under which the other Western

Powers later obtained analogous privileges. The 1535 Treaty provided, *inter alia*, for the following:

'That all French subjects and tributaries who wish may freely and safely navigate in armed or unarmed ships, travel on land, reside, remain in and return to the ports, cities and all other places . . . and the like shall be done to their merchandise' (Art. I). 'That only the ordinary customs and ancient dues and taxes' should be levied (Art. II). 'That their Consul shall hear, judge and determine all suits, causes and differences, both civil and criminal, which might arise between merchants and other French subjects. . . . The Qadi or other officer of the Grand Seigneur may not try any difference between French subjects' (Art. III). 'In a civil case against Ottoman subjects French subjects shall not be summoned without the consent of the Consul and only in the presence of a Consular dragoman' (Art. IV). All criminal suits involving a French and an Ottoman subject were to be referred to the Sublime Porte and not tried locally (Art. V). French subjects were to have freedom to practise the Christian religion (Art. VI). French subjects dying in the Ottoman dominions could have their property bequeathed according to their testamentary dispositions (Art. VII). French subjects only to pay Ottoman taxes and only to be subject to Ottoman military conscription after ten years' continuous residence in the Ottoman dominions (Art. XV).[2]

The French treaty also provided that other European Powers, including England, would be entitled to adhere to the treaty if they exercised their option to do so within eight months. None of them did so but, in 1553, Anthony Jenkinson, an English merchant adventurer, obtained, at Aleppo, a declaration from the Sultan which entitled English merchants in the Ottoman Empire to privileges 'in like sort as the French and Venetians use and enjoy, without enforcing any other customs or tolls whatsoever, save only the ordinary duties.'[3] Apart from this more or less unofficial arrangement, the first English capitulations treaty was ratified in 1583, two years after the foundation of the Levant Company. This treaty was on the lines of the French treaty and provided, *inter alia*:

'That English peoples and subjects may safely and securely come to our princely dominions with their goods and merchandise and ladings and other commodities by sea, in great or small vessels, and by land, with their carriages and chattels, and that no man shall hurt them, but they may buy and sell without hindrance and observe the customs and order of their own country' (Art. I). 'If they shall at any time be taken, they shall be delivered and enlarged without any excuse or cavillation' (Art. II). 'If their ships accost any of our ports and harbours, it shall be lawful for them to do so in peace and from there again to depart without any let or impediment' (Art. III). Art. VIII provided that no Englishman was to be arrested for another Englishman's debt, 'except he be the surety'. Art. IX provided for testamentary, and Art. XI for religious, freedom. Art. XIII provided that no Englishman was to be made a slave and Art. XIV that no Englishman should be called upon to pay poll-tax or head-money. Art. XVII provided that 'if any variance or controversy shall arise among the Englishmen and thereupon they shall apply to their own Consul, let them freely to do that the controversy may be finished according to their own customs'. Art. XIX provided that 'if Ottoman ships of war shall find any English ship laden with merchandise they shall use them friendly and do them no wrong'. The concluding Art. XX provided that 'even as we have given and granted privileges to the French, Venetians and other Kings and Princes, so also we have given the like to the English'.[4]

This treaty was successively renewed and extended in 1603, 1606, 1624, 1641, 1666 and 1675. The 1675 treaty repeated the provisions of the 1583 treaty and added a number of Articles:

'Duties shall not be demanded or taken of the English or of the vessels sailing under their flag on any piastres or sequins they may import into our dominions.' (Art. XXI. The English and most Western nations normally had what we should now call an adverse balance of trade with the Ottoman dominions and the excess of imports over exports was paid in coin.) 'The English may buy, sell and trade in our dominions and, except arms, gunpowder and other prohibited commodities, load and transport in their ships every kind of merchandise at their pleasure, without experiencing the least obstacle or hindrance from anyone, and their ships may at all times safely and securely come, abide in and trade in the harbours of our sacred dominions and with their own money buy provisions and take in water without any hindrance or molestation from anyone.' (Art. XXIII). 'If an Englishman shall be involved in a lawsuit, the Judge shall not hear or decide thereon until the Ambassador or Interpreter shall be present, and all sums exceeding £4,000 shall be heard at the Sublime Porte and nowhere else' (Art. XXIV). 'The Consuls shall never be imprisoned nor their houses searched, nor themselves sent away, but all differences in which they may be involved shall be reported to the Sublime Porte where the Ambassador shall answer for them' (Art. XXV). 'The English merchants, having once paid the customs at Constantinople or other port in our dominions, not an asper more shall be taken or demanded from them at any other place' (Art. XXX). 'The English merchants or other subjects of that nation may trade in our dominions on paying according to ancient custom a duty of 3% on all their merchandise' (Art. XXXIV). 'Customs shall not be demanded or taken on merchandise brought in their ships to Constantinople or any other port which they shall not of their own free will land with a view to sale' (Art. XXXIX). 'In case any Englishman, or any person navigating under their flag, commit manslaughter or any other crime, the Governor shall not proceed to the case until the Ambassador shall be present' (Art. XLII). Art. XLV provided for immunity for interpreters and other Ottoman subjects acting under the Ambassador's orders. Art. LIV provided that 'the English merchants, having paid duty on their merchandise at the rate of 3%, no one may demand or exact from them anything more without their consent'.[5]

These, and other, capitulations treaties were applicable, not only to the subjects of the European nations concerned, but to all persons sailing under those nations' flags. In practice, this led to a certain amount of abuse.

Up to the end of the eighteenth century British trade with Egypt, under the capitulations regime, never seems to have been very flourishing. In 1719 the British 'factory' in Cairo was described by the French Consul as 'three people comfortably installed, living well, but doing little business.'[6] In 1756 the British Consulate in Cairo was closed and in 1768, when James Bruce, the explorer, visited Cairo, there was no British resident there to offer him hospitality.

This lack of interest on the part of the Levant Company, which was fairly active in most other parts of the Ottoman dominions, derived from the increasing lack of security for Christian foreigners in Egypt owing to the conditions prevailing there.

Egypt had become part of the Ottoman Empire in 1516 after the Ottoman Sultan Selim had put an end to the Mamluk Empire by his victory over the Mamluk Sultan Qansuh-al-Ghuri on the field of al-Dabiq, near Aleppo. But, although the Mamluk dominions in Syria were brought under direct Ottoman rule, the Mamluk Beys in Egypt were allowed a measure of self-government. An Ottoman Pasha, or Governor, was appointed but, under him, the administration was carried on by a Mamluk Shaikh-al-Balad or Head of State appointed by the Pasha, and a Council composed of the commanders of the Ottoman garrison stationed in the country, of the Mufti or principal religious dignitary, and of several leading Mamluks. The country was divided into twenty-four Provinces, each of which was administered by a Mamluk Lieutenant-Governor, or Bey. An annual tribute was payable to Constantinople and Egypt was required to ship certain quantities of cereals annually to the Ottoman capital. The Mamluks were allowed to maintain their own army up to a maximum of 14,000 men and to mint their own coins, provided that the name of the Ottoman Sultan appeared on them.

This semi-independence naturally increased as Ottoman power declined. By the second half of the eighteenth century the Mamluks were once again the real masters of the country. In 1766 Ali Bey, the Mamluk Shaikh-al-Balad, having eliminated his domestic rivals by assassination or exile, drove out the Ottoman Pasha and, for a few years, became master of a virtually independent Egypt. In 1772 he was ousted by another Mamluk usurper and from then until Bonaparte's invasion, except for a short interval in 1786 when the Turks momentarily re-asserted their authority by the despatch of a military expedition, Egypt was given over to a series of internal struggles between rival Mamluk leaders. The consequent lack of security made the Levant Company unwilling to reopen the British Consulate in Cairo after its closure in 1756 and, when it was re-opened in 1786, it was, as we shall see, at the instance of the

India Board and in face of Levant Company opposition.

The Levant Company's attitude towards trading in Egypt is apparent from a Report on Trade in the Levant compiled by the Office of the Committee for Trade and issued in October 1790.[7] 'The trade of Egypt, which flourished for many centuries, is now on the decline. Many canals are now either wholly dried up or so decayed that they no longer answer the wise purposes for which they were made. It is computed that more than one-third of the land of Egypt which was formerly cultivated is now changed into a sandy desert. Egypt, from its fortunate situation between the Mediterranean and the Red Sea, is able to trade either with the rich countries of the south coast of Asia or with Europe. It was for many centuries the entrepôt and only channel by means of which any commercial intercourse between these distant parts of the world could be carried on. The wealth it derived from foreign trade was immense; it still continues to trade with many parts of Africa by means of caravans, but there is no country which has at present so little communication with foreign nations either in Asia or Europe and its commerce by way of the Mediterranean or Red Sea is now inconsiderable. The members of the Turkey Company say that there is little or no trade directly between Great Britain and Egypt but that British merchants still trade considerably through Leghorn and that there had been sent from Europe to Alexandria cargoes of lead, tin and arms which had been sold to advantage and that the returns were made principally in senna. The commerce of France with Egypt has for many years been greater than that of England but has of late diminished and is still on the decline. Leghorn and Venice are the ports which carry the greatest trade with Egypt. The country continues to provide in abundance many articles which might be exported with great profit, e.g. silk, flax, saffron, senna and many other drugs, and Egypt still produces a much greater quantity of grain and rice than the inhabitants can consume; their export would afford a very profitable freight to British subjects. Egypt would take in return many of our manufactures, particularly our fine cloths and stuffs, cotton goods, hardware, tin and firearms. The population of Egypt is still rich notwithstanding the oppressive government; Bengal and other parts of India were in former times enriched by commerce carried to ports of the Red Sea. The merchants of the Turkey Company, being asked why the British merchants had now so little trade with Egypt, answered that they attributed it principally to the disturbed state of the country. The authority of the Grand Seigneur in Egypt is now merely nominal and cannot give effect to the capitulations privileges. A Pasha is sent from time to time by the Porte to reside at Cairo who frequently amasses a great fortune, but who has no power except such as the Egyptian government allows him to enjoy. They dismiss them often and oblige the Grand Seigneur to send a new one as often as suits their interest or inclination. The natives of Egypt have an inherent aversion to European Christians residing therein, so that when Ali Bey endeavoured to encourage a commercial intercourse with Europe, and to commit himself particularly to the Russians, he grew unpopular and on that account was dismissed from Cairo. . . . If the trade of Egypt should be revived by a restoration of Turkish authority, the privileges granted to British merchants by the capitulations will be sufficient for their protection. If it should ever happen that a more perfect government should be established in Egypt by any other Power, it will then be time enough to think of making some Treaty with that Power.'

This Report does not denote a very high degree of official British interest in Egypt. But, ever since the position of Great Britain as the paramount European Power in India had been confirmed by the Treaty of Paris in 1763, there had been some intermittent British interest—official and unofficial—from the points of view of developing trade between India and Egypt, and, more particularly, of expediting despatches and correspondence between England and India by way of Egypt. The interest in trade was exhibited almost entirely by private individuals; the interest in the expedition of mail was manifested by the East India Company and, after its inception in 1784, by the India Board of Control, a Department of Government formed to supervise the administration of India by the East India Company.

Interest in the India trade was first stimulated by the explorer James Bruce, who visited Cairo in 1768, during the time of Ali Bey. He formed no very favourable opinion of Ali Bey's administration, and wrote: 'A more brutal, unjust, cynical, avaricious set of infernal miscreants there is not on earth than the members of the government of Cairo.'[8] Of Ali Bey himself he wrote: 'Ali Bey, with all his good sense and understanding, was still a Mamluk and had the principles of a slave. Three men of different religions possessed his confidence and governed his councils. . . The one was a Greek, the other a Jew and the third an Egyptian Copt, his secretary. It would have required a great deal of discernment and penetration to have determined which of these was the most worthless and the most likely to betray him.'[9]

In spite of these opinions, Bruce, going on to Jidda, discussed with the captains of several British merchant ships plying between India and Jidda the possibility of landing Indian goods at Suez instead of Jidda. As a result of a long-standing Ottoman embargo on the navigation of the Red Sea by Christian vessels north of Jidda, imposed in the interest of the Sherif of Mecca who derived a profit from the overland transit of India goods to Europe via Jidda, there was at that time no European commerce with the Egyptian Red Sea ports of Suez and Qusair. It seems that Ali Bey was anxious to divert the Jidda trade to Egypt and was quite prepared to defy the Ottoman ban in order to do so. The British captains, full of complaints at the treatment accorded to them by the Sherif of Mecca, listened favourably to Bruce's proposals. 'They complained grievously of the manner in which they were oppressed by the Sherif of Mecca and his officers. The duties and fees were increased every voyage and their privileges all taken away. . . . I asked them if I should obtain from the Bey of Cairo permission for their ships to come to Suez and whether there were merchants in India willing to undertake the voyage. Captain Thornhill promised for his part that the very season after such permission should arrive in India he would despatch his ship the *Bengal Merchant*. . . . The scheme was concerted between me and Captain Thornhill only.'[10]

Bruce then departed for Abyssinia on his famous journey to the sources of the Blue Nile and appears to have done nothing to develop the proposal until his return to Cairo in 1773, by which time Ali Bey had been deposed by Mohamed Abu Dahab, who ruled in his stead.

Bruce immediately started negotiations with Mohamed Abu Dahab for the opening of trade between Egypt and India via Suez. When he complained of the extortions of the Sherif of Mecca, the Bey expressed surprise that the ships of so powerful a country as England did not use their guns and beat Jidda down about the Sherif's ears. Bruce replied that in countries belonging to strangers the English never used force unless obliged to in their own defence. Eventually, after several meetings, Bruce agreed with the Bey that British ships could come to Suez and import cargoes from India against payment of duty at the rate of 8 per cent instead of the 14 per cent which was being charged at Jidda.[11]. On 1 February 1773 Bruce wrote to Thornhill from Cairo advising him of the arrangements he had made. 'At the desire of several of the gentlemen trading to Jidda in the year 1769 I have spoken to the Bey of Cairo that he would give permission for bringing the India ships directly to Suez. . . . Mohammed Bey expressed all the desire possible to have this speedily executed. He despatched this express in which I enclose the terms of our agreement. You will see that he renounces all presents which, however, it will be prudent to give. . . . He seeks 8 per cent customs and leaves to your option to pay this in goods or money, and 50 pataques anchorage for each vessel. Arrived at Suez you will do well to give notice to any of the houses you choose to attach yourself to. There are three French houses of note here . . . there is also an Italian house of credit equal to theirs but not so rich. You know what Turks are. I never saw one of them to be trusted in money affairs. You must keep your eyes open and deal for ready money. . . . There are no British merchants at Cairo, but there comes from time to time a wandering sort of sharper under that name either from Port Mahon, or from the Greek Islands, or from Leghorn and, after an establishment of one year, breaks and disappears. Be careful of having anything to do with them, for they will either rob you themselves or betray you to the Government or both. . . . If you address yourself to the Government . . . you may do it through the Venetian Consul, immediately on your arrival putting yourselves under his protection. He does not trade, but is very well-affected to our nation, and there is no Consul here but the French and the Venetian.'[12]

When Bruce returned to England, no enthusiasm was expressed either by the Government or by the East India Company for his initiative. He commented: 'It seemed very strange, considering the immense Empire which belonged to the British in the East Indies, that the East India Company and their servants should be so ignorant of the Red Sea and so indifferent to being better informed about a sea which washed the shore of their conquests and comes at the same time within two days' journey of the Mediterranean.'[13]

21

But in India there was great interest. Much of this arose from the desire of individual servants of the East India Company to repatriate the fortunes they had made in India. A convenient way of doing this was to export India goods for their own account to Europe via Egypt, thus evading both the East India Company monopoly via the Cape and the Levant Company monopoly of British trade with the Ottoman Empire. On receipt of Bruce's news a Suez Adventure was formed by three merchants, Albert Thornhill, Robert Holford and David Killican. A vessel, the *Bengal Merchant*, was freighted, with William Grieg as Captain and John Shaw as Supercargo, and instructed to proceed to Suez. The interest of Warren Hastings, the Governor of Bengal, was obtained, and a schooner, *Minerva*, belonging to the Bengal Government, was detailed to accompany the *Bengal Merchant* to 'assist in the navigation' and to make charts of the northern part of the Red Sea.[14]

Mr Shaw and Captain Grieg were charged by Warren Hastings to proceed to Cairo and to draw up a formal agreement with the Bey ratifying the arrangements made with Bruce. This was duly negotiated in 1773 with Jean Cassis, a Greek, who occupied the position of Chief of Customs in Egypt and who, in the absence of a British Consul, appears to have been used from time to time by Mr Murray, the British Ambassador in Constantinople, as his Agent. The agreement, hereafter referred to as the Warren Hastings Treaty, provided that Bengal goods could be imported into either Suez or Tur[15] against payment of $6\frac{1}{2}$ per cent customs duty, and that Bombay and Surat goods could be similarly imported against payment of 8 per cent duty. Anchorage dues were laid down and it was provided that British merchants could export goods from Egypt without payment of export dues.

This treaty opened the way to the despatch of several more British cargoes from India and provoked angry protests to Constantinople both from the Sherif of Mecca and from various Aleppo merchants dealing in India goods by way of the alternative overland route via the Persian Gulf and the Euphrates Valley. The Porte reminded Abu Dahab, through their Pasha in Egypt, of the traditional Ottoman ban on this trade, and also appear to have protested to the British Ambassador in Constantinople.[16]

The opening of trade between Egypt and India enabled the more rapid transit of private letters and public despatches between England and India. Merchant ships arriving at Suez from India invariably carried mail for England which was sent overland across Egypt and then onwards by one of the frequent sailings from Alexandria to a European port. Almost as invariably such ships, on returning to India, carried mail sent out from England to Egypt. Apart from the trading vessels, sloops and other small vessels of the Indian Navy began to come to Suez with couriers and official despatches for England. The East India Company, while objecting to trade between India and Egypt for the reasons given, were not insensible of the advantages of speedy communication. Up to that time the regular method of communication with India had been by sea round the Cape of Good Hope which took anything up to six months. Urgent mail was despatched fairly regularly overland by the Euphrates route via the Persian Gulf, Basra (where the Company had an agent), Baghdad, Aleppo, Constantinople and thence, in times of peace, by the ordinary mail route to England via Semlin, Vienna and Ostend. This was speedier than the Cape but slower than the Suez route and was subject to continual interruptions by banditry between Basra and Constantinople. Hence the East India Company's interest in the Suez route which, in 1775, led them to appoint George Baldwin as their agent in Egypt, with the principal task of trying to organize a regular mail service between England and India via Egypt.

George Baldwin was a member of the Levant Company. He had gone in 1760 to Cyprus where his brother was established as a merchant. In 1763 he opened a branch of the family business in Acre. In 1767 he returned to England and in 1768 went again to Cyprus as British Consul. In 1773 he went to Egypt with the intention of proceeding from there to India. This plan miscarried and he remained in Egypt, becoming interested in the possibilities of trade with India. In 1775 he went to Constantinople, where he made himself known to Murray, the British Ambassador, and from there to London where he obtained his appointment from the East India Company. He arrived back in Egypt in 1776 at about the same time as Mohamed Abu Dahab was killed in battle in Syria and just after Murray had been replaced at Constantinople by Sir Robert Ainslie.

Mohamed Abu Dahab was succeeded as Shaikh-al-Balad by Ibrahim Bey. But the Mamluk Beys were divided between support of Ibrahim, of the house of Abu Dahab, and Ismail, of the house of Ali Bey. For some time there was civil war between the two factions. At first Ismail succeeded in displacing Ibrahim, but soon afterwards he and his adherents were defeated and Ismail went into exile at Gaza. Since he had been supported by the Turkish Pasha, his defeat contributed still further to the decline of Ottoman authority in Egypt.

Baldwin's position was equivocal in that, as a private merchant, he was anxious to develop the India trade with Egypt, while the East India Company, whose agent he was, disapproved of this trade as an infringement of their monopoly. In a letter dated 22 January 1777 he addressed Ainslie, whom he had not yet met, 'entreating your countenance and protection at the Porte. I am established in a lawless country, and may be in need of it, though our best defence I believe is in a cautious demeanour'. He reported that a party of British-Indian officers had arrived at Suez in the sloop *Swallow* on their way to England and that their baggage had been seized and searched on their way through Egypt by order of Ibrahim Bey. He told Ainslie: 'Redress should be obtained. We are entitled to pass through any part of the Grand Seigneur's country with freedom and without molestation. Our ships by the capitulations can go into all the ports and trade. As communication via Suez is likely to become so important for intelligence and for other national concerns I should hope I might insist upon a proper exertion to ensure for it a future and I hope Your Excellency will obtain commands for this purpose.' Baldwin went on to explain that transit of mail only without trade would cause difficulty with the Beys, who would derive no profit from mail, and he advocated an insistence on the provisions of the capitulations treaties which allowed English merchants to trade anywhere in the Ottoman dominions. 'I say this with the knowledge that steps have been taken to prevent it, but I know also that in some disguise or other it will peremptorily be carried on and the Turk cannot prevent it. The first ground of complaint from the Porte is that the Sherif of Mecca will lose his revenues, and one answer to that is that the Sherif has already lost them by his tyranny to the English trade and that, though the Porte should deny us the port of Suez, they cannot force us back to Jidda. . . . The capture of Basra by the Persians has now stopped up this channel of supplies. . . . It may appear a disadvantage to the East India Company to permit it, but they cannot prevent it.' Baldwin ended his letter with a complaint against Jean Cassis, the Chief of Customs. 'The Levant Company has refused to appoint a Consul in Egypt and do disavow having anyone acting under their authority as such in this country. Now the Doganier (Chief of Customs) of Cairo is possessed of a letter from the deceased Mr Murray virtually empowering him to protect and act for the British nation, which he does in a very unfair and tyrannical way and unfortunately to my prejudice and to that of the members of the Levant Company who do me the honour to trade with me. The Doganier however persists in acting notwithstanding the verbal disavowal of the Company and says he will only be diverted by the authority who invested him. I depend on Your Excellency's justice to relieve me from this oppression.'[17]

Ainslie protested to the Porte about the infringement of the capitulations involved in the treatment of the three British officers. He told Lord Weymouth, the British Foreign Secretary: 'I have received the strongest assurances from the Reis Effendi (Turkish Foreign Minister) that the Porte will use every means to punish the officials. . . . He confirmed that the government of Egypt is in a state of anarchy which gives very little hope of their being able to accomplish it. . . . I am very apprehensive that they will form complaints against our ships going to Suez as we have no right to proceed farther up the Red Sea than to Jidda, and that would be the more disagreeable as I am informed that a large English ship is expected at Suez laden with Indian goods.'[18]

Ainslie was a servant of the Levant Company as well as of the British Government, and the hostile attitude he adopted towards the Suez trade from the beginning appears to have been influenced by the Levant Company's similar attitude. In stating to Weymouth that 'we have no right to proceed up the Red Sea farther than Jidda' he was ignoring the capitulations treaties and resting on the subsequent Ottoman prohibition, presumably because this was what suited the interest of the Levant Company. And, because the Levant Company were not interested in the question of mail, he was not very interested in this either. In reply to Baldwin's letter he wrote: 'The pretended right of navigating in the Red Sea for Frank[19] ships has already been the subject of much negotiation and occasional dispute at the Porte, but I do not think that this Court ever acknowledged such a right, or that she ever granted to HM's subjects, or to those of any other Christian Power, a privilege so visibly disadvantageous to the revenues of Mecca and Medina. The capitulations give to our ships the same right to navigate and trade in the ports of the Empire that were then enjoyed by the subjects of France, but this concession was never understood to be unlimited, as the ports on the Red Sea, as well as those on the Black Sea, have always been excepted. The matter was discussed during the embassy of my predecessor, Mr Murray, and the Porte did at that time notify all the foreign Ministers of their resolution that no Frank ship should in future be admitted into the port of Suez. On this account I have had the greatest difficulty in obtaining redress in the case for which you have made application.' With regard to Baldwin's complaint about Cassis, Ainslie replied that he would have to consult the Levant Company.[20]

In another despatch to Weymouth Ainslie wrote that the trade between India and Suez was carried on 'by private merchants or interlopers independent of the East India Company; it is equally disadvantageous to them as it obstructs their sales at home as it is to the Levant Company as it interferes with the export of East India goods, particularly muslins, from England, for which reason I have not thought it proper to object to the Porte insisting upon obedience being paid to the commands that henceforth no Frank ships shall be admitted into the port of Suez. But I have obtained a promise that proper indulgence shall be shown to such ships belonging to HM's subjects as may touch there in the interval necessary for making this resolution known. In the meantime I have written to Captain Paxton of the *Swallow* and to the C-in-C HM's Squadron in the Indian Ocean acquainting them with the determination of the Porte.'[21]

During the next few weeks Ainslie wrote several times to Baldwin and to the Foreign Office complaining of the embarrassments he was suffering as a result of the continual arrival of British merchant ships at Suez. (Ainslie was receiving regular reports from Egypt from an Italian correspondent named Brandi, who was Swedish Consul in Alexandria. When Baldwin got to hear about this, it became another source of grievance with him.) He sent to London a copy of a formal Note of Protest he had received from the Porte which drew attention to the recent British infringements of the Ottoman prohibition, asked for these infringements to stop and stated that the reasons for the prohibition were protection of the revenues of the Sherif of Mecca and the existence of dangerous reefs in the north of the Red Sea.[22] The Note concluded: 'Wherefore the Sublime Porte desires the Ambassador to take into serious consideration the reasons alleged in this friendly representation, to write to his Government with earnestness and to employ his diligence in preserving the constant friendship between the two Courts.' To Baldwin Ainslie wrote that the recent arrival of six British merchant ships at Suez had caused a crisis in relations with the Porte which 'went so far as to endanger the property of all HM's subjects established in the Empire'. He told him that he had sent a copy of the Porte's Note to London and that he had not 'the least doubt but that effective orders will be sent to India to put a stop to a practice which tends to hurt the interest of the East India Company and the Levant Company and to diminish HM's revenue'.[23]

Ainslie, in reply to his despatch enclosing the Turkish Note, was informed by Weymouth that 'the most positive orders have now been despatched by the East India Company Directors to their several Presidencies. They have strictly prohibited all persons in India employed in their service from trading to any part of the Red Sea except Jidda and Mocha; it is earnestly hoped that such orders may be despatched by the Ottoman Porte as may effectively secure from seizure and confiscation all vessels and cargoes which may have been despatched from the East Indies with British property for the port of Suez any time before 1 May next. . . . Your Excellency will use your most earnest endeavours that the East India Company may be secured in the privilege of passing despatches under their seal to and from the East Indies by way of Suez and that all vessels carrying such despatches and furnished with the Company's passport be suffered to enter that port and remain there without molestation provided that they have no goods or merchandise on board. This point is of so much importance to the Company that I must in the most particular manner recommend it to your attention.'[24]

Ainslie was not optimistic. Replying to this despatch on 17 September he wrote that the Sherif of Mecca, whom the Porte 'dare not disoblige', would probably object and that the Porte also feared that the granting of such a privilege to the East India Company would lead to a similar application from the French.[25] In a subsequent despatch he wrote that the Reis

Effendi had offered to carry the Company's despatches between Jidda and Suez by Ottoman vessels: 'I do not know how far this proposal may suit the purpose of the East India Company, but it is certain that the Porte will to the utmost obstruct the passing of packet boats to Suez in future.'[26] A few days later the Ambassador triumphantly reported: 'It is with real satisfaction that I have to inform Your Lordship that I have at last obtained from the Porte that all ships belonging to HM's subjects which arrive at Suez until the end of next season will be admitted to enter and in every respect treated with the same indulgence and courtesy as formerly.'[27]

But, early in the New Year, Ainslie warned the Foreign Office that 'no argument whatsoever will engage this Court to tolerate the free navigation of Christian ships to the port of Suez unless the Sherif of Mecca withdraws his opposition, nor would anything less than superior force protect such ships and their cargoes from the violence and extortion of the Beys of Egypt who have hitherto been their protectors only in consideration of the valuable presents made and the high duties paid to them.'[28] In fact, cargoes arriving at Suez after the death of Mohammed Abu Dahab paid much higher duties than those laid down in the Warren Hastings treaty. This did not prevent the goods from being imported and sold at a considerable profit.

Meanwhile, Baldwin had been bombarding Ainslie with letters, urging the advantages of the India trade, complaining of the oppression of the Chief of Customs, and bewailing the paucity of the support which he was receiving from the Ambassador. The tone of some of these letters offended Ainslie and, on 27 January, he replied sharply, reminding Baldwin that, 'when you formed your establishment in Egypt you knew the difficulties you had to encounter. To complain of them at present would be as uncalled-for as it would be needless. If you can engage the Levant Company to change the system I shall gladly concur in it. Thus far you have only dropt desultory hints that Egypt abounds in resources for trade and have made unsupported complaints against the Doganeer.' He then, somewhat unreasonably, having heard from Brandi about the high duties paid on the Indian cargoes which had arrived at Suez, requested Baldwin to obtain from the 'Doganeer' a refund between the duties charged and those permitted under the capitulations treaties.[29]

Baldwin, in reply, told Ainslie that he had tried to persuade the Levant Company to reopen a Consulate in Egypt, as British trade with Egypt was considerable and capable of great expansion. Since his arrival in Egypt two years before, and in spite of all the disadvantages under which he laboured, he had freighted fifteen ships and kept four in almost constant employment. (This appears to have been independent of any interest he had in the India trade.) He then referred to an interview he had had with the Turkish Pasha and gave Ainslie a budget of local news. He told him that, since the recent defeat of Ismail Bey, instructions from Constantinople about allowing British ships at Suez until the end of the following season would have no weight with Ibrahim Bey, whose position was that British ships would be received indefinitely at Suez provided that they paid the same high duties as before but that, unless these duties were agreed to, not one single bale of cargo would be landed. He added that Cassis was Ibrahim's adviser in these matters and indicated the futility of any attempt to recover from him the surplus duties paid on previous cargoes. 'The commands of the Porte have no sort of operation unless they favour the inclinations of the Bey; to attempt the contrary is ensuring his displeasure and the consequence, either immediate or remote, is always ruinous and disgraceful. . . . The status of the present government of Egypt is very unsettled. The remains of the former Ali Bey's house, who were principally instrumental in raising Ismail Bey, finding his intention of destroying them in order to remain alone, deserted and, by uniting with the fugitives, returned triumphant into Cairo. The power is now divided between Mohamed Bey's house, whose chief is Ibrahim, and some of Ali Bey's house, whose chief is Rozoum, but not without manifest signs of disagreement. Ismail Bey has retreated to Gaza with a body of 1,500 men and, it is thought, will wait the moment of their separation to take advantage of it and return to Cairo. The Pasha, who cannot be easy while this party reigns, having taken an open and vigorous part against them, will naturally favour Ismail Bey's return.'[30]

Ainslie's reply to this letter was in a more friendly tone. He congratulated Baldwin on his commercial success, promised him all the protection and help in his power, sent him a letter for the 'Doganeer' formally divesting him of his pretensions to act on behalf of the British Ambassador, informed him of the outbreak of war between England and France, asked him to

29

convey the news to India if a suitable opportunity occurred, and concluded by requesting him to send some coffee and 'medals, engraved stones or other antiquities'.[31] Baldwin answered in a style of sarcastic impudence at which he was adept and which cannot have contributed to the amity of his relations with Ainslie. Referring to Ainslie's request to transmit news of the outbreak of war to India, he made it clear that he had already heard the news from his own sources before receiving Ainslie's letter, and went on: 'On 7 May I despatched Captain Praen from Suez to Bombay and on 14 May Captain Barrington for Madras and Bengal with all the extracts relating to what had happened and I suppose that by the 20th of this month all India will be apprized of it. I was afraid I might have been too sanguine and too hasty in forwarding such advices until I had received the sanction of public authority. Your Excellency's injunction has relieved me in this particular and flatters me that the time which will have been anticipated by my spontaneous action on this occasion will enhance the degree and merit of the service.' He went on to draw the moral. 'The circumstance of our apprizing our settlements in India of an impending danger before any premeditated stroke can take effect is an irrefutable argument for the utility of the passage and will plead my excuse for insinuating to Your Excellency the necessity for applying for a new permission from the Porte for the packets and passengers of next season. . . . If the Porte could be reconciled also to the prosecution of the trade to Suez they would find their advantage in it. . . . I am persuaded that I could prove how little reason the Levant Company has to complain of it. . . . Mr Hastings, the Governor of Bengal, has declared that he considers the trade to Suez a matter of infinite importance and I am told he has remonstrated strongly to HM's Ministers and to the Court of Directors in support of it. It provides a market for a very great consumption of the manufactures of Bengal and thus employs the natives and enables them to discharge the principal taxes. . . . It unquestionably presents to us innumerable advantages in the surprising celerity which it affords to our despatches.' He went on to castigate, not unjustly, the Levant Company's objection on the ground that it hindered the re-export of India goods by them from England. He pointed out that the Levant Company had been given its monopoly for the export of English-made woollens and not for the re-export of India goods brought into England by the East

India Company. In answer to a query from Ainslie he told him that his own imports into Egypt from England were running at the rate of £20,000 a year and 'under proper encouragement would increase to double that amount'. He then requested Ainslie to use his influence to have him appointed British Consul in Egypt. He pointed out that the Consulage dues on imports approved by the Levant Company were divided 50/50 between the Consul and the Ambassador and estimated that, on this basis, Ainslie's share out of the India trade to Suez since 1775 would have amounted to 20,000 piastres. He con-concluded with his usual budget of local news. The expected fracas between Mohamed Bey's house and the dissident supporters of Ali Bey had taken place; the latter had been routed with great loss and Ibrahim Bey was now undisputed master of Egypt; Rozoum Bey had been arrested and Ismail Bey had sent his submission from Gaza.[32]

Meanwhile Ainslie had sent a despatch to London expressing the hope that the Directors' orders to India about stopping ships to Suez would be strictly observed, 'thus preventing complaints and putting an end to a very dangerous abuse'.[33]

In November Governor Reinhold of Madras sent Baldwin a letter which must have given its recipient great satisfaction: 'I have been favoured with your several letters by the sloop of the season from Suez. The intelligence you sent of the probability of war was the first and enabled me to prepare everything for the event.' He then described how this early intelligence had enabled him to capture the French settlement of Pondicherry immediately on the outbreak of war. 'I return you my particular thanks, Sir, for the early intelligence you gave me and have not failed to make favourable mention of it to the Company.'[34]

Towards the end of 1778 Baldwin went to Constantinople to tackle Ainslie in person about the Consulship and the India trade. While he was there the Sultan issued a Firman in very strong language forbidding any ships 'either with English colours, or with those of any other Christian Power' from navigating in the Red Sea except to the ports of Jidda and Mocha. After calling on all Moslem people to take warning from the example of India, where the Europeans, starting by trade only, had ended by occupying the whole country, the Firman declared that any Franks who dared to disobey this order would be looked upon as having disobeyed the orders of their own governments, and threatened that they would be treated as rebels and pirates: 'not only the vessels but the merchandise and effects will be confiscated and the captain and seamen will be made slaves.' Ainslie, reporting this to London, indicated that the only protest he had made about the Firman, which was in several respects contrary to the provisions of the capitulations treaties, was to provide that the prohibition and the penalties were extended to all Frank ships and not to British ships only as in the original draft. He does not appear to have protested against the implication in the Firman that the British government were in agreement with the prohibition and the threatened penalties. He mentioned, however, that he had obtained a verbal promise from the Reis Effendi that 'during next summer no molestation or hindrance should be given to English ships despatched from India under the restrictions mentioned in Your Lordship's order (i.e. no goods). Had I argued the thing further there is reason to believe that this concession would have been retracted.'[35]

In the light of this Firman, and of Ainslie's attitude towards it, any attempt by Baldwin to advance the cause of the India trade while in Constantinople was foredoomed to failure. In fact, he seems to have confirmed Ainslie in his view of the illegality of the trade by telling him: 'no orders sent out by the East India Company Directors will be effective to hinder the illicit exportation of goods in which even the chiefs of each Department have a direct interest, being the only means left for them to transmit their acquired fortunes to Europe.'[36] He also told Ainslie that 'the ruling powers of Egypt, the Beys, from motives of interest, for they receive large sums from the duties, besides large presents, will obstruct the views of the Porte and continue to prevent the execution of the commands they send for stopping the trade to Suez, and that, in case navigation stopped in English bottoms, the same would be carried under French or Imperial colours and, if necessary, those of some Nabob who, being Moslem, cannot be objected to by the Sherif of Mecca.'[37]

Baldwin's journey to Constantinople was not entirely fruitless from his point of view. He obtained from Ainslie an appointment (apparently unpaid) as his Wakil (agent) in Egypt. In a letter addressed to Baldwin at Smyrna, when he was on his way back to Egypt, Ainslie wrote: 'I send you with this packet the strongest commands for your protection which could be obtained from the Porte in favour of any person who has not a Consular patent. This I hope will answer the purpose intended, as well as for what immediately regards yourself as for those of HM's subjects who may go into Egypt. You will also find enclosed a letter by which I appoint you as my Wakil or Lieutenant in Egypt until such time as the Levant Company think proper to change their present system. . . . In case you find it necessary to appoint an agent at Suez in order to enforce my recommendation for obstructing to the utmost the trade carried from India and for the purpose of carrying the East India Company's despatches to and from these settlements, you have my full liberty to do it.'[38] In reply, Baldwin promised to 'use every means possible to suppress the trade now carried on from India to Suez so highly offensive to the pleasure of the East India Company and the Sublime Porte', but again made his point that it would be very difficult to get the Beys to facilitate the passing of despatches, from which they made no profit, unless these were accompanied by a certain amount of merchandise, from which duties and presents would accrue to them.[39]

Soon after Baldwin's return to Cairo two British officers crossing Egypt with despatches were arrested. Being informed of this by Baldwin, Ainslie procured orders for their release and pointed out that the incident underlined the necessity of adhering strictly to the requirements of the Ottoman Firman. Soon afterwards, Baldwin got himself into serious trouble. 'In May two Danish ships arrived at Suez, one under the direction of Mr Moore (English) which brought letters of recommendation from the Governor of Bengal to the Supreme Bey. . . . The other had several adventures (i.e. cargo) on board and the supercargo was a German, van der Velde. As they came under Danish colours and were recommended to the French house of Magellon, Noel & Olive, I did not interfere. Application was made for orders from H.E. the Pasha to land the goods, which was granted. Mr Moore, being the first ready, came safe and in good order to Cairo. But van der Velde's party, consisting of himself, St Germain (French), O'Donnell, Jenkins, Barrington and Waugh (English) were attacked. All died except St Germain and O'Donnell.' Baldwin then related how Ibrahim Bey, while pretending to cooperate in the capture of the bandits, seized the two ships and arrested Moore, O'Donnell and Baldwin himself, 'together with five gentlemen from London, some of them with public despatches. Mr Moore is yet in prison in the castle; Mr O'Donnell and I are arrested on parole.'[40] At about the same time, Ainslie received an independent report about the incident from his correspondent Brandi in Alexandria which alleged Baldwin's complicity and revealed that the intention had been to load the two Danish ships with a return cargo imported into Egypt from France and Italy.[41] Ainslie, in reply to Baldwin's letter, wrote to him somewhat tartly: 'I had already received private accounts of the affair and must note my surprise in not having had a line from you until regard for your personal safety induced you to apply for my protection. Although you have not attempted to give any reason for your being in company with a caravan, which was inconsistent with your situation as a member of the Levant Company, Agent for the East India Company, and my Wakil, I have nevertheless, with great difficulty, obtained the enclosed command for the release of such British subjects as are confined in Egypt, in which you are particularly mentioned. The determined resolution of the Porte to suppress the trade so long and so ineffectively complained of, increased my difficulties. I hope that what I have been able to obtain may serve to procure your immediate release as well as that of the other British subjects you mention.'[42]

But Baldwin, having asked for Ainslie's protection, had been making his own arrangements, which he detailed in a letter which did not arrive until after Ainslie's letter had been sent. 'The ships have been released and Mr Moore set at liberty and all the gentlemen permitted to proceed to their destinations. The government of Cairo did not consent to this without exacting from everyone of us a condition that we should never, collectively or separately, claim damages which had been sustained, nor commit any act of hostility or reproach against the government, that we should not even remonstrate to the Porte, nor demand any sort of satisfaction. Mr. Andrew Skiddy and myself are being kept as hostages for the punctual observance of this agreement. . . . The government here pretends to have acted in consequence of commands from the Porte to which Your Excellency was privy and had acquiesced in. Our liberty hangs on this—that Your Excellency should obtain a command from the Porte absolving the government of Cairo from any responsibility or restitution for the damage sustained as a result of their seizure of the ships and effects, and ordering a specific release of our persons.'[43]

Ainslie, not unnaturally, was furious. He told London: 'The whole tenour of Mr Baldwin's conduct appears to me to be highly improper. As a member of the Levant Company and as my agent for protecting the Levant Company's concerns and for obstructing by all legal means the trade carried between India and Suez, he could take no interest and much less a personal engagement in order to procure the restitution of two ships under Danish colours. . . . The request addressed to me by Messrs Baldwin and Skiddy amounts to no less than demanding the sanction of my approbation to a treaty con-cluded between a knot of adventurers composed of different nations and the Beys of Egypt. . . . The article on which these gentlemen say their liberty hangs would be equally impos-sible for me to obtain and absurd for me to demand.' He added that he hoped nevertheless to obtain their release 'as there is little appearance after what has happened that any further attempt will be made to prosecute a trade so dangerous in itself and so directly contrary to orders given in India'.[44]

In the event Baldwin broke parole and took ship from Alexandria to Smyrna. From there he advised Ainslie of his escape and made a bitter attack on Carlo Rosetti, the Venetian Consul in Cairo, 'as the man who has principally suggested and directed all the mischief and to whom I attribute the disgraceful necessity of leaving Egypt and many interesting affairs in a manner unbecoming my status and the credit I have always enjoyed'.[45]

The facts behind this incident, which created some stir in Europe and which, as Ainslie predicted, put a stop to the trade between India and Suez for some time to come, are obscure. It is clear from several letters sent by O'Donnell, one of the survivors, to Ainslie[46] that the 'adventure' was a private enterprise by various individuals who were interested in transferring their private fortunes from India to Europe. It is almost certain that Baldwin himself had a commercial interest in the adventure. It seems improbable that Baldwin's suspicions of Rosetti were justified, but it does seem that there was some kind of plot. The Privy Council Trade Report already referred to stated that 'suspicions have been entertained that the disaster was brought about by the contrivance of those who for interested motives wished to prevent the opening of a trade with India by way of Suez.' There were many who apprehended that the manufactures of India brought by this channel into the countries bordering on the Mediterranean might be sold there cheaper than the like goods imported round the Cape in England, France and Holland and re-shipped to the Mediterranean.

From Smyrna Baldwin proceeded to Constantinople, where his first action (in company with Mrs Baldwin who had shared her husband's adventurous residence in Egypt) was to attend a ball given by the Neapolitan Envoy in honour of the King of Spain's birthday, which was boycotted by the British colony on account of England being at war with Spain. For some weeks afterwards Baldwin indulged himself in a violent quarrel with Ainslie. In a formal Petition[47] to the British government, he blamed Ainslie for his acquiescence in the terms of the Ottoman Firman and claimed compensation for the losses he had sustained. In a long letter to the Foreign Office he repeated his complaints against Ainslie and expatiated on the utility of the Suez route from the point of view of the national interest, mentioning especially the early information he had been able to give to the Governor of Madras about the war with France.[48] Ainslie, apparently nervous about Baldwin's possible influence in London (he mentioned in one despatch that Baldwin was an intimate friend of Mr Edmund Burke), defended himself against Baldwin's accusations and roundly declared that Baldwin's enthusiasm for the Suez route was due to the fact that 'under the promise of immense profits he (had) engaged some gentlemen at home and in India to advance money and pay him commission for the Indian trade through Egypt' and that, as his view 'was merely interested and highly profitable, he dissimulated the risks and represented the trade as perfectly secure.' He attributed his 'late conduct', that is to say his accusations and his demands for compensation, to a desire 'to skreen himself from the pursuit and resentment of his deluded friends over the immense losses incurred by them'.[49]

The strange quarrel dragged on until October, when Baldwin and his wife left Constantinople for London via Vienna. At one point there was a physical scuffle between Baldwin and Ainslie when Baldwin tried to force his way into a meeting of the factors of the Levant Company held in the British Embassy. After that Baldwin was debarred from the Embassy building and was seen often at the French Embassy, where Ainslie suspected that he was intriguing for a renewal of the Suez trade under French auspices. He also suspected that, in his passage through Vienna, Baldwin had conversations with the Imperial authorities 'of a nature most dangerous to the interests of the East India Company'.[50]

While Baldwin was still in Constantinople, Ainslie received a letter from Cairo from a certain Richard Hughes, advising him that Skiddy had escaped from Egypt to Gaza, telling him that he was the only Englishman left in Cairo, and asking to be appointed as Ainslie's Wakil and East India Company agent in place of Baldwin.[51] This letter does not appear to have been answered and there was no British Consular, East India Company, or Levant Company representative in Egypt for the next six years, except for Brandi, who acted as British Agent in Egypt 'for the service and protection of HM's subjects who occasionally or accidentally pass through that Province and of British shipping trading to Alexandria'.[52] The India trade came to a standstill, although occasional despatches were passed through Egypt by way either of Suez or Qusair. But the principal means of rapid communication, such as it was, was the Euphrates Valley route.

But there was still some interest in the India trade via Suez. Possibly as a result of Baldwin's conversations in Vienna, the Imperial government began to concern themselves with it. In 1782 Cassis, the Chief of Customs, became an Imperial subject and was appointed Imperial Consul-General in Egypt. It was soon rumoured that he and Carlo Rosetti, the Venetian Consul whom Baldwin had blamed for the 1779 incident, were, with the connivance of the Beys, actively engaged in arrangements for the revival of the Suez trade. There then occurred one of those incidents which always seemed to crop up to defeat this trade. Cassis somehow got himself into trouble with the Beys, fled from Egypt by way of Palestine, and was eventually reported as having settled down in retirement at Leghorn. That was the end of the Imperial attempt (if indeed it ever existed) to revive the India-Suez trade.[53]

In the autumn of 1784 Saint-Priest, the French Ambassador in Constantinople, who had continually, although unsuccessfully, pressed upon his government the desirability of a French occupation of Egypt, but who was not particularly interested in the development of the India trade, was replaced by Choiseul-Gouffier, who was interested not in an occupation but in the trade. Towards the end of November Ainslie noted that the French packet boat commanded by Chevalier Truguet, attached to the French Embassy, had 'slipped out of the harbour and proceeded down the canal (i.e. the Bosphorus). A departure so unexpected is sufficiently remarkable.'[54] Some weeks afterwards there was news from Egypt that Truguet had arrived in Cairo on a mission from the French Ambassador and was in negotiation with Ibrahim and Murad, another Mamluk Bey who was associated with Ibrahim in the government of Egypt. Ainslie assumed that the French were negotiating for a revival of the India trade and obtained an assurance from the Grand Vizier that the Ottoman opposition to this trade was unaltered. Reporting to London, he suggested that the French might be aiming at introducing the flag of some Moslem potentate—perhaps Tipu Sahib, France's protégé and England's enemy in India—to the Suez trade. He recognized that 'the Beys of Egypt, in fact independent of the Porte, will have no objection to close proposals so particularly calculated to raise both their importance and their revenues'. He went on to lament that, having no Consul in Egypt, it was difficult to get accurate information, and suggested that the East India Company might be interested in making a grant, so that 'proper steps may be taken to defeat the dangerous views of our rival'.[55]

In London great interest was taken in Ainslie's news about the Truguet mission. During the course of 1784 the India Board of Control, under the Presidency of Henry Dundas, had been formed as a Department of government to supervise the East India Company's administration of India which, it was now beginning to be realized, had to take into account other matters besides the sometimes narrow commercial interests which actuated the East India Company's Court of Directors. The Board of Control's initiative led to a renewed official insistence on the desirability of arranging for a regular service of despatches to and from India via Suez and a less unfavourable official attitude towards the question of trade between India and Egypt. This initiative was due partly to the news of the Truguet negotiations, and partly to the views of Baldwin, who was in touch with Dundas and who, during 1784, had submitted to him a Note entitled *Speculations on the Situation and Resources of Egypt*, in which he warned him against French ambitions in Egypt and emphasized the importance of Egypt to England as a channel of communication with India.[56]

The India Board asked the Foreign Office for full particulars of the past history of the trade between India and Egypt.[57] The Foreign Office, in a despatch to Ainslie, told him: 'It becomes of great importance to us to prevent the attainment of France's views in Egypt', and referred to current rumours of French acquiescence in a Russian occupation of Constantinople in return for Russian acquiescence in a French occupation of Egypt.[58] This apprehension, which was short-lived, was no doubt inspired by Baldwin's conversations with Dundas, but the rumours did have some basis of truth. Ainslie reiterated that the Porte were still unalterably opposed to the idea of Christian navigation to Suez and reported that the French Ambassador had denied knowledge of any French attempt to circumvent this opposition. But he admitted that the Porte had no effective authority in Egypt and that he had reason to doubt Choiseul-Gouffier's sincerity.[59]

In August the India Board told the Foreign Office that the whole question of trade between India and Egypt had been the subject of their consideration and that papers on the subject had been put before Mr Pitt, the Prime Minister, who had suggested a conference between Dundas, the President of the India Board, and Lord Carmarthen, the Foreign Secretary.[60] The Foreign Office continued to express their anxiety to Ainslie about French designs in Egypt and to ask for more information. Brandi had now retired and Ainslie had no regular correspondent in Egypt. He therefore prevailed on Brandi, who was living in Constantinople, to take up some of his old Consulships and return to Alexandria. Meanwhile, he reported that, apart from one French packet which had arrived at Suez with despatches and was waiting there for return despatches, no French vessel had lately been to Suez.[61]

Soon after Brandi had returned to Egypt, he succeeded in obtaining a copy of a treaty which had been concluded between Truguet and Ibrahim and Murad Beys in February. He immediately sent it to Ainslie who forwarded it to London.[62] It was on much the same lines as the Warren Hastings treaty. It provided for the free access of French vessels to Suez, for the transit of goods through Egypt against payment of 3 per cent customs dues, and for the import of Eastern goods into Egypt against a duty of 6 per cent—4 per cent for the Beys and 2 per cent for the Turkish Pasha. The Chief of Customs in Cairo was designated as 'protector, supervisor and adviser' of the French merchants, and provision was made for the escort of French goods across the desert between Suez and Cairo. The treaty was subject to ratification by the Porte, but there was provision for importing goods immediately in anticipation of its being ratified. Ainslie, correctly as it turned out, played down its importance: 'I continue to be of the opinion that the same conditions for the sale and transit of Indian and European goods in Egypt might easily be obtained by any other nation who is disposed to deal with the government of Egypt and also that the mention of the Hatti Sherif (i.e. Ottoman ratification) and the stipulation in favour of the Turkish Pasha, who was not even consulted in this transaction, were only intended as a salve for the Ambassador and as an inducement for the Indian speculators to engage in this trade with the French flag.'[63] A few weeks later Ainslie informed London that the Porte were determined to 'devise the most certain and most expeditious mode of defeating the pretended commercial treaty with France' which was recognized 'as an insidious attempt to advance their own (i.e. French) interests by encouraging the Beys to slough off all dependence on the Porte'. He went on to quote Sir Richard Worsley, a recent English visitor to Cairo, as saying that the French in Egypt 'had little hope of commercial advantage' from the treaty.[64]

Meanwhile, things were moving in London. Early in 1786 Dundas obtained Foreign Office approval for the reopening of a British Consulate in Egypt and for the appointment of Baldwin as Consul-General. The Levant Company, which had got wind of negotiations to this end between the India Board and the Foreign Office, although they were apparently not consulted, protested to Ainslie that the intention to open a Consulate in Egypt on behalf of the East India Company was in breach of the Levant Company Charter and that they were 'anxious to prevent the mischief which may arise from the appointment of a Consul in Egypt with a view to opening a trade with India via Suez'. Ainslie, who had not been consulted either, wrote indignantly to the Foreign Office, enclosing copies of his correspondence with the Levant Company. 'I am bound to appoint such Consuls at the Levant Company's recommendation for the benefit of their trade in the Ottoman Empire. . . . I cannot suppose that a Consular appointment unconnected with the interests of the Levant Company . . . can depend from this Embassy.'[65]

Dundas, unperturbed by the protests of Ainslie and the Levant Company, continued with his preparations for the appointment. (Although it was a Foreign Office appointment, all the initiative came from the India Board, which drafted the instructions eventually given to Baldwin and Ainslie in connection with it.) In May he told the Foreign Office that 'the great end of Mr Baldwin's residence in Cairo is the opening of a communication to India through Egypt'. He stressed 'the importance and necessity of removing the present obstacles to that communication. It is a matter of great concern that at all seasons of the year we might avail ourselves of the opportunity which has hitherto been and which we trust will be again in our power for sending our despatches without interruption to India and for keeping up a constant and uniform succession of correspondence with India. This might be accomplished by the three ways of the Cape, Bussorah and Suez. The two former are always open to us, but, being excluded from the latter, a material interval occurs from the months of April to July when no other route can be performed as soon by nearly two-thirds of the time.' Dundas then referred to the past history of this communication and recalled that the British government had acquiesced in the prohibition of Christian trade to Suez but had been 'particularly insistent that communication should be kept open for the purpose of conveying the Company's despatches'. Although the prohibition on trade had been 'acquiesced in for a time, and while the prohibition was understood to be generally against the Franks, yet should we not consider such acquiescence to be a dereliction of the rights which HM's Government holds under the capitulations treaty of 1675. . . . For this treaty repeats and asserts in the most decisive and unequivocal terms the right, not only for the ships of England, but for all nations and merchants who come under the protection of England . . . to sail at all times in the seas leading to the Ottoman domains.' 'How is it that the Porte acquiesce in the treaty lately made between the government of Egypt and M. Truguet? We conceive that HM will not approve of such a treaty being concluded with the knowledge of the Porte if that treaty is to give preference to a rival nation and to exclude HM's subjects from all the privileges to which they are entitled by the existing capitulations.' (In fact, the Porte had not been consulted over, much less approved, the Truguet treaty.) 'You will probably inform Sir Robert that HM has been advised to appoint a Consul-General in Egypt who will set out immediately to fulfil the purpose of his appointment and forthwith negotiate such a treaty as shall put HM's subjects at least on an equal footing with those of the French King. Sir Robert will easily perceive the reasons for this treaty being carried on with the Egyptian government in the first instance are not from any motive unfriendly to the Porte, not from any inattention to the role of HM's Ambassador, but from the present weak and disordered state of the Turkish government, from the great delay which the negotiation of such a treaty would necessarily meet with at Constantinople, and above all from the recent precedent which has been set by such a treaty having been entered into and successfully concluded between the French and the Beys under the proposed sanction and confirmation of the Porte, which we infer from its being concluded in the name of a person deputed by the French Ambassador at the Porte. . . . Sir Robert should therefore be directed to obtain in the same way the final authority of the Porte to the treaty we are now about to set on foot in Egypt.' After stating that Baldwin had agreed to let bygones be bygones as far as Ainslie was concerned, and expressing confidence that Ainslie would do the same, Dundas went on: 'If the treaty with the Beys should finally fail, and if it should not be practicable after it shall have failed to obtain one from the Porte to the same purpose and to carry it into effect . . . Sir Robert should nevertheless immediately and peremptorily insist upon a right to the navigation for packets, though it should be offered separately and independently of the right to trade, but he should take care that in no edict to be issued by the Porte, and still less in any agreement to which by his signature he should make HM a party, should the right to trade be given up or called in question.' After approving the expenditure of up to £600 by Ainslie for such 'palm-grease' as might be necessary in Constantinople, Dundas ended by referring to the probability of Ainslie receiving instructions from the Levant Company to continue obstructing the India trade with Egypt, and stated that the interests of the Levant Company must not be allowed to override those of the nation, and that 'what has happened before may happen again, and perhaps it is not putting the case in too strong a light when we say that to the single circumstance of communication to India by this route being fortuitously open at the beginning of the last war with France, we owe the possession of all our establishments on the coast of Coromandel.'[66]

To Dundas' memorandum was annexed a draft of instructions to be given to Baldwin by the Foreign Office. These instructions, in their final form, were set out in a despatch to Baldwin, who was still in England, dated 20 June 1786. He was told, first and foremost, 'to make it your constant attention to discover the motions of the French within the limits of your Consulship'. He was then told that 'one of the most important objects of your mission is that of forming a treaty with the government for carrying on the trade of the East India Company through that country', and instructed to 'give your serious attention to the means of accomplishing this with as little delay as circumstances will permit. . . . Though there can be little reason to suppose that the Beys will object to give the English every commercial privilege which they have given to the French, and which it is in their interest to enlarge and extend, yet if they should not do so, you will still consider yourself at liberty to obtain a permission to forward the Company's despatches, taking care that no such permission contains any Article detrimental to the right which HM enjoys under the capitulations to trade in these seas. And when such a treaty or permission is settled you are to send it to Sir Robert Ainslie for the signature of the Porte in the same way as was done by Chevalier de Truguet.'[67] The instructions went on to forbid Baldwin to trade for his own account, to lay down his Consular duties in respect of protecting British subjects and property in his Consular area (which consisted of Egypt and Palestine) and of supporting the rights of the East India and Levant Companies. He was instructed to try to reconcile the Sherif of Mecca to Christian trading to Suez and try to induce him not to make any complaints to Constantinople when such trading was resumed. He was authorized to appoint agents at Gaza, Jidda, Tur and Qusair in connection with the service of despatches, for which a comprehensive plan was already being worked out between the India Board and the Post Office.

Baldwin left Falmouth in the middle of August in the sloop *Weymouth* and arrived at Alexandria on 18 December, having called in at Smyrna to obtain the Consular Patent which Ainslie had been instructed to obtain for him.

Ainslie was officially advised of Baldwin's appointment in a despatch dated 1 September,[68] although he had known of it unofficially for some time. He was told that it had been made with the two particular objects of 'concluding a treaty of commerce with the government of Egypt and obtaining permission to forward the East India Company's despatches via Suez'. All the arguments which had been set out in Dundas' memorandum were reiterated and Ainslie was instructed to inform the Porte and the government of Egypt of Baldwin's appointment.

Meanwhile there had been notable changes in Egypt. In March 1786 a Venetian vessel arrived at Constantinople from Alexandria bearing a protest from the European Consuls there against the proposed destruction by Murad Bey of the church and convent of the Fathers of the Holy Land, an Order of Christian monks.[69] The Porte, temporarily at peace, resolved to use this complaint as an opportunity to bring the rebellious Beys to heel. At the beginning of May Hasan, the Capitan Pasha (Admiral of the Fleet), left Constantinople for Alexandria with 'several ships of the line, three frigates, two sloops, a bomb-ketch, three galleys and two gunboats'[70] on a punitive expedition. According to Ainslie, Choiseul-Gouffier tried to prevent the departure of this expedition which, if successful, would have restored the reality of Ottoman control over Egypt and nullified the Truguet treaty.

Ibrahim and Murad put up little resistance. Cairo was captured at the beginning of August and, in September, Ainslie, kept advised of events in Egypt by Brandi, told London that Ibrahim and Murad had asked Baron de Thonus, the Russian Consul-General, to negotiate their submission to the Capitan Pasha.[71] The following month he reported that Ibrahim and Murad had been driven into Upper Egypt above Asyut and that the Porte were considering the abolition of Egypt's semi-autonomous status and the division of the country into a number of Pashaliks under the direct control of Constantinople.[72]

This turn of events, which suited the policy Ainslie had been pursuing, helped him to regard Baldwin's appointment with equanimity. He told the Foreign Office that it had provoked some surprise at the Porte but that he had reassured the Reis Effendi by talking of 'the great advantages which it was natural to expect from a commercial connection in the rich Province of Egypt' now that it was under the direct control of the Porte.[73] To Baldwin he wrote genially, enclosing his Consular Patent

(Berat), telling him of his desire to assist him in his mission, and commending the Capitan Pasha to him.[74]

The Capitan Pasha's success had not been so great as Ainslie had believed, and hoped. After the capture of Cairo he had appointed Ismail Bey, Ibrahim's old rival, as Shaikh-al-Balad and left to him and his adherents the conduct of operations in Upper Egypt. He himself remained in Cairo where he devoted himself primarily to self-enrichment by plundering the property of the absent Beys. Eventually a truce was agreed between Ismail on the one hand and Ibrahim and Murad on the other by which the latter were allowed the administration of Egypt above Girga provided they remained there with their followers. A garrison was stationed at Girga to see that the truce was observed and, so long as the Capitan Pasha remained in Egypt, Ismail, the Ottoman nominee, remained secure in the possession of Lower Egypt.

Baldwin, having set up his establishment in Alexandria (throughout the period of his mission he never opened an office in Cairo), proceeded to Cairo in February 1787 to present his credentials to the Capitan Pasha. He told him: 'HM has sent me to Egypt to resume the exercise of our rights in accordance with the sacred capitulations . . . including the right of navigating the Red Sea and of frequenting all the ports along its coasts', and requested him to assist the English nation in the free exercise and enjoyment of these rights. . . . 'The Capitan Pasha replied that most certainly the English should be protected in all that the capitulations warranted; with regard to Suez, he must consult the Porte.'[75] In spite of several further conversations with the Capitan Pasha, Baldwin got nothing more from him than vague promises and expressions of goodwill. In Constantinople Ainslie also did his best with the Porte. 'I urged that the only reasonable objection to the passage of our ships was removed by the extirpation of the rebel Beys. . . . I also said that it would assist Ottoman rule in Egypt to allow trade with India, which would increase the prosperity of Egypt.' The Grand Vizier replied that 'until the beast was killed he could not dispose of the skin' and presciently warned Ainslie that the rebellion in Egypt was by no means at an end.[76]

In the autumn of 1787 the complexion of affairs in Egypt again changed. War had broken out between Turkey and Russia and, in October, the Capitan Pasha and his fleet were recalled from Egypt. With them departed the precarious basis of Ottoman authority. By the end of the year the country was in a state of civil war, which lasted for four years and was accompanied by an outbreak of famine and plague. Ismail, installed by the Capitan Pasha as Shaikh-al-Balad, died of the plague in 1791. His troops had already been decimated by the disease, but those of Ibrahim and Murad, in Upper Egypt, had been able to keep themselves immune by drawing a *cordon sanitaire* across the Nile Valley south of Cairo, an action which, involving the withholding of food supplies from Upper Egypt to the capital, contributed to the famine. After Ismail's death Ibrahim and Murad occupied Cairo. The Porte, unsuccessfully at war with Russia and Austria, were in no position to assert their authority in Egypt. They recognized Ibrahim as Shaikh-al-Balad and gave Murad, who had become Commander of the Mamluk armed forces, the honorific title of Amir-al-Hajj (Leader of the Pilgrimage). The victorious pair, although they made no formal attempt to declare their independence of Constantinople, governed, or misgoverned, Egypt as they chose for the next seven years.

For some time after Baldwin's appointment the British government continued energetically to press the question of expediting despatches through Egypt. In April 1788 Baldwin assured London that he had 'succeeded with the actual government of Cairo in gaining permission that all despatches and passengers who may arrive in the Company's packets may freely land and pass through the country without molestation', and expressed his confidence that he would be able to obtain similar facilities from any government which might displace that of Ismail.[77] In Constantinople, the Porte continued to procrastinate in face of Ainslie's representations. By the end of 1788 the British government were beginning to lose interest in Egypt. Occasional British and French vessels arrived at Suez bringing and collecting, without molestation, official mail and passengers. Some of these vessels also carried small quantities of merchandise. But there was nothing like a regular service of mail or exchange of trade.

Baldwin tried in vain to maintain British official interest in Egypt. He warned London about (mostly imaginary) French, Russian and Austrian designs on that country. He made much of an attempt by Baron de Thonus, the Russian ex-Consul General, to return there in 1788 at the instance of Ibrahim and

Murad. He made a great to-do about mysterious French emissaries passing through Egypt on their way to India. He protested over British dilatoriness at organizing a mail service. He expatiated on the advantages of trade with Egypt, and sneered at the cautious attitude displayed by the Levant Company.

Ainslie, from 1788 until his retirement in 1793, absorbed in the problems which arose from the war with Austria and Russia and from subsequent peace negotiations, completely ignored Baldwin and almost completely ignored Egypt.

In February 1793, so minimal had British official interest in Egypt become, it was decided once more to abolish the British Consulate-General there. In a curt note from Grenville, the Foreign Secretary, Baldwin was told that 'HM has no further occasion for your services as Consul-General in Egypt' and was informed that his allowances as Consul-General would cease as from April of that year.[78]

At the beginning of 1794 Baldwin, ignoring, or possibly still ignorant of, his dismissal, and encouraged by Ainslie's replacement at Constantinople by Mr (afterwards Sir Robert) Liston, concluded a formal treaty with Ibrahim and Murad on the lines of the Truguet treaty of 1785. With a despatch dated 20 May 1794 sent to England by the hand of a Major Macdonald, who had arrived at Suez from India by the sloop *Panther*, he enclosed a copy of his treaty, explaining that 'the government of Egypt, after the death of Ismail, having acquired a degree of stability under Ibrahim Bey, now Shaikh-al-Balad, and Murad Bey, and a new Ambassador having been appointed to the Porte, Mr Baldwin immediately reverted to the object of his mission and concluded the treaty in question, fully persuaded that Mr Liston will find it far from a difficult problem to obtain the sanction which the Beys request from the Porte. The utility of the passage to the East India Company has been so fully proved by the military events, but the Beys have no interest in providing the conveyance of letters. The re-establishment of the trade therefore will always ensure the Company's free correspondence with their settlements.'[79] The enclosed text of the treaty, after referring to the capitulations by which British ships were authorized to trade with all parts of the Ottoman dominions, provided (a) for the British to be treated on a 'most favoured nation' basis in Egypt; (b) for British ships to enter and leave any port in Egypt; (c) for disputes between

Moslems and British subjects to be dealt with according to the capitulations treaties; and (d) for 3 per cent import duty to be paid to the Porte and 6 per cent to the Beys in respect of India goods, and only 3 per cent import duty on other goods. As in the Truguet treaty provision was made for ratification by the Porte, but 'fearing the impatience of the Beys upon every arrival of empty packets at Suez', Baldwin sent his secretary, Willis, to India on the return voyage of the sloop *Panther* with letters to the Presidents and Councils of Bombay, Bengal and Madras, enclosing a copy of the treaty, stating that the Porte's ratification was merely a formality, and asking them to expedite the sending of cargoes to Suez.[80]

As it happened, Willis died on the voyage to India and no cargoes were despatched as a result of Baldwin's treaty. In Constantinople, Liston, whose letter of instructions on his appointment[81] had contained no special reference to Egypt, and who does not appear to have been informed of Baldwin's dismissal, was somewhat alarmed at being told by Baldwin that 'confident of Your Excellency's dispassionate candour and patriotism, I have taken it upon me to give the Beys the assurance that the treaty will receive the sanction of the Porte'.[82] He asked London for instructions and, tracing the history of previous negotiations with the Porte, pointed out the unlikelihood of their ratifying Baldwin's treaty. He suggested that it would be unwise to ask them to do so since 'it appears possible that the Porte will not only refuse but issue rigorous orders to prevent the reception of the ships expected'. He added that he had informed Baldwin of the difficulties, 'but it appears very uncertain whether my advice will be attended with effect'.[83]

Early in 1795 a messenger bearing Indian despatches across Egypt, who had arrived at Suez by the sloop *Panther*, was murdered in the desert.[84] This incident gave point to Baldwin's warning that the Beys would not tolerate the traffic in despatches, from which they derived no profit, unless it were accompanied by trade. But the British government was no longer interested in Egypt. The Baldwin treaty, like the Truguet treaty, remained a dead letter, although the transit of passengers and mail across Egypt went on intermittently, with Baldwin's assistance, until his departure in 1798.

It was not until the end of March 1796 that Baldwin acknowledged having received official intimation of his dismissal in the form of a duplicate of the original despatch, said by him to have been received on 10 March 1796.[85] Not unnaturally, he requested that the emoluments of his office should be paid up to that date, a request which was not granted at the time. He continued to act as East India Company Agent in Egypt, at a salary of £500 a year, and, in that capacity, corresponded with Dundas (who was now Secretary of State for War, although Baldwin apparently thought that he was still President of the India Board) and arranged for the transit of such occasional East India Company despatches and passengers as continued to be routed through Egypt. He protested, vigorously but in vain, both to Grenville and to Dundas against the abolition of the Consulate, stating that neither the prestige nor the emoluments of the East India Company agency were sufficient to provide adequately for the duties he was performing. He also, with equal vigour and equal lack of success, pressed upon Grenville and Dundas a scheme for the bulk buying of corn from Egypt.[86]

During his last few years in Egypt Baldwin had a difficult time with Ibrahim and Murad, which he ascribed to the British failure to implement his treaty. In May 1796 he wrote to the Governor of Bengal: 'The ill-humour strongly and frequently expressed by the Beys at our making of their country a mere conveniency . . . may make it advisable to proceed with great caution in coming to Suez.'[87]

He left Egypt in March 1798, only a few weeks before the arrival of Bonaparte's invading army. Writing to Dundas from Greece soon after his departure, he told him that 'the Beys hold all authority but their own in contempt', expressed the view that all Europeans should be advised to leave the country, and concluded that 'what may then ensue is a question to which it may be proper for a Ministry having the safety of India confided to its watch to keep in constant regard'.[88]

CHAPTER TWO

THE FRENCH INVASION OF EGYPT

From the time of St Louis's Crusade in the thirteenth century France had always shown considerable interest in Egypt. After the discovery and development of the Cape route to the Indies, the powerful Marseille trading interest, with a view to off-setting the diversion of the Eastern trade by the long-sea route, had tried to encourage the development of Egypt as an entrepôt for this trade. Throughout the seventeenth and eighteenth centuries the French government received several proposals, from their Ambassadors in Constantinople, from their Consuls in Egypt, and from numerous individuals actuated by commercial, missionary or idealistic motives, for a French occupation of Egypt. Successive French governments paid no attention to these proposals but were interested in developing trade between France and the Levant generally. France was the first nation to conclude a capitulations treaty with Turkey (in 1535) and held the lion's share of the trade between Egypt and Europe.

After the Seven Years' War had ended in 1763 with the Treaty of Paris, French interest in Egypt was sharpened by the possibilities of using that country both as a means of harrassing the British in India and as a colony (i.e. as a source of raw materials and as a market for manufactures) to replace her lost possessions in the West Indies. Saint-Priest, their Ambassador in Constantinople, was an ardent protagonist of a French occupation of Egypt. In 1777 he sent an Hungarian adventurer, Baron de Tott, temporarily in the French service, to Egypt, ostensibly on a tour of inspection of the French *échelles*, or trading stations, there, but in reality to draw up a plan for a possible French invasion. In 1783 Mure, the French Consul-General in Cairo, in a long report, recommended a French military occupation and drew up a detailed scheme for the subsequent administration and exploitation of Egypt. The views and ambitions of these French diplomats 'on the spot', which coincided with those of French merchants in Egypt, were known to, or suspected by, locally resident Englishmen such as Baldwin, who was tireless in warning the British government of French designs on Egypt and of the importance of Egypt from the point of view of British communications with India.

But pre-Revolutionary French governments were little more interested in Egypt than contemporary British ones, and were not prepared to risk precipitating a European crisis by any adventure there. Choiseul-Gouffier, who replaced Saint-Priest in 1784, although suspected of all kinds of mischief by Ainslie, was in fact opposed to any idea of a French occupation, and the object of the Truguet treaty was genuinely commercial, without any imperialist *arrière pensée*. As we have seen, this treaty came to nothing, mainly because Ibrahim and Murad, by their exactions against the foreign merchant communities, soon reduced all foreign trade to a trickle.

After the Revolution in France and the departure from Egypt of Mure, the Consul-General, Charles Magellon, a French merchant long established in Cairo, who had assisted Truguet in the negotiation of his treaty, assumed the unofficial leadership of the French community. In 1791 he went to France to report on the state of French trade in Egypt and, in 1793, he returned there as Consul-General. By that time Ibrahim and Murad had made the position of all the foreign communities in Egypt almost impossible by their exactions and, in 1795, Thainville, an emissary from the French Embassy in Constantinople, visited Egypt in an unsuccessful attempt to arrive at some *modus vivendi* between the Beys and the French merchants. Baldwin was highly suspicious of 'Tinville's' activities (England and France had been at war for the past two years), but he appears to have had no ulterior designs.

Magellon was a strong advocate of a French occupation of Egypt as a means both of getting the French merchants out of the clutches of Ibrahim and Murad and of carrying on war against the English. For he was convinced that the English, unless the French forestalled them, would inevitably occupy Egypt themselves as a means of safeguarding their communications with India. He reported to Paris in this sense after the failure of the Thainville mission and was invited to return home for consultations with the Directory. He arrived in Paris in 1797, just after Talleyrand had replaced Delacroix as Foreign Minister.

By that time the Directory had made peace with Prussia and was engaged in peace negotiations with Austria after Bonaparte's victorious campaign in northern Italy. Only England remained as an active enemy. At the end of September the Treaty of Campo Formio was signed with Austria. For some months afterwards Bonaparte occupied himself with preparations for a sea-borne invasion of England. While he was thus engaged Magellon was writing a memorandum on Egypt for Talleyrand. In this[1] he expressed the view that it was necessary 'either to renounce the French position in Egypt or establish it by force'. After stating that there would be no serious military resistance from the Beys, he discussed the proposed occupation in the light of the war with England. He recalled that the English had always been sensitive to the presence of the French in Egypt and described the British diplomatic efforts to prevent the development of the French transit trade. He wrote that the English had only 15,000—20,000 troops in India and that a French occupation of Egypt, followed by the despatch of 15,000 French troops to India via Egypt, would be sufficient to destroy the British position there. They would have the assistance of Tipu Sahib, the Sultan of Mysore, who was at war with the British and in contact with French agents. Magellon ended his memorandum by pointing out that, if Egypt was essential to France in order to get at the British in India, it was, a *fortiori*, essential to the English in order to enable them to retain their position in India. 'The British must realize that Egypt must not be allowed to fall into French hands. When they see that the moment is favourable for occupying it, they will send a squadron there on the pretext of protecting it from a French attack. They could send a force of 1,500 natives with some 5,000—6,000 British troops which would be more than sufficient both to occupy Egypt and to make any subsequent attempt at occupation by us much more difficult.'

Talleyrand, adopting Magellon's thesis, recommended[2] the occupation of Egypt to the Directory and expressed the opinion that Turkey would not regard it as a *casus belli*. At the same time Bonaparte, returning from an inspection of the Channel ports, advised the abandonment of any attempt to invade England and recommended an expedition either into Germany or to the Levant in order to threaten the English position in India.[3]

There was no very good strategic reason for the French expedition to Egypt. But the abandonment of the project for the invasion of England, and the end for the time being of hostilities on the continent of Europe, meant that Bonaparte and a sizeable French army were without occupation. Bonaparte was anxious for military glory; the Directory, probably, was anxious to get him away from France. If England could not be directly invaded, it was desirable to strike a blow against her elsewhere. There were imponderable historical pressures in favour of a French invasion of Egypt. Magellon's memorandum was the last of a long line of plans and recommendations to this end. But, unlike the earlier ones, it was produced at a particularly opportune moment, chiming both with Talleyrand's caution and with Bonaparte's ambition. For Talleyrand, an expedition to Egypt appeared to promise an easy conquest which, by giving France a bargaining weapon, might facilitate the negotiation of peace with England. And Bonaparte 'knew that, when a man was not born in the purple, he had to captivate men's imaginations in order to govern them. The war carried into Africa, into an almost fabulous country, would heighten his prestige, would appeal to the "friends of liberty" who longed to shatter the fetters of the nations of the East, to bring back within the fold of civilization the country where science and art first saw the light, to change the face of the earth.'[4]

The ostensible object of the expedition was a blow against England. On 12 April 1798 the Directory, on Talleyrand's recommendation, ordered Bonaparte to prepare and command it. In their orders[5] the Directory accused the Mamluk Beys of having allied themselves with the British and of having, as a result of this alliance, grossly oppressed French interests and maltreated French nationals in Egypt. Referring to the recent British occupation of the Cape of Good Hope, which had made French access to the Indies difficult, they stressed the necessity of opening an alternative route to the Indies by means of which the French could 'attack the British satellites and take away from England the source of her corrupt riches'. The Commander-in-Chief of the Army of the East (as the expeditionary force was called) was ordered to 'expel the British from all their possessions in the East, wherever they may be, and, in particular to destroy all their trading stations on the Red Sea, to cut a canal through the isthmus of Suez, and to take all necessary steps to ensure the free and exclusive use of the Red Sea by French vessels'.

During 1797 the British Navy had been considerably weakened by a series of mutinies. During that year no British squadron and only an occasional British warship had entered the Mediterranean. The believed French intention of invading England or Ireland had dictated the concentration of the British Navy in the neighbourhoods of Brest and Cadiz in order to shadow the French and Spanish fleets in these ports, and in the North Sea to shadow the Dutch Navy in the Texel. At the end of 1797, after the Treaty of Campo Formio with Austria, France was in a strong position in the Mediterranean. She was allied with Spain; Austria had been defeated; the Republic of Venice had been extinguished; the Ionian Islands and part of the Dalmatian coast had been annexed; the Ottoman Empire had been impressed with the recent French victories in northern Italy, with the French proximity to the Ottoman territories on the Adriatic, and with the absence of British warships from the Mediterranean. Malta, held by the *fainéant* Knights of St John, seemed a fruit ripe for the French plucking; the ramshackle Kingdom of Naples maintained a cowed and precarious neutrality. To all appearances France shared the dominion of the Mediterranean with the pirates of the Barbary Coast who themselves were learning to respect the might of the French flag.

By 1798 things were beginning to improve from the British point of view. In December 1797 the Dutch had been decisively defeated by Admiral Duncan off the Texel. The French fleet in Brest was in bad condition. It was known that the French fleet in Toulon, under Admiral Brueys, was being refitted for an expedition and that a French military force was being got together to accompany it. Bonaparte was at some pains to create the illusion that a junction between the Brest and Toulon fleets was intended as a preliminary to a descent upon either England or Ireland. In April 1798 Lord St Vincent, commanding the British fleet off Cadiz and the British naval station at Gibraltar, was ordered to send a small force into the Mediterranean to watch Toulon. St Vincent sent Nelson, who had recently joined his command, with three ships of the line and accompanying frigates. Subsequently, on receipt of further orders from the Admiralty, together with reinforcements from the Channel fleet, he sent a further nine ships of the line. On 19 May, just before Nelson received this reinforcement, and while his flagship was temporarily crippled as the result of a storm, Brueys slipped out of Toulon with the French fleet, escorting the Army of the East, a force numbering some 35,000 men commanded by Bonaparte. Nelson's frigates had parted from him during the storm which had dismasted his flagship. This seriously handicapped him in his pursuit of the French fleet.

The destination of the French expedition was unknown to the British government. St Vincent, in his orders to Nelson, relaying the opinion of the Admiralty, told him that 'the object appears to be either an attack on Naples or Sicily, the conveyance of an army to some part of Spain to invade Portugal, or to pass through the Straits with a view to proceeding to Ireland'. In fact, the expedition, after receiving convoys from Genoa and Corsica, sailed for Malta, which capitulated on 12 June after a faint show of resistance. Nelson, on 17 June, at Naples, heard of Bonaparte's arrival at Malta, and, on 20 June, at Messina, of that island's surrender. On 22 June, off Cape Passaro, he learnt that the expedition had left Malta for an unknown destination. He made up his mind that this destination was Egypt and immediately set sail for Alexandria with a following wind, arriving there on 28 June.[6] Meanwhile, the French expedition was proceeding more slowly towards Egypt on a more northerly course via Crete, which it reached on 27 June. Nelson, not finding the French at Alexandria, left that port on 29 June, sailing north to the coast of Asia Minor and thence westward to Syracuse, which he reached on 19 July. From there he wrote to the British Minister at Naples that, 'having gone a round of 600 leagues with the utmost expedition', he was as ignorant of the position of the enemy as he had been four weeks before. Meanwhile, the French expedition had arrived off the Egyptian coast on 1 July, and Bonaparte started landing his army just west of Alexandria the same evening. Murad, the Commander of the Mamluk forces, was in Cairo, and Alexandria was in no condition for more than a token resistance. The city was in French hands by midday on 2 July. Disembarkation of the French troops was completed by 5 July. By that time the march on Cairo had started. Two columns set out from Alexandria, one for Damanhur and one for Rosetta. After occupying these places, they marched to join forces at Rahmaniya, a village on the Rosetta branch of the Nile some 15 miles east of Damanhur. The column from Rosetta was accompanied up the river by a flotilla of gunboats and some supply ships. The two columns duly met at Rahmaniya on 11 July. Meanwhile, Murad was advancing down the Rosetta branch from Cairo with a force of several thousand cavalry and foot-soldiers, supported by a flotilla of gunboats. The first encounter between the French and Mamluk forces took place at Shubrakheit, a village on the Nile a few miles up-stream of Rahmaniya. The Mamluk flotilla, manned by Greek sailors, more than held its own against the French gunboats, but on land the Mamluk force was routed. It was the first time that the Mamluks had faced a Western army.

Shubrakheit was only a skirmish. The Mamluk army got away and retreated up the river. The decisive battle took place on 21 July at Embaba, on the west bank of the Nile opposite Cairo, where Murad and his army were utterly defeated. Ibrahim Bey, who was in Cairo on the other bank of the Nile with another Mamluk army, made no attempt to come to the aid of his coadjutor and, after he had seen the issue of the battle, fled with a few of his followers into Syria, leaving a deputation of *Ulema* (religious leaders) from al-Azhar to surrender the Citadel of Cairo to Bonaparte.

On 3 July, before leaving Alexandria, Bonaparte—who knew, or guessed, that Nelson was after him—ordered Brueys to take his fleet into the Old Port (i.e. the western port) of Alexandria if possible. If the larger ships could not enter, he was to investigate whether he could defend his fleet against a superior force in Abuqir Bay, some twelve miles east of Alexandria. If this were not possible either, he was to sail his fleet to Corfu, at that time in French hands. Brueys decided that the Old Port was impracticable and, on 7 July, took his fleet into Abuqir Bay. He had been there for over three weeks when Nelson, who left Syracuse on 24 July, arrived once more off Alexandria on 1 August and saw the French flag flying over the city. At first he thought that the French fleet had again given him the slip, but, at one in the afternoon, one of his ships signalled that it was lying in Abuqir Bay. Despite the lateness of the hour, he decided to attack immediately.

When taking up a defensive position in Abuqir Bay, Brueys's object had been to deploy his ships in line across the mouth of the bay with his vanguard and rearguard ships sufficiently near to the shoal water, and with all his ships close enough together, to prevent an enemy fleet from outflanking him by passing either across his rear or van or through his line. In fact, there remained enough room between his van ship, *Guerrier*, and the shoal water off Abuqir Island at the north-west entrance to the bay, to enable *Goliath* and *Zealous*, the two leading ships of the British fleet, to cross the French van and get inside the enemy fleet. There was also enough room between the French ships to pass between them. Brueys, whose fleet was inferior both in gunnery and seamanship to the British, and who appears to have been taken by surprise at Nelson's decision to attack shortly before nightfall instead of waiting until next morning, was thus caught between two fires. Within a very few hours the issue had been decided and, by daybreak next morning, the battle was over. All the French fleet, except three ships which escaped, was either destroyed or captured. Brueys himself was killed when his flagship, *Orient*, caught fire and blew up. The British fleet suffered fairly heavy casualties and a good deal of damage, but no ships were lost.

By this one great stroke, England achieved naval command of the Mediterranean, which she was not again to lose for over 100 years. The most immediate effects of the victory were to deprive Bonaparte of reinforcements from, and regular communication with, France, and to encourage Turkey to react strongly against the French invasion of part of her dominions.

Both Great Britain and France were represented at Constantinople at this time by Chargés d'Affaires—M. Ruffin representing France and Spencer Smith, a relation of Lord Grenville, Great Britain. Talleyrand, in charge of Foreign Affairs in the Directory, did virtually nothing to try to reconcile Turkey to the French invasion of Egypt, no doubt assuming that she would accept the *fait accompli*. Before the Toulon expedition set out he wrote to Ruffin[7] telling him that the expedition was designed for Egypt and that its object was to bring the Beys to heel since the Porte had not the means to do so themselves. He acknowledged that the invasion would create an unfortunate impression at Constantinople, but stressed that its only purposes were to chastise the Beys and to give the French facilities for attacking the British in India. 'The invasion of an Ottoman Province detached from the Ottoman Empire by rebellion should not be a reason for hostility between the Porte and France. If the Porte detaches itself from France it will become the prey of Russia and Austria. As a proof of its sincerity, France is prepared to send an Ambassador to the Porte.'

When news of the departure of the Toulon expedition was received in Constantinople Ruffin was questioned about its destination by the Reis Effendi. He first told him that he had no information from Paris about it, but subsequently advised him of the contents of Talleyrand's despatch. At about the same time, Talleyrand was telling the Turkish Ambassador that the expedition had no other object than the capture of Malta.[8]

Before the end of July news was received in Constantinople that the French had landed in Egypt and captured Alexandria.[9] In an interview with Spencer Smith the Reis Effendi pointed out (what Ruffin had presumably told him) that the French invasion was directed against the British possessions in India and took the initiative in suggesting an alliance between England and Turkey against France.[10] Spencer Smith, delighted that 'my wearisome efforts towards opening the eyes of the Porte with respect to the common enemy of mankind'[11] were at last bearing fruit, immediately took up the proposal and sent to Grenville the draft of a Convention worked out with the Reis Effendi, and asked for authority to conclude a Treaty on these lines. The draft provided: (a) that the Porte should raise an army of 100,000 men and mobilize the whole Turkish navy to fight the French; (b) that the British should maintain a 'respectable fleet of warships' in the Levant; (c) that the two parties would consult each other regarding the employment and destination of their respective armaments; (d) that neither party should make peace with France without the consent of the other and that, in particular, England would not lay down arms until the territorial integrity of the Ottoman Empire was restored as the result of the recovery of all Ottoman territory invaded by the French.

These negotiations took place before the news of Nelson's victory had reached Constantinople and while the Porte was still in diplomatic relations with France. As soon as the news of this victory had been confirmed at the beginning of September, the Porte declared war on France and sent Ruffin and his staff to the Castle of the Seven Towers.[12]

Neither British diplomacy in Constantinople, nor the French lack of it, were important factors in deciding Turkey's attitude towards France. The most important factor was the attitude of the Russians, who were alarmed by French ambitions in the eastern Mediterranean and who were already, through their Ambassador General Tamara, negotiating with the Turks for an alliance which would allow Russian warships access to the Mediterranean through the Straits. The Porte was even more frightened of Russia than of France, and the destruction of the French fleet at Abuqir still further weighted the balance of terror in favour of Russia. At the same time, Nelson's victory not only opened up the prospect of a British offset to Russian influence in the Levant, but also opened up the agreeable possibility of recovering Egypt with British rather than Russian help.

The British government, anxious to see the Russians committed to active hostility against France, did what they could to encourage the conclusion of a Russo-Turkish alliance, and instructed Spencer Smith to use his good offices in that direction.[13] When they received Spencer Smith's draft Convention they approved its terms subject to a stipulation that it should take the form, not of a separate treaty but of a British accession to a treaty of alliance which, as the Russian Chargé d'Affaires informed Grenville, was on the point of being concluded between Russia and the Porte. The counter-project embodying this stipulation was on the lines of Spencer Smith's draft but, as a result of Nelson's victory, was able to be more definite about the British naval contribution. The British intention was 'to maintain a superiority of maritime force wherever the enemy may be found, and by this means to provide, in concert with her allies, for the defence of the Ottoman Empire and for acting offensively against the enemy, particularly in Egypt'. Spencer Smith was also instructed to add the verbal explanation that it was the British government's intention 'to maintain in the Mediterranean a considerable fleet . . . and, by cruising off the coasts of France and Italy, to fulfil the double object of recovering, if possible, Malta and of preventing reinforcements from being sent to Egypt'. Grenville's instructions concluded with an admonition to 'bring the treaty to an immediate conclusion on the ground of the counter-project'.[14]

It was only too likely that the proposals embodied in the

counter-project for military cooperation between the British and Turks would remain without much practical application unless the resources of diplomacy could be supplemented. It was decided to do this in two ways. First, a British military mission, headed by Brigadier-General Koehler, and consisting of a number of British engineer and artillery officers and a supply of military equipment, was ordered to Constantinople with the object of instructing the Turkish army. In the event there were delays in getting the mission together and it did not arrive in Constantinople until March 1799. The other way was less orthodox. Spencer Smith who, as has been related, was a connection of Lord Grenville, had a brother, Sir Sidney Smith, a naval officer who had just been appointed to command the battleship *Tigre*. Although still a young man (in his early thirties), and comparatively junior in the Service, he had already gained an extraordinary reputation for ability, for bravery, and for eccentricity. He had acted for a time as Naval Adviser to the King of Sweden, had distinguished himself in the Swedish service and received a Swedish order of knighthood. Later, when serving in the Royal Navy during the French war, he had been taken prisoner, escaped, and found his way back to England. He had something of the reputation acquired, nearly a century later, by General Gordon and, like Gordon, he was recklessly brave, highly individual, and grossly insubordinate. It was arranged by Grenville, with the very dubious concurrence of Earl Spencer, the First Lord of the Admiralty, that this officer 'shall proceed to Constantinople with the eighty-gun ship *Tigre*, to the command of which he was recently appointed. His instructions will empower him to take command of such of HM's ships as may be found in these seas unless it should happen that there should be among them one of HM's officers of superior rank. And he will be directed to act with such forces, in conjunction with the Russian and Ottoman squadrons, for the defence of the Ottoman Empire and for the annoyance of the enemy in that quarter'. Grenville also arranged that Sir Sidney should receive the same powers as his brother as Minister Plenipotentiary accredited to the Sublime Porte and that he should be associated with him on equal terms both in the signature and implementation of the proposed treaty.[15]

The object of Sir Sidney's elevation to the rank of Minister was to give him more authority than that possessed by a naval

Captain in negotiating with Russian and Turkish officials over the implementation of the military and naval clauses of the treaty. But, given the British naval sense of hierarchy, it would have created difficulties with Lord St Vincent, and with Nelson, even had Sir Sidney been a model of tact. As it was, there was a good deal of friction, arising mainly out of Sir Sidney's habit of using his position as Minister, even in operational matters, as a means of circumventing his lack of seniority in the Service.

Sir Sidney did not arrive in Constantinople until the end of December, on the same day that Tamara, the Russian Ambassador, received 'such answers from Petersburg as remove all difficulty in the way of negotiations'.[16] All the detailed work of negotiation had been done. The Porte had undertaken that Jezzar, the Pasha of Acre, and the Pasha of Damascus, with 50,000 and 60,000 troops respectively, should march on Cairo; it had been arranged that a Turkish, possibly reinforced by a Russian, naval squadron should join in the British blockade of the Egyptian coast. The tripartite treaty was signed on 6 January 1799. By its terms England acceded to the defensive alliance already concluded between Turkey and Russia and, in addition, guaranteed for a period of eight years the territorial possessions of the Ottoman Empire as they existed immediately before the French invasion of Egypt.[17]

Sir Sidney immediately got down to detailed discussions with the Russians and Turks about the implementation of the treaty. It soon became apparent, first that the Russians had no interest in Egypt and were principally intent on driving the French out of Corfu,[18] and secondly that Bonaparte had no intention of passively awaiting the advent of a Turkish invasion of Egypt from Syria. At the beginning of February Bonaparte, with a force of 13,000 troops—rather more than one-third of the total fighting strength of the Army of the East—marched into Syria, successively capturing al-Arish, Gaza and Jaffa, and from there advancing on the fortified town of Acre, the headquarters of Jezzar Pasha and the key to the control of Syria.

Sir Sidney, having received news from the Porte of Bonaparte's advance, left for Acre in *Tigre* to give such assistance as he could to Jezzar Pasha. He was accompanied by Colonel Philipeaux, a French engineer officer and a Royalist, who had assisted Sir Sidney in his escape from captivity and who was to perform invaluable service in strengthening the defences of

Acre during the forthcoming siege. Sir Sidney wrote a succinct description of the siege, immediately after it had been raised, to Rear-Admiral Blankett, commanding the British naval squadron in the Red Sea[19]:

'Bonaparte, finding his power and resources diminishing in Egypt, made an incursion into Syria in hopes of making himself master of the treasure accumulated by Jezzar Pasha. Having taken Gaza and Jaffa after a feeble resistance, he advanced to Acre which he laid siege to on 18 March last. The Porte had sent me timely information of his approach and I hastened to the anchorage and arrived before the French army in time to put the place in some sort of defence to resist Europeans. I was enabled to furnish the Pasha with heavy guns and ammunition without dismantling the ships,[20] having the good fortune to intercept Bonaparte's battering train of artillery on board his flotilla from Alexandria and Damietta, the whole of which, to the number of eight sail, while of great help to the enemy, afforded us the most effectual means of annoying them in their approaches. The town standing on a rectangular point of land in the form of a square, of which two sides are washed by the sea, HM's ships could likewise afford the protection of their guns to the garrison and to the work-parties detached from it to throw up two ravelins, which, taking the enemy's nearest approaches in flank, considerably impeded him in his operations. It would be useless to go into the events of this most singular siege. Suffice it to say that we have been within a stone's throw of each other for more than two months, the enemy very early making a lodgment on the crown of the glacis and mining the tower forming the inland angle of the town walls, which are composed of curtains and square towers after the manner of the twelfth century. Bonaparte, having transported cannon from Jaffa, effectuated a breach on the fourteenth day of the siege, attempted to storm and was repulsed. Since when he has made no less than eleven desperate attempts to carry the place by assault. In the end he has been unsuccessful and obliged to return south, with the flower of his army, and eight General officers, killed or wounded. The army, totally dissipated and worn down with fatigue and disease, refused to mount the breach any more over the putrid bodies of their comrades. They were consequently paraded yesterday and furnished with shoes and water gourds to enable them to cross the desert again. My emissaries in the French camp assured me that Suez is mentioned there as the object of Bonaparte's speculations'. Sir Sidney went on to assure Blankett that the state of the French force was such that it could no longer constitute a menace to India. In a further letter to Blankett[21] Sir Sidney described how the French army had been harassed in its retreat from Acre and how the French wounded, embarked at Jaffa for Damietta, had voluntarily surrendered to the British Navy.

Bonaparte's failure to take Acre was his first defeat. He was afterwards to refer to Sidney Smith as having stood between him and his destiny. He did not realize, and was never to learn, that what had really defeated him was British naval supremacy, which had destroyed Brueys's fleet, captured his siege train, prevented him from receiving reinforcements, and ensured succour and supplies to Jezzar Pasha in Acre.

Bonaparte returned to Egypt in June, having lost about half his Syrian expeditionary force either before Acre or on the march back. He found Murad engaged in guerilla warfare against the French in Upper Egypt and the French garrison in Cairo suffering severely from disease in the summer heat. In July, about a month after his return, a Turkish force under the command of Mustafa Pasha, consisting of five battleships, three frigates, and between fifty and sixty transports, arrived off Abuqir. This expedition was the result of the conferences which Sir Sidney, in his capacity as Minister Plenipotentiary, had had with the Ottoman government after the signature of the treaty, when he had urged the despatch of a sea-borne Turkish force to Egypt. This force, consisting of about 9,000 troops, landed and captured the fort, garrisoned by a small French force, at the eastern tip of the Abuqir peninsula. Ten days later, the Turkish force, having made no attempt to exploit its initial success, was defeated with very heavy casualties by a French force of about 10,000 men led by Bonaparte in person. Their commander, Mustafa Pasha, was taken prisoner. Some 2,500 Turks continued to hold out in the fort (the remainder having re-embarked), but surrendered on 2 August after a week's siege.

Meanwhile Sir Sidney, commanding *Tigre*, and in his capacity as a naval Captain under the direct command of Nelson, had taken over the blockade of Egyptian waters from Captain Troubridge, commanding *Zealous*, who had rejoined Nelson's fleet further west. In negotiating an exchange of prisoners after the Turkish defeat he took care, whether out of courtesy or craft, to see that Bonaparte was provided with newspapers giving up-to-date news of events in Europe, where matters were going badly for the French. Austria had declared war in March after the French had occupied Naples (from whence the Neapolitan royal family had been conveyed to Sicily by Nelson); the Directory's armies were being hard-pressed by the Russians and Austrians in Germany and Italy; Malta was blockaded by the British navy; Corfu had fallen to a Russo-Turkish force, and the British had captured Minorca from Spain. Admiral Bruix, commanding the French fleet in Brest, had been ordered to proceed to the Mediterranean, join the Spanish at Cartagena under the command of Admiral Mazarredo and, with their combined fleet of forty-two ships of the line, relieve Malta, recapture Corfu, and reinforce Bonaparte with French troops transferred from various Italian ports. Later, in May, with the tide of war turning against the French in Europe, these orders were amended to provide for the evacuation instead of the reinforcement of the Army of the East, since this army was now needed for the reinforcement of the French armies in Europe. Bonaparte was to judge whether he could safely leave behind some small part of his force to hold Egypt and was ordered to return with the main body of his force and to leave the rest under the command of anyone he saw fit.[22] In the event the Directory's plans miscarried as a result of Mazarredo's refusal to cooperate with Bruix in any enterprise save the re-capture of Minorca, and Bruix stayed in Brest. By the time of Bonaparte's return to Egypt, therefore, any immediate prospect of relief or reinforcement had departed.

After hearing the news from Europe Bonaparte appears to have been anxious to liquidate the Egyptian adventure on the most advantageous terms possible and to return to Europe either to shore up or to replace the tottering Directory. On 17 August he addressed a letter to the Grand Vizier (at that time commanding a Turkish force advancing through Syria towards Egypt) suggesting negotiations with a view to a French evacuation. A week later he slipped away from Alexandria in the sloop *La Muiron*, which had been kept in readiness for him by Admiral Ganteaume, commanding that small part of the French fleet in Egyptian waters which had survived the battle of Abuqir. He succeeded in evading the Anglo-Turkish blockade and arrived safely in Toulon after a forty-nine-day voyage. Sir Sidney, who told his brother Spencer that he 'made an opening for Bonaparte in order to catch him at sea', blamed the Turkish Admiral for his failure to do so and added: 'If I had not considered the object of the campaign, in conjunction with the Grand Vizier, for the emancipation of Egypt of more consequence than the capture of his person, I would have gone to the west with *Tigre* rather than have sent *Theseus*.'[23]

The 'campaign' mentioned by Sir Sidney to his brother referred to a rather motley force of some 100,000 troops, led by the Grand Vizier, which had been assembled in Syria after the raising of the siege of Acre and which was, by that time, encamped at Jaffa, with vanguards in front of the fortress of al-Arish on the frontier of Egypt.

Bonaparte left General Kléber in command of the French army in Egypt and, in a farewell letter of instructions to him (he deliberately avoided a personal meeting) authorized him to follow up his peace offer of 17 August to the Grand Vizier. Consequently, on 17 September, Kléber wrote to the Grand Vizier renewing Bonaparte's offer of negotiations. (This letter, which was not answered, was taken to the Grand Vizier by Mustafa Pasha, the Turkish General captured in July at Abuqir.) At the beginning of November another Turkish force, under the command of Said Ali Bey, supported by Sir Sidney in *Tigre*, made a landing at Damietta. Like the Abuqir landing four months previously, it was defeated, but the Turks succeeded in retaining a foothold on the shore and the fighting ended in a truce.[24] During the course of this truce, Kléber again put out peace feelers to the Grand Vizier and, as a result, Sir Sidney, who was in close touch with the Grand Vizier in his camp at Jaffa, received authority from him to conduct negotiations on behalf of the Porte with French representatives appointed by Kléber.

Ever since coming to the Mediterranean Sir Sidney had been convinced that a combination of Turkish military force and a British naval blockade would never defeat the French in Egypt and that the object of the campaign must be to harass the French sufficiently to induce them to agree to a negotiated evacuation. He saw this harassment as taking the forms of (a) repeated, comparatively small-scale, Turkish landings on the Egyptian coast which, although almost certain to be defeated, would act as a drain on French manpower and resources; (b) encouragement to Murad and the Mamluks to keep up their guerrilla warfare in the interior of Egypt; and

(c) sapping the morale of the French army by propaganda and by the encouragement of Royalist elements in that army.

In his assumption of the overriding importance of getting the French out of Egypt Sir Sidney did not reflect the views of the majority of the British Cabinet. As early as May 1799 Earl Spencer, the First Lord of the Admiralty, had expressed his perturbation to Grenville at the tone of despatches sent to him by Sir Sidney after his conferences with the Porte at Constantinople. In one of these despatches, written off Alexandria on 6 March 1799, just before he sailed for Acre, Sir Sidney, referring to the blockade of Egypt, had written: 'I shall pursue the plan which Troubridge's experience points out to me, with the difference that, according to the measures adopted as a result of the conferences at the Porte, we shall no longer keep the enemy dammed up in Egypt, but allow him to evacuate the territory by all means except that of permission to return with arms in their hands at liberty to use them elsewhere.' In commenting on this to Grenville, Spencer remarked that it would be impossible to guarantee that the French garrison, if returned to France, would not be used elsewhere, and concluded that he would be 'entirely sorry if any considerable portion of that force were ever to return on any conditions'.[25]

In Constantinople, the overtures of Bonaparte and Kléber to the Grand Vizier were promptly and loyally reported by the Reis Effendi to the British and Russian representatives. Spencer Smith told Grenville that the Porte was in favour of a French evacuation provided that their allies agreed and reported that Tamara, the Russian Ambassador, had signified that the Russian fleet in the Mediterranean would not oppose a negotiated evacuation.[26] At that time Spencer Smith was unaware of the part which his brother was taking in the negotiations. He was also awaiting the arrival of Lord Elgin, who had been appointed British Ambassador at Constantinople (he had already arrived at the Dardanelles) and who would be assuming responsibility for the implementation of the policy to be pursued. He therefore made no recommendations and asked for no instructions.

Elgin, on his arrival, was informed by Spencer Smith of the peace negotiations and asked by the Reis Effendi to confirm that the British government would be prepared to grant safe-conducts to the returning French army in the event of the

negotiations succeeding. A few days after his arrival he wrote
to Dundas, the Secretary of State for War, and one of the few
members of the Cabinet who wanted to get the French out of
Egypt at almost any cost, that he could not 'entertain a doubt
of its being at all times the wish of France to form an establishment in Egypt and that such establishment must necessarily
and at all times be directed against our own interests. I can
conceive no way in which the same number of Frenchmen can
be so dangerous to us as by fixing themselves in Egypt.'[27] To
Mornington, the Governor-General of India, he wrote in the
same vein and assured him that 'as our interests in India are
so nearly concerned in defeating the attempts of the French
to establish themselves in Egypt . . . every facility will be
afforded on the part of British influence in this part of the world
to remove the French troops now there.'[28] Writing a month
later to Grenville, whose views were almost diametrically
opposed to those which he had expressed to Dundas and
Mornington, Elgin was more circumspect. He told him[29] that
the French force, numbering some 18,000 French and 10,000
natives, was firmly established in Egypt and had nothing to
apprehend either from the local inhabitants or from the
Turkish army, and that the recent British successes in India
(Tipu Sahib, the Sultan of Mysore, had been defeated and
killed in May) had 'removed one great object of apprehension
to our interests from the French expedition to Egypt'. He asked
for instructions about the line to be taken over the negotiations
and referred obliquely to a Turkish plan, which had apparently
been communicated to and approved by Tamara, according
to which, in the event of an evacuation being negotiated, the
evacuating French force would be ambushed and massacred
on its way back to France, thus eliminating any fear lest it
might be used elsewhere against the allies.[30]

A week later Elgin reported that he had approved a Turkish
request for Sir Sidney Smith to represent England in the
Grand Vizier's negotiations with the French and quoted
Tamara as saying that he agreed with the negotiations provided
that 'there was caution on our part should it be agreed that the
French army were to be sent back to France' and provided
that the French army were not allowed to land anywhere
except in France.[31]

Grenville, having received Elgin's first despatch, immediately
warned him to use 'the utmost caution in entering into any

positive engagement of whatever nature'.[32] He followed this
three days later with definite instructions[33]: 'You should in any
case decline all applications for passports for the transport of
the French army in Egypt from that country to France; the
power of concluding capitulations and of granting passports
resting with the proper officer of HM's fleet and not with his
Ambassador or Minister. HM's orders have been sent to the
C-in-C Mediterranean not to consent to the return of the French
army to France or to permit of their capitulating otherwise
than jointly to the allied Powers or on any terms short of their
surrender as prisoners of war and of their actual detention in
the territory of the allied Powers until exchanged. Enemy
vessels at Alexandria must be surrendered in like manner.
. . . You should impress upon the Porte a proper sense of
the immediate danger and future insecurity that would result
(i.e. from such an arrangement as was proposed by the Turks).
The conditions on which the present conflict is terminated
and upon which the security of all the governments of Europe
must depend will be regulated not by the transitory occupation
of a particular portion of territory which the events of war have
placed in the hands of the enemy, but in the comparative
strength or weakness of the French Republic. With this in
view, the situation of a veteran army of 18,000 men in an
isolated position and cut off from all possibility of cooperation
or communication with France, affords to the allies a circumstance of so much greater comparative advantage than could
result from any other employment of the same force, and this
advantage must not lightly be thrown away in compliance
with the wishes of a single member of the alliance. HM's naval
force in the eastern Mediterranean will be augmented, and
other means of annoying the enemy pursued as may induce
them to such desire of capitulation as is suited to their present
situation and to the dignity of the Turkish government.' At
the same time, orders in this sense were despatched to Lord
Keith, who had taken over from St Vincent as C-in-C Mediterranean.

Meanwhile Sir Sidney Smith was busy negotiating with the
French on behalf of the Grand Vizier, unaware that the ground
for negotiations had been cut from under his feet by the decision
of the British government. For the evacuation of the French
garrison could not be carried out unless the British fleet in the
Mediterranean were prepared to let it pass. Furthermore, the

decision that a capitulation was the responsibility of the C-in-C deprived Sir Sidney of any *locus standi* (even supposing that he still had the authority of Minister Plenipotentiary, which the British government later decided that he had not), since he had no authority from the C-in-C to conduct these negotiations, which had been entrusted to him by the Grand Vizier in the belief that the British, as well as the Turkish, governments were committed to whatever he might arrange.

Talks were started on board *Tigre* on 23 December between Sidney Smith on the one hand and the French delegates Desaix and Poussielgue on the other.[34] The truce, agreed at Damietta in November, under cover of which the negotiations were being carried on, was of uncertain duration, and nearly came to an end as a result of the Grand Vizier's army, now being assisted by some British officers and equipment from Koehler's mission, having stormed and captured the fortress of al-Arish. But both parties were anxious for an agreement and negotiations continued, being adjourned early in the New Year from *Tigre* to the Grand Vizier's camp near al-Arish. Agreement was reached on 24 January and, on 28 January, the Convention of al-Arish was ratified by Kléber on one side and the Grand Vizier on the other. It was in the form of an agreement between the two army commanders. It provided that the French garrison, with its arms, baggage and effects, should concentrate on Alexandria, Abuqir and Rosetta, and that it should be evacuated from these ports to France within three months under shipping arrangements to be made by the Porte. The Convention laid down dates for a phased withdrawal from the interior of Egypt during this period and for the phased occupation by the Turkish army of the areas evacuated by the French. Detailed provision was also made for the exchange of prisoners, restitution of property, the supplying of the French army during the period of evacuation, etc. It was laid down that passports would be provided as necessary by the British, Russian and Turkish governments to provide for the free passage of the evacuated garrison back to France. The Convention was signed by Desaix and Poussielgue on behalf of Kléber and by two Turkish officers on behalf of the Grand Vizier. Neither Sidney Smith nor a Russian officer who was with the Grand Vizier and who was associated with, and apparently approved of, the negotiations, was a signatory. Sidney Smith who, at the time of the signature and ratification of the Convention, was unaware of the British government's views, as communicated to Elgin and Keith, immediately sent both Elgin and Nelson (his immediate superior officer) copies of the Convention, with the request that the provision about passports for the evacuating French garrison be honoured as far as the British navy were concerned.

In a covering despatch to Nelson[35], whom he had previously (on 8 November) advised of the opening of negotiations, Sidney Smith wrote: 'The proposition from a General at the head of an unbeaten army and not even hard-pressed on any side, had my decided support. . . . The Grand Vizier wrote to General Kléber referring him entirely to me. . . . It was not until 23 December that we could open the desired intercourse. The first proposals were inadmissible, being no less than the restoration of the Venetian (i.e. Ionian) Islands in exchange for Egypt, the guarantee of Malta to France, the transport of the army of Egypt to these islands, and the rupture of the triple alliance. I did not however break off the negotiations . . . a gale of wind drove *Tigre* off the coast and the Grand Vizier proposed the adjournment of the conference to his camp. . . . Your Lordship will note that I have not signed (the Convention), the execution of most of its Articles depending solely upon the Ottoman government and on the discipline of the Turkish army. I have however reserved to myself the right of arbitration. The great object . . . (is) . . . the recovery of Egypt for our allies and the security of the British position in India, advantages not to be compared to trifling sacrifices. . . . The utmost has been obtained by negotiations that could have been acquired by victory.'

During the course of the negotiations Elgin, in Constantinople, was becoming progressively more irritated with the Smith brothers. Spencer, who resented his supersession, obstructed him at every turn, concealing correspondence from him and negotiating independently with the Ottoman authorities. And, long before he had received Grenville's despatch of 22 December, he was expressing nervousness at Sir Sidney's negotiations, and sent him two agitated despatches, telling him that the question of a French evacuation 'involves the highest considerations of general politics requiring infinitely more recent information than can possibly have reached you'[36] and warning him that he was exceeding his powers. At the same time he sent J. P. Morier, a member of the Embassy staff who was acquainted with the Turkish language, to the Grand Vizier's camp 'to establish a regular and authoritative system of communication with me in all matters concerned with the operations under the Grand Vizier' and to furnish him 'with every information, however minute, on the plans of the Turks with regard to Egypt'. He instructed him that 'every degree of respect' was to be accorded to Sir Sidney, and provided him with a letter of introduction to the Russian representative with the Grand Vizier.[37]

These evidences of Elgin's displeasure reached Sir Sidney during the two or three weeks immediately following the ratification of the Convention. Much more important was a communication from Lord Keith telling him that he had received positive orders from the Admiralty to disregard any agreements reached between the Grand Vizier and the French over evacuation and that any French troops evacuated under such an agreement would be intercepted by the British navy and treated as prisoners of war. Sir Sidney immediately, and honourably, informed both Kléber (through Poussielgue who had remained with him as Armistice Commissioner) and the Grand Vizier of the contents of Keith's communication. He also wrote to Keith, putting the case for the Convention and asking for his views to be forwarded to the British government. 'It never entered into my ideas that we could put any obstacles in the way of an arrangement very beneficial to us in a general view and which evidently could not take place on any terms disgraceful to a veteran, unbeaten and uninvested army.'[38]

The British government's attitude towards a negotiated evacuation had been affected by correspondence, both official and unofficial, from the French garrison in Egypt which had been intercepted by the British navy and which gave to them an impression of the weakness of the garrison and the discontent and dissensions prevailing in it. This impression, together with a probable overestimate of the effectiveness of the Grand Vizier's army, reinforced the British view that it was for Turkey, with such naval and other assistance as they were getting from England, to recover Egypt by military means without setting the French garrison free to fight against the allies elsewhere. This presumed weakness, in conjunction with the defeat of Tipu Sahib the previous year, also relieved British fears lest the presence of the French in Egypt might constitute a threat to India. Sir Sidney's estimates of the strength of the French garrison and the weakness of the Grand Vizier's army were more nearly correct than those of the British government, although he certainly underrated the probability of the repatriated garrison being used against the allies elsewhere. (He seems to have thought that the anti-revolutionary temper of Kléber and many of the French Generals in Egypt would have rendered the repatriated garrison more of an embarrassment than a reinforcement to the French.)

Elgin derived from the intercepted correspondence an even more extreme and erroneous view than that taken in London. On 26 January he forwarded extracts from it to Morier at the Grand Vizier's camp, instructed him to 'impress on the Grand Vizier the weakness of the French as revealed by this correspondence' and expressed the 'anxious hope that the Grand Vizier may by his own army punish the French as they deserve and enable the inhabitants of Egypt to resume their allegiance to the Sultan'.[39] Nevertheless, on receiving news of the Convention, Elgin, in a despatch to Grenville, expressed 'infinite satisfaction . . . that on 24th ult. a capitulation was signed at the Grand Vizier's camp at al-Arish in consequence of which the French are to evacuate Egypt within three months'.[40] On the same day Elgin wrote to Nelson that 'although terms of capitulation so far below our expectation have been granted to the French, no hesitation can exist as to the importance of the recovery of Egypt and Your Lordship will no doubt provide them with the assistance that they require.'[41]

From this it does not appear that Elgin received Grenville's despatch of 22 December, or a copy of the orders given to Keith, until towards the end of February. At all events, he did not communicate their contents to the Porte until the beginning of March, after the Porte had been advised of the terms of the Convention. He then told Grenville[42] that the Porte were embarrassed by the orders given to Keith and that the Reis Effendi had protested to him, saying (correctly) that the negotiations had been undertaken with the knowledge and consent of the British and Russian Ambassadors and that the Convention had actually been negotiated by Sidney Smith as Minister Plenipotentiary to the Porte. The Reis Effendi had asked Elgin that Keith's orders should be countermanded. Elgin pointed out to Grenville that these orders had only been communicated to Sir Sidney a month after the Convention had been ratified and indicated his view that the British government should accept and implement the terms of the Convention.[43] On the same day Elgin wrote to Keith giving the history of the Convention and making it clear that the Turks had acted in good faith in negotiating it.

On receipt of Elgin's recommendation Grenville, having consulted the Cabinet, replied that: 'HM has signified his disapprobation of the terms of the Convention', and that Sidney Smith had exceeded his powers, but agreed that the C-in-C Mediterranean 'should abstain from any action inconsistent with the engagements to which Sir Sidney Smith has erroneously given the sanction of HM's name'.[44] Keith was given orders accordingly.

But by then it was too late. Sidney Smith, having told the Grand Vizier and Kléber at the beginning of March of the orders given to Keith, did his best to keep the armistice going pending the result of his representations, through Keith, to the British government, and to persuade both parties to proceed with the phased evacuation provided for in the Convention. At first, both parties were willing enough[45], but Kléber was under strong pressure to use the opportunity presented by Keith's orders to denounce the Convention. In France Bonaparte had overthrown the Directory in the coup of 18 Brumaire and become First Consul and virtual dictator. Within the French garrison in Egypt there was a strong minority party, led by General Menou, Kléber's eventual successor, against the Convention and in favour of holding on to Egypt. This party used such opportunities as were open of communicating its views to the First Consul and it seemed possible that Bonaparte might disavow the Convention in spite of the fact that, before leaving Egypt, he had authorized Kléber to open negotiations. (Bonaparte was not remarkable for keeping faith with subordinates.) In mid-March Kléber refused to evacuate Cairo Citadel in accordance with the terms of the Convention. The Grand Vizier's army, undisciplined and probably out for plunder, did not wait until the difficulties raised by the British government had been settled. They took over the city of Cairo, excluding the Citadel. Whereupon Kléber, on 20 March, denounced the Convention and attacked and defeated the main body of the Grand Vizier's army at Heliopolis, on the north-east outskirts of Cairo, driving it back to Salhieh on the edge of the Sinai desert.

Two days before he attacked the Turks Kléber had received

a personal letter from Keith dated 8 January curtly notifying him that the British government would not consent to capitulation on any terms except unconditional surrender.[46] It seems that this letter, which he quoted to the French army in a Proclamation announcing the end of the armistice, was the excuse rather than the reason for the resumption of hostilities.

Although the main body of the Turkish army had been thrown back to the frontier of Egypt, part of it remained in possession of Cairo, and it took the French until the end of April to recapture the city. In this they were assisted by Murad who, up to that time, had been harassing the French in Upper Egypt, sometimes penetrating as far north as the Delta and the outskirts of Cairo. But, at the beginning of March, alarmed at the prospect of a Turkish occupation of Egypt, he opened negotiations with the French and, at the beginning of April, concluded an agreement with them to join in keeping the Turks out of Egypt.

Thus ended the first phase of the Anglo-Turkish alliance, brought into being as a result of the French invasion of Egypt, and having as its principal ostensible object the recovery of Egypt from the French. It was to take eighteen months, a British military expedition, and several thousand British and Turkish casualties, to obtain a French evacuation of Egypt on almost precisely the same terms as had been agreed by Sidney Smith at al-Arish.

CHAPTER THREE

THE ENGLISH INVASION OF EGYPT

In July 1800 Kléber was assassinated in Cairo by a Moslem fanatic and succeeded as C-in-C by General Menou, the leader of the 'colonizing' party in the French garrison, who had been opposed to the evacuation negotiations, not merely because he regarded the occupation of Egypt as a bargaining counter to be used in peace negotiations for the recovery of the Ionian Islands or Malta (which surrendered to the British in September 1800), but also because he saw Egypt as a permanent French colony. Menou was a genuine Arabophile, who had adopted the Moslem religion, taken a Moslem name—Abdallah —and married a Moslem wife.

In Europe, Bonaparte's coup, and his assumption of the First Consulate, were soon followed by a revival of French military fortunes. Tsar Paul of Russia changed sides and attempted to form a Northern League of Baltic States in opposition to the British blockade of Continental ports. Austria, after a crushing defeat at Hohenlinden, made peace with France. The Second Coalition was at an end; only England and Turkey remained at war with France. Both London and Paris were anxious for peace, but it was clear to the British government that, so long as the French remained in Egypt, they could use it as a powerful bargaining counter in peace negotiations. Therefore, since there were no military campaigns in Europe, and since the return of the French garrison no longer represented a possible threat from that point of view, they would have been disposed, had it been possible, to negotiate an evacuation on the terms agreed in January at al-Arish. But it was no longer possible. Bonaparte was not interested in getting the French garrison back to Europe, and even succeeded in slipping a few frigates past the British blockade to reinforce it.

Menou had quite different ideas from Kléber about the desirability of the French remaining in Egypt and proclaimed the country a permanent French possession. The agreement with Murad and the rout of the Grand Vizier's army at Heliopolis had stabilized the internal position, and Menou's administrative reforms were beginning to have some effect in reconciling the inhabitants to a continuance of French rule.

In January 1800 General Sir Ralph Abercromby had been sent by the British government to Minorca to take command of the British troops there and to use them, in cooperation with Lord Keith, C-in-C Mediterranean fleet, to preserve British interests in the Western Mediterranean pending further orders. At the end of July 1800, Dundas, advising Abercromby of the conclusion of an armistice between France and Austria, informed him that, as his troops would no longer be required for operations in support of Austria, 'our immediate exertions should be directed to the destruction of the enemy's naval forces as affording the best chance now remaining either of carrying on the war or of adding to the security of the peace'. He ordered him to proceed to Gibraltar with all the troops he could spare after providing for the security of Minorca and indicated that he would shortly receive orders for an attack on Spain.[1] But when he did receive orders, on 6 October, they were for an attack not on Spain but on Egypt.[2] He was ordered to proceed to Rhodes, via Minorca and Malta (which had just been captured), with the force of some 16,000 men under his command, and there prepare for a descent on the coast of Egypt. At Rhodes he was to obtain as much information as possible about Egypt by sending his Quarter-Master-General, Lieutenant-Colonel Anstruther, to Constantinople, to settle some plan of cooperation with the Turkish naval and military commanders, and to arrange for the provisioning of the expedition.

Abercromby's force, escorted by part of the Mediterranean fleet, arrived at Rhodes at the end of December. Sidney Smith, still commanding *Tigre* and in charge of the blockade of the Egyptian coast, was made responsible for the naval side of the expedition, which was delayed for two months at Rhodes owing to the dilatoriness of Turkish supply arrangements. Abercromby got very depressed. Sidney Smith, on whom he relied for information about Egypt, was away for most of the time investigating a rumour (which proved to be unfounded) about the departure of a French squadron from Toulon. The C-in-C described his troops as being 'certainly less sickly than could have been expected, considering how long they have been embarked, how ill-clothed they are, how ill-provided with necessities, and how often wet for days together'.[3] He complained about the Turkish supply arrangements and the Grand Vizier's army, which was in Syria and which was supposed to march on Egypt simultaneously with the British landing. He sent an officer to the Grand Vizier's Headquarters who reported that the Turkish army 'afforded no hope either of a speedy or effective cooperation. . . . It does not amount to 15,000 effective men and does not at present possess the means of moving forward across the desert. I have relinquished every idea of assistance from that quarter.' He told Dundas that he had asked Elgin to try to arrange for the embarkation of 7,000— 8,000 Turkish troops with the Capitan Pasha's fleet, which was to accompany the British expedition, and remarked that the presence of the Capitan Pasha would be useful 'as he has the character of being vigorous and energetic'. He feared that the Navy had been unable to supply sufficient gunboats either for disembarkation or for subsequent navigation on the Nile. He lamented that his information about the French strength in Egypt was uncertain, the estimates varying from Sidney Smith's figure of 30,000 to his own of about 12,000 plus 3,000—4,000 auxiliaries. His own strength was about 15,000 and he warned Dundas that 'if it is the intention of HM's government finally to extirpate the French from Egypt', it would be necessary to reinforce him.[4]

Abercromby's force left Rhodes on 22 February 1801 and arrived off Alexandria on 1 March. He told Dundas just before sailing that 'all cooperation on the part of the Turkish government has failed', that 'the army of the Grand Vizier is without discipline, numbers or resources', that the Capitan Pasha, 'although earnestly requested to join us, has delayed his departure from Constantinople', and that his force was 'in a very imperfect state of preparation'.[5]

In spite of these disadvantageous circumstances, a landing was successfully effected and a bridgehead formed on the peninsula of Abuqir. On 16 March Abercromby sent his first despatch to Dundas from the field: 'On 2 March the fleet anchored in Abuqir Bay; until 7 March the sea ran high and no disembarkation could be effected; on 8 March the troops forming the First Division got into the boats in the small hours. They had five or six miles to row and did not arrive at the point of landing until 10 a.m. The point of disembarkation was carried but a hill which dominated the whole seemed inaccessible. The enemy were fully aware of our intentions, were in force and had every advantage on their side. Our troops, however, under a severe cannonade and fire of grape, made good their landing, ascended the hill, and forced the enemy to retire. The disembarkation of the army continued on that and the following day. The troops who landed on 8 March advanced three miles on the same day, and on 12 March the whole army moved forward and came within sight of the enemy, who were now formed up on an advantageous ridge with their right to the canal (i.e. the canal joining Alexandria to the Rosetta branch of the Nile) and their left to the sea. It was determined to attack on 13 March with the intention of turning their right flank. Our troops had not long been in motion before the enemy descended from the heights and attacked the leading battalions.' The despatch then described how the enemy, after a stiff fight, had retired westward to 'the fortified heights which form the principal defences of Alexandria', where they occupied a position about a league from the city with their left flank on the sea and their right flank on the canal and Lake Mariut. From this position, the despatch concluded, it was impracticable immediately to dislodge them. In their advance the British forces had by-passed the fort of Abuqir, defended by a small French garrison which surrendered on 19 March. In the course of the action the British lost about 100 killed and 500 wounded.

On 21 March the French, who had been reinforced from Cairo and who numbered some 11,000—12,000 according to British estimates, attacked the British positions and were repulsed after some heavy fighting in which the British lost some 250 killed and 1,100 wounded. Abercromby was severely wounded and died of his wounds a few days later. He was succeeded as C-in-C by Lieutenant-General Sir John Hely Hutchinson.

It was now apparent that the British force would not be able to take Alexandria by assault unless reinforced. As the new C-in-C wrote: 'The French still occupy their entrenched position in front of Alexandria; it would be extremely imprudent to hazard an attack, as the enemy is nearly as numerous as we are and his front is covered with a great number of pieces of heavy ordnance. Our present great deficiency is in cavalry which prevents us from watching the motions of the enemy and pressing him.'[7]

By this time the Grand Vizier's army had advanced across the desert from Syria and entered Egypt, and the Capitan Pasha had arrived off Alexandria with six sail of the line, some frigates and 3,000—4,000 troops, of which 1,200 were regulars.[8] Hutchinson had inherited his predecessor's lack of faith in the efficacy of the Grand Vizier's army and, in the course of the campaign, was to acquire an intense dislike for every aspect of his Turkish allies which was to colour the immediate future of British policy in Egypt.

Faced with a stalemate in front of Alexandria, Hutchinson prepared to move towards Cairo, along the Rosetta branch of the Nile, in order to join up with the Grand Vizier's army, advancing from the north-east. A force of British-Indian troops from Bombay was also on its way to Suez. Hutchinson hoped that it would arrive in time for a joint advance on Cairo. He also hoped for the adhesion of Murad and the Mamluk forces, with which he was already in touch. 'We do not know on what terms we stand with Murad; he is the doubtful ally of the French and certainly not the friend of the Turk, although he recently sent a confidential message to the Capitan Pasha praying pardon and forgiveness.'[9]

As a first step, Hutchinson sent a small mixed Anglo-Turkish force to capture Rosetta. The next step was to be an attack by land and water on Rahmaniya, up-stream from Rosetta, commanding the narrow supply route between the desert and the sea which linked Alexandria with the Nile Valley. 'It is the point from which the French draw all their supplies and, deprived of it, they would be driven entirely into the desert.'[10]

Hutchinson, a more sanguine character than Abercromby, was reasonably optimistic about the prospects of the campaign. 'Circumstances are more favourable than we could have hoped for; physical difficulties are less than expected; we have found water, provisions abound, the troops are healthy, the heat is not great. But there are still obstacles, perhaps insuperable. The French are probably as numerous as we are, much more inured to the climate and in a position from which it is impossible to drive them unless we receive considerable reinforcements. The Turks are in a deplorable state, suspicious of their friends, fearful of their enemies, you cannot place the smallest reliance on them. The Capitan Pasha is an honourable exception, but he has to contend with the sloth of his countrymen.'[11]

In the same despatch Hutchinson began to speculate on the future of Egypt after the French had been driven out. 'It will be necessary to leave a British garrison in Alexandria and other places, otherwise the Turks will not be able to hold Egypt. I doubt whether they would retain it even against the remains of the Mamluks and the inhabitants of the country who, though they may hate the French, dislike the Turks extremely. . . . I think no event so unlikely as that Egypt will long continue to belong to the Turks; it will probably fall to the lot of some European Power.' He went on to point out the absolute necessity of securing that Egypt should not again fall into French hands, 'although their evacuation at present appears to be a distant, although not impossible, event'.

The question of Egypt's future having been raised by Hutchinson, it was incumbent on the British government to lay down a line of policy for him to follow. This was done by Dundas in a despatch dated 19 May: 'The great object for the attainment of which the expedition to Egypt was undertaken was the expulsion of the French from the country. This object was originally founded and stands on the principle of good faith towards an ally. . . . The total expulsion of the French having been effected . . . it is necessary to determine what forces to keep there to guard against a renewed French occupation. Our sole object is to guard against French designs on Egypt and we are neither bound by our engagements to the Turks nor led by any view of our own to look beyond this object. The possession of Alexandria with such a force there as would enable us to maintain a position at Abuqir seems all that would be necessary.'[12] Dundas went on to stress that the British force in Egypt would be needed elsewhere as soon as it could be spared, and suggested that such a garrison as might be necessary after the expulsion of the French could be found from the Sepoys in the British-Indian force on its way from Bombay.

Meanwhile the campaign was going on successfully. Rosetta was captured by an Anglo-Turkish force under Lieutenant-Colonel Spencer. The Grand Vizier's army had occupied Damietta and was said to be approaching Cairo. A British force of 5,000—6,000 men under Major General Coote had been left in front of Alexandria in a defensive position to contain the French garrison. The rest of the British force, together with the Turkish troops under the Capitan Pasha, were switched to Rosetta for the advance up the Nile. Rahmaniya was captured after bitter resistance on 10 May and the enemy retired towards Cairo. They were followed somewhat slowly by the Anglo-Turkish force, which was having supply difficulties owing to its lengthening line of communications.[13]

There was still no sign of the British-Indian force which, instead of going on to Suez, had landed at Qusair. It arrived in Cairo, after a long and exhausting march, after all the fighting was over. But the Grand Vizier's army was, by this time, on the outskirts of Cairo and his cavalry defeated the French in a skirmish on 16 May. Hutchinson, while admitting that, if the French had won this skirmish ('and I can't think why they didn't') his own force would have found itself in difficulties, ungenerously referred to the Grand Vizier's army as 'the worst that ever existed in any country'.[14]

About this time Murad Bey died and was succeeded in the leadership of the Mamluk forces by Osman Bey Bardissi. (The aged Ibrahim Bey and his much smaller body of Mamluks had been with the Grand Vizier's army ever since he had fled to Syria after the French capture of Cairo three years before.) Bardissi Bey, seeing which way the tide of war was turning, deserted the French, with whom Murad had become reconciled fifteen months previously, and joined the British force with 1,500 Mamluk cavalry.

Bardissi's adhesion, to which Hutchinson attached great importance, was secured at the price of a British guarantee of protection given by Hutchinson, 'which they positively demanded before they would come forward, and I am sure would never have joined us unless they had received it. They prefer the French to the Turks, on whose promises they place not the smallest reliance because they are perfectly convinced that they intend to put an end to their power in this country and even to extirpate the whole race of them.'[15]

The details of Hutchinson's undertaking to Bardissi were given by Lieutenant-Colonel Anstruther, Quartermaster-General to the British force, in a note written some months later: 'Early in May a confidential person arrived at the camp at Rosetta from Osman Bey, the new chief, with positive assurances that the whole body of Mamluks would join us on the road to Cairo provided they might be assured that, in the event of the expulsion of the French, they should be reinstated in their privileges and property. These assurances were given in the fullest measure by the Capitan Pasha and guaranteed by Lord Hutchinson.[16] This went a good way beyond the guarantee of 'protection' mentioned by Hutchinson and virtually amounted to an undertaking to restore the Mamluks to the *status quo ante* the French invasion.

This pledge to Bardissi added a further complication to the problem of Egypt's disposal after the French had been compelled to evacuate. After giving it, Hutchinson became more and more critical of the British government's policy of leaving Egypt to the Turks. He wrote to Lord Hobart, Secretary of State for War in the Addington administration which had just come into office: 'Should the French be driven from the country the settlement of its government becomes a matter of the most serious importance. I stated in a letter to Mr Dundas that the Turks would never be able to keep it. I am more and more convinced in that opinion. The Mamluks, the Arabs, the Copts, the Greeks—everyone in the country—look upon them with horror. If they were as strong as they are barbarous they might exterminate half the people and then govern in their manner those that remained, but I think that, the moment the British and French are out of the country, the Mamluks, Arabs and Greeks would be an entire overmatch for the Turks.'[17]

Dealing with the military situation, Hutchinson told Hobart that, in order to cut the French in Alexandria off from supplies, they had been forced to cut through the narrow neck of land running between Lake Mariut and the sea and to let the sea into Lake Mariut. This operation had also involved destroying the canal which ran through this neck of land from the Nile and supplied Alexandria with fresh water. As a result Alexandria was invested by the sea on three sides and the garrison and inhabitants driven to rely for fresh water on the contents of the rock cisterns underneath the city.[18] He went on to express regret that the British-Indian force had not taken advantage of the favourable winds during April and May to land at Suez instead of Qusair.

By the time the Anglo-Turkish force arrived at Giza, on the west bank of the Nile opposite Cairo, the French garrison of Cairo, about 5,000 strong, had shut themselves up in the Citadel and Hutchinson clearly expected that he would have to besiege them.[19] But General Belliard, the French Commander, capitulated without a struggle on 28 June. Under the terms of the capitulation, which was made jointly to Hutchinson, the Capitan Pasha and the Grand Vizier, the French agreed to evacuate the city and Citadel of Cairo, the fortresses of Giza and Bulaq, and 'all the parts of Egypt which they occupy at the moment' except Alexandria. The French garrison was to march by land with arms, ammunition and baggage to Rosetta, and from there be embarked for France 'avec leurs armes, artillerie, caissons, munitions, bagages et effets, aux frais des puissances alliées'. It was provided that the embarkation was to be completed within fifty days of the capitulation. About 6,000 French troops were involved.[20]

Menou, who had taken over command of the Alexandria garrison, bitterly criticized Belliard for his surrender, but he followed suit himself on 4 September, after a British force had landed west of Alexandria and started attacking the city from that, comparatively undefended, direction. The terms of the capitulation, which involved about 8,000 troops and 1,300 sailors, were similar to those granted to the Cairo garrison.[21]

The campaign had lasted just six months and the terms of the French evacuation were substantially the same as those which had been agreed under the terms of the Convention of al-Arish twenty months previously. And, according to the British government's intention at the time, the future status of Egypt was to be the same as that envisaged at the time of the al-Arish Convention—its return to Turkey for governing as the Porte thought fit, subject to such minimum British naval and military assistance as would ensure against a French re-occupation.

At the time of the surrender of Cairo, Hutchinson set out his proposals about the future government of Egypt: 'The Turks should possess exclusively Alexandria, Rosetta and Damietta and should have a garrison in Cairo Citadel. A Pasha should be named as formerly by the Porte, who should have the general government of the country. The tribute should be augmented. The Beys should be reinstated in all their property and should have the entire management of it, subject to certain limitations in regard to taxes to be levied, and to be under the obligation of keeping up a certain number of men in proportion to their property. These stipulations were at first complained of by the Beys as placing them on a footing much inferior to their original establishment, but at length they agreed to them, and the Grand Vizier, after some hesitation, also agreed.'[22]

The Addington government took the same view as their predecessors about the future of Egypt. In a despatch dated 22 July Hobart expressed to Hutchinson his unease about the commitment entered into with Bardissi and enjoined him to observe great caution in dealing with the Beys. In a further despatch dated 18 September, acknowledging and approving the terms of the capitulation of Cairo, he reiterated that 'after the expulsion of the French it is HM's intention to confine his views to the one object of providing against the danger of a renewed invasion by the French and that the British forces to be left in Egypt are to be proportioned to the protection of Alexandria and such other ports as necessary.[23]

But the British were to find it difficult to dissociate themselves to this extent from the future government of the country they had just conquered. The Porte were by no means anxious to assume complete responsibility and requested Elgin to ask the British government 'to permit the British army now in Egypt, or a considerable part of it, to remain in that country, together with an adequate force of HM's ships as long as the French danger should last.' They also asked Elgin to advise them about the 'authority to be given to the Beys and Mamluks, the nature and form of the military establishment necessary for internal tranquillity and external defence, and whether the Province should be divided into a number of Pashaliks.'[24] Elgin asked for instructions in the light of these requests, and received in return a statement of policy, a copy of which was sent to Hutchinson.[25] This laid down:

(1) That the rights, privileges and territorial jurisdiction of the Mamluk Beys should be ascertained, the nature and extent of their military service defined, and the performance of that service made a condition of their privileges;

(2) That the revenues of the State should be placed under fixed regulations to preclude the officers of government from extorting any payments other than the regular dues;

(3) That a stated proportion of the public revenue should be devoted to the upkeep of a military establishment, with British officers;

(4) That the Turkish regular troops already in Egypt should remain there;

(5) That an additional corps of Turkish troops should be raised in Albania for duty in Egypt;

(6) That all military forces in Egypt should be under a British C-in-C who should have powers of remonstrance with the Porte in cases where the above principles of administration were not observed in respect of the privileges of the Mamluks, the rights of the people in respect of taxation, etc.;

(7) That Alexandria should be garrisoned by British troops paid by the Porte.

The object of the proposed settlement was stated as being 'to ameliorate the condition of the most oppressed people on earth, to counteract the French in one of the most extensive projects on which they have ever embarked, and to open to the commerce of Great Britain the markets of Egypt, restored to some degree of that prosperity and greatness she formerly enjoyed'.

This statement of policy envisaged a considerably greater degree of British involvement than had previously been contemplated by any British government. Apart from the assumption of British responsibility for the defence of Egypt, it meant, in effect, that the British should also assume responsibility for the observance of certain standards in the domestic administration of Egypt.

In the event the projected policy was abandoned almost as soon as enunciated as the result of the opening of peace negotiations with France in the autumn of 1801. These negotiations, which culminated in the Treaty of Amiens in February 1802, affected the position of Egypt in two ways. First, they diminished, in the eyes of the British government, the immediate importance of providing for the defence of Egypt against a French reoccupation; secondly, from the point of view of France and Russia, who was also represented at the negotiations, the prospect of a permanent British presence in Egypt was objectionable and inadmissible, and one of the conditions of the Treaty of Amiens, on which both the French and Russians insisted, was that the British should evacuate Egypt within twelve months.

Thus Hutchinson found himself trying to honour his undertaking to the Mamluks in face of a diminishing and, ultimately, disappearing British presence in Egypt. Writing to Hobart in September, he referred to this undertaking as 'reasonable in the extreme. They have desired nothing but protection for their lives and security for their property under the guarantee of HM's government. They furthermore agree to increase considerably the amount of tribute paid to the Porte, that the Turks should keep a garrison in the towns, and that the Pasha should be the actual and efficient Governor of Egypt. . . . The Grand Vizier and the Capitan Pasha both promised me to agree to these conditions and seemed to be perfectly satisfied with them. Notwithstanding, so far from restoring the Mamluks to the villages they possessed, it was only by the strongest remonstrances that I prevailed with the Grand Vizier to suffer them to enter their own houses in Cairo. . . . I have most studiously avoided interfering in the internal concerns of the country. Save in the instance of the Mamluks, the Turks have done exactly what they wished without any remonstrance from me and have acted not at all to their honour or with any view to the good or happiness of the country. . . . The Turks themselves are incapable of possessing Egypt. The army of the Grand Vizier is rapidly dispersing itself. The Mamluks declare that, if reasonable conditions are not granted to them, they will return to Upper Egypt and organise the Arab tribes; and, were we to retire from the country, they would soon drive the Turks out. Nothing but a wise arrangement between the two parties can give the country a short respite. . . . I shall leave Egypt convinced that, without an arrangement with the Mamluks, it will be impossible for the Turks to possess it. . . . The Mamluks were so useful as an ally, and so formidable as an enemy, that it was absolutely necessary to make them declare.'[26]

One suspects that Hutchinson was exaggerating the value of the Mamluks as allies in order to justify the undertaking which Bardissi had extracted from him and which he was in honour bound to press upon the British government to observe. If the Mamluks were as powerful as he implied, and if the Turks were as useless as he believed, it is difficult to see why the Mamluks should have required protection. In fact, as Hutchinson mentioned in another despatch,[27] the Mamluks, by the time of the British invasion, had been reduced to 'between 1,800 and 2,000 men, many of them dispersed all over the country, and not nearly so well armed or mounted as formerly'. Ibrahim Bey, a virtual prisoner of the Turks, had for some time been a negligible quantity, but the main body of the Mamluks, under the prestigious leadership of the aged Murad, had remained in being throughout the French occupation as an organized force with its base in Upper Egypt, at first fighting against, and then, under the threat of a Turkish occupation, enjoying a virtual autonomy in alliance with, the French. When the threat of a Turkish occupation was renewed, and when it appeared that the French were on the verge of being driven out of the country, Bardissi quite naturally threw in his lot with the British as an insurance against the Turks, in the same way as Murad had done with the French. For the Turks, in the light of their experience over the previous fifty years, were undoubtedly determined to dispose of the Mamluks once and for all. But, so long as the Mamluks could remain united under a strong leader, as they had done under Murad, they might well have enjoyed, in Upper Egypt, a condition of autonomy even in face of an effective Turkish occupation of the country. But, with Murad dead and Ibrahim discredited, it was almost inevitable that they would start contending and fighting among themselves, and so fall an easy prey to the Turks.

After the surrender of Alexandria, and as soon as the evacuation of the French garrison was under way, the process of British withdrawal began. Egypt was reduced to the status of a Major-General's command and placed under Lieutenant-General Fox, C-in-C British forces in the Mediterranean, with his Headquarters at Malta. Hutchinson, who was raised to the peerage in recognition of his services in Egypt, was replaced as C-in-C Egypt by Major-General the Earl of Cavan. The British-Indian force, which had by this time arrived in Cairo, was incorporated into the Egypt garrison, and its Commander, Major-General Baird, appointed Second-in-Command to the Earl of Cavan. Most of the survivors of the original expeditionary force were transferred to Malta.

In October 1801, just before Hutchinson left, the Capitan Pasha in Alexandria and the Grand Vizier in Cairo, in accordance with an arrangement concerted between them, succeeded in luring the principal Mamluk Beys into conference, under the pretext of discussing the future government of Egypt, but with the intention of assassinating them en masse. The plot was foiled as the result of a forcible British intervention. In Alexandria five of the Beys were murdered by order of the Capitan Pasha before Brigadier-General Stuart, acting under

Hutchinson's orders, insisted successfully on the release of the remainder. In Cairo the British, forewarned, were in time to intervene with the Grand Vizier and avert the massacre altogether.

Hutchinson, whose worst suspicions of the Turks were thus confirmed, told Hobart all about it in a despatch written from Malta on 24 December.[28] He explained how the Mamluks had ignored his warnings, given to them in July, of Turkish treachery and refused his suggestion that they should concentrate their whole force at Giza under the protection of the British garrison there. Ibrahim and his followers remained with the Grand Vizier; those who had been followers of Murad dispersed themselves all over the country. 'Early in October I received information that the Turks were determined to seize the Beys and send them to Constantinople and disarm their followers. I again offered them British protection and recommended them not to enter any Turkish boat. On 15 October Osman Bey (Bardissi), successor of Murad, and several others, visited the Capitan Pasha and encamped their troops in the midst of the Turks in spite of British warnings of treachery. On 23 October the Capitan Pasha invited the Beys to dinner and got them all into a boat.' Hutchinson then described how the Capitan Pasha had made an excuse to get out of the boat and how, as soon as he had left, the boat changed course and made for a large Turkish gunboat. On getting alongside it was fired on. Five of the Beys were killed. The Capitan Pasha said that he had given no order to assassinate the Beys, but that he and the Grand Vizier had arrested them on the orders of the Sultan and that Lord Elgin had assured the Porte that the British government would not interfere. Hutchinson insisted that the Capitan Pasha set the surviving Beys at liberty. He intimated that he would use force if necessary and ordered Brigadier-General Stuart to hold his Brigade in readiness. 'I then sent to demand those Beys in the possession of the Grand Vizier, a mean tool in the hands of the Capitan Pasha. He raised every possible difficulty, using the same arguments as the Capitan Pasha. I was then obliged to send General Baird to Fort St Julien and turn out the Turkish garrison. General Baird was then ordered to threaten to march on Cairo. The Grand Vizier eventually gave up his prisoners on 13 November after the arrival of General Stuart. I thought it impossible to act otherwise without leaving an indelible stain on the national honour.

The Beys are now at perfect liberty and camped at Giza and Alexandria.'

This incident still further complicated British relations with Turkey, which were already strained as a result of events arising out of the peace negotiations with France. In October 1801 the British government, advising Elgin that preliminaries of peace had been signed in London between Great Britain and France, instructed him to tell the Porte that their interests in respect of Egypt and the Ionian Islands would be safeguarded[29] and expressed the hope that the Porte would agree to entrust their interests at the forthcoming peace conference to Lord Cornwallis, the British negotiator.[30] At the same time, the French government, anxious to separate Turkey from the British, and to pave the way towards a resumption of France's previous friendly relations with Turkey, negotiated preliminaries of peace with the Turkish Ambassador in Paris (who had remained there throughout the state of war between France and Turkey), providing for a French evacuation of Egypt (the negotiations took place before the news of the French capitulation had reached Paris) and the guaranteeing to France of rights and privileges there equal to those granted to any foreign Power. These 'preliminaries of Paris' were followed by the despatch to Constantinople of Colonel Sebastiani, a special envoy from the French government, bearing a personal message from Bonaparte to the Sultan which, in defiance of protocol, he insisted on, and eventually succeeded in, delivering to the Sultan in person.[31] To make matters even more complicated, the Russian government, with the connivance of France, was pressing the Porte to negotiate peace terms with France in Constantinople, with the Russians acting as guarantors. In the event Turkey signed a separate peace with France in June 1802, four months after Great Britain and Russia had signed the Peace of Amiens with France in February.

Another source of discord was the apparent British intention, proclaimed in the preliminaries of London, to hand Malta back to the Knights of St John, a move which, the Turks feared, would open the way to another French invasion of Egypt. Elgin urged that the British should keep Malta in order to retain Turkish good-will. Thereafter, continued British possession of Malta became, in some sense, a condition of blocking the Franco-Turkish alliance for which Bonaparte was angling. The British refusal to evacuate it in accordance with the terms of the Peace of Amiens was the principal reason for the renewal of war between Great Britain and France in the Spring of 1803.

The first news of Hutchinson's undertaking to the Beys reached Elgin, without details, from Turkish sources, in October 1801. The Porte took the view that this undertaking was limited to a promise of security for the Beys' lives and personal chattels and suggested that it could be honoured by allowing the Beys to go into exile, taking their chattels with them. They went on to suggest that the Mamluk followers should be enlisted into the Turkish army and requested Elgin to remind the British government that Hutchinson had no power to interfere with Turkish plans for the future government of Egypt. Simultaneously with these approaches from the Porte, Elgin received the British government's statement of policy for the future government of Egypt (see p. 84), which had obviously been influenced considerably by Hutchinson's views. Elgin's reaction was that the Porte would never consent to the presence of a British C-in-C in Egypt and, more particularly, that the future role of the Beys, as adumbrated in the statement of policy, 'would be hard to correlate with the degree of security wished by the Turks'. He thought, however, that some of their 'more obnoxious privileges' might be traded for 'more essential advantages' and proposed to go to Egypt himself to try to straighten things out.

As the complications over the peace negotiations prevented Elgin himself from going to Egypt as he had intended, he sent Alexander Straton, the First Secretary at the Embassy, who left for Alexandria in the middle of December. In his instructions to him[32] Elgin wrote that Hutchinson's engagements to the Beys 'having so early as the month of September created Ottoman apprehensions', he had offered to go to Egypt for the purpose of reconciling Hutchinson's promises (a) with the British government's determination not to interfere in the internal affairs of Egypt, and (b) with the Porte's views about the Beys. 'Unfortunately the Ottoman Ministry has been so imprudent as to direct the Grand Vizier to execute by strategem what they proposed to me to recommend (i.e. the exile of the Beys). Subsequent events have increased difficulties in the way of a proper adjustment.' He went on to say that the 'prospect of peace and evacuation make the consequences of a dissension between the Beys and the Turks discreditable to HM's conquest and dangerous to the tranquillity of the Province'. He did not know the exact terms of Hutchinson's undertaking and instructed Straton, first of all, to ascertain this, and then to enter into discussions. 'It has ever been the object of HM to restore Egypt to the Turks and no question can be admitted into consideration of delivering it to the Beys rather than to the Turks. The French have always represented it as their object to exterminate the Beys for the benefit of the Turks.'[33] 'The Porte must be expected to insist on the removal of the Beys from Egypt. Use every means in your power to effectuate such an arrangement as may serve the objects of the Porte and of the British government.' In a covering note Elgin told Straton that, if Hutchinson's undertaking was inconsistent with the British policy of returning Egypt to the Porte, it could not be implemented. The British would soon be evacuating Egypt and the Beys would therefore be well-advised to accept a British guarantee of protection for their goods and chattels. Their removal from Egypt was indispensable and he authorized Straton to offer them asylum either in England or in India, with pensions equal to those offered them by the Porte in return for exile anywhere in the Ottoman dominions.[34]

When Straton arrived in Alexandria he first tried to persuade the C-in-C, the Earl of Cavan, to agree to the Turks arresting the Beys and taking them off to Constantinople.[35] When Cavan refused, Straton informed the Grand Vizier and suggested that they try to persuade the Beys to accept voluntary exile and pensions. He also tried to get him to agree to a possible alternative by which the Beys might be induced to accept a settlement in Upper Egypt, but the Grand Vizier told him that this was excluded by specific instructions from the Sultan himself. In the negotiations which followed, the Beys rejected the idea of exile on any terms and, in Straton's words, 'appeared to be under the impression that they were not only under the immediate protection of HM's government, but that that government would support their claim in opposition to the views of the Porte.' He therefore 'took particular pains to convince them of the error into which they had fallen.' The meeting ended on the Beys declaring that, if they were not granted an establishment in Upper Egypt, 'there remained nothing but to thank Great Britain for the protection hitherto afforded . . . and to endeavour to provide a place of retreat for themselves.' When Straton asked them what they meant by 'Upper Egypt', they made it clear that, for them, it meant all Egypt south of a line some 12 leagues above Cairo.

In subsequent negotiations the Beys indicated that they would be content with the grant of all territory in Upper Egypt above Girga and that they were prepared to continue to acknowledge themselves as the Sultan's subjects and to pay monetary tribute to the Porte. Then, suddenly and without warning, they left Giza, where the negotiations were taking place, and withdrew with their followers into Upper Egypt. The Grand Vizier asked Cavan for British armed assistance in pursuing them and for a public statement that British protection of the Beys did not amount to siding with them against the Porte Cavan refused both of these requests.

Straton, reporting to Elgin on his mission, commented that personal relations between Cavan and the Grand Vizier were very bad indeed, that a letter written by Hutchinson to Bardissi contained 'very strong assurances', and that similar verbal assurances had been given to Ibrahim. He told him that the Grand Vizier had complained of Cavan's interference in the internal affairs of Egypt and of 'the extreme partiality which the British officers had shown on every occasion for the Beys in opposition to the views of the Porte'. He indicated that he was in general agreement with the Grand Vizier's criticisms and 'was a good deal puzzled how to answer some of his remarks'. He added that the Mamluk forces were about 2,000 strong and that the Grand Vizier had detailed Taher Bey (made a Pasha for the occasion), at the head of 4,000 Albanian troops, to pursue the Beys into Upper Egypt.

By this time, the Turks, realizing for the first time the amplitude of Hutchinson's promises, were extremely angry with their British allies. The Reis Effendi sent a bitter note to Elgin complaining of the British government's attitude over the Convention of al-Arish, when they had lost the opportunity of getting the French out of Egypt without any bloodshed at all, attacking Hutchinson's promises to the Beys and Cavan's support for these promises, and justifying the Porte's separate peace negotiations with France.[36]

Meanwhile, news of the attempted assassination of the Beys, and the Anglo-Turkish recriminations proceeding from it, had reached London. In a despatch to Elgin dated 29 January,[37] Hawkesbury, the Foreign Secretary, reiterated the British Government's 'fixed determination to return the whole of the

Province of Egypt to the Porte and to take no other part in the direction of it than the stationing, until the general peace, of a sufficient British force upon the coast for defence against any invasion from France'. Then, referring to the statement of policy of October 1801, which might have seemed inconsistent with this, he explained that 'if the British government have expressed any views on the lines on which the Porte should act,' this was because the Porte had asked for their advice. He added that it was not the British intention to dictate to the Porte, who should however realize that they would find it difficult to support their authority against the Beys if the Beys were disposed to resist them. For that reason a settlement with the Beys was desirable. He denied that Hutchinson had shown any disposition to interfere in the internal affairs of Egypt but, quoting Hutchinson as attributing the success of his campaign as 'in great measure due to the cooperation and assistance of the Beys', stated that something was due to the Beys for that assistance. He had been shocked to learn that they 'should by false pretences have been first ensnared into the hands of the Turks and then cruelly murdered'. He instructed Elgin to represent to the Porte 'in a cautious and temperate manner' his feelings on the subject.

Towards the end of 1801 the War Office called Brigadier-General Stuart, who had distinguished himself in the negotiations over the release of the Beys, to London for consultations. In an (undated) note to Hobart while in London[38] Stuart advised the restoration of the Mamluk government in Egypt, 'increasing perhaps the tribute of the Beys under the guarantee of the British government. To render the guarantee more effective and the obligations of the Mamluks more secure, a British officer might be established as an agent in the country, who would be instructed to remonstrate against infractions and even to receive tribute for the Grand Seigneur. . . . Whenever British troops are withdrawn the Beys will recover Lower Egypt for themselves; by becoming accessories to their re-establishment we shall, while confirming the sovereignty of the Porte, retain all our influence in Egypt. Could we succeed in restoring the Mamluks to their proper preponderance in Egypt we might be able to assume an efficient barrier against French invasion. . . . The Beys are prepared for any modification of their privileges short of exile. In re-establishing the Mamluks we should meet with tractability to our views and

93

might then dictate at discretion; in leaving the Turks in dominion we leave a country under oppression of which the inhabitants would consider any invading Power a welcome instrument of delivery.'

While in London, Stuart received a letter from Ibrahim and Bardissi reminding him of the promises given by Hutchinson and stating that they would be satisfied with the guaranteed possession of Upper Egypt above Girga; they also declared their immediate intention of leaving the British camp at Giza and retiring to Upper Egypt pending the result of Stuart's efforts on their behalf.[39]

The Peace of Amiens, under the terms of which the British undertook to evacuate Egypt, was signed with France in February. It therefore became a matter of some urgency to try to settle the Egyptian imbroglio. It was determined to send Stuart to Constantinople on his way back to Egypt, where he was to take over from Cavan as C-in-C, to cooperate with Elgin in 'arranging with the Turkish government some eligible and effective means of terminating the differences that subsist between them and the Beys of Egypt and of restoring tranquillity to Egypt'. Elgin was requested to 'exert his utmost endeavours to prevail upon the Ottoman Ministers to accede to one of the plans suggested by HM's government'.[40] These 'plans' were contained in instructions given to Stuart by Hobart, the Secretary of State for War.

They[41] outlined a policy totally at variance with that laid down by Hawkesbury to Elgin in January. Hobart told Stuart that he had been 'selected for the purpose of endeavouring to effect an amicable arrangement between the representatives of the Ottoman government and the Beys. As the embarkation of British troops from Egypt is fixed to take place within a limited period, the Ministers of the Porte, as well as the Beys, may possibly be induced to perceive that, unless an accommodation be effected between them through our mediation, the contest for power may be converted into a war of extermination. The best arrangement would be to replace things as they were at the time of the French invasion of Egypt, with an augmentation of the tribute. The Beys may be induced to consent to such an augmentation and be more punctual than before in the payment of it. . . . But the Porte would be very reluctant to consent to the re-establishment of Mamluk authority over the whole of Egypt'. He went on to suggest that the Porte might be induced to agree to an arrangement which would restrict the Beys to Upper Egypt above Girga, 'an arrangement which the Beys have already stated would be agreed to by them'. He ended by stressing that 'nothing but indispensable necessity will induce the British government to prolong the British occupation after July, and something must be settled by then'.

Stuart achieved nothing in Constantinople. He told Hobart[42] that both he and Straton were 'convinced that the Porte would accept no solution which admitted the Mamluks into participation, however limited and qualified, in the government of Egypt', and refused to give the Beys autonomy in Upper Egypt above Girga as 'tending to continue in Egypt the existence of an evil which had for so long been a source of uneasiness'.

In August Stuart left Constantinople and returned to Egypt to take over from Cavan command of the few British troops remaining there. It was thus left to him to clear up as best he could the political debris left by the campaign. Writing to Hobart immediately after his return[43] he informed him that the Mamluks had advanced north of Girga and defeated the Turks between there and Cairo. A few days later, after expressing his dissatisfaction that the British had so far been unable to keep their promises to the Beys, he stated that he was about to try to negotiate some agreement with Khosrev Pasha, the Turkish Governor, who had succeeded the Grand Vizier as the principal Ottoman representative in Egypt. He later reported that these negotiations were without result, although 'the Mamluks still desire peace on any terms short of exile'.[44]

In the same despatches Stuart reported that Colonel Sebastiani had arrived in Egypt and expressed surprise that the British evacuation had not been completed. He told Stuart that the object of his mission was to visit Cairo and all the other French échelles in the Levant and to reestablish French commercial activity. Stuart, however, suspected that Sebastiani's objects were 'totally foreign to those which he has declared and are of a more important nature; the French meditate, either by negotiation or by some more open means, some plan for the reestablishment of their preponderance and authority in Egypt'.

In fact, Sebastiani had been instructed by Bonaparte to spy out the land in Egypt—to report on the strength of the British and Turkish forces there, the state of the fortifications, and the condition of the inhabitants.[45] On his return to France he gave the First Consul a full account of all these things and, *inter alia*, revealed that he had been in correspondence with Bardissi and had tried, without success, to mediate between the Beys and the Turks. He concluded his report by stating that the Turks were very unpopular, that the country was ill-defended and in a state of great discontent, and that a force of 6,000 Frenchmen would be able to re-conquer it.[46] This report was published in the French official *Moniteur* on 30 January 1803 and the implied suggestion that France might again invade Egypt was one of the British government's reasons for refusing to evacuate Malta in accordance with the terms of the Peace of Amiens. This refusal was the principal cause of the renewal of war between France and England in May 1803.

By the end of October, when Stuart's negotiations with Khosrev had finally broken down, there was a state of open war between the Turks and Mamluks. On the Turkish side the fighting was carried on principally by the Albanian troops, under Taher Pasha, who had come to Egypt the previous year with the Capitan Pasha. On the whole they had not fared well against the Mamluk forces, who were in possession of the whole of Upper Egypt and part of the Western Delta. But, in spite of their successes, the Mamluk resources, as Stuart reported, were failing. 'They have no means of subsistence except what they extract from the country, their losses of men are irreplaceable, and the Arab tribes are beginning to transfer their allegiance to the Porte.'[47] At Bardissi's request, he arranged for negotiations between Mohamed Bey Elfi, the leader of the Ibrahim faction, at the head of the Mamluk force which had penetrated into the Western Delta, and the Capitan Pasha. These negotiations, which took place near Damanhur, with Captain Ernest Missett, a member of Stuart's Staff, and 'an officer of my family' as intermediary, failed, and Stuart told the Capitan Pasha that he 'neither would nor could exert any authority with the Beys to prevent them from taking measures for their defence'.[48]

On 26 November Hobart sent orders for the immediate evacuation of all remaining British troops from Egypt.[49] But Stuart was anxious to arrive at some political settlement first. He sent his ADC, Lord Blantyre, to Constantinople to try to get Elgin to arrange something with the Porte. He sent Missett (now promoted to Major) to Cairo to negotiate again with

Khosrev. He indicated to Hobart that these negotiations would delay his embarkation by at least three weeks. He invited Elfi Bey to stay with him in Alexandria, after having received a letter from him intimating that he would seek French protection unless he obtained some British support. At the end of February he apologized to Hobart for the continued delay in completing the evacuation owing to his awaiting the result of Blantyre's mission.[50] He told him that Missett's mission to Khosrev had only produced further proposals of exile and pensions for then leading Beys and that 'the whole of Lower Egypt west of the Nile is involved in the misery of civil war. . . . The Mamluks and the numerous tribes of Beduin attached to them are living on the country'. Stuart himself had been to the Mamluk camp, warned them that the British were on the point of evacuating, and pleaded with them to return to Upper Egypt. This they had agreed to do in a letter to Stuart signed by all the leading Beys, which emphasized that they were still relying on the British government for protection.

At the beginning of March Blantyre returned from Constantinople with the news that Elgin had persuaded the Porte to offer the province of Aswan to the Beys. As was no doubt foreseen by all concerned, this offer was rejected on the ground that the province was too poor to support them. Advising Hobart about this, Stuart told him that he proposed to complete the evacuatoin and that 'the whole of the troops would be on board tomorrow morning'. Before leaving he arranged with the Turks for (a) a remission of arrears of taxes for the inhabitants of Alexandria; (b) a guarantee of non-discrimination against local inhabitants who had been employed by the British forces; (c) a guarantee of security for the European inhabitants of Alexandria; (d) a political amnesty for all local inhabitants; (e) permission for European vessels to use the Old Port of Alexandria.[51]

Stuart made other dispositions before leaving. He arranged for Elfi Bey to visit England. In advising Hobart of this he stated that Elfi, 'who has already made large provisional remittances to England', had asked to come as a representative of the Mamluks. He recommended agreeing to this request on the two grounds that 'he may be a formidable instrument in the hands of HM's government to counteract any projects of the French', and that he might be 'a source of influence for our future preponderance in the country'.[52] He arranged for Major

Missett to remain in Egypt 'in the ostensible character of British Agent in Cairo.'[53] He appointed Captain Hayes RE (who had surveyed the Nile from the First Cataract to the sea) as Missett's assistant in Alexandria. He appointed Mr Briggs, 'a partner in a responsible English house in Alexandria', as 'provisional Vice-Consul' in that city. In his instructions to Missett Stuart wrote: 'You will use every influence in your power to counteract the progress of French intrigues . . . and you will suggest every obstacle to the employment of Frenchmen among the Turks. . . . As to the question of the Mamluks, I recommend you to abstain from all further interference in this delicate subject or in any of the internal affairs of the country except by orders from home. Captain Hayes has been instructed by me to consider you as head of the British Establishment in Egypt and to make his ordinary communications through you.' He added that he had opened a credit of £15,000 for him with Briggs & Frampton, British merchants in Alexandria. Similar instructions were issued to Captain Hayes.[54]

On 7 April 1803 Stuart advised Hobart from Malta that the British evacuation of Egypt had been completed on 11 March, almost exactly two years after Abercromby's force had landed at Abuqir.

CHAPTER FOUR

THE ADVENT OF MOHAMED ALI

For about six years before the French invasion Ibrahim and Murad had exercised a tyrannical but reasonably effective control over Egypt. In March 1803, after the British evacuation, there was no effective control. The government was contested between the Turks and the Mamluks. Khosrev Pasha, the Turkish Viceroy,[1] had little control over, and no means of paying, the various Turkish army corps which were garrisoning the country, and of which the most important was the Albanian corps, some 4,000 strong, commanded by Taher Pasha. These army corps, undisciplined, their pay in arrears, with empty bellies and arms in their hands, attracted to fighting only by the chances of loot, and loyal to their commanders only to the extent that these could provide loot and pay for them, battened mercilessly on the wretched inhabitants who, plundered alternately and sometimes simultaneously by the Turks and Mamluks, soon looked back with nostalgia at the relative orderliness of the French occupation. The Mamluks, deprived of the military prowess of Murad, who was dead, and of the political sagacity of Ibrahim, who was old and ailing, were once more splitting up into quarrelling and intriguing factions. Their principal leaders, Osman Bey Bardissi, head of the Murad faction, and Mohamed Bey Elfi, head of the Ibrahim faction, both of them men much inferior to Ibrahim and Murad in their prime, were jealous of each other, intriguing one against the other, and soon, after Elfi's return from England, at open war with each other. Their European encounters had enfeebled the Beys militarily and debauched them morally. Elfi, in London, behaved like a spoilt, greedy and very unpleasant child, disgusting and disillusioning those who had cherished romantic ideas about the Mamluks. He and Bardissi and the other Beys thought almost entirely in terms of restoring themselves to power, neither by fighting, nor by an accommodation with the Turks, but by a process of intrigue with the British and French, either of whose clients they were prepared to be provided that their personal privileges were restored to them. The Mamluks, like the Turks, lived off the country, as they had no other resources. Their own diminishing military strength was augmented by the support of the Arab tribes from Upper Egypt and the Western Desert, who were principally interested in loot and whose depredations during the next few years greatly increased the misery of the Egyptian villages, both in Upper Egypt and in the Western Delta.

At the beginning of May 1803, less than two months after the last British troops had left Egypt, the Albanians under Taher Pasha, who were supposed to be fighting the Mamluks, mutinied in protest against their mounting arrears of pay and occupied Cairo. Khosrev Pasha, the Viceroy, fought his way out of Cairo with a small bodyguard and made his way to Alexandria, which he put in a state of defence against the rebels, with the assistance of Captain Hayes, who told Hobart that he was advising Khosrev in 'such measures as circumstances may require for the speedy restoration of his authority'.[2] He added that he was advising Khosrev to come to terms with the Mamluks with a view to joining forces with them to crush the Albanians. (Hayes died of fever during the course of the summer.)

The Mamluks, taking advantage of the situation, marched north from Minia and blockaded Cairo from supplies from the south. At the beginning of June, Taher Pasha, the commander of the Albanians, was murdered by the Turkish Janissaries, who had declared for Khosrev. Civil war broke out in Cairo between the Albanians and Janissaries. The Albanians managed to secure the Citadel and called on the Mamluks to join them. The Beys accepted and were soon reestablished in Cairo. But the Albanians, under their new leader, Mohamed Ali, who had been Taher's second-in-command, and the Beys were deeply suspicious of each other. They occupied different quarters of the city and the Albanians continued to occupy the Citadel. But some semblance of a united front was necessary in face of Khosrev, who had moved his headquarters to Damietta and was said to be waiting for reinforcements from Constantinople and the advent of the Nile flood before moving against Cairo.

100

In the early summer of 1803 a French 'Commissioner for Commercial Transactions', Mathieu de Lesseps, arrived in Cairo. Missett was intensely suspicious of his activities, particularly after he had heard of the renewal of war between England and France in May.[3] In accordance with his instructions from Stuart, and the realities of the situation, he was concerned about the possibility of a French reoccupation of Egypt, and vigilant both to discover and to defeat French activities in Egypt which might be directed towards this end. This vigilance was to lead him into many mistakes and miscalculations. He became convinced that Lesseps had been sent to Egypt to form a 'French party' in anticipation of another French invasion. In order to offset this presumed activity, and to recruit support for a possible British reoccupation, he busied himself trying to form a 'British party'. The relations of the British military authorities with the Mamluk Beys made it inevitable that this 'British party' should consist of these Beys.

In fact, Lesseps pursued no such activities as were attributed to him by Missett. Talleyrand had instructed him to avoid becoming involved in internal Egyptian politics.[4] Immediately on his arrival in Egypt, he had been approached by Bardissi,[5] who had maintained contact with the French throughout his dealings with the British and who was trying to play one off against the other. He gave him no encouragement, but Bardissi's approach caused Missett to redouble his efforts to prevent the Beys from succumbing to those French 'intrigues' which were becoming an obsession with him. Later, when Mohamed Ali and his Albanians were in control of Cairo, and when Lesseps, for prudential reasons connected with his own safety and that of the French colony in Cairo, tried to ingratiate himself with them (*inter alia* by supplying them with cheap liquor), Missett became convinced that this was part of a French plot to obtain control of the country.

Thereafter, his activities in support of the Beys, and his recommendations to London and Constantinople, were based on the conviction that Mohamed Ali was a French agent. This mistaken conviction had an appreciable effect on the course of British policy in Egypt.

In his support for the Beys Missett was continuing the tradition started by Hutchinson. Although partly due to liking and sympathy for the Beys, this tradition was based mainly on the belief that the Turks were unable to control or defend Egypt by themselves, that a British 're-entry card' was necessary to guard against the possibility of another French invasion, and that an alliance with the Beys provided such a card. This military idea of an alliance with the Beys was not viewed with favour by the Foreign Office, the cornerstone of whose policy in the Eastern Mediterranean was the maintenance of the territorial integrity of the Ottoman Empire. Consequently they wished to enhance rather than weaken Turkish control over Egypt and at all costs to avoid throwing Turkey into the arms of France by any suggestion that England wished to supplant Turkish influence in Egypt with her own.

The opposing policies of the Foreign and War Offices inevitably produced ambiguities and muddles. Stuart had invited Elfi to England on his own initiative and Elfi had to spend some time in Malta before the British government agreed to receive him.[6] During his time in Malta he negotiated with the British Commissioner, Sir Alexander Ball (previously one of Nelson's Captains), with a view to the provision of disguised British assistance to the Beys.[7] Nothing came of it, but Elfi was certainly encouraged to expect some British military assistance as part of a plan to reestablish the rule of the Beys in Egypt under British protection. As a by-product of the negotiations, Captain Vicenzo Taberna, a Piedmontese and ex-Mamluk, was sent to Egypt by Ball to join Missett's staff and act as intermediary between him and the Beys. In effect, Taberna became Missett's principal adviser and a sort of Oriental Secretary. The British government knew nothing about these negotiations, from which Ball eventually had to withdraw at the cost of some embarrassment.

Elfi's visit to England was viewed with grave suspicion in Constantinople and Drummond, the British Ambassador, protested against it in a despatch[8] which expressed with clarity the traditional Foreign Office view towards Egypt: 'Any connection which we desire to keep with that country may be more effectually and easily maintained through the medium of the Porte than through that of the treacherous chiefs of lawless banditti. . . . Great Britain is the ally of the Porte. It can never be to her interest to consent to the partition of the Ottoman Empire, and therefore she can never desire that one of the finest and most productive Provinces of the Turkish Empire shall be lost to it.'

Elfi, when he arrived in England in October 1803, presented a Petition addressed to the King by all the principal Beys,[9] asking for confirmation and implementation of the promises which Hutchinson had made to them. He received an encouraging reply, indicating that HM's government would 'use their influence and good offices at the Sublime Porte to effect a reconciliation upon a basis not less advantageous than at the period of the French invasion'. This was a large promise and indicates the ambiguity into which British policy in Egypt had fallen as a result of conflicting pressures from the Foreign and War Offices. As it turned out, the Mamluks had once more split into factions and civil war was to break out between them on Elfi's return to Egypt. The only result of the assurance given to Elfi was to identify the British, for the time being, with one particular faction of the Mamluks and still further to reduce the viability of the policy which Missett was trying to pursue.

To return to events in Egypt in the summer of 1803. Missett was impressed with the Mamluks in their alliance with the Albanians. He told Hobart: 'Soon after they entered Cairo they reduced the Albanians to the condition of mercenaries',[10] and described how they had captured Rosetta and Damietta and taken Khosrev prisoner. 'No measure has been taken to restore the authority of the Porte and Alexandria is the only place left in their hands.' In view of their possession of two of the three ports of entry into Egypt from the Mediterranean, and of the possibility of a French invasion, Missett, apparently not knowing that Bardissi was still in communication with the French, recommended the Beys to fortify these ports.

After Khosrev had been taken prisoner, the Porte, which was not altogether unused to such a situation, sent Ali Pasha to Egypt, with 'an inconsiderable force', as the new Viceroy. Since Ali had previously lived in Egypt under the rule of Ibrahim and Murad, this appointment was regarded by Missett as an indication that the Turks had 'realized the futility of coercive measures' against the Beys who, he reported, were 'in possession of nearly the whole country and have signified their resolution of submitting to no form of government but that which existed before the French invasion.'[11] But he added that the Turks were still masters of the sea and continued to hold Alexandria, and expressed the fear lest, since neither side could effectively conquer the other, one of them might call upon the

French. He had by this time become suspicious of Bardissi, who was still in touch with the French, partly with a view to eliminating Elfi.

By the end of the year, Ali Pasha, the new Viceroy and representative of the nominal Suzerain, was in possession of Alexandria 'with an inconsiderable force', but was unable to proceed to Cairo because of the opposition of the Mamluks and Albanians, who were united in an uneasy alliance, likely to be broken at any moment, and particularly precarious in that the Mamluks were unable to satisfy the Albanians about their arrears of pay. Ali Pasha, anxious to conciliate one of the two factions as a preliminary to establishing his own mastery, started with the Mamluks and offered to reinstate Ibrahim Bey as Shaikh-al-Balad and restore the Beys to their former position on condition that the whole of the revenues of Egypt were remitted to the Porte. When the Beys rejected this, Ali Pasha started negotiating with the Albanians. Whereupon the Mamluks determined to get rid of him. Under pretence of reopening negotiations, they lured him to Cairo and took him prisoner. A few weeks later, when they were escorting him out of Egypt towards Syria, a dispute broke out between the Pasha's bodyguard and his Mamluk captors and, in the course of a fight, Ali Pasha was killed.

By this time the Mamluk forces had been split as a result of Elfi's return from England. In February 1804, armed with the British government's reply to his petition, he arrived at Malta, en route for Egypt, in a British warship. Before his arrival Ball had received a letter from Bardissi and some of the other Beys, requesting military and financial assistance, and asking that Elfi be prevented from returning to Egypt. Neither of these requests was complied with and Elfi was sent on to Rosetta on another British warship. Bardissi, by encouraging Elfi to go to England, had no doubt hoped to eliminate him altogether and establish himself as undisputed leader of the Mamluks. When Elfi arrived in Egypt he was able to rally some of the Ibrahim faction to his support and fighting immediately broke out between him and Bardissi.

This Mamluk split encouraged the Albanians to assert themselves. In March 1804 they took possession of Cairo and drove the Mamluks out of the city, incidentally acquiring the custody of Khosrev Pasha who had been a prisoner of the Mamluks. At about the same time Khurshid Pasha, the Governor of Alexandria, was appointed by the Porte as Viceroy in place of the deceased Ali Pasha.

The confusion which arose in Cairo as a result of the Albanian coup, and the fighting which accompanied it, caused Missett and Lesseps, and most of the European colony, to quit Cairo for Alexandria, where Missett was to remain for the next three years. His stay in Cairo of about a year cannot have been a very happy one; he told Hobart that 'no consideration but the strongest sense of duty could have induced me so long to endure the treatment I have frequently met with from the government'.[12] He may possibly have been relieved to hear, at about this time, of his impending supersession in Egypt by Mr Charles Lock, who had just been appointed Consul-General.[13] The appointment of a Consul-General responsible to the British Ambassador in Constantinople was a necessary step towards the effective recognition of Egypt as part of the Ottoman Empire, since Missett, the Chief British representative in Egypt, was under the War Office, which was pursuing a totally different policy. There was a good deal of muddle over the appointment. It will be remembered that Briggs, a British merchant, had been appointed by Stuart as Pro-Consul in Alexandria. He was subsequently recognized as Consul by the Levant Company, which had the power of nominating Consuls in the Ottoman Empire, but not by the Foreign Office who, in the autumn of 1803, appointed Mr Morier. In January 1804 Lock's appointment was decided on and Morier, on the eve of his departure for Egypt, was appointed Consul-General in the Morea.

In his instructions Lock was told that he was accredited to the Ottoman Pasha of Egypt but that 'as there is occasion to believe that an arrangement has or is about to be made by which the actual powers of government . . . are vested in the Beys . . . you will conduct yourself towards the Beys in such a manner as to obtain their confidence without giving cause for jealousy to the Ottoman Porte'.[14] In the light of these equivocal instructions Lock was in no hurry to proceed to his post. Writing from Malta, he referred to reports from Egypt of 'violent and prolonged contentions between the Turks, the Mamluks and the Albanians' and indicated the difficulty of deciding to which of the several claimants to the post of Pasha he was supposed to be accredited.[15] While in Malta he appears to have been influenced by Ball's ideas about the desirability of having a British force in Egypt. At the end of June, anxious still further to delay his arrival in Egypt, he went to Constantinople to sound the Porte about their reactions to the presence of such a force. He was warned by Straton, the British Chargé d'Affaires, that the Porte were sensitive on the subject. After an interview with the Reis Effendi he noted that it would be 'vain to expect any previous consent of a Minister of the Porte to any measure HM's government may judge advisable . . . (but) . . . I have no doubt of their acquiescing in any step when they are apprised that it is already taken'.[17] From Constantinople he returned to Malta, where he died early in September before he had been able to proceed to his assignment in Egypt.[18]

Missett, who had been instructed by Hobart to remain as War Office representative in Egypt after Lock's arrival, but 'to take no measure whatever without (his) prior knowledge and concurrence',[19] stayed on as chief British representative in Egypt. Two years later, after assiduous lobbying on his behalf by friends in England,[20] he was appointed Consul-General.[21] As such he was accredited to the Ottoman Pasha. By the time Missett heard of his appointment, Mohamed Ali had been confirmed in this position by the Sultan, a circumstance which makes it difficult to justify his hostile attitude towards Mohamed Ali and his intrigues with Elfi after that date.

Mohamed Ali, commander of the Albanians and, from the time of his coup in March 1804, master of Cairo, released Khosrev from captivity and appears at first to have been inclined to recognize him as a puppet Viceroy entirely under his control. But this idea did not commend itself to some of his Albanian officers. So Khosrev was sent out of Cairo to Rosetta and Khurshid was recognized as Viceroy. Khurshid, having asked for reinforcements from Constantinople, then proceeded to Cairo to carry on a battle of wits with Mohamed Ali, who was beginning to emerge as the dominating figure from the murk of civil war. Missett managed to convince himself that Lesseps had 'actively promoted' the Albanian coup in Cairo.[22] This conviction is certainly erroneous and the evidence of the French archives was that Lesseps had no more to do with Mohamed Ali's rise to power than Missett had.[23]

The Mamluks under Bardissi soon regrouped after their expulsion from Cairo and, in spite of the feud with Elfi, who was plundering the Delta with his followers. remained in secure possession of Upper Egypt. Khurshid was in Cairo, waiting for reinforcements from Constantinople to enable him to deal with the Albanians, and trying to persuade Elfi to fight Bardissi. Khosrev had left Rosetta for Constantinople to try to get himself reappointed as Viceroy. Mohamed Ali was already thinking in terms of the Viceroyalty for himself and, through his agents, spending money in Constantinople to that end. Missett, in the course of his tortuous efforts to counter French and promote British influence, asked the Constantinople Embassy to support Khosrev's claims.[24] In the same despatch he described the position in Egypt as he saw it: 'Four different factions . . . each of which aspires to supreme authority. Osman Bey (Bardissi) will never agree to any arrangement depriving him of Cairo, but he would readily sacrifice the Mamluks themselves. Elfi, notwithstanding having made a treaty with Khurshid, is quite capable of taking over the leadership of the Mamluks if opportunity presents itself. Mohamed Ali, guided by the French Agent, must oppose every measure tending to the restoring of a steady and firm administration. . . . Khurshid's party is the weakest. Khosrev, having no troops, must ally himself with one of the Mamluk factions or with Mohamed Ali.' He concluded that there was 'no well-grounded hope of tranquillity or safety', except in the event of a British reoccupation.

In July 1804 Elfi and Bardissi patched up their feud and the combined Mamluk forces surrounded Cairo. Missett considered that if the Beys captured the city, war would immediately break out again between Elfi and Bardissi for the mastery of Egypt. If the Beys failed to capture Cairo, 'Mohamed Ali would soon acquire the government of Egypt, an influence which cannot fail ultimately to prove fatal to the interests of Great Britain in this country.'[25] He went on to propose that the British should use their influence in Constantinople to 'suggest the propriety' of Mohamed Ali's 'removal from his present situation'.

Towards the end of July the onset of the Nile flood compelled the Mamluk forces to withdraw from the neighbourhood of Cairo. During their enforced inactivity Elfi and Bardissi again started quarrelling. Missett, who now mistrusted Bardissi almost as much as he mistrusted Mohamed Ali, continued corresponding with Elfi (which he had done since Elfi's return from England) on the ground that 'the goodwill of the Mamluks, or at least that of one party amongst them, must ever prove beneficial'.[26]

When the Nile flood subsided, the Albanians resumed operations against the Mamluks in Upper Egypt. Matters between Mohamed Ali and Khurshid were approaching a crisis but, in the meantime, it was necessary to keep the Mamluks at bay. The campaign in Upper Egypt lasted all through the winter with indecisive results. Meanwhile, the reinforcements for which Khurshid had asked were beginning to arrive by way of Damietta. With their help Khurshid hoped to be able to disband the Albanians and so rid himself of Mohamed Ali. But, with the countryside in the hands of the Mamluks, he was no more able to pay the reinforcements than he was to pay the Albanians, with the result that the wretched inhabitants of Cairo were subjected to plundering both by the newly-arrived troops and by the Albanians. Mohamed Ali, returning from Upper Egypt in the spring, was able both to win the commanders of the reinforcements over to his side and to convince the Ulema, as representative of the civilian inhabitants of Cairo, that Khurshid was responsible for the depredations of the troops and for the shortage of foodstuffs imposed by the Mamluk blockade. He was now ready to act against Khurshid, using as pretext the old question of arrears of pay. In April 1805 he made a formal demand of Khurshid for the immediate payment of four million Turkish piastres, representing six months' arrears of pay, for his Albanians. He told him that he would not allow the inhabitants of Cairo to be mulcted by special levy to satisfy the demands of his followers, and insisted that the ordinary revenues of Egypt (which of course Khurshid had been unable to collect) were adequate for the purpose. Khurshid replied calling on Mohamed Ali to account for all the sums which he and his troops had already stolen from, or levied upon, the inhabitants, alleging that, so far from being owed money by the Porte, he owed money to them. After some further negotiations, Khurshid promised Mohamed Ali that his pay claims would be met and asked him to return to Upper Egypt with his Albanians to fight the Mamluks. This Mohamed Ali refused to do, and the Ulema, instigated by him, presented a petition to the Viceroy demanding (a) that all troops should be withdrawn from Cairo; (b) that no more taxes be levied on the inhabitants; (c) that escorts be provided for the annual Mecca caravan; and (d) that communications with Upper

Egypt be restored. Khurshid rejected these demands, which were indeed impossible to fulfil. Mohamed Ali, on promising to meet them, was immediately proclaimed Pasha of Egypt by the Ulema and inhabitants of Cairo.

Having secured almost unanimous military and civilian support in Cairo, and the Mamluks being for the moment immobilized in Upper Egypt by internecine quarrels, Mohamed Ali demanded of Khurshid that he leave Egypt after handing over to him an account of the public revenues. Khurshid refused and barricaded himself in the Citadel with his few remaining followers. Mohamed Ali then besieged the Citadel with his troops but made no attempt to assault it. The reason for these Fabian tactics was that both parties were in communication with Constantinople and were awaiting the Porte's reactions. Khurshid hoped for reinforcements to relieve him, Mohamed Ali for confirmation of the Viceroyalty. The Ottoman reaction was characteristic. First, the Sultan's Master of the Horse was sent to Cairo to offer Mohamed Ali the Pashalik of Salonica as a means of getting him out of Egypt. On this being declined, the Capitan Pasha was sent to Alexandria with a small force to appraise the situation, to recognize the *fait accompli* if necessary, and to make plans for the future. As a result of his visit it was decided to leave Mohamed Ali in command of the situation in Cairo pending the outcome of his struggle with the Mamluks, and to ensure that Alexandria remained in effective Turkish occupation.

Soon after the Capitan Pasha's return, an emissary from Elfi Bey was received in Constantinople. The object of his mission, according to Missett, was 'the re-establishment of Mamluk power in Egypt through the mediation of HM's Ambassador'.[27] Missett, in his letter to Arbuthnot, the British Ambassador, added that 'Egypt cannot enjoy any permanent tranquillity unless the Mamluk government be re-established', and expressed the view that the Beys as a whole, except for Bardissi, would accept Elfi as head of such a government. But he made it clear that its establishment would necessitate the prior evacuation of the Albanians, which could only be brought about by force, and suggested that Great Britain might be prepared to assist the Porte over this. Arbuthnot refused to mediate on the ground that the Porte would never agree to foreign interference in such a matter, and was sceptical of the possibility that the Turks might agree to the reinstatement of

109

the Mamluks. But he seems to have been convinced by Missett
of Mohamed Ali's French affiliations and told the Foreign
Office that, should the Porte be persuaded to recognize the
Beys, 'much benefit may be expected to arise from it to British
interests, notwithstanding that we have had no share in the
transaction.'[28]

Elfi's emissary, partly as a result of bribes given and promised,
and partly, no doubt, as the result of a 'hedging bet' by the
Porte, succeeded in getting a Firman confirming the Beys in
all their former privileges, and in getting the Capitan Pasha
sent on a second mission to Alexandria with the ostensible
object of carrying out the intention expressed in the Firman.
On hearing the news Missett sent a fulsome letter of congratulation to the Beys.[29]

The Capitan Pasha arrived at Alexandria in July 1806 with
a seventy-four-gun line of battleship, six frigates and corvettes
and a small military force. He also brought with him a Firman
which appointed Mohamed Ali Pasha of Salonica, and a
certain Musa Pasha with a Firman appointing him Viceroy of
Egypt, for use in the event of his considering it practicable to
induce Mohamed Ali to exchange Egypt for Salonica. The
Capitan Pasha soon satisfied himself that the Mamluks were a
spent force and that Mohamed Ali was firmly in the saddle. He
returned to Constantinople in October, taking Musa Pasha
with him. Before he left Mohamed Ali had received a Firman
confirming him in the Viceroyalty of Egypt. Missett regarded
this as the result of French intrigues; in reality, it was a well-
timed recognition of the realities of the situation.

Under the terms of the Firman the Mamluks were assigned
certain districts in Upper Egypt for their residence, but it was
left to Mohamed Ali to enforce this on the Beys, who were
actually in possession of areas much wider than those allotted
to them. Although they still remained in the field with their
Beduin allies, they had done nothing seriously to challenge
Mohamed Ali's position. They had split into several quarrelling
factions and Elfi, still marauding in the Delta, was the most
powerful single leader. And he was little more than a bandit,
a nuisance without being a menace, both to Mohamed Ali and
to the Turks, interrupting communications, plundering villages,
and cutting the canal which supplied Alexandria with water.
He was enough of a nuisance to induce Mohamed Ali to ask
Missett to act as intermediary in trying to arrange terms of

submission. Missett, with that rather puerile Machiavellianism which characterized his diplomacy, accepted this request with the objects of restraining Mohamed Ali 'from manifesting too great a partiality for the French by the fear of my instigating Elfi to insurrection', and of preventing an alliance between Mohamed Ali and Elfi so that Elfi's cavalry might be available to help the British in the event of a British invasion.[30] As it happened, Elfi died towards the end of 1806, within a week or two of his rival Bardissi.

It is convenient at this point to trace the course of events at Constantinople since the signature of the Peace of Amiens in February 1802. After the conclusion of peace with England and Russia, the French were particularly anxious to repair their relations with Turkey. In June 1802 Bonaparte, as we have seen, sent Sebastiani on a mission of friendship to Constantinople. This was followed by the appointment of General Brune as French Ambassador to the Porte with instructions to 'regain by every possible means the dominance which France has been enjoying in Constantinople for 200 years'.[31] In May 1803 war between England and France was resumed. This made the British government particularly anxious to remain on good terms with Constantinople and to counteract General Brune's efforts there. This meant, *inter alia*, that they were particularly anxious not to offend Turkish susceptibilities over Egypt, which had already been wounded by British military relations with the Beys.

In the wider context of European affairs, the British were anxious to make common cause with Russia, against France, at Constantinople. Both governments were agreed on the desirability of excluding French influence but, whereas British policy was based on protecting Turkish independence and territorial integrity, the Russians were thinking in terms of a partition of the Ottoman Empire between themselves, England and Austria, with Russia taking the lion's share as 'protector' of the Slav racial and Orthodox religious minorities in the Balkans. British policy was to resist this threatened Russian expansion into the Mediterranean, but not to the point of preventing a common front against France. The diplomatic struggle became concentrated on the French Ambassador's efforts to secure Ottoman recognition of Napoleon as Emperor of the French. The great British fear was lest the Porte should seek French protection against the predatory designs of Russia.

The fact that she did not was due, not so much to British diplomacy as to the relative strength and proximity to Constantinople of the French and Russian armies. From 1803 to 1805 the Turks were more frightened of the Russians than they were of the French.

Turkish belief in Russian strength secured their resistance to French blandishments; British diplomacy succeeded in moderating Russian designs on Turkey. In the result, Russia and Austria, in a *Declaration d'Alliance Intime* concluded in October 1804, solemnly affirmed the integrity of the Ottoman Empire. Brune was withdrawn from Constantinople in December 1804 and, in September 1805, a Treaty was signed between Russia and Turkey which, although it provided for the passage of Russian warships and transports through the Straits, did not provide for what Russia had previously been insisting on—the right of intervention in favour of Christian minorities in the Balkans. Nevertheless, by the end of 1805, 'Turkey was in the grasp of Russia. The provinces were agitated by Russian agents, Russian squadrons were passing to and fro under the windows of the Seraglio, the Divan was daily humiliated by arrogant demands, and the Ministers were not allowed the liberty of taking the most ordinary measures.'[32]

This picture was entirely changed by the campaign of Austerlitz in 1805–6, when Napoleon successively defeated the armies of Austria, Prussia and Russia on the fields of Austerlitz, Jena and Friedland, breaking up the Third Coalition and bringing the French armies in force to the borders of the Ottoman dominions.

The progress of this campaign both emboldened the Turks into resisting Russian encroachments and chastened them into paying some attention to French demands. Sebastiani returned to Constantinople as Ambassador and was treated with great respect. In August 1806 there were rumours that Russia had concluded a separate peace with Franch.[33] The Turks reacted by dismissing the two notoriously pro-Russian Hospodars (Greek princes) of the Danube Provinces of Moldavia and Wallachia, on the boundary between the Ottoman Empire and Russia, over whom the Russians claimed rights of protection. Italinsky, the Russian Ambassador, immediately demanded their reinstatement. Arbuthnot associated himself with this demand,[34] in a note to the Reis Effendi in which he complained (a) of the Porte's refusal to renew the 1799 treaty of alliance with England; (b) of the 'unprecedented honours' paid to the French Ambassador; and (c) of the violation of British rights under the capitulations.

The Russians were determined to use the occasion to reaffirm their dominance in Constantinople. In addition to the reinstatement of the Hospodars, to which the Porte eventually acceded, Italinsky was instructed to demand the expulsion of Sebastiani and the reaffirmation of the Russian right, to which Sebastiani was objecting, of free navigation through the Straits for her warships. In December Russian troops invaded Moldavia and Wallachia. In the light of the new military situation in Europe they were overplaying their hand. Italinsky was ordered to leave Constantinople and Turkey declared war on Russia. The Russian Ambassador left on a British warship which Arbuthnot put at his disposal. The British Ambassador who, during the previous few months had associated himself almost entirely with Russian demands, now blamed them for invading Moldavia and Wallachia and remarked that 'the Porte has now become thrown into the hands of France'.[35]

As early as September, Arbuthnot had asked Sir Sidney Smith, commanding a naval squadron in the Mediterranean, to cruise off the Dardanelles, expressing his conviction that 'nothing can preserve HM's interests . . . but the immediate appearance of some ships of war'.[36] In November, Lord Howick, the new Foreign Secretary, approving Arbuthnot's general line of support for Russia, told him that 'an additional naval force is preparing to be sent to Lord Collingwood (C-in-C Mediterranean) which may enable him to detach a sufficient squadron to give weight to, if not enforce acquiescence in, your representations'.[37] Ten days later he was informed that a powerful squadron was on its way to Constantinople. On its arrival he was instructed to insist on Turkish observance of their obligations to England and Russia, and particularly on the reinstatement of the Hospodars and the right of Russian warships to pass through the Straits. 'On these two points you will immediately and peremptorily insist. If they are not met you are to declare your mission at an end and leave with the squadron and signify to the British Admiral that hostilities are to commence. If war has already begun with Russia, you will offer your mediation on the ground of immediate compliance with the two above-mentioned demands.'[38] At the same time Howick sent a note to the Admiralty stating that the hostile

113

Turkish attitude had determined HMG to 'adopt prompt and decisive measures suitable for the occasion' and asked them to send such reinforcements to Collingwood 'as would enable him to act offensively against Constantinople'. He stated that the Admiral commanding the squadron should be guided by Arbuthnot over the question of hostilities which, if determined on, should take the form of a demand for the surrender of the Turkish fleet, followed by a bombardment of Constantinople if that demand were not complied with. He added that instructions had been sent to General Fox, C-in-C Malta, to prepare a force of 5,000 men to occupy Alexandria as soon as he had been informed that hostilities had started off Constantinople.[39]

Meanwhile, in response to Arbuthnot's earlier request, Rear-Admiral Louis arrived off Tenedos on 1 December with three ships of the line. At Arbuthnot's request he proceeded himself with one of these, *Canopus*, to Constantinople, leaving the other two at Tenedos. After evacuating Italinsky towards the end of December, *Canopus*, at Arbuthnot's request, returned to Constantinople. In spite of the Rear-Admiral's increasing restiveness, Arbuthnot insisted that his squadron remain in Turkish waters all through January, with *Canopus* at Constantinople and the other two ships at Tenedos. At the beginning of February, feeling himself isolated, and fearing that his communications would be cut off by the Porte, and even that he himself might be sent to the Seven Towers, Arbuthnot arranged for the British community to assemble on *Canopus* under the pretence of an evening entertainment, and then caused it to leave Constantinople under cover of darkness and join the rest of the squadron at Tenedos.[40] Apparently the British wives and children were left in Constantinople.[41] Thus, rather ingloriously, did Arbuthnot's mission come to an end, before the arrival of the 'powerful squadron', which was already on its way, and the British government found themselves at war with Turkey.

While the crisis in Constantinople was working towards its climax, the new Viceroy of Egypt received orders from the Porte to make his peace with the Mamluks and put the country in a state of defence against the possibility of a British invasion. Alexandria was still lightly garrisoned with Turkish troops, had never been occupied by Mohamed Ali, and was not included within the limits of his Viceroyalty. In the event of a British landing there, it was therefore open to him to enter into negotiations with the invaders. But he seems to have decided to let the British and Turks fight it out in Alexandria and to defend the rest of Egypt if the British moved inland. He judged, correctly, that the Mamluks neither would nor could give effective assistance to the British. His decision was probably due to his desire to consolidate himself in the Viceroyalty by proving his ability, or at all events willingness, to defend Egypt from a foreign invader. If his efforts should prove more effective than those of the Turkish garrison of Alexandria, so much the better.

The strength of the British force being assembled at Malta for the expedition to Alexandria was dictated by three considerations. First, its commander, Major-General Fraser, was ordered to take Alexandria only and on no account to advance into the interior. Secondly, Missett's (mainly correct) information about the state of the fortifications and garrison of Alexandria indicated that little resistance would be offered. Thirdly, Missett's (entirely incorrect) information about the state of Egypt generally indicated that there would be no difficulty in obtaining supplies from the interior and little possibility of an attack from Mohamed Ali's forces. As a result the total strength of the expedition was six regiments only, of which three were composed of almost untrained foreign mercenaries.

Vice-Admiral Duckworth, commanding the squadron ordered to Constantinople, arrived at Tenedos about a week after Arbuthnot's flight. Immediately he learned what had happened he sent word to General Fox at Malta suggesting that he despatch Fraser's force to Alexandria.[42] Then, after some abortive negotiations with the Capitan Pasha (whose return from Egypt in October had been caused by the crisis brewing up nearer home), his squadron, with Arbuthnot on board, sailed through the Dardanelles without loss on 19 February and anchored in the Sea of Marmora. After a fortnight of inconclusive negotiations, during which Arbuthnot was 'in an agony of fear' for his four infant children,[43] and during which he and Duckworth appear to have encouraged one another in their increasing reluctance to take any decisive action, the squadron withdrew. This time they had to fight their way through the Dardanelles, incurring casualties amounting to forty-two killed and thirty-five wounded. The Turks had been encouraged by Sebastiani in their resistance to British demands and the consequent failure of the expedition 'led to the consummation it was intended to prevent, namely, the predominance of France in Constantinople'.[44]

On 14 March, a few days after Duckworth's ignominious return to the Aegean, a British brig arrived at Alexandria with a letter to Missett from General Fraser, who was on his way from Malta with his expedition. Missett was invited to leave Alexandria in the brig and join the expedition in order to give them the benefit of his local knowledge. But he decided to stay on at Alexandria. Informing Fraser of his decision, he gave him detailed information about the fortifications, landing beaches, etc., and expressed his opinion that the landing would meet with little or no resistance.

Part of the expedition, consisting of fourteen transports escorted by *Tigre*, arrived off Alexandria on 16 March; the rest, consisting of nineteen transports escorted by *Apollo*, had parted company in a gale. Fraser sent an officer ashore under a flag of truce to invite the Governor of Alexandria to surrender the town; this invitation was not accepted. He also, in gross breach of the flag of truce, sent a message to Missett informing him of the depleted state of his force and asking his advice about whether or not to land immediately. Missett advised him that delay would give Mohamed Ali an opportunity to reinforce the garrison. Fraser followed his advice and, on the evening of 17 March, landed a small force on the west side of Alexandria, near Marabout Island, where Bonaparte had landed nine years before. On 18 March this force advanced on the town and carried a palisaded entrenchment covering the inner defences and stretching from the Western Harbour to Lake Mariut. This was effected with little loss against a heavy fire of cannon and musketry and brought the invaders to the walls of the town near Pompey's Gate. They found the gate barricaded and the walls manned with defenders. Fraser decided not to storm the town with his small landing force of 1,000 men. Instead, he landed the rest of his force east of the town and occupied the fort at Abuqir and the narrow isthmus between the sea and Lake Mariut, thus cutting Alexandria off from reinforcement from the Delta. The next day, 20 March, he sent the Governor another invitation to surrender which was accepted, and capitulation terms were arranged. British losses in the whole operation were six killed and eight wounded. The Alexandria garrison consisted of four hundred and sixty seven men; of these, two hundred and twenty seven surrendered. Most of the rest had already deserted.[45] On 21 March, the day after the surrender, the rest of Fraser's force, escorted by *Apollo*, arrived.

Missett seems to have been taken aback to learn that Fraser's orders confined him to the capture of Alexandria only, and that he had no authority to advance into the interior. He had evidently envisaged an expedition of much larger scope, having as its object the defeat of Mohamed Ali and the reinstatement of the Beys in Cairo. He told Fraser that it would be impossible to keep Alexandria supplied either with food or water (Elfi had cut the canal linking Alexandria with the Nile during his depredations in the Delta) without capturing Rosetta and Rahmaniya. He also told Fraser that the Beys, then in Upper Egypt, to whom he wrote, with Fraser's agreement, advising them of the British landing, would expect active British assistance in occupying Cairo.

The Consul-General and the Commander-in-Chief were clearly at cross-purposes. Fraser was disturbed to learn of the extent of Missett's commitments to the Beys and, having been led to expect that the inhabitants of Egypt would welcome his arrival with open arms, was annoyed to find that further military operations would be necessary in order to maintain himself in Alexandria. Writing to Windham, the Secretary of State for War, on 27 March, he told him that he was reluctantly taking Missett's advice about the occupation and garrisoning of Rosetta and Rahmaniya, and asked him whether he should afford assistance to the Mamluks in taking Cairo and in expelling the Albanians from Egypt, 'on which the Mamluks are intent and which they have been encouraged by Major Missett to hope that the British will assist them in effecting'. He added that Missett had given assurances to the Beys that they would be restored to the government of Egypt and that he had done this on the ground that otherwise the Beys would have joined Mohamed Ali in resisting the British invasion.[46] Fraser seems to have accepted Missett's conviction that Mohamed Ali was being supported by the French. He told Windham that Drovetti, the French Consul-General,[47] had gone from Alexandria to Cairo before the British landing and was encouraging Mohamed Ali, then in Upper Egypt, to use his Albanians, consisting of 12,000 troops, to march on Alexandria. In fact, Drovetti was able materially to assist Mohamed Ali by advising him and by warning the Mamluks of the weakness of the British expedition.[48] This may have

117

served as the basis for the great influence which he later had with Mohamed Ali.

Two attempts were made to capture Rosetta, both ending in disaster. In the first, a British force of 1,400 men under Brigadier-General Wauchope marched straight into the town without previous reconnaissance, found, when it was too late, that it was held in force by Albanian troops recently arrived from Damanhur, and retreated in some disorder after incurring casualties amounting to 170 killed, including General Wauchope, and 251 wounded. The second attempt was even more disastrous. A force of 2,400 men under Brigadier-General Stuart was forced to retreat from the outskirts of the town after several days fighting with the Albanian garrison, which had been further reinforced, and after some 700 men, under Lieutenant-Colonel MacLeod, had been cut off and taken prisoner.

In a series of unedifying messages, Missett and Fraser blamed each other for the disasters. Missett, whose interpreter and principal assistant, Captain Taberna, had been captured with Colonel MacLeod and his men, complained that the attacks had been mismanaged. Fraser considered that Missett's information had been misleading. Both agreed that the situation was dangerous. The Albanians had been encouraged by their victories. The Mamluks had been discouraged by the British defeats and were likely to remain passive in Upper Egypt. The supply situation in Alexandria was becoming desperate. After the failures at Rosetta there was no possibility of supplies from the Delta; the Arabs of the Western Desert, another possible source of supply, were, like the Mamluks, cautious about assisting an apparently defeated invader. There was a possibility that the Albanians might follow up their success at Rosetta by an attack on Alexandria. Fraser was in favour of evacuation 'to save not only ourselves, but the miserable inhabitants of Alexandria, from starving.'⁴⁹ Missett was in favour of staying on. 'We shall meet with great difficulty in obtaining supplies, but, sooner than abandon so important a post, the Army should submit to every possible privation. To regain our influence in the country it will be necessary to compel the Albanians to evacuate it.'⁵⁰ He tried to impress Fraser with 'the lively interest which Great Britain takes in this country, the anxiety which HM's Government feels lest this key to our East Indian possessions should fall into the hands of the

French'. He reminded him that the French in Alexandria had sustained a blockade of five months 'in conditions much more disadvantageous than those in which the British force is now placed.'[51]

Fraser was unimpressed. He told Windham: 'We have possession of this place only so long as the enemy may allow us to receive supplies . . . (it) cannot be held as a British port in enemy country. Although we might, with immediate reinforcement of men and supplies of money and provisions, keep possession of it for a time, yet it must ultimately be evacuated.' But, before evacuating, it was necessary to try to arrange for the release of the British prisoners captured at Rosetta and to guard against the possibility of an attack in the meantime. He therefore gave orders once more to cut through the isthmus between the sea and Lake Mariut in order to deepen the lake 'which has been found fordable for cavalry and infrantry'.[52] As a result of Fraser's recommendations, General Fox, C-in-C Malta, was authorized to arrange for the evacuation of Alexandria as a preferable alternative to reinforcement, which might have led to the abandonment of Sicily.[53] Meanwhile, events were moving elsewhere. Both England and Russia were anxious to make peace with the Turks, whom the French were trying to persuade into an offensive and defensive alliance. In May 1807 the Russians sent Pozzo di Borgo to Constantinople for negotiations. He arrived just after a domestic revolution in which Sultan Selim was deposed and a number of Ministers murdered in an outburst of reactionary resistance to the Sultan's attempts to replace the lawless and semi-independent military corps, such as the Janissaries, by a disciplined Nizam Jedid (New Model) under his direct control. But the imbroglio did not much affect the customary Ottoman processes of trying to play off one Power against another as a condition of survival. At the end of July, Pozzo di Borgo, who had not been able to accomplish anything, was joined at Constantinople by Sir Arthur Paget, a British diplomat sent by Canning, the new British Foreign Secretary.[54] In September, while Paget was in Constantinople, news was received of the Treaty of Tilsit concluded between Napoleon and the Tsar of Russia. This treaty, which appeared to presage the partition of the Ottoman Empire between France and Russia, put an effective end to the British mission.

In Egypt, Mohamed Ali was determined not to embroil

himself with the British more than necessary. He sent Lieutenant Matthews, one of the British officers captured at Rosetta, back to Fraser under a flag of truce to arrange for an exchange of prisoners. Matthews told Fraser that the British prisoners were being well treated and that they owed much to the kindness of Drovetti, the French Consul-General.[55] He also told him that the Mamluks had made their peace with Mohamed Ali.[56]

With Lieutenant Matthews, Mohamed Ali sent a confidential interpreter to 'discover the real intentions of HM's Government regarding Egypt'. From this interpreter it was learned that Mohamed Ali had intercepted a letter from Fraser to the Beys in which it was made clear that his orders were confined to the occupation of Alexandria. On this basis, Mohamed Ali indicated through the interpreter that he would be prepared to come to some arrangement enabling the British force to remain in Alexandria for the time being. Missett scouted the idea of 'an alliance with so mercenary and faithless a set of men as the Albanians' and expressed the view that any such arrangement, even if genuinely intended by Mohamed Ali, would mean that the Mamluks would turn against England and be assisted by the French.[57] He was still in correspondence with the Beys and still pinning his faith to them, and continued to bring forth arguments against evacuation, pointing out that Mohamed Ali's forces did not exceed 7,000 men, of which 2,000 had to be kept in Cairo to defend that city against the Mamluks.

But Fraser was intent on getting out of the country and confined his negotiations with Mohamed Ali to the question of prisoners. Their release was eventually arranged, in spite of Missett's conviction that Drovetti was trying to persuade Mohamed Ali to retain them, and an agreement signed with Mohamed Ali providing for the evacuation of Alexandria. According to the terms of this agreement, which was signed on 9 September, all hostilities were immediately to cease, all prisoners of war, including those who had been made slaves, immediately released and sent to Rosetta to be embarked on a British ship. The British were to complete their evacuation within ten days, leaving all fortifications in their existing state. A general amnesty was provided for the inhabitants of Alexandria, which was occupied by Mohamed Ali's troops after the British evacuation.[58]

Missett left Alexandria with the British force. In a despatch to the War Office he wrote: 'The Mamluks as a political body may now be regarded as nearly extinct. Shortly before the evacuation they fought and nine Beys fell in the action. Ibrahim Bey will try and make his peace with Mohamed Ali, having now no longer any hope of support from HM's Government.'[59]

Thus ended one of the most depressing episodes in British military history. However ill-conceived the expedition, and however disastrous its execution, it is clear that the British government's object was a demonstration against Turkey. It is unlikely that they believed in the possibility of a French attempt to invade Egypt and Fraser's expedition was almost certainly not an attempt to forestall this. There was no British intention to restore the Mamluks or to drive the Albanians out of Egypt. Missett's politicking with the Beys and against Mohamed Ali was a residue of Hutchinson's and Stuart's attitudes during the British occupation and received no countenance or encouragement from the British government.

For Mohamed Ali, the fiasco of the British expedition provided the finishing touch to the complicated process by which he had risen to attain the mastery of Egypt. He had arrived as Second-in-Command of the Albanian Corps which had come to Alexandria with the Capitan Pasha in the spring of 1801. His political career started when he took command of the Albanians after the death of Taher Pasha in June 1803. Thereafter, by the processes of intrigue and violence, which we have described, he secured his elevation to the Viceroyalty. But his position was still precarious and rested on the loyalty of his turbulent and not very reliable Albanians. The Mamluks were still in the field; the Porte were anxious to remove him before he became too powerful. But, by the time Fraser had left Alexandria, he had consolidated his position. He had, to all appearance, successfully defended Egypt against invasion by a foreign army. By negotiation on equal terms with a British General he had secured British evacuation, and his own occupation, of Alexandria, the key to Egypt, which the Turks had withheld from his Viceroyalty, and which they had failed themselves to hold. The Mamluks, despairing of effective intervention on their behalf, were suing for peace. He had no more active enemies within Egypt. He was too powerful, and too useful, for the Turks either to achieve, or even desire to achieve, his removal. The governments of Great Britain,

121

France and Russia were all prepared to regard him as the *de facto* master of Egypt.

Despite Missett's suspicions, Mohamed Ali owed nothing to French influence in the course of his rise to power. France was in no better position than England to influence the course of events in Egypt. Neither Lesseps nor Missett had the prescience to see that Mohamed Ali was the coming man. Lesseps' complaisance towards Mohamed Ali, such as it was, had no more effect in promoting his cause than Missett's hostility had in retarding it. Mohamed Ali's confirmation as Viceroy was likewise unaffected by any representations either from the British or from the French governments. It was simply, in the Ottoman fashion, the recognition of a *fait accompli*.

CHAPTER FIVE

THE RISE OF MOHAMED ALI

The Treaty of Tilsit between France and Russia provided, *inter alia,* for French mediation between Russia and Turkey. In the event of Turkey refusing this, or of peace negotiations leading to no satisfactory result within three months, it provided that France and Russia would strip Turkey of her European Provinces. But, in the event, nothing much happened. The Tsar, who regarded Tilsit merely as a breathing-space to enable Russia to recover from her defeat at Friedland, was not disposed to give up his designs on Turkey, and Napoleon had no intention of letting him have a free hand there. And the Turks, as always, in spite of another instalment of the May revolution in September, which cost ex-Sultan Selim and his successor Mustafa IV their lives and elevated Mahmud II to the throne, showed great diplomatic virtuosity in playing France and Russia off against each other.

In February 1808 the Porte indicated to HM's Government that they were prepared for a resumption of diplomatic relations. So Canning sent Sir Robert Adair to Constantinople with instructions to try to reconstruct the Triple Alliance of Great Britain, Russia and Turkey against France.[1] He was not to run any risk of offending Ottoman susceptibilities by any reference to the possibility of a British occupation of Egypt, which in any case, as Canning stated, would 'require a larger army than HM could appropriate for that object'.

Adair arrived in Constantinople in September 1808 and, after some three months of negotiation, concluded, in January 1809, the Treaty of the Dardanelles,[2] in spite of continual warnings and threats to the Porte from the French Chargé d'Affaires. This Treaty did not renew the guarantee of Turkish possessions given in the 1799 Treaty. One of its most important

123

provisions (Article XI) stipulated that the Straits between the Mediterranean and Black Seas should be closed at all times to foreign warships of all nations. This clause was insisted on by the British with a view to preventing the possibility of a union between the Russian and French fleets in the Mediterranean.

For the next three years British diplomatic efforts at Constantinople were devoted to putting a stop to the war which again broke out between Russia and Turkey late in 1809 and to reconstituting the Triple Alliance of Britain, Russia and Turkey against France. Eventually, in May 1812, mainly on account of Russian anxiety about Napoleon's imminent invasion of their territory, a treaty of peace was signed at Bucharest by which Russia restored to Turkey Moldavia and Wallachia, Servia, and all their conquests in the Caucasus. Stratford Canning, then a young man of twenty four, who was acting as Chargé d'Affaires during most of these three years, afterwards regarded this treaty as his greatest diplomatic success. Much of the credit was, however, due to Sultan Mahmud II, who had come to the throne under such inauspicious circumstances, but who had made a good start by salvaging his Empire from the *Stürm und Drang* of the Napoleonic Wars. But the major contributor was Napoleon, whose designs on Russia necessitated the withdrawal of Russian troops from the Caucasus and from the Balkans.

To return to Egypt. Fraser, when he evacuated Alexandria in September 1807, left behind as an agent P. Army, a Maltese, who sent reports from time to time. In one of these, written in October 1808, Army indicated that Mohamed Ali was extremely annoyed with the British because of the blockade which they were maintaining in Egyptian waters as a result of their still being at war with Turkey.[3] Earlier he had reported that there was nothing to be hoped for by the British from Mohamed Ali as he was entirely committed to the French.[4]

Soon after the Treaty of the Dardanelles had been signed, Samuel Briggs, who had been Pro-Consul in Alexandria and Agent of the Levant Company in Egypt before the Fraser expedition, and who had departed from Alexandria with it, returned to Alexandria in his previous position. One of the principal reasons for his return was the organization of purchases of wheat from Egypt for the British Army. Mohamed Ali was pleased to help him in this, in spite of protests from Constantinople, where Egypt was accustomed by tradition, and indeed by treaty, to ship her annual surplus. The Viceroy made a considerable profit out of these sales, buying the wheat from the fellahin at 15-20 piastres an ardeb[5] and selling it to the British at 80-90 piastres as compared with the market price of about 25 piastres. Drovetti made continual but unavailing protests about these purchases. Mohamed Ali maintained that they were necessary, both for Egypt's economy and because, if he did not sell it to the British, the British would invade Egypt. The sales were continued until 1815, while France was virtually cut off from Egypt by the British blockade. They formed the basis of the substantial British trading interest in Egypt which developed after the war.

In one of his early reports, Briggs lamented the absence of a British representative in Cairo and complained that 'the French Consul has been suffered for too long to maintain an uncontrolled sway in the capital'.[6] He also reported that 'Mohamed Ali, though professing nominal allegiance to the Porte, has long been virtually independent in the same degree as the Mamluks were prior to the French invasion'. Civil war was still raging. 'After several months' cessation of hostilities between the Pasha and the Beys, war has suddenly recommenced. The house of Elfi Bey, which has been at peace with the Pasha ever since the British evacuation, has now been prevailed on to join the other Beys, who have all decamped with many tribes of Arabs towards Upper Egypt, where protracted warfare may be expected.'

Briggs, who was dissatisfied with the British government's treatment of him financially, left Egypt towards the end of 1810.[7] A few months later, in June 1811, Missett returned to Egypt as Consul-General.

In January 1811, just after Briggs' departure, Captain Waldegrave RN, commanding HMS *Thames*, came to Alexandria to negotiate over the use of the Western Harbour by British vessels, over which there had been some difficulty. (One of the terms of the British evacuation agreement in 1803 stipulated that the Western Harbour should be open for the use of European vessels.) Waldegrave was able to get Mohamed Ali to agree that British ships could use the Western Harbour freely, but that no more than two British warships should be allowed there at one time. On his return he reported that the Viceroy had sounded him about the British attitude in the event of his declaring his independence of the Porte. 'The Viceroy's secret wish is that the Porte may be annihilated and that he may declare his independence and proclaim his sovereignty from Damascus to the Yemen.'[8] He also reported that the Viceroy was much concerned with getting more land into cultivation so as to increase the taxable capacity of the country and so in turn enable him to pay his troops which, Waldegrave estimated, at that time amounted to 6,000–7,000 cavalry and 5,000 infrantry.

These troops had inflicted a decisive defeat on the Mamluks in August 1810,[9] which had put an end to them as a military threat and cleared the way for Mohamed Ali's projected expedition to Arabia against the Wahhabis. The Wahhabis were members of a fanatical and puritanical sect of Islam which had been founded in the deserts of Central Arabia by a certain Mohamed ibn-el-Wahhab during the eighteenth century. The ruling family of Nejd, the Banu Sa'ud, and their followers, had been converted to the Wahhabi faith and, under the impulse of its fanatical élan, had made themselves masters of most of the Arabian Peninsula. In 1803 they had caused consternation throughout Islam, and grave prejudice to trading interests in Egypt and Syria, by invading the Hijaz and capturing and sacking the Holy Cities of Mecca and Medina. The recovery of the Hijaz from the Wahhabis was desirable to the Porte for reasons both of prestige and of trade and the task of recovering it appeared to be one which would absorb the energies and occupy the armies of the ambitious Viceroy of Egypt. Mohamed Ali, for his part, was not unwilling. The campaign would get his Albanians away from Cairo and either provide loot for them or get most of them killed. For these predatory and undisciplined soldiers, with whose help he had climbed to power, were now a source of anxiety to him with their perpetual intrigues and their inflated demands for back-pay.

In September 1808 Mohamed Ali asked Army, the unofficial British Agent, to inform the British government that he intended to capture Yenbo, Jidda and the Yemen. In May 1810 Briggs reported that the Viceroy was building thirty large ships at Suez and had sent an armed ship of 400 tons to the Red Sea via the Cape. After his defeat of the Mamluks in August 1810 had stabilized the internal situation in Egypt, he began making his preparations in earnest.

The expedition to Arabia was to be commanded by Tusun, Mohamed Ali's second son. The occasion of his departure from

Cairo at the head of his troops in March 1811 was used by the Viceroy in order to rid himself of most of the remaining Beys who, since their defeat in Upper Egypt the previous August, had been allowed to return to their houses and live there with some of their followers. Although they no longer represented a military menace, they were still likely sources of intrigue, either with the British, with the French,[10] with the Porte or with the Wahhabis, and the Viceroy determined to get rid of them once and for all. So, pretending to be reconciled with them, he invited the leading Beys, together with the principal notables of Cairo, to the Citadel to take part in the procession with which Tusun was to leave Cairo. The Beys accepted the invitation and, once inside the Citadel, were massacred almost to a man. One of the Beys, Hasan, escaped to Acre. By this massacre the whole of Elfi's house was eliminated. Some of the rival house of Ibrahim survived for some years in Upper Egypt. They gradually retreated further and further up the Nile, leading a precarious existence as bandits. About 300 of them settled in Dongola and their presence there was one of the reasons, or pretexts, for Mohamed Ali's Sudan expedition in 1820.

Soon after Missett, now a Lieutenant-Colonel, returned as Consul-General and British Resident in June 1811, he reported that 'the present Governor of Egypt respects none of the privileges accorded by the Capitulations. He has sold or taken into his hands various monopolies; the old duties have been increased and new dues exacted on all articles of import and export. . . . It would be vain to apply for redress to the Porte for, though he acknowledges the authority of the Sultan, he refuses to obey any order from him which may stand in opposition to his own private interest.'[11]

Mohamed Ali was raising money by every possible means in order to strengthen his army and form a navy with a view to declaring and maintaining his independence of the Porte. The monopolies to which Missett referred, and which were to become an essential feature of Mohamed Ali's internal policy, consisted of a system by which the government reserved to itself the right to buy produce from the cultivator at a price fixed by itself and to sell that produce to the merchant at a much higher price, also fixed by itself. The wheat sales to the British government, which have already been mentioned, was a good example of how it worked in practice. These monopolies, and the various customs duties and dues, bore very heavily both on the cultivators and on the merchants, but this oppression was partly offset by the great increase in public security which the Viceroy's rule brought all over Egypt, after the continual disturbances of previous years. The Mamluks and their Beduin allies were defeated and dispersed. The Albanian and other troops were subjected to stricter discipline and had, most of them, left the country to fight in Arabia. There were no longer two or more Viceroys contending for power. There was no more street-fighting in Cairo or cannonades from the Citadel. The lot of the cultivators was also being eased by Mohamed Ali's land 'reforms'. These consisted of abolishing all the dubious land titles already in existence, of appropriating to the State all the titles so abolished, and of making the sitting tenants direct tenants of the State. This involved, *inter alia*, the confiscation of the estates of the Mamluk Beys, the dispossession, against compensation in this case, of the 'multazimin' or tax-farmers, who, under the old system, had received titles to land in return for collecting taxes, and the alienation to the State of many 'awqaf', or religious trusts, in which much land had been vested, ostensibly for charitable purposes, but usually in order to avoid taxation. These reforms, although they did not, owing to increasing taxation, much relieve the cultivator, ensured that he was subjected only to a single oppressor, and that the State received the total benefit of what was extracted from him, either in the form of taxation or of forced sales of produce to a State monopoly.

The restoration of public security, the institution of monopolies, and the introduction of land reforms were all under way by the time Missett returned to Egypt. Mohamed Ali had also made a small start with building and acquiring a navy. His plans for industrialization, for a European-trained army recruited from Sudanese negroes and Egyptian peasants to replace the mutinous Albanian and other levies, for the development of cotton-growing for export, and for the modernization of Egypt's administration in the fields of education and public health, were still to come. But he was gradually building up an administrative machine, manned mainly by Turks, to relieve him of his previous reliance on the Albanians, who were being antagonized by the Viceroy's insistence on stricter discipline, and on the Ulema, who were being antagonized by the weight of taxation and by the land reforms. His principal collaborator was his Kiaya-Bey, or Minister of the Interior, Mohamed Lazoghlu, who was responsible for public security and who, in 1813, while the Viceroy was absent in Arabia, put down the last serious internal challenge to Mohamed Ali's rule. This took the form of an attempted coup by Latif Pasha, who had almost certainly been sent to Egypt by the Porte to overthrow Mohamed Ali. The attempt failed and, after a few days of disturbance, Latif Pasha was captured and beheaded and order restored.

Sultan Mahmud II and Mohamed Ali were, and remained, suspicious and mistrustful of one another. Mohamed Ali wanted to get rid of Ottoman suzerainty; the Sultan wanted a more subservient Viceroy in Cairo. But each realized that there were difficulties in the way of getting rid of the other. The Sultan could not, from his own resources, get rid of Mohamed Ali; Mohamed Ali knew that there would be reactions from the Powers in the event of his declaring his independence. In the meantime, the Sultan could use Mohamed Ali to fight the Wahhabis, and the Viceroy could use the Wahhabis as a means of battle-training his army and obtaining a foothold east of Suez, nearer the great overland trade-routes, on which his eyes, like those of all the great rulers of Egypt, were already fixed.

Mohamed Ali had already grasped that a condition of a successful assertion of independence was the goodwill of Great Britain. For that Power, with its command of the sea, was in a position either to guarantee or to frustrate that independence. In 1807 with Fraser[12] and in 1811 with Waldegrave he had raised the question of an alliance with Great Britain. During the course of 1812 he sounded Missett about the British attitude in the event of declaring his independence and indicated that he would be prepared to assist the British in the event of their becoming involved in war with Turkey.[13] He was told in reply that the British government could not 'enter into any engagements inconsistent with good faith . . . towards a Power in alliance with HM'.[14] At the same time, Mohamed Ali was negotiating with the Porte with a view to obtaining, as a first instalment of the independence which he wanted, the same semi-independence as was enjoyed by the Ruler of Algiers.[15]

Meanwhile, the campaign in Arabia, under the command of Tusun, was proceeding. Yenbo was captured but, between Yenbo and Medina, Tusun's army was ambushed in a defile by the Wahhabis and, after a three-day battle, defeated and compelled to withdraw to Yenbo. After reinforcement, the Egyptians again advanced and, after a siege lasting several weeks, captured Medina in November 1812. Mecca and Jidda were captured soon afterwards. The first stage of the campaign was over; the Wahhabis had been driven out of the Holy Cities, the trade and pilgrimage routes to and from Syria had been liberated. But the Wahhabi power remained unbroken and the object of the second stage of the campaign was the invasion of Nejd and the capture and destruction of Dariya, the Wahhabi capital.

The Viceroy himself took charge of the start of the second stage. He arrived in the Hijaz in the autumn of 1813 and visited Mecca in October. He then began preparing for a campaign in the interior of the peninsula. These preparations took the whole of the year 1814 and it was not until January 1815 that he began his advance. On 20 January he met the main Wahhabi force, 30,000 strong, at Bisel, on the road from Mecca to the Nejd. Aided by the possession of artillery, which the Wahhabis lacked, he won a decisive victory. Then, hearing news of the European crisis caused by Napoleon's return from Elba, he returned to Cairo, leaving Tusun to make peace with Abdallah ibn Sa'ud, the Sultan of Nejd (who had succeeded his father, Sa'ud ibn Sa'ud, in May 1814). By the terms of the peace treaty, Abdallah made his submission to the Porte and renounced all claims to the Hijaz. But this peace was no more than a truce. Mohamed Ali was determined to crush the Wahhabis, whom he regarded as rivals for that dominion over the Arab world which had already become his ambition. For the Wahhabi power and the Wahhabi faith, born, like Islam itself, in the deserts of Arabia, posed a threat to the Ottoman Empire similar to that which Islam had originally posed to the Byzantine Empire. Its raids and its propaganda affected all the lands of the Fertile Crescent bordering on Arabia, and the conquest of these lands, ill-defended as they were, by the Wahhabi armies and the Wahhabi faith would have forestalled Mohamed Ali in his own designs.

Ibrahim, the Viceroy's eldest son, was placed in command of preparations for a new and, it was intended, final campaign against the Wahhabis. Dariya, the Wahhabi capital, was some 500 miles SE of Medina, and separated from it by an almost waterless desert inhabited by nomad Arab tribes mostly sympathetic to the Wahhabis. Its reduction presented difficult problems both of supply and diplomacy. Ibrahim, then a young man of twenty-six, dealt with them patiently and successfully. After nearly two years of preparation, he set out from Medina in October 1817 and, in April 1818, reached Dariya without having had to fight a major battle. He had with him an army of 7,000 men and a siege train commanded by a French officer. In spite of a near-disaster due to a fire and explosion in the Egyptian ammunition-dump, Dariya surrendered to Ibrahim in September. The Wahhabi capital was razed to the ground and Abdallah ibn Sa'ud sent as a prisoner, first to Cairo, and then to Constantinople, where he was beheaded.

The Arabian campaign brought Mohamed Ali into direct contact with the government of Bombay which, at that time, was engaged in putting down piracy and the slave trade in the Persian Gulf and, by means of Protectorate treaties with the various Shaikhdoms of the Gulf, laying the foundations of that British hegemony which was to last for the next 100 years or so. This contact was, at first, friendly.

As in most unpoliced narrow waters through which trade passes, piracy was endemic in the Persian Gulf. Towards the end of the eighteenth century the lack of any strong central authority in Persia, and the invasion of the littoral Shaikhdoms on the Arab side of the Gulf by the Wahhabis, had encouraged this piracy. It fell to the British, as the only strong naval power in the area, to deal with it. In 1809, and again in 1816, the British-Indian Navy attacked and destroyed the pirate stronghold at Ras al Kheima, but piracy seemed likely to continue so long as the fanatical Wahhabis controlled the Arab shores of the Gulf.

The British and Mohamed Ali thus had a common interest in the destruction of the Wahhabis and Ibrahim's capture of Dariya was welcomed by the government of Bombay. On hearthe news they sent an emissary, Captain Sadleir, to Medina in 1819 to congratulate Ibrahim on his victory and to propose that the British, the Egyptians and Imam of the Yemen should enter into an agreement to keep the peace in Central Arabia.

The Yemen, situated at the SW corner of the Arabian Peninsula, was the most important part of Arabia both strategically and economically. Its mountainous interior, which just catches the monsoon winds, is fertile, and was known as Arabia

Felix by the Romans. Its principal production at that time was coffee, exported from the port of Mocha on the Red Sea coast. The port of Aden commanded the Straits of Bab-al-Mandeb, the entrance to the Red Sea from the Indian Ocean.

The Yemen was nominally part of the Ottoman Empire; it was ruled by a quasi-independent Imam, who was the religious leader of the Za'idis, a Moslem sect to which most of the highland inhabitants of Yemen belonged. In view of its economic and strategic importance it was of interest to the Turks, to the Egyptians, and to the British, as well as to the marauding Arab tribes of the surrounding deserts. The Turks were anxious to establish their effective authority and to exact some tribute from the Ruler. Mohamed Ali, now that the Wahhabis had been dealt with, was awaiting a suitable opportunity to invade it for his own benefit but in the name of his Suzerain. The British were interested because of the profitable Mocha coffee trade and, in the light of their nascent interest in the overland route through Egypt between England and India, because they wanted themselves to have the means of controlling entrance to and egress from the Red Sea. A few years before, when Mohamed Ali had been preparing for the Arabian expedition, the British had intercepted one of his corvettes which he had despatched round the Cape for service in the Red Sea, and this had served to warn him about British sensitivity towards his activities in the area.

Sadleir's proposal to Ibrahim from the Bombay government was communicated to the Porte by the British Ambassador at Constantinople. The Porte saw this proposal, probably correctly, as a British attempt to secure a 'sphere of influence' in the Yemen and told Mohamed Ali to have nothing to do with it. Mohamed Ali, who had his own plans for the Yemen, obeyed his Suzerain and rejected Sadleir's proposal, using as pretext the fatigue of his troops after their campaign in the Nejd.

The Egyptian presence in Arabia was probably one of the reasons for a treaty, concluded between the Bombay government and some of the Persian Gulf Shaikhs in 1820, which virtually established a British Protectorate over the Shaikhdoms of what had become known as the Pirate Coast between Qatar and Musqat. This presence was also probably one of the reasons for the British armed demonstration against the Imam of the Yemen in the same year. There was already in existence a treaty between the Bombay government and the Imam conferring various trading privileges and a British Resident was established at Mocha to supervise its observance and to look after British trading interests there. On the Resident's complaint that these interests were being infringed, two British warships arrived at Mocha from Bombay on 3 December 1820 and, after an intermittent bombardment lasting for most of the month of December, received the surrender of the Yemeni garrison and imposed a new treaty on the Imam which provided, *inter alia*, for (a) the stationing in Mocha of a guard of British-Indian troops for the Resident; (b) free access by the Resident to Sana'a, the capital, which was in the mountains in the interior; and (c) the application of the Ottoman Capitulations to British trade and British merchants in the Yemen. Both Mohamed Ali and the Porte complained about the British action, and both the British government and the government of Bombay made it clear that they had no territorial designs on the Yemen. Bruce, the British Resident, was told by the government of Bombay in September 1821 that his duty was 'strictly confined to the superintendence of our commercial concerns and the transmission of intelligence of a political nature'.[16]

British imperial policy in Asia has always been suspicious of the rise of any strong or stable authority in the area of British trading or strategic interests. The idea seems to have been that the existence of such an authority would correct the military weakness, administrative fragmentation, and local rivalries on which the British relied for making, and for being able to implement with a minimum of armed force, the agreements and treaties which were the favoured British method of imperial penetration. For the British only reluctantly assumed 'the White Man's Burden' of direct administration, if and when indirect methods of control failed. A strong and stable authority, like that of Mohamed Ali, represented increased bargaining power which would necessitate a higher price being paid for commercial and strategic advantages. In this respect the Ottoman regime suited the British perfectly. On the one hand, the great principle of the territorial integrity of the Ottoman Empire, which was, in theory, subscribed to by all the Great Powers, could be invoked against any serious derogation from Ottoman sovereignty, either by another Great Power or by an Ottoman vassal; on the other hand the Ottoman Empire's weakness, particularly in its outlying dominions, could be exploited for the securing of such local advantages as could be reconciled with the maintenance of theoretical Ottoman sovereignty. On the commercial plane, the Ottoman Capitulations—judiciously expanded here and there by the exercise of local pressures—which restricted the amount of duty payable, and conferred a large measure of extraterritoriality on resident British merchants, gave very favourable terms for British trade, much more favourable than anything which could be expected from the Ruler of a strong and stable independent State. On the strategic plane, the doctrine of the inviolability of Ottoman territory could be conveniently stretched to justify such naval and military demonstrations as might be necessary to keep local rulers in order.

The same game as the British were playing in the Red Sea and the Persian Gulf was being played by the other Great Powers in their 'spheres of influence' on the outskirts of the Ottoman Empire—by the Russians in the Black Sea, by the French in North Africa, and by the Austrians in the Adriatic. And, just as the Powers used the integrity of the Ottoman Empire as a cloak for their penetration, so Mohamed Ali used his nominal Ottoman vassalage as a cloak for his penetration, first of Arabia and, later, of Syria.

The naval demonstration at Mocha in 1820 had the ostensible object of enforcing the observance of the Ottoman Capitulations. Three years later, an attempted invasion of the Yemen by Mohamed Ali was ostensibly intended to restore order and to bring the country back to effective Ottoman suzerainty. This invasion was abandoned in 1826, partly because of the demands of the campaign then being fought by Egyptian troops in the Morea (for the ostensible purpose of restoring Greece to effective Ottoman suzerainty), and partly because of Mohamed Ali's appreciation that he could not afford seriously to clash with British interests, either in Arabia or elsewhere. The Viceroy was always acutely conscious of the necessity of accommodating himself to the reality of British sea power, in the Mediterranean and the Red Sea and the Indian Ocean, which had been a decisive factor in the defeat of Napoleon and which had been confirmed and consolidated by his downfall.

After Arabia, Mohamed Ali's next military adventure was in the Sudan. Since Pharaonic times, the Upper Nile valley had been one of the natural lines of Egyptian expansion. There was believed to be gold there. Apart from the profitable trade in slaves, Mohamed Ali was already thinking in terms of recruiting the inhabitants of the Sudan into his army, as being likely to prove cheap, docile and brave soldiers. There were cattle in the Sudan, of which there was a shortage in Egypt. There were other commodities, such as ivory and ostrich feathers, for which there was a ready market in Europe. The Sudan had never formed part of the Ottoman Empire, and there was no need either for the formality of Ottoman permission or for the pretence that its conquest was in the name of, or for the benefit of, the Sultan. Also there was, at that time, no interest in the Sudan on the part of any of the Great Powers. Mohamed Ali discussed the intended expedition with Salt, who replaced Missett as Consul-General in 1816. Salt warned him against any designs on Abyssinia, on the ground of British objection to the conquest of a Christian by a Moslem people, but otherwise expressed no objection.

The expedition assembled during the first half of 1820. At the end of June Salt reported: '5,000 troops are already assembled at the Second Cataract where they await the arrival of Ismail Pasha (Mohamed Ali's third son), who is to command the principal body. They will follow the course of the river and conquer Senaar, while a detachment under the Deftardar Bey is to march across the desert to Darfur. The troops are then to meet in Kordofan. . . . The professed objects of the expedition are to avenge an insult offered many years ago to the Pasha by the Sultan of Darfur, to collect a body of black slaves, to take possession of the gold mines, and to open up trade routes into the interior.'[17]

During the course of the Sudan expedition (1820-1822), the whole of the Northern Sudan was conquered as far as Kawa and the Abyssinian frontier on the White and Blue Nile respectively. To the west Kordofan was occupied, but the expedition against Darfur, and a projected expedition up the White Nile, were abandoned. In 1822 the prospective military needs of the Greek war caused Mohamed Ali to abandon further advances and consolidate gains already made. In October 1822 his son Ismail who had on several occasions during the campaign behaved with great barbarity, was ambushed and murdered at Shendi on his way back to Cairo.

The conquest of the Sudan did not bring all the economic benefits expected. The gold found was negligible. The slave trade was hampered by competition from the East African ports and by increasing British objections. Mohamed Ali's other preoccupations prevented any adequate exploitation of his conquests. An administrative capital was established at Khartum, at the junction between the White and Blue Niles, but Egyptian authority seldom extended beyond the garrison towns. Mohamed Ali's idea of recruiting Sudanese for his army was followed up to a certain extent, but the Albanian and other foreign mercenaries on which he originally had to rely were mainly replaced, not by Sudanese negroes, but by Egyptian fellahin.

During the years covered by the Arabian and Sudanese campaigns, British commercial interests in Egypt flourished. In 1817 Salt reported that, for the year September 1815 to September 1816, 125 British merchant vessels had arrived at Alexandria and 214 merchant vessels had sailed from Alexandria for English ports.[18] This increasing British commercial interest was due less to the enterprise of the Levant Company than to the initiatives of individual British merchants. Since the beginning of the nineteenth century the Levant Company had lost much of its importance. In Egypt, the end of the old ghetto-like existence which the foreign communities had led under the Mamluks, and the opening of the country to European influences, had rendered the old 'factory' system obsolete. And, in English commercial thinking, the old system of monopolistic trading companies was being replaced by a concept of individual free enterprise. Politically, too, the atmosphere had changed as a result of the subordination of commercial to political interest in the Ottoman Empire. In the eighteenth century the British Ambassador at Constantinople had been appointed jointly by the British government and the Levant Company, and the British Consuls in the Ottoman Empire had been nominated and paid by the Levant Company. But, as the affairs of the Ottoman Empire became more and more involved in European politics, and in British imperial interests, this became an unworkable arrangement. As from 1804 the Levant Company ceased to have any voice in the nomination of or in the instructions given to, the British Ambassador. In 1825 the Levant Company surrendered its Charter to the Crown and its existence came to an end.

Henry Salt, who was much more favourably disposed towards the Viceroy than Missett, arrived in Egypt as Consul-

General at the beginning of 1816. The war was by that time over and the task of the British Representative was no longer dominated by the necessity for discovering and combating real or supposed French intrigues. In his instructions[19] he had been told to use his best endeavours 'to maintain all the privileges and immunities of the Levant Company and to preserve inviolate the capitulations which already exist in favour of their trade and enlarge the same as far as possible'. He was also instructed to avoid interfering in the internal affairs of the country and to 'maintain a good understanding with the agents of all other Powers and endeavour to penetrate into any designs that may be entertained by them prejudicial to the interests of HM'. He was enjoined to keep in close touch with HM's Ambassador at Constantinople, with HM's Minister at Naples, with the British Resident at Corfu, with the Governor of Malta, and with the C-in-C Mediterranean Fleet. This is an indication of the extent to which the British government had come to regard Egypt as part of the Mediterranean world.

Over the next few years Salt, in accordance with his instructions, was to complain and protest against the incidence of the monopolies and against various infringements of the Capitulations. But, as he pointed out to the British Ambassador, the merchants' complaints were really invalid in that, if Ottoman rule in Egypt had been effective and the Capitulations strictly applied, the export of most of the monopolized products would, under Ottoman regulations, have been forbidden altogether, and that the cotton, indigo and sugar subject to monopoly would not have been produced in Egypt at all but for Mohamed Ali's enterprise.[20] The English merchants, like most business men, wanted it both ways; they wanted, on the one hand, the advantages, without the disadvantages, of being under direct Ottoman rule and, on the other hand, the advantages, without the disadvantages, which they actually derived from being under Mohamed Ali's rule. As Salt put it, they seemed to think that the Capitulations acted as a positive prohibition against the Ruler of the country standing between the merchants and the cultivators.[21] He expressed the view, and Stratford Canning, the Ambassador, agreed with him, that 'it could not have been intended by the Porte to concede the right of control over its own regulations', and pointed out that Mohamed Ali would have been within his rights to prohibit the export of cotton (in which the British merchants were principally interested) altogether.

In fact, a great many extensions to the extraterritorial privileges enjoyed under the Capitulations were introduced for the benefit of European residents and those living under the protection of European Consuls. Article 16 of the Capitulations treaty with Britain was interpreted as providing, not only that all criminal cases, as well as civil disputes, involving European nationals were exempted from the local jurisdiction, but that all civil cases in which a European national was a defendant against an Ottoman subject should be tried in the defendant's Consular Court. Salt reported that 'European subjects accused even of robbery or forgery are by usage handed over to the Consul. . . . It would be considered a great disgrace to his country and to the European character in general should the Consul give up a debtor or a criminal to the local authority, as the strict sense of the Capitulations would seem to prescribe.' He went on to explain that this 'established usage' had arisen 'out of the base and mercenary character of Turkish Courts of Justice', and because 'the affairs of merchants and shipping are not, as in Europe, regulated by any formal law, but all is decided according to the caprice and, often, the interested maliciousness of the local authority'. The extensions to the Capitulations described by Salt did to a great extent shield the foreign merchants from this caprice and, behind this shield, the foreign merchant community increased greatly in numbers and affluence. A petition addressed to the Consul-General by the British merchant houses in Alexandria in 1825 indicates that there were 15 such houses. During the year September 1823—September 1824 goods to the value of £178,723 were exported from Egypt to Great Britain against imports worth £35,198 from Great Britain to Egypt. The comparable figures for all Mediterranean ports were £41,080 exported from Egypt and £27,242 imported into Egypt.[22] Much of the exports, particularly to Great Britain, consisted of cotton, the cultivation of which as an export crop was being promoted by Mohamed Ali. Egypt's 'favourable trade balance' as revealed by these figures, was no doubt assisted by Mohamed Ali's monopolies, which enabled him to maximize export and minimize import prices, and resulted in a regular flow of specie into Egypt, which Mohamed Ali needed for paying the troops engaged in his numerous and expensive wars.

One of Mohamed Ali's most ambitious enterprises was the digging of the Mahmudieh Canal (completed in 1819), from

Atf, on the Rosetta branch of the Nile, to Alexandria. There had been in existence a small canal between Rahmaniya and Alexandria for supplying fresh water to Alexandria, until it was destroyed by Elfi during the civil wars. But the Mahmudieh was a navigation canal, the completion of which enabled cargoes to be carried direct by water between the interior of Egypt and the port of Alexandria.

Mohamed Ali was a keen student of European techniques and, in his quest for increased productivity, and consequent increased taxable capacity, was indiscriminately anxious to import these techniques into Egypt. In 1812 he was expressing interest in the possibility of using steam engines for the pumping of irrigation water, and asked Missett to get him a specimen steam engine from England.[23] He also imported much machinery for cotton ginning mills, textile factories etc., motivated by animal or water power. Few of these experiments were successful, owing mainly to lack of trained local *main d'oeuvre* and the Viceroy's lack of appreciation of the necessity for such training. Consequently, much money was wasted.

Mohamed Ali was more successful in his introduction of European techniques into military matters, which he understood better. His principal concern was to build up a well-armed army and navy. To replace his Albanians, he recruited Egyptian peasants and Sudanese negroes into his army and engaged European instructors to train them. Such instructors were plentifully available after the Napoleonic wars, and most of them were ex-officers of the French army. The most famous of these was Colonel Sève, who came to Egypt in 1817 and who, in 1820, was placed in command of a training depot at Aswan, which was the nucleus of Mohamed Ali's Nizam Jedid (New Model) and which, in ten years' time, was to conquer Syria and advance to the walls of Constantinople. An infantry school, a cavalry school, and a school of artillery were also established in Lower Egypt and manned with European instructors. Modern arms were necessary as well as modern training and, again with the assistance of European experts, a gunpowder factory and several foundries were set up.

In addition to modernizing his army, the Viceroy was determined to acquire a modern navy. Acutely aware of the role which the British Navy had played in the Eastern Mediterranean during the first fifteen years of the century, and of the importance of sea communications in his increasingly ambitious designs, he wanted an adequate navy both in the Mediterranean and the Red Sea. Until he established a naval shipyard in Alexandria in 1830, after his first fleet had been destroyed at Navarino, he had most of his ships built in European shipyards. He was anxious to have them built in England, but the British government, from the beginning, were suspicious about his naval activities. They stopped one of his corvettes going round the Cape.[24] After the outbreak of the Greek War of Independence in 1821, they uncompromisingly turned down a request for two frigates, telling Salt: 'It is entirely out of the power of HM's Government to comply with this request, as it would be a direct violation of the neutrality which HM has declared it to be his intention to observe during the present unhappy conflict between the Ottoman Porte and the Greeks.'[25]

In the early years of his reign most of the European experts engaged by Mohamed Ali were military instructors and most of these were French. This was partly because of the number of unemployed French officers available after 1815, partly because of the interest in Egypt displayed by France as a result of the work of the Institut d'Egypte founded during the French occupation, but mainly, perhaps, because of the policy of Drovetti, who remained as French Consul-General—with a break between 1814 and 1819—until 1829.[26] During his second term as Consul-General—from 1819 to 1829—Drovetti got the support of successive French governments in achieving a gradual French cultural penetration of Egypt, by associating France with the Viceroy's desire for modernization, and by supplying French experts, French techniques, and French products to meet this desire. His policy, which was very successful, and in marked contrast to the subsequent blunderings of French *haute politique* over Egypt, does much to explain the distinctively French *ambience* assumed by Egypt during the first half of the nineteenth century.

The French government gave facilities for many young Egyptians to be educated in France. Many of the principal civilian experts—Clot Bey in medicine, Linant de Bellefonds in irrigation, Gallice Bey in engineering, Champollion in the new science of Egyptology—were French and introduced French methods and French assistants. The French language became the principal vehicle of communication between educated Egyptians and Europeans, and between Europeans of different nationalities. The Viceroy was more than ready to accept any help he could get and the French preoccupation with cultural influence forged strong bonds between France and the Egyptian government. The British preoccupation with trade, on the contrary, tended to predispose successive British governments against the regime. Although infinitely more favourable to foreign trade than any of its predecessors, and generally more favourable than the regimes in most of the other Ottoman Provinces, by reason of the security and relative prosperity which Mohamed Ali had brought to Egypt, it was, somewhat perversely, regarded in British official circles as being unfavourable to foreign trade on account of the monopolies and other restrictions. These predispositions did not determine, but they almost certainly influenced, the respective positions taken up by the British and French governments when the events of the Greek War of Independence once more brought Egypt into the forefront of international affairs.

CHAPTER SIX

THE GREEK WAR OF INDEPENDENCE

Ever since the capture of Constantinople by the Turks in 1453 it had, theoretically, been an ambition of Christian Europe to liberate the Christian lands and peoples which had fallen under the Moslem yoke. In the eighteenth century France and Austria were joined in this ambition by Russia which, from the time of Peter the Great onwards, ranked as a European Great Power. But this theoretical ambition was frustrated by rivalries between these three Powers, which prevented them from combining with each other against Turkey and which, on occasion, led one or more of them to make common cause with Turkey against the others. Thus a theoretical determination to liberate Christians subject to the Turks became transmuted into a practical policy of sustaining the Ottoman Empire in Europe for fear lest one or other of the Christian Powers might gain disproportionately as a result of its dissolution and so upset the precarious balance of power in Europe.

During the second half of the eighteenth century the Russian drive southwards towards warm water ports and access to the Mediterranean involved them in two wars with Turkey and brought them considerable accessions of Ottoman territory round the coasts of the Black Sea. These wars also led to Russian contacts with the Christian peoples of Turkey in Europe, including the Greeks. In 1770, during the first Russo-Turkish war, there was a Russian-inspired Greek insurrection, which the Russians supported inadequately in spite of the presence of a Russian naval squadron in the Mediterranean, and which was mercilessly suppressed by the Turks. At the Peace of Küchük Kainarji, in 1774, which concluded this war, the Russians stipulated, and obtained from the Turks, an amnesty for Christian subjects of the Porte who had revolted

during the course of it. They also obtained a Turkish acknowledgement of Russia's right thenceforward to make representations on behalf of these Christian subjects. It was the thin
end of a substantial wedge. In 1787, when Russia was again at
war with Turkey, she was joined by Austria, and a partition of
European Turkey between these two Powers might well have
taken place had it not been for the French Revolution and for
the menacing attitude of the French revolutionary armies in
the Low Countries, which caused Austria hurriedly to make
peace with Turkey in 1791. A year later, Russia followed suit.

For the next twenty years European affairs were dominated
by the French wars which, *inter alia*, resulted in the emergence
of England as a major Power in the Mediterranean. During
these wars, the continued existence of the Ottoman Empire in
Europe was ensured by the desire of both sides to secure the
alliance of the Porte and by the virtuosity of Turkish Ministers
in taking advantage of this situation. As the result of a series
of delicate and complicated balancing acts, the Ottoman
Empire emerged, in 1815, with its European territory almost
intact.

The peace settlement of 1815 was dominated by the desire of
all the negotiators to restore Europe, as far as possible, to the
status quo ante Napoleon. In particular, the subversive forces of
nationalism and democracy which had been bred by the
French Revolution and fostered by Napoleon, were to be
discouraged and, if necessary, repressed as posing a threat to
the old-established, recently-endangered, and now restored
monarchies of Europe, of which the principal one was the House
of Hapsburg, whose capital, Vienna, was the seat of the peace
conference, and whose Foreign Minister, Metternich, was the
principal architect of the peace settlement. Soon after the
settlement, on the initiative of Tsar Alexander I of Russia, the
'Holy Alliance' of Russia, Austria and Prussia was formed with
the principal object of intervening in favour of the *status quo*
against any revolutionary movement in any European State.

The restoration of the balance of power and the discourage-
ment of national movements of insurrection imposed the necessity for restraint in the pursuit of Russian and Austrian designs
on European Turkey and, to that extent, acted as a guarantee
against further Russian and Austrian encroachments. The immediate threat to the Ottoman Empire in Europe came from a
more or less spontaneous insurrection by the Greeks, which

broke out in 1821. It was seen by the European Powers primarily as an unwelcome manifestation of that nationalist and revolutionary spirit which they were concerned to discourage. But, from the point of view of public opinion in Christian Europe, it was impracticable for Christian Powers to ally themselves with a Moslem Power in suppressing the insurrection of a Christian people oppressed by that Moslem Power. Therefore, unless the Turks were themselves able to deal with the insurrection, some compromise would have to be arrived at.

The other nascent threat to the *status quo* in Eastern Europe was beginning to come from Egypt. While the French wars were still on, Mohamed Ali, in conversations with both the British and the French Consuls-General, had made no secret of his ambition to make himself independent of the Porte. During these wars, the desire of both Britain and France to stand well at the Sublime Porte had prevented either Government from encouraging him in this ambition. And, after 1815, they both realized that a formal declaration of independence by Mohamed Ali might start a chain of events leading to a dissolution of the Ottoman Empire, and a consequent disruption of the balance of power in Europe. Mohamed Ali, always sensitive to the nuances of European diplomacy, eventually realized this, and ceased to think in terms of British or French sponsorship for an act of independence which would separate him from the Ottoman Empire. Instead, he concentrated on aggrandizement within the framework of the Ottoman Empire, possibly with a view to himself and his heirs succeeding to the leadership of an Empire regenerated by his creative enterprise.

Ambitious vassalage aiming at independence was no new phenomenon for the Sublime Porte. Mohamed Ali was but the latest of a long line of powerful adventurers who had temporarily elevated themselves into positions of virtual independence and who had eventually come to grief. Fakhreddin al Ma'ani of Lebanon, Ali Bey of Egypt, Jezzar Pasha of Acre, Ali Pasha of Yanina—to name but a few—had all either been defeated, decapitated, diminished or deposed. The classic Ottoman prescription was to set a potentially rebellious vassal at the throat of an actually rebellious one, in the hope that one would be destroyed and the other weakened. This is what the Sultan had done with Mohamed Ali against the Wahhabis. The Wahhabis were indeed destroyed. But Mohamed Ali, instead of being weakened, was strengthened.

144

After his victory over the Wahhabis, Ibrahim, who was made Pasha of Mecca by the Turks, was regarded by his father almost as a partner in his plans for the future. These plans may indeed have been influenced by Ibrahim, who was almost as remarkable a man as his father. As he had already shown in Arabia, and as he was later to prove in Greece, Syria and Asia Minor, he was an outstanding General. He was an efficient, although harsh, administrator. He spoke Arabic well, which Mohamed Ali did not, had Arab affinities which were quite foreign to the Viceroy, and regarded himself as almost an Arab. These Arab proclivities may have been formed, and had in any case been strengthened, by the years of fighting, negotiating and ruling among the Beduin of Central Arabia. As a statesman he never had the opportunity to act entirely independently of his father, but he was probably responsible for channelling his father's ambitions in the direction of the Arabic-speaking peoples of the Ottoman Empire. At all events, these ambitions seem to have become concentrated on Syria from about 1820 onwards. He had, for years, been in close touch with men and events there. He was on intimate terms with Emir Beshir Shihab of Lebanon, who had spent a period of enforced exile in Egypt. In 1823 Salt reported that the Viceroy was 'in secret correspondence with the Kurds and has the Pashas of Acre and Damascus and the Emir Beshir under his control'.[1] In January 1825 he reported that 'the possession of the Pashaliks of Acre, Aleppo and Damascus is certainly his (i.e. the Viceroy's) first aim'.[2] Mohamed Ali's principal reason for coming to the assistance of his Suzerain in the Greek insurrection was the calculation that this would enable him successfully to demand the grant of the three Syrian Pashaliks in return. That this ambition was well known, and that it was not at that time regarded by the British government with any particular concern, is shown by the fact that Stratford Canning, when British Ambassador in Constantinople, offered his good offices to try to obtain the Syrian Pashaliks for him on condition that he used his influence at the Porte in the direction of British mediation in the Greek war.[3]

Mohamed Ali's assistance to his Suzerain in the Greek war was to bring him for the first time into the arena of European politics, and to make him and his regime an object of interest and concern to the governments of Europe. From 1824 to 1841 he and his son Ibrahim, up to that time almost unknown to the man-in-the-street in London, Paris or Vienna, were always somewhere near the centre of the European stage.

The Greeks were easily the most important and influential Christian community in European Turkey. In so far as the Turks had become Europeanized, they had become so by absorbing the *mores* of the Byzantine Empire which they had supplanted. There was a large Greek community in Constantinople and the Greek Orthodox Patriarch enjoyed an almost extraterritorial status. By tradition, the Principalities of Moldavia and Wallachia, on the Danube, had Greek Hospodars, or Governors. Many of the Greek islands had almost completely autonomous administrations. The mountain districts on the Greek mainland also enjoyed a large measure of autonomy. Nevertheless, the Greeks were regarded by the Turks as *Rayahs*—second-class, because Christian, Ottoman subjects— under the rule and subject to the authority of a Moslem master race. Although generous in the concessions which they were prepared to grant to non-Ottoman Christians living in the Ottoman dominions, the Turks greatly resented any European attempt to claim, or any *Rayah* attempt to assert, an extension of these concessions from non-Ottoman to Ottoman Christians. The Greeks, on their side, could never forget that they had been rulers where they were now ruled. To them Constantinople was what Jerusalem was to become for the Zionists. Their desire for independence had, moreover, been sharpened by recent events, by the successive Turkish defeats at the hands of Russia, by the nationalist and liberal aspirations released all over Europe as a result of the French Revolution, by the romantic cult for the Greeks which was beginning to grow up among the intelligentsia of Western Europe, and by the alluring, although deceptive, quasi-independence enjoyed, since 1815, under British protection, by the inhabitants of the Ionian Islands.

The outbreak of the Greek insurrection early in 1821 marks the beginning of that 'Eastern Question' which, now that the overriding Napoleonic threat had been exorcized, was to agitate European politics for the next fifty years or so, in much the same way as, over 100 years later, the 'Cold War' was to agitate European politics after the removal of Hitler and the Nazis. The roots of the Eastern Question lay in the rise of Russia, in the decline of Turkey, and in the fear of the other Great Powers lest the combination of these facts should result in the absorption of European Turkey by Russia. In face of this threat Austria maintained a fairly consistent policy of trying to preserve, as far as possible, the territorial integrity of the Ottoman Empire. France, recovering from its Napoleonic debauch, was anxious to re-assert its traditional position in the Eastern Mediterranean. This had been compromised by British naval supremacy in that area, a by-product of the French wars which had resulted, *inter alia*, in British possession of Malta and the Ionian Islands. French attempts to re-assert their traditional position oscillated between efforts to restore the position of the French Representative at Constantinople as *primus inter pares* at a rejuvenated Sublime Porte, and the development of close relationships with the Greek and Egyptian heirs presumptive of the Ottoman Empire. The French saw that, in the event of the dissolution of the Ottoman Empire, an independent Greece and an enlarged and independent Egypt, bound by ties of friendship and obligation to France, would do much both to offset Russian influence at Constantinople and the British influence in the Eastern Mediterranean conferred by their naval superiority. The French, therefore, were less than whole-hearted in their desire for the preservation of the Ottoman Empire, and oscillated between two diametrically-opposed policies—between preserving the *status quo* and pre-empting as large a share as possible of the Ottoman heritage. On the one hand they tried to outbid the other Powers in obtaining influence at Constantinople; on the other hand they endeavoured to undermine Ottoman influence in Egypt, Greece, Syria and elsewhere.

The British position was based firmly on the maintenance of the territorial integrity and unimpaired authority of the Ottoman Empire as being the best available means of keeping the Russians out of Constantinople and the French out of Egypt and so of preserving the balance of power in Europe and the security of British communications with India. The basic weakness of this policy lay in the weakness of the Ottoman Empire; its successful implementation (and it was, on the whole, successfully implemented) lay in the dexterity and flexibility with which the British both shielded the Porte from some of the most formidable pressures operating against it and induced the Porte to bend sufficiently before these pressures in order to avoid being buckled under their weight.

The centre of the Greek insurrection was in the Greek

islands of the Aegean and, particularly, Hydra which, in the early years, was the rebel headquarters. The ability of the Greek marine to harass Turkish sea communications, to prevent the sea-borne reinforcement of Turkish garrisons on the Greek mainland, and to provide such reinforcement for their own armies, was the essential factor which saved the Greeks from defeat and, by ensuring European intervention, brought about their ultimate independence.

On the mainland the principal rebel areas were Missolonghi, in Western Greece, and the Morea which within a few months was, with the exception of the fortress of Patras in the north-west corner, entirely under Greek control. An attempted rising, under Greek leadership, in Moldavia and Wallachia, rapidly fizzled out after Russia had made it clear that the rebels could not expect her support.

When the news of the rebellion reached Constantinople there was a popular outburst of Moslem fanaticism and several hundred Greeks living in the city, including the Greek Orthodox Patriarch, were massacred. The Russian government reacted strongly. Relying on previous treaties, which conferred on them the right to make representations on behalf of Christian subjects of the Porte, they demanded the cessation of persecution, apology and restitution. On these demands not being met they withdrew their Ambassador. The resources of European diplomacy were immediately deployed to prevent the outbreak of a war between Turkey and Russia which would probably have resulted in a Russian occupation of Constantinople. There is no need here to follow the proceedings of the various conferences which followed. None of the Powers welcomed the Greek rebellion; they saw it as a disturbing influence which had already precipitated a crisis in relations between Russia and the Porte. The best solution, from the point of view of all the European governments, would have been for the Turks to deal successfully with the rebellion themselves either by concession or by conquest, and without the accompaniment of those atrocities to which the Turks were prone and towards which, when applied to Christians, European consciences were becoming increasingly sensitive. But it soon became apparent that the Turks by themselves were neither able to crush nor willing to compound with the rebels and that the fighting on both sides was being conducted with appalling savagery. Also, the fact that much of the fighting took place at sea was beginning to affect European commerce in the Eastern Mediterranean, mainly as a result of the activities of the Greeks who, taking a large view of the necessities of war, were engaging in activities indistinguishable from piracy against shipping of all nations.

War between Turkey and Russia was, for the time being, averted. As conference succeeded conference, and as the rebellion dragged on, the attitude of the Powers towards the struggle began to clarify. Austria's attitude was consistent from beginning to end. Metternich desired no concessions whatever to be made to the Greeks, encouraged the Turks to put down the rebellion by all possible means, and used all the resources of diplomacy to try to prevent any European attempt either to assist the Greeks or to restrain the Turks. The Russians were not interested in Greek independence but, at the beginning of 1824, produced a plan for a settlement involving the creation of three or four autonomous Greek Provinces under Turkish suzerainty which, like the Principalities of Moldavia and Wallachia, would inevitably have become Russian protectorates. France became involved in negotiations intended to lead to the installation of a French Prince onto a Greek throne. England, under the impulse of a more liberal policy adopted by Canning, who became Foreign Secretary after Castlereagh's death in September 1822, and under the influence of increasingly vociferous philhellenic public opinion, was moving in the direction of forcible intervention in favour of the Greeks.

In March 1823 the British government made a declaration of neutrality in which belligerent rights were conceded to the Greek insurgents, thus, in effect, elevating the rebellion into a war of independence. At the beginning of 1824 the Greek Provisional Government raised a loan of £800,000 in London. At the end of 1824 Canning, in a letter to the Head of the Greek Provisional Government, assured him, 'not only that Great Britain would not be concerned in any attempt to force on them a plan of pacification contrary to their wishes but, if they should at any time hereafter solicit our mediation, we should be ready to tender it to the Porte and, if accepted by the Porte, do our best to carry it into effect conjointly with other Powers'. The letter, however, went on to warn the Greeks that the British government were 'connected with the Porte by the established relations of amity and by the ancient obligation of treaties which the Porte has not violated', and that it could not be expected that they should 'engage in unprovoked hostilities against that Power in a quarrel not her own'.[4]

At first, Mohamed Ali was not called upon by his Suzerain to provide any considerable assistance in the Greek war. In the autumn of 1821 Salt reported the Viceroy as having told him that 'whatever difficulties previously existed between him and the Sublime Porte are now entirely removed and that his whole disposable force of 18,000 men under the command of Ibrahim Pasha is at the Sultan's disposal. Were he assured that England would secure the passage of his troops by sea in case of emergency he would soon show the Grand Seigneur what he was capable of doing. . . . He has already sent twenty-two armed vessels to join the Turkish fleet and has furnished two million dollars' worth of supplies.'[5] A year later, in a reference to the large Greek population of Alexandria, Salt reported that 'the Pasha, in everything that concerns the Greeks, has evinced a degree of humanity and consideration that does honour to his government'.[6] At the beginning of 1824, when it had become apparent that the Turks, unaided, would be unable to put down the insurrection, the Sultan signified the need for the Viceroy's assistance by appointing him to the supreme command of operations in the Morea. Mohamed Ali thereupon started preparing an expeditionary force, to be commanded by Ibrahim. There was a good deal of delay in its setting out, due mainly to Mohamed Ali's mistrust of the Capitan Pasha, who was none other than Khosrev, ex-Pasha of Egypt, whom Mohamed Ali had expelled in 1805. However, at the end of July, the Egyptian force, consisting of 63 warships, 100 transports, and 16,000 men, set out from Alexandria for Rhodes to join the Capitan Pasha in the Aegean. They never made their junction. The Turkish fleet was engaged by the Greeks, severely mauled, and forced to retreat through the Dardanelles. Ibrahim postponed his attempt on the mainland and retired for the winter to Candia, where a Greek rebellion was being put down and where the Turks were more or less in control.[7]

This delay reduced Turkish hopes to a very low ebb, since all their hopes depended on the success of Ibrahim's expedition. Meyer, the British Consul in Albania, reported that 'all the extraordinary Turkish reverses of the campaign, combined with the recent blockade of Patras and Lepanto by the Greeks, have produced an extraordinary depression in the minds of the Turks. . . . They now openly express the wish that the Morea, if irrevocably lost to them, should be ceded to England or to any other Power rather than that they should acknowledge a Greek government under any form.'[8] But the Greeks did not take advantage of their favourable position. The army quarrelled with the navy. Russophiles quarrelled with Anglophiles. The blockade of Patras and Lepanto was raised. Something like a state of civil war developed.

In February 1825 Ibrahim, taking advantage of the situation, landed his force at Modon in the south-west of the Morea and, within a few months, defeated the Greeks in several pitched battles. By the time winter put a stop to active operations, he was threatening the fortress of Nauplia, in the north-east of the Morea, the seat of the Greek Provisional Government. In the following spring he took part of his army into Western Greece and, in conjunction with the Turkish General Rashid Pasha, captured the fortress of Missolonghi, which had been a stronghold of Greek resistance since the beginning of the war. This campaign was the first which had been fought by Mohamed Ali's Nizam Jedid and their victories were evidence of the beneficial effect of the European training and weapons which had been introduced. As a British observer wrote: 'It has been shown that men of no personal prowess . . . of whom one Greek is more than a match for ten, are able, with the advantages of discipline, of modern arms, of good officers, and of unity of command, to restrain the impetuosity of the bravest Greek soldiers.'[9]

The Greeks, under the impulse of these misfortunes, closed their ranks and presented something like a united front towards the enemy. In a gesture almost of despair, the Greek Provisional Government, in July 1825, made a communication to the British Government in which they 'voluntarily placed their liberty and their political existence under the protection of Great Britain'.[10] The Provisional Government's choice of Great Britain as a protector had been influenced by several factors. The British philhellenes, under the aegis of the London Greek Committee, had been extremely active in organizing moral support and material assistance for the Greek cause. The romantic death of Byron at Missolonghi had created a great impression. The English loan had enabled desperately needed supplies to be bought for the Greek marine. The British administration of the Ionian Islands under a new High Commissioner, Sir Frederick Adam, was proving more sympathetic to the Greek cause than the previous administration under Sir Thomas Maitland. Two British naval officers—Admiral Cochrane, acting unofficially, and Captain Hamilton, acting semi-officially—had rendered great assistance to the Greek cause at sea. The British recognition of Greek belligerent rights, and Canning's subsequent policy, had demonstrated that the British were more sympathetic than any other of the Great Powers.

This sympathetic attitude was resented by the Turks and the Egyptians as much as it was appreciated by the Greeks. In November 1825 Salt reported that Admiral Cochrane's activities were causing great alarm in Egypt where it was feared that, if he were placed in command of the Greek navy, he would, 'with the vessels and steam-boats promised in England', be able to blockade the Egyptian coast and prevent reinforcements being sent to Ibrahim in the Morea. He added that, in spite of the British government's declaration of neutrality, it was common knowledge that the burden of the war was being carried by individual Englishmen forming the Greek Committee, who furnished 'arms, ammunition, vessels, money and officers. Such is the view taken by Mohamed Ali and the Capitan Pasha (who was visiting Egypt) who have severally declared to me that, had it not been for the English, the war would have been terminated.' He concluded his despatch with the following reflection: 'The Turks are too removed from civilization to understand the nice distinction between a neutral being at peace and its subjects being permitted to carry on a war.'[11]

The British government rejected the Greek request for protection, but British diplomacy devoted itself to the task of bringing the Powers round to an agreement by which pressure would be brought on the Porte to end the conflict on terms acceptable to the Greeks. Stratford Canning, a cousin of the Foreign Secretary, was appointed Ambassador to the Porte in place of Lord Strangford who, while in Constantinople, had shown himself almost entirely subservient to the views of Russia and Austria. In the summer of 1825, before proceeding to Constantinople, Stratford Canning was sent to Petersburg to try to induce the Russian government to resume diplomatic relations with the Porte as a preliminary to a joint Anglo-Russian attempt at mediation. At the beginning of 1826, on his way to Constantinople, he stopped at Hydra, where he met several of the Greek leaders and secured their consent to British mediation.

Towards the end of 1825 Tsar Alexander I died and was succeeded by Nicolas I. Alexander, as the principal architect of the Holy Alliance, while quite prepared to insist on Turkish observance of existing treaties with Russia, had been most reluctant to separate himself from Austria by any action calculated to assist the Greek cause. His successor had no such inhibition and, in April 1826, as a result of a mission by the Duke of Wellington to Petersburg, the Russians signed a Protocol with the British in which it was agreed that the two governments should propose to the Porte a settlement based on a single autonomous Greek State under Ottoman suzerainty. The implementation of this Protocol was, however, delayed by the fact that, a few days before its signature, the Russian government had presented to the Porte an ultimatum calling for satisfaction in various matters of Russo-Turkish relations unconnected with Greece. This ultimatum, which the Turks accepted in principle, led to a series of negotiations which delayed by several months the arrival of a Russian plenipotentiary at Constantinople.

The Turkish acceptance of this ultimatum was due in part to events in Turkey which, for the time being, made it impossible for them to conduct any warlike operations anywhere. Twenty years before, Sultan Selim III had attempted to replace his mutinous praetorian guard, the Janissaries, by a modern army, and he and his successor, Mustafa IV, had been murdered in the disturbances which followed. Sultan Mahmud II, as soon as he had consolidated his position on the throne, renewed his predecessors' attempts to build up a Nizam Jedid to replace the Janissaries. He was more successful than they had been. In the summer of 1826, having prepared the ground with care, he took advantage of an attempted mutiny by the Janissaries to exterminate that body, together with their sympathizers. For several weeks the streets of Constantinople almost literally flowed with blood. At the end of the slaughter the Janissaries had been eliminated as completely as the Mamluks had been in Egypt sixteen years before. But, for the time being, Turkey was weakened, and this weakness was an important factor in the events which followed.

Throughout 1826 Stratford Canning, pending the settlement of the Russo-Turkish dispute, which was being discussed at a

153

conference at Akkerman on the Russo-Turkish border, and the arrival of a Russian plenipotentiary at Constantinople, tried, vainly and single-handed, to extract from the Porte an agreement to mediation on the lines of the Anglo-Russian Protocol. Since it was apparent that Turkish ability to carry on the war depended entirely on the Egyptian army and navy, he sought to influence Mohamed Ali in favour of a settlement. In June 1826 he wrote to Salt informing him that he had been authorized to mediate between the Turks and Greeks: 'If the Viceroy of Egypt could be made to understand his own interests so far as to enter into our views, there is no doubt that his concurrence might tend to further the success of my negotiations; it would surely be better for him to look for a share of the tribute to be paid by Greece and to a Pashalik for his son in Syria than to persist in wasting his resources on the reduction of a stubborn population which must be exterminated, leaving an unproductive possession in his hands as an infallible subject of quarrel between him and the European Powers. I have little doubt that the influence of the Embassy would reasonably be lent to him in return for his prevailing on the Porte to accept our mediation and to proceed at once to the pacification of Greece. There is no intention of insisting on the independence of Greece; what is proposed is autonomy under the Sultan's suzerainty.'[12] Salt replied that 'the Viceroy would be most happy to find an excuse to retire from the contest if he could do so with honour'. He told the Ambassador that he had discussed the question with Boghos Yusef, an Armenian who was the Viceroy's Chief Interpreter and unofficial Foreign Minister. Boghos had told him that the Porte 'would look with great disfavour on any initiative by the Viceroy in favour of mediation'. Mohamed Ali had entered the war 'with the sole object of showing that he could accomplish what the Porte was unable to do'. He thought that he would have had an easy conquest 'but for the secret influence of HM's Government'. Salt added that the Viceroy had no territorial ambitions in Greece, that he was anxious to get his army out of the Morea, but that 'he would not be satisfied until he obtained the Pashaliks of Syria for his son'.[13]

About six weeks later Salt had a long audience with the Viceroy in which he again asked him to use his influence at the Porte in favour of British mediation. In a note of the conversation sent to Stratford Canning, he recorded the Viceroy as saying that the Sultan was too much of a bigot to consider peace. He thought that he could have beaten the Greeks himself by attacking Nauplia and Hydra but had been prevented from doing so by the refusal of Khosrev, the Capitan Pasha, to cooperate with him. The Viceroy then, after expressing, in his characteristically veiled way, his mistrust of the Porte, of the Russians, and of the French, hinted that he would be willing to fall in with the British government's views if the British government showed some complaisance towards him. Pressed to be more specific, he said that he wanted a credit to enable him to buy ships in England and an assurance that the British would look with favour on Egyptian expansion towards the Yemen and the Persian Gulf. Salt added that what he really wanted was an assurance of British support for a declaration of independence should matters come to a rupture between him and the Porte. If he got such an assurance he would withdraw his forces from Greece. If not, Salt quoted the Viceroy as saying: 'I will collect all my forces, get the command of the Ottoman fleet, secure the dismissal of the Capitan Pasha, and finish the business.'[14]

A Russian plenipotentiary, Ribeaupierre, arrived in Constantinople in February 1827, but negotiations with the Porte made no progress, partly because of the attitude of the Austrian Internuncio and the Prussian Minister, who did their best to persuade the Porte to reject all demands for mediation. Another emissary of Metternich's, Prokesch-Osten, had arrived in Egypt in October 1826 in order to try to persuade the Viceroy to carry on the war in the Morea.[15]

Meanwhile, the French government had come round almost completely to the British and Russian views as expressed in the Petersburg Protocol of April 1826. In July 1827, the Treaty of London was signed between England, Russia and France. By its terms the three contracting Powers offered to the Porte their mediation for a settlement on the lines laid down in the Protocol, called on both belligerents to agree to an immediate armistice, and provided that, in the event of an armistice not being arranged within a month, the three Powers would interpose naval forces between the combatants 'without actually taking part in hostilities themselves'.[16] In effect, this last provision meant that communications between Ibrahim and his bases in Candia and Egypt would be cut off and movements of Turkish and Egyptian transports and ships of war towards Greek ports would be intercepted.

A British naval squadron under Vice-Admiral Sir Edward Codrington, and French and Russian squadrons under Admirals de Rigny and de Heyden, were sent into Greek waters and furnished by their respective Ambassadors in Constantinople with necessarily rather equivocal instructions to enforce the armistice if necessary. Codrington, whose nickname of 'Go it Ned' does not indicate a particularly pacific disposition, asked Stratford Canning for elucidation and received the following answer: 'I have considered and talked over with my colleagues, Count Guilleminot and M. de Ribeaupierre, the several questions mentioned in your letter. . . . Although the measures to be executed by you (in the event of the Porte's rejection of our proposals) are not adopted in a hostile spirit, and although it is clearly the intention of the allied governments to avoid, if possible, anything that may bring on war, yet the prevention of supplies, as stated in your instructions, is ultimately to be enforced, if necessary, and when all other means are exhausted, by cannon-shot.'[14]

By the time of the signature of the Treaty of London, the Greeks were in a desperate state. In June 1827 Athens had fallen to Rashid Pasha. A fleet was being fitted out at Alexandria under the command of Moharrem Bey, the Viceroy's son-in-law, for an attack on Hydra. At Constantinople the Turks utterly refused to consider the allied offer of mediation. The Viceroy, having secured his demands for Khosrev's dismissal and for his investment with the command of the whole Turco-Egyptian fleet, listened to the exhortations of the various representatives of the Powers. On the one hand Prokesch-Osten was urging him to action against the Greeks. On the other hand Salt and Drovetti were urging caution. The drawing together of Britain, France and Russia was making the Viceroy pause. In June Salt reported that he only wanted a suitable pretext for withdrawing his troops from the Morea and recommended that, if the Powers had decided to compel the Porte to accept their mediation, they should arrange for a naval demonstration off Alexandria to insist on an Egyptian withdrawal from the war. A few days later, Salt expressed the fear lest news of the capture of Athens, which had just reached Alexandria, might precipitate the sailing of the Egyptian fleet to attack Hydra. In July, Salt told Stratford Canning: 'Whatever may be determined on, it is desirable that an immediate and friendly communication be made to the Pasha, who will probably be prepared to comply with whatever line of conduct may be suggested to him. Should any hostile exhibition of interference be made against his shipping away from Alexandria, it might altogether prevent his recalling Ibrahim Pasha, a step he has promised to take if he is treated in a conciliatory way. The force he is about to send will consist of two line of battle ships, about fifteen frigates, twenty corvettes and brigs, with fireships and transports and about four thousand troops.'[18]

After the signature of the Treaty of London, the Foreign Office sent Colonel Cradock, of the British Embassy in Paris, to negotiate with the Viceroy. He arrived at Alexandria on 8 August. But the Egyptian fleet had sailed on 2 August. According to Salt, 'the Pasha had become wearied by the state of suspense in which he was kept by its remaining in port and, on a sudden impulse, sent it away'.[19] Referring to Cradock's mission, he described it as 'a proof of the friendly intentions of HM's Government', but added: 'HH having as it were staked himself to the Grand Seigneur to the performance of something of importance, we have to ask from him a neutrality which may compromise him altogether with the Porte and have nothing to offer him in return. If the Porte should throw its whole force on the Pasha, will HM's Government support him in his view of independence? Will it acknowledge him as a separate Power?' When Cradock asked the Viceroy to give orders for the recall of the fleet, he refused, but suggested that the allied Admirals should send a joint note to Ibrahim requesting him to abstain from attacking Hydra. He went on to explain that Ibrahim would submit this request to Constantinople before taking any further action and that, in this way, time would be gained.[20]

On 8 August Canning, who had been Prime Minister since April, died. He was succeeded by the Duke of Wellington. The Earl of Dudley, who had succeeded Canning as Foreign Secretary in April, remained in this office for the time being.

At the end of August Salt reported the result of another audience with the Viceroy. He quoted him as saying that, if the Syrian Pashaliks were placed at his disposal by the Sultan, he would be prepared to risk the loss of his fleet to obtain 'these long-desired possessions', 'always reserving to himself the power of separating himself from the Ottoman Empire if he can obtain from the British government, or rather from the allied

Powers, what he would esteem still more highly—a positive assurance of support in his plans for independence and aggrandisement. HH is daily expecting the arrival of some person of distinction from Constantinople to acquaint him with the Sultan's final resolution. . . . Should the Syrian Pashaliks be given to him . . . it may induce him to take up the Sultan's cause with such fervour as to face the possibility of a religious war that may last for fifty years . . . trusting that the Powers, now united, would ere long disagree among themselves and one or more retire from the contest. . . . On the other side, HH is trying to ascertain what he has to hope from HM's Government and, if we would sanction his independence and connive at his taking Damascus, HH would be well content to renounce the glory of being at the head of the Moslem world and content himself with remaining the ally of Christendom. . . . Should the Grand Seigneur not come forward as liberally as he expects, HH would be ready . . . to withdraw immediately his fleet and to recall his son and army and take his chance of what may follow. He is evidently gratified that matters have been brought to this point by the allied Powers, as it seems to place the Grand Seigneur so much at his mercy. . . . I recommend, as soon as the Grand Seigneur's final determination is known, if it be adverse to mediation, that a naval force be sent to Alexandria to bring HH to a decision. Should he be determined to act with us, the necessary measures should be devised for bringing back Ibrahim Pasha and his army and for bringing the fleet home. If he should be determined to shape his conduct in conformity to the orders of the Grand Seigneur, the means should be afforded for removing HM's Consulate, and such British subjects as may choose to quit the country.'[21]

This was Salt's last important despatch. At the end of October, just before leaving Egypt for sick leave in Europe, he died. John Barker, British Consul in Alexandria, took over as Consul-General. Before he had done so, the resources of diplomacy had been overtaken by the arbitrament of war. On 20 October 1827 the combined Turkish and Egyptian fleets were attacked and destroyed in the harbour of Navarino, on the west coast of the Morea, by the combined British, French and Russian squadrons.

The Greek war of independence was a religious war—between the Cross and the Crescent—as well as a struggle for national freedom. This fact helps to explain both the obstinacy with which the Sultan refused all offers of mediation from Christian Powers and the sympathy with which the Greeks were regarded in most European countries. It also helps to explain the Viceroy's hesitancy in withholding aid from the Sultan and his reluctance to appear either to be making common cause with the Christian Powers or taking advantage of the Sultan's difficulties by declaring himself independent. For the Sultan was also Khalif-ul-Islam and, in this capacity, attracted allegiance all over the Moslem world which he would not have attracted merely as Sultan. Had the Viceroy contravened the Sultan's wishes on this issue, either by withdrawing his aid or declaring himself independent, he would have run the risk of exciting hostility against himself in the Moslem world as a whole, in Egypt itself, and even among his own officers and officials.

There is no reason to suppose that the Viceroy was insincere in his statements to Salt that he would be willing to defy the Sultan if he could be assured of the support of the allied Powers. (He was saying much the same thing to Drovetti.) At that time Mohamed Ali was still thinking in terms of the possibility of cutting Egypt off from the Ottoman Empire and making an enlarged Egypt, including Syria and, possibly, Candia, into an independent state. It was only when this possibility was seen by him to be impracticable, owing to the reluctance of the Powers to support his designs, that he finally abandoned his European ambitions and began to think in terms, not of declaring his independence of the Sultan, but of superseding the Sultan in the leadership of the Moslem world. It can be seen from Salt's reports of the Viceroy's conversations during the events leading up to Navarino that he was balancing these two alternatives in his own mind and, as his custom was, thinking aloud before the British Consul-General. Navarino helped to decide the question for him.

The British and French governments were almost equally reluctant to take seriously the Viceroy's offers of cooperation in return for an assurance that they would recognize his independence. In the case of France, such an assurance would have been consistent with one facet of that double policy they were pursuing in the Eastern Mediterranean, But, as always, when it came to the point, they were unprepared to 'go it alone' in opposition to the other Powers and to face the implications

159

of a probable dissolution of the Ottoman Empire. For the British, refusal to give any assurances to Mohamed Ali was consistent with their policy of preserving the territorial integrity of the Ottoman Empire as far as possible. The pressure of events, which included the Russian threat to Turkey contained in the ultimatum which has been mentioned, the tenacity of Greek resistance, the military weakness of Turkey which had been temporarily intensified by the extermination of the Janissaries, and the widespread sympathy which the Greek insurrection had aroused in Christendom—dictated the necessity of saving the Ottoman Empire from itself by putting an end to the Greek war on terms more or less acceptable to the Greeks themselves and to Christendom as a whole. But the total objective, which was the preservation of the Ottoman Empire and the neutralization, so to speak, of the Eastern Mediterranean, also dictated the necessity of saving for the Ottoman Empire what could be saved. The secession of Egypt, followed almost certainly by an Egyptian seizure of Syria, coming on top of the concessions in Greece which were in process of being enforced by the Powers, would have been a fatal blow to it.

The case of Mohamed Ali was different from that of the Greek insurgents. There was no actual or incipient popular revolt against Turkey either in Egypt or Syria—only the ambition of a powerful Pasha of a kind which, for the past 100 years and more, had posed similar and ephemeral threats which the effluxion of time and the operation of local rivalries had invariably dissipated. In the Ottoman Empire, in so far as religion was a factor, it was against the Viceroy and on the side of the Sultan. In Christendom, there was for Mohamed Ali no particle of that sympathy which existed for the Greeks. On the contrary, Christian indignation against the Moslems for their proceedings in Greece had been largely diverted from the Sultan and concentrated on Ibrahim as a result of widely disseminated, although mainly mendacious, reports of atrocities committed by Egyptian troops in the Morea. It was generally believed in Europe that Ibrahim was pursuing a deliberate policy of killing the adult male population of the Morea, of transporting the women and children into slavery, and of re-populating the country with Moslem settlers from Egypt. To some extent this belief was the result of deliberate British propaganda. Canning, in a despatch to his cousin, the Ambassador, dated 6th January 1826[22] wrote: 'I think I see . . . a new ground of interference much higher than any we have yet had open to us—I mean the manner in which the war is now carried on in the Morea—the character of barbarism and barbarization which it has assumed. Butchering of captives, forced conversions, the dispeopling of Christendom, recruiting from the countries of Islam, the erection in short of a new Puissance Barbaresque in Europe—these are facts . . . new in themselves, new in their principle . . . which I do think may be made the foundation of a new mode of speaking . . . which I confess I would like the better because it has nothing to do with Epaminondas nor (with reverence be it spoken) with St Paul.' Ibrahim's methods were certainly rough. In order to demonstrate his loyalty to the Sultan and the efficacy of his operations against the rebels, he was in the habit periodically of sending to Constantinople sacks containing the heads or ears of slain Greeks as trophies of war. Individual officers and men were allowed to take prisoners, to kidnap women and children, and either retain them or sell them as slaves. But this was in accordance with the barbarous Turkish practice of the time when making war against infidels. There was no deliberate policy of extermination, no mass enslavement, no Moslem colonization. But the rumours had their effect on European public opinion.

When the month's grace provided in the Treaty of London had expired and the Porte had not acceded to the allied demand for an armistice, the instructions given to the three Admirals were put into effect. The Turkish and Egyptian fleets were lying in Navarino harbour. Ibrahim Pasha was with them. On 20 September, in accordance with the suggestion made by the Viceroy to Cradock, Admiral de Rigny saw Ibrahim, told him that he and Admiral Codrington had orders to prevent the Egyptian fleet from sailing in any direction but towards Alexandria, and suggested that he should agree not to carry out any further offensive operations unless he received positive orders either from the Sultan or his father. Ibrahim gave his reply to de Rigny and Codrington five days later. He told them that, as a servant of the Porte, he had received orders to carry on the war and make an attack on Hydra, that he had no authority to accept any other orders, but that, in the circumstances, he would refer to his father and to Constantinople. He undertook that, pending receipt of their replies, he would not take the fleet out of Navarino. But he made it clear that, if his previous orders were confirmed, he would carry them out, whatever the consequences.[23]

The Admirals calculated that it would take at least twenty-five days for Ibrahim to receive replies from Alexandria and Constantinople. Meanwhile, the British and French squadrons (the Russian squadron had not yet arrived) cruised off the Morea. At the beginning of October some Turkish ships tried to sail from Navarino to Patras, but were turned back by the British squadron. The Admirals regarded this as a breach of faith by Ibrahim, who was in supreme command of the Turkish and Egyptian land and sea forces. Moreover, Turkish and Egyptian troops were still fighting in the Morea. On 13 October the Russian squadron under Admiral de Heyden joined the British and French squadrons. By that time the Admirals' patience with Ibrahim was wearing rather thin. On 20 October the allied squadrons, with the British squadron in the van, the French second and the Russian third, entered the harbour of Navarino where the Turkish and Egyptian fleets lay at anchor. It is not clear if they went in to shelter from the weather, which was becoming stormy in the open sea, or in accordance with de Rigny's recommendation to his government a week before, with a view to compelling the Turkish and Egyptian fleets to weigh anchor and return to their respective bases. Whatever the reason, 'it might fairly be said', to quote Stratford Canning,[24] 'that to take so large a force without previous agreement to a port which, belonging to a friendly government, was already occupied by a numerous fleet bearing that government's flag, was in the first place a flagrant breach of courtesy, and in the second a provocation. . . . Sir Edward might as well have kept the tompion in each of his guns, which would have looked like a denial of hostile intentions without causing the slightest impediment to their discharge in case of attack. One thing is certain; that, whatever the justification the Admirals might derive from local circumstances, neither the letter nor the spirit of their instructions could be cited to warrant their hazardous but effective decision.'

What happened was this. The Turkish and Egyptian fleets were anchored in a semi-circle parallel to the shore. Codrington, in the van, anchored his flagship between the Turkish and Egyptian flagships, which were anchored side by side in the middle of the line. A British Lieutenant, bearing a flag of truce, was fired on and killed. This led to some return fire and soon the action became general. In the result the Turkish and Egyptian fleets were almost entirely destroyed.

In Constantinople the news of the battle was received with some consternation by the allied Ambassadors, but with resignation at the Porte, which still remained adamant on the subject of mediation. The British, French and Russian Ambassadors left Constantinople on 8 December, having apparently exhausted all possibilities of a peaceful settlement.

In Egypt the Viceroy received the news quietly. Barker reported that 'the Viceroy is evidently in a most delicate situation. He is probably awaiting the course of events which he hopes, in case of war, will present some conjunction which he may, with his usual address, use to secure the advantages of neutrality without incurring the weighty consequences of a rupture with the Porte. Meanwhile he omits no preparation for defence that is in his power.'[25]

The British government, appalled at the news of Navarino (described in the Speech from the Throne at the opening of Parliament as 'an untoward event') sent a message to the Viceroy expressing regret at 'a conflict in which the Admiral would not have engaged unless compelled by the rash conduct of the Turks', and concern at the recollection of 'how large a share of the loss was sustained by the forces of the Pasha of Egypt with whom they have always desired to sustain an unbroken friendship'. The message went on to explain 'how little HM is inclined to go to war with the Ottoman Empire or to avail himself of the disaster to extract from the Porte conditions different from those which he has already proposed in conjunction with his allies'. The hope was expressed that the Porte would now accede to the terms of the Treaty of London for the pacification of Greece, and the offer made that 'HM, without interfering in any other respect with the relations which exist between the Pasha and the Sultan, is willing to respect HH's complete neutrality upon his entering into an engagement to observe strictly that neutrality during any war between the allies and the Porte'. The message concluded: 'The catastrophe at Navarino has deprived the Pasha of his fleet and left his son Ibrahim Pasha exposed to the chances of famine and defeat in a country entirely hostile. His return to Egypt is impossible if opposed by the combined squadrons, whose annihilation of the only force which could have been brought up against them

163

has rendered them absolute masters of the sea. If the Pasha embraces neutrality, HM engages not only to throw no impediment in the way of Ibrahim Pasha's return, but to facilitate it.'[26]

At about the same time as he received this message, the Viceroy also received despatches from Constantinople advising him that 'his friends had obtained from the Porte the formal promise that, in case of war with the Franks, he should be invested with the government of the three Pashaliks of Syria and his son Ibrahim with the supreme command of all the Provinces of Turkey in Europe'.[27]

For some time the Viceroy continued to waver between the two courses open to him. In the middle of January 1828, Barker, replying to Stratford Canning's notification of his having left Constantinople, explained that, pending a clarification of the Viceroy's attitude, he had not yet struck his Consular flag in accordance with the Ambassador's instructions. The Viceroy had indicated to him that, in the event of a formal declaration of war by Turkey against the allies, he would not allow the allied Consuls to continue their functions, 'from which it must be inferred that HH is determined to make common cause with his Sovereign. I entertain the opinion that he will sacrifice his army as he has sacrificed his fleet and support all the evils of a strict blockade rather than incur the weighty consequences of separating his interests from those of his Sovereign.'[28]

In February Colonel Cradock arrived in Egypt on a second mission to try to persuade the Viceroy to adopt a policy of neutrality in face of a Hatti Sherif from the Sultan announcing a state of war between Turkey and the allies, and to try to obtain from him the release of the Greek slaves who had been transported from the Morea to Egypt. Barker was not hopeful of the results of Cradock's representations about either the slaves or neutrality. Writing to Sir F. Adam in Corfu he expressed the view that 'our applications must fail and for the same cause that produced the failure of Colonel Cradock's first mission—HM Government's misconception of the character of the Egyptian government and of the position in which Mohamed Ali is vis-à-vis the Grand Seigneur'.[29] Writing to the Foreign Office on the same subject he stated: 'HH cannot be prevailed on to listen to any overtures which should require his slightest deviation from the Porte'.[30]

164

But by this time the situation at Constantinople had changed as the result of a Russian invasion of the Danubian Provinces. The Porte immediately signified to the British and French Ambassadors, then resident at Corfu, that they would negotiate with them on the basis of the Treaty of London. This provided the Viceroy with the loophole he had been seeking. If the Porte were prepared to negotiate he might do likewise without being accused of disloyalty. Arrangements were made, through Drovetti, for Codrington to come to Egypt to negotiate an agreement with the Viceroy on the terms of an Egyptian evacuation of the Morea. Codrington arrived at Alexandria at the beginning of August and an agreement was signed on 6 August. This provided: (1) for the release of all Greek slaves who had been shipped to Egypt; (2) for the release of all Turkish and Egyptian prisoners of war in Greek hands in the Morea; (3) for the Viceroy to send all available shipping to the Morea to assist in the evacuation; (4) for the evacuation to be supervised by the British and French squadrons which would escort evacuating ships to within sight of Alexandria; (5) that no Greeks were to be evacuated.

The evacuation proceeded according to plan and, at the beginning of October, Ibrahim Pasha himself returned to Egypt with the last of his troops. In September, Stratford Canning, on his way back to Constantinople from Corfu, visited Navarino and met Ibrahim Pasha, who was supervising the evacuation of his army. He described the meeting in a letter to his wife: 'I have just been making acquaintance with Ibrahim Pasha. Figure to yourself a fat, short man, sitting like a Christian with his legs down, a large clear blue eye, a high forehead, a brownish-reddish beard straggling from beneath a face much marked with small-pox, and the whole appearance, in spite of shortness and corpulency, that of an active, intelligent man, full of enterprise, subject to humours good and bad, and eager for instruction. Considering that he is on the point of being turned out of his Province, bag and baggage, he was in excellent spirits. He shook me heartily by the hand and hobanobbed with a glass of the Admiral's Constantine.'[31]

The subsequent events of the Greek war can be briefly told. In September 1828 a French force under General Maison landed in the Morea and occupied the whole peninsula. In October the British and French Ambassadors, still at Corfu, visited Poros, an island in the Aegean near Nauplia, for discussions with members of the Greek Provisional Government, on the basis of which they drew up a detailed plan for a settlement. This proposed boundaries for an autonomous Greek State under the more or less nominal suzerainty of the Sultan. The new State was to consist of the Greek mainland northward to a line stretching east-west from the Gulf of Volo to the Gulf of Arta, plus Negreponte and the Cyclades, but excluding Candia. This plan was the subject of long discussions between the allied Powers in London. During the course of these discussions Stratford Canning was replaced as Ambassador at Constantinople as the result of a disagreement with the new Foreign Secretary, Lord Aberdeen. His successor was Aberdeen's brother, Mr (later Sir) Robert Gordon. The result of the London discussions was contained in a Protocol dated 29 March 1829 which confirmed the plan drawn up at Poros. The British and French Ambassadors then proceeded to Constantinople to secure the agreement of the Porte. The Porte were still reluctant, but their hands were forced by the success of the Russian armies which, by the end of August, were approaching Constantinople. The Turks sued for peace, which was concluded at Adrianople, in a Treaty signed on 16 September, by the terms of which the Porte, *inter alia*, agreed to the terms of the London Protocol. It then occurred to the British government that the autonomous Greek State provided for in the Protocol would enjoy approximately the same status as Moldavia and Wallachia and, like them, would inevitably come under the influence and protection of Russia, particularly since it was the Russian invasion of Turkey, and not the diplomacy of Britain and France, which had secured the Porte's acceptance of the Protocol. So Lord Aberdeen made an abrupt *volte face* and, in agreement with the French government, proposed that the autonomous Greece of the Protocol be replaced by an independent Greece with boundaries drawn somewhat south of the Volo-Arta line. This revised plan was incorporated into another Protocol drawn up in London in February 1830 and signed by representatives of the British, French and Russian governments.

The new arrangement satisfied neither the Greeks nor the Turks. Greece drifted into a state of anarchy, with the Turks holding aloof and the Greeks fighting each other. In 1831, Stratford Canning, who had been dismissed so ignominiously by Lord Aberdeen to make room for his brother, was sent to

Greece and Constantinople by Lord Palmerston, then Foreign Secretary, on a special mission to try to get both sides to agree to an arrangement by which an independent Greece would be established with boundaries as per the first Protocol (i.e. the Volo-Arta line) with the Greeks paying the Turks an indemnity in return for the additional territory conceded. After a strenuous negotiation, agreement was arrived at and the new Greek State came into being. Stratford Canning attributed his success partly to the fact that 'just at this time Mohamed Ali was acting in a manner to make him more than usually an object of suspicion at Constantinople', and that 'fear of danger from Egypt' was making the Sultan less reluctant than usual to obtain a settlement of the Greek question.[32]

CHAPTER SEVEN

THE EGYPTIAN CONQUEST
OF SYRIA

Immediately after the disaster at Navarino, Mohamed Ali set about building a new and more powerful fleet. He constructed a dock and naval arsenal at Alexandria and engaged M. Cerisy, a French shipbuilder from Toulon, to run them. He also continued to buy ships from abroad. In order that his navy should be as efficient as possible he had the larger vessels commanded by European captains and partly manned by European officers and petty officers. At first, the captains were mainly French but later, impressed as he always had been by British sea-power, he did his best to recruit British officers. By the beginning of 1832 he had a new fleet comprising two one hundred and four-gun line-of-battle ships, seven frigates, six corvettes, ten brigs and schooners, thirteen gunboats, eight fireships, seven rocket ships and twenty-three transports. Another one hundred and four-gun and a seventy four-gun line-of-battle ships were under construction.

The Viceroy was particularly keen on his navy, regarding it as a personal hobby as well as a form of national defence. From the windows of his palace at Ras-el-Tin, overlooking the Western Harbour, near where Ptolemy Philadelphus had built the Pharos, he loved to look out and see his vessels at anchor or cruising off the coast. He had a special room built for himself at the naval arsenal and used to spend hours there watching the progress of the shipbuilding. He delighted in accepting invitations to inspect British and other foreign warships that came to Alexandria, and plied the captains with questions about sail-making and other nautical matters. He liked going to sea himself. He took a great interest in the development of the steamship and, in the 1820's, acquired one for his own use. He had a shrewd appreciation of the importance of sea-power. In spite of the fiasco of Fraser's expedition in 1807, he never forgot that it was British sea power which enabled Fraser to get to Egypt at all and, once there, to get away again. He compared this with the fate of Bonaparte's expedition, and this helped to determine his attitude towards Great Britain and France respectively. He realized that British would be more effective than French support for his expansionist designs, because of the factor of sea power, and that British opposition would nullify French support. But, much as he tried, he could never obtain British support. The French were, at times, more forthcoming but, for the Viceroy, the limited French support sometimes offered or promised was no real substitute even for that British neutrality which would have kept his sea lanes open and protected his coast from a blockade.

While building up his navy, the Viceroy continued to strengthen his army. He aimed at creating a disciplined force of 100,000 men, raised by conscription from the Egyptian villages and trained according to European methods. His policy was to have no Europeans in any positions of command, but to use his European officers for advisory and training purposes. The senior officers were mostly Turks, and Mohamed Ali counted on retaining their loyalty by giving them extremely high rates of pay. At least one of his senior officers was an ex-Mamluk and some of them had been sent to Europe for their education. Some of the officers commanding regiments were his own relatives, including two nephews, Ibrahim and Ahmed. By the middle of 1829 his army strength amounted to about 62,000, including 15,000 Beduin irregulars. Barker, the British Consul-General, described the infantry as being 'well-armed, well-dressed, well-supplied, in the highest discipline and equal to the best European soldiers except in experience'.[2] He thought less of the cavalry, which were 'very badly mounted' but described the artillery as 'excellent' and armed with cannon cast in Cairo by Egyptians under the supervision of an English engineer.[3]

In the light of Mohamed Ali's expansionist policy, he needed a large army. He had garrisons to maintain in Arabia, in the Sudan, and in Candia. He needed troops in Egypt both to maintain his own authority and to man the coastal defences against a possible invasion, either by a foreign Power, or by his Suzerain. He did not conceal his eventual determination to march his troops into Syria. He was, as we shall see, interested for a time in an invasion of North Africa. And he needed a navy to guard

169

the Egyptian coasts and to keep his communications open in all his actual and projected adventures overseas.

In spite of Egypt's increasing productivity, brought about by Mohamed Ali's irrigation works and his development of cotton cultivation, this continuing naval and military expenditure placed a very heavy burden on the country, in terms both of taxation and manpower. There was a great deal of discontent. Whole villages became depopulated as a result of the inhabitants fleeing either from the tax-gatherer or the press-gang. In the summer of 1829 Ibrahim Pasha, whom the Viceroy was gradually bringing forward as his deputy and eventual successor, presided at an Assembly held in Cairo of 'all the principal officials of the civil and military departments, the governors of districts, sheikhs and aghas of towns and elders of villages, to deliberate on the correction of abuses and to consider how the present wretched state of the peasantry can be ameliorated without causing any diminution in the amount of money that is annually extorted from them.'[4] The problem remained insoluble, since the Viceroy's needs increased *pari passu* with increasing productivity, and the oppression continued. Barker who, in 1829, estimated Mohamed Ali's annual revenue at about five million sterling, expressed astonishment that he could go on spending as much as he did and was forced to conclude that his real revenues must be greater than they appeared to be.

Mohamed Ali's relations with his Suzerain began to deteriorate from the time of the battle of Navarino. He had some reason to believe that he would be granted the Syrian Pashaliks in return for his assistance in the Greek war. He received instead only peremptory demands for the despatch of an army to fight the Russians, and for the placing of the remains of his fleet at the Sultan's disposal. The first demand was eventually waived against the payment of a sum estimated by Barker at between one and two million Spanish dollars. In response to the second demand, Mohamed Ali, after the Russian war was over, sent back to Constantinople the eighteen survivors of the Turkish fleet which had come to Alexandria after Navarino, but refused to send any of his own fleet. The Turkish ships, which were in very bad condition, were escorted as far as the Dardanelles by eight Egyptian ships, 'to aid them in distress', as the Viceroy contemptuously remarked.[5]

During the war with Russia, the Viceroy must have thought

it possible that the Ottoman Empire was on the verge of breaking up. He showed no disposition to try to prevent this from happening, evaded all requests from Constantinople for assistance, hardly concealed his satisfaction at news of Turkish defeats, and expressed his intention of sending an army into Syria to forestall its occupation by the Russians. He began to prepare public opinion in Egypt for the possibility of a break with Constantinople. In April 1829 he presided at an assembly of Ulema and notables held in Cairo, asked them to adjudicate on the Porte's demand that he send Egyptian troops to help against Russia and obtained from them a unanimous declaration that no troops should be sent.

After the Peace of Adrianople, the Porte began to look askance at the powerful vassal who, however helpful he had been over Greece, had done little or nothing to assist against Russia. Signs of Imperial displeasure began to become apparent. Ibrahim, who had been created Pasha of Mecca by the Sultan, but who spent the whole of his time in Egypt, was ordered back to Arabia. He took no notice. Taher Pasha, who had been the Turkish Admiral at Navarino, and was an enemy of Mohamed Ali, was sent to govern the Province of Adana, from where the Viceroy was accustomed to obtain his timber for shipbuilding. Taher Pasha forbade the export of timber from there to Egypt. In the time of the Mamluks the Pashalik of Egypt had not included the ports of Alexandria, Rosetta and Damietta, or the island of Marabout, which were traditionally the appendages of the Capitan Pasha. But, since 1807, the annual Firman of confirmation had invested Mohamed Ali with these places as well. Then, in 1830, the annual confirmatory Firman, while investing Mohamed Ali with the governorship of 'the capital of Egypt and its dependencies', pointedly omitted to mention the names of the maritime towns.

The Viceroy's reply to all this was to strengthen his fortifications on the Mediterranean coast, and to make speeches in open Divan denouncing the treachery and ingratitude of the Porte, which he accused of fitting out an expedition for the invasion of Egypt. While he admitted privately that he was not really afraid of any attempt at a Turkish invasion, the Viceroy's real object in these public pronouncements was, in the opinion of the British Consul-General, to 'habituate his people to the idea of an eventual conflict with the Sultan for the maintenance of his power in Egypt'.[6]

The British government's attitude towards this defiance was disapproving. After the surgical operation in Greece and the advance of Russian forces to the gates of Constantinople, and intent as always on 'neutralizing' the Eastern Mediterranean by maintaining the territorial integrity of the Ottoman Empire, they were anxious that no further assaults should be made on that integrity. Gordon, the British Ambassador in Constantinople, instructed Barker to try to persuade the Viceroy to defer to the Porte in the matter of the fleet, and it may have been due to Barker's intervention that Mohamed Ali did send the remainder of the fleet back to Constantinople after the end of the war had deprived him of any reasonable excuse for keeping it any longer. Mohamed Ali was disappointed at the British attitude, and told Barker that 'if the King of England is so interested in the preservation of the Ottoman Empire, it is for him and not for Mohamed Ali to defend it'.[7]

Barker, reporting the result of his intervention to the Ambassador, said that no similar intervention had been made by Mimaud (the French Consul-General who had recently replaced Drovetti) and expressed the fear lest the unsympathetic British attitude might lead the Viceroy to turn towards France.

This fear was not altogether unfounded. Soon after Navarino, the French government, alternating as usual between two policies in the Eastern Mediterranean, and seeing the prospect of predominant Russian influence at Constantinople as a result of Russian successes in the war then being waged against Turkey, began to lean towards the establishment of a friendly understanding with Mohamed Ali. They had in mind, generally, the regeneration of French political and commercial influence in the Eastern Mediterranean and, specifically, Mohamed Ali's assistance in a contemplated invasion of the Barbary Coast. In a policy document prepared in the French Foreign Ministry in 1829[8] it was pointed out that Russian territorial proximity to Turkey on the one hand and British naval supremacy on the other meant that France could never expect to play more than a secondary role at Constantinople, and that it was in the French interest to support Mohamed Ali's ambitions and, by doing so, remove the centre of gravity in the Moslem world from the Bosphorus to the Nile, and from a Russian or British-dominated Constantinople to a French-dominated Cairo. The document pointed out that Mohamed

Ali's natural lines of expansion from the Nile Valley were eastwards into Syria and westwards along the Barbary Coast, and expressed the view that community of language, customs and origins would enable a single State to be created in these areas, and recommended that such an expansion should be supported and protected by France.

This Egyptian policy owed much of its inspiration to Drovetti who, after handing over the Consulate-General in Egypt to Mimaud in June 1829, returned to France to promote his plan, which he had maturing for some time, for a joint French and Egyptian conquest of the Barbary Coast. The Barbary Coast, consisting of the Provinces of Tripoli, Tunis and Algiers, was nominally part of the Ottoman Empire but had, for many years, been autonomous under local rulers. Algiers, under its ruler, or Dey, had for long been notorious as a nest of pirates. The French government, partly with a view to suppressing the piracy (in which they could count on the support of most of the European Powers) and partly with a view to that expansion into the Sahara which they later undertook (a project in which they could count on the benevolence, or at least the indifference, of the European Powers), were in 1829 meditating an occupation of Algiers. Drovetti's plan was for an Egyptian occupation, financed by France, which would put an end to the piracy, facilitate the development of French commercial and other interests, and lay the foundations for a French protectorate over Egypt. The plan was approved by Polignac, the French Foreign Minister, although few of the other members of the government were enthusiastic. Polignac was at this time trying to interest the Russians in the partition of the Ottoman Empire[9] and his principal object in the Algiers plan was to forge bonds between France and Mohamed Ali in order to consolidate future French influence in the Levant after that partition.[10]

In November 1829 M. Huder, a junior diplomat, ADC to Count Guilleminot, the French Ambassador at Constantinople, arrived in Egypt on a mission to discuss the terms of a joint expedition to Algiers. The Viceroy agreed to send a force of 40,000 men—20,000 regulars and 20,000 Beduin—under the command of Ibrahim Pasha, to take possession of Algiers, on condition that the French government (a) supplied him with four eighty-gun ships-of-the-line and a loan to finance the expedition, and (b) undertook to protect him from any hostile intervention by Turkey or any of the European Powers which might object to the enterprise.[11] The French at first agreed to the Viceroy's proposals, except that they substituted a sum of eight million francs instead of the four warships for which he had asked. They sent Huder back to Egypt with the news in January 1830, and then sounded the Porte for their reactions. The Porte objected and the British government, which had not been consulted, but which had heard about the plan from their Ambassador at Constantinople, objected violently.[12] They instructed Sir Robert Gordon, their Ambassador at Constantinople, and Barker in Egypt, to make representations accordingly. In a despatch to Barker, Aberdeen, the Foreign Secretary, wrote: 'The prospect of the Viceroy making war upon a State vassal and tributary to his lawful Sovereign could not be viewed with indifference by HM's Government. . . . The particular character of the plan, in which the Viceroy concerts with one of the Powers of Europe . . . to effect an entire change . . . on the coasts of the Mediterranean render it in the highest degree objectionable to HM . . . who cannot believe that the Viceroy has maturely considered all the important consequences'. After stating that HMG were not unaware of all the provocations which France had suffered from the Dey of Algiers, Aberdeen went on to protest against the French proposal to 'have recourse to an alliance of so questionable a nature', which would upset 'the existing relations of countries whose geographical positions render it impossible that any essential changes concerning them should be effected in the interests of any one Power without giving just cause of uneasiness to other European States'. Barker was instructed to bring this view to the attention of Mohamed Ali, 'who has had too many proofs of the goodwill of HM's Government and of the satisfaction with which they view the progress of that prosperity which he has so largely promoted in Egypt' to regard the British attitude as being dictated by any unfriendliness towards himself.[13] A few days later, having heard from his brother, Sir Robert Gordon, that the Porte also objected, Aberdeen instructed Barker, in his representations to the Viceroy, to lay especial stress on the fact that the Algerian project was 'an act of insubordination towards the Sultan'.[14]

Meanwhile, the French government, having been apprized of British and Turkish objections, got cold feet and sent another diplomat, Langsdorff, who was senior to Huder, post-haste to

Egypt to cancel the agreement conveyed by Huder. Instead, he was instructed to propose that the French themselves should undertake the conquest of Algiers and that Mohamed Ali, assisted by a French loan of ten million francs, should confine himself to a simultaneous invasion of Tripoli and Tunis. Mohamed Ali turned this proposal down on the ground that he could not associate himself with the conquest of Algiers by a Christian Power. His real reason was almost certainly disillusionment at the vacillating French attitude, which had already manifested itself over the Greek war and which was again to manifest itself over Syria.

Barker had noted the comings and goings of Huder and Langsdorff, and had gathered that they were connected with a projected invasion of Algiers. He does not appear to have received Aberdeen's instructions until the end of February, by which time the Viceroy had turned down the amended French proposal and had, for the time being, dismissed France from his mind as a possible ally. As far as he was concerned, the conquest of Algiers had only been a second-best compared with the project nearest his heart—the occupation of Syria. But he had been prepared to cooperate with the original French proposal as a means of securing that support from a European Power which was necessary for the fulfilment of his ambitions. But France's precipitate retreat in face of British objections had persuaded him of the desirability of making one more effort to secure the benevolent interest of the British government. Therefore, when Barker came to see him at the beginning of March with Aberdeen's message about Algiers, he was received with great *empressement*.

The Viceroy gave the British Consul-General a carefully-edited version of the Algerian project. He explained that Drovetti had originally tried to persuade him to conquer Tripoli, Tunis and Algiers, and that he had told him that British consent must first be obtained. After Drovetti had left, Huder had come and told him that the British had no objection. As soon as he had heard that the British did object, he had decided to have nothing more to do with the project. He then proceeded to develop his theme of an alliance with Great Britain. Referring to the British policy of supporting the Sultan's authority, he told Barker: 'Do they not see that it is not possible? You may prop here and prop there, but all will be to no purpose. What can you do with a government which has lost the confidence of its people? The British government should realize that the only way to strengthen the Sultan is to support me. By supporting me they would soon have at their disposal a disciplined army of 125,000 men ready to form a barrier against the Russians both in Constantinople and in Persia. . . . The Porte is gone and England must prepare to raise a force in Asia to meet the Russians. Where can she find it but with me and my son after me? You have tried the Persians[15] and the Porte and you have found that they can do nothing for you. . . . Your frontier force—the Turkish army in the Balkans—disappointed your hopes of resisting the Russians. The people in every part of the Empire have lost confidence in the Porte. . . . They would all flock to my standard if the English would but come forward and support me and answer for my plans being those of a man jealous for the honour of his Sovereign and the religion of his country. I shall soon have an army of 125,000 men, but with the alliance of the English I could make it 200,000. But the hostility of the British government paralyzes all my efforts.' He went on to boast of his agricultural improvements in Egypt. 'Soon I shall have 200,000 feddans more under irrigation; I am prepared to supply England exclusively with cotton in the event of a war with America.' He concluded by reminding Barker of how, ten years before, he had kept out of Abyssinia in deference to the British government's wishes as communicated to him by Salt.[16]

There seems little doubt that the Viceroy was sincere in his efforts to come to an understanding with England. He repeatedly asked Barker whether he had received an answer from the British government to his proposals for an alliance. In June 1830 Boghos Yusef had an interview with Barker in which he developed the Viceroy's ideas. Boghos Yusef was an Armenian and the Viceroy's principal *homme de confiance* in dealing with Europeans. He came from Smyrna, where he had been a Dragoman at the British Consulate. He had probably influenced Mohamed Ali in his desire for an understanding with England. He was a frequent confidential channel of communication between the Viceroy and the British Consul-General. On the occasion of this interview Boghos pointed out how Mohamed Ali was showing his goodwill towards England by refraining from pushing his Arabian conquests towards the Persian Gulf and how he had resisted 'the most urgent and reiterated

176

solicitations to throw himself into the hands of France and, latterly, the no less eager pursuit of the same object by the Russians'. He referred to the British government's cold reception of the overtures made by Mohamed Ali to Salt during the Greek war, and blamed Salt for not having taken them seriously owing to 'the artful intrigues of Drovetti . . . who had had the impudence to give out that he was the intimate counsellor of HH, who was consequently devoted to the French'. He said that HH preferred to ally himself with England rather than France because of England's 'naval superiority and her vital interest in creating a barrier to the advance of the Russians into Turkey'. He expatiated on Egypt's financial, naval and military strength, saying that the Viceroy did not need money, ships or military aid from England. He assured Barker that the Viceroy was satisfied with *de facto* independence, which he had enjoyed since he became Ruler of Egypt, and had no intention of throwing off his allegiance to the Sultan.[17]

The British government made no reply to any of these proposals from Mohamed Ali. A few weeks later, when the French invasion of Algiers was about to start, the Viceroy and Boghos, in separate interviews with Barker, insinuated that a French occupation of Algiers would be contrary to British interests and that it would be much better for the British if Algiers were occupied by Egypt instead. But, in the event, neither the British government nor the Porte objected to the French invasion. The real objection of both was the proposed participation of Mohamed Ali.

During the second half of 1830 Mohamed Ali's relations with his Suzerain took a temporary turn for the better. In July, Pertew Effendi, previously Reis Effendi, paid a goodwill visit to Egypt, bringing with him a Firman investing Mohamed Ali with the Pashalik of Candia. Mohamed Ali thereupon sent two regiments of 3,200 men there to complete the pacification of the island and a present of 50,000 Spanish dollars (about £10,000) to the Sultan.

But, from the beginning of 1831, relations again began to deteriorate. The Viceroy recruited another 23,000 troops in Egypt and pressed ahead with his naval building. Barker surmised, correctly, that an attack was being prepared against Acre 'in order that the Pashaliks of Acre and Damascus should be added to the Viceroyalty'.[18] As far back as 1827 Barker had attributed to the Viceroy the determination to make himself

177

master of Acre. He had told Codrington: 'The possession of Acre is evidently the goal to which he tends: that important fortress could effectively cover Egypt from attacks by land while his fleet would protect him from a blockade by sea'.[19] The Viceroy also had a ready-made excuse for attacking Acre without necessarily involving himself in direct hostilities against the Porte. Abdullah Pasha of Acre was by no means a loyal subject of the Sultan, and hostilities between rebellious Pashas were rather encouraged than frowned upon at the Porte as a means of reducing the strength of both. Mohamed Ali had a grievance against Abdullah in that the Pasha of Acre had been in the habit of giving asylum and encouragement to Egyptian fugitives and deserters. This grievance gave the Porte the opportunity to ignore any attack on Acre by Mohamed Ali, or even to assist him in such an attack, without immediate loss of prestige.

The Viceroy let it be understood that his preparations were being undertaken at the Sultan's request and that he had been promised the Pashaliks of Damascus, Aleppo and Baghdad in return. Barker thought that he was not without hope of prevailing on the Sultan to grant him the Syrian Pashaliks. There was some question of the Capitan Pasha coming to Egypt to negotiate with the Viceroy. Presumably in the hope of coming to some arrangement, preparations for the expedition were suspended in July. They were resumed in August and it was given out by the Viceroy that the Capitan Pasha was coming to Egypt with a Firman granting him the Syrian Pashaliks and to make plans with him for the capture of Acre, whose Pasha was in rebellion against the Sultan. But Barker expressed the correct view that the Viceroy was preparing for the conquest of Syria 'not with the concurrence of the Porte but in open defiance of the Sultan'.[20]

The Viceroy had a powerful ally in Syria in the person of the Emir Beshir Shihab, the quasi-independent Ruler of Lebanon. In 1822, when the Emir, in alliance with Abdallah Pasha of Acre, was in revolt against the Porte, he had spent a short period of exile in Egypt before being pardoned by the Sultan. In his expedition against Abdallah, who had meanwhile quarrelled with the Emir, Mohamed Ali relied on, and was to receive, assistance from the Emir and his Druze and Maronite mountaineers.

The Egyptian military expedition was due to leave Cairo on

20 August but was delayed owing to an outbreak of cholera. On 14 October, when the cholera had subsided, it set out for al-Arish. From there it was to advance to Haifa and there join the Egyptian fleet preparatory to laying siege to Acre, on the other side of the bay. The Egyptian land force consisted of the Viceroy's bodyguard of 3,350 men, four regiments of infantry comprising 13,250 men, four regiments of cavalry, about 1,000 Beduin, one regiment of artillery 600 strong, a battery of six field pieces, and 7,000 camels. Soon afterwards an Egyptian fleet set out from Alexandria to rendezvous with the army at Haifa. Ibrahim Pasha, who was in command of the whole expedition, accompanied the fleet, sailing in the frigate *Kafr-esh-Sheikh*, commanded by an Englishman, Captain John Prissick. There was no longer any pretence that the invasion was being undertaken with the concurrence of the Porte, although Barker surmised that 'on becoming master of Acre, Palestine and Damascus, (the Viceroy) will probably offer a large sum of money for a legal possession and the Porte will then condescend to grant him the usual Firman'.[21]

At about the same time as the expedition set out, Palmerston had replaced Aberdeen at the Foreign Office, and Gordon, at Constantinople, had been replaced as Ambassador by Stratford Canning. Pending Canning's arrival, Mr S. H. Mandeville was acting as Chargé d'Affaires.

At first, it appeared that Barker's surmise would prove correct. The Sultan went through the motions of sending a message to the Viceroy forbidding him to invade Syria, and of issuing a Firman depriving him of all his Pashaliks. But he did not appoint anyone in his place and, at the same time, sent a Commissioner to Egypt to treat with him. News of the Firman was suppressed in Egypt and Ibrahim, by this time before the walls of Acre, published a forged Firman appointing Mohamed Ali to the Pashalik of Acre. During the siege which took place, the Porte took no steps to relieve or to reinforce Acre and, in February 1832, the Turkish Commissioner and Mohamed Ali sent a joint message to Constantinople recommending that the Viceroy be recognized as Pasha of Acre against a money payment. There had been no reaction from the Powers and it seemed possible that all might end fairly peaceably, with the Porte recognizing Mohamed Ali's possession *ex post facto*. But such a possibility, if it ever existed, came to nothing as the result of the unexpectedly tough resistance put up by the

179

defenders of Acre who, for the second time in less than half a century, upset the calculations of an ambitious conqueror.

Although the Porte made no direct attempt to relieve Acre, Osman Pasha, who had been made Pasha of Tripoli,[22] landed in north Syria and started raising local forces to march on the town of Tripoli, which had been occupied by Ibrahim with a small force. The Porte was also encouraging other local Pashas to attack Ibrahim and lethargically preparing an expeditionary force to march through Asia Minor to Syria. Ibrahim, at the end of March, learning of these preparations, left two regiments only in front of Acre, marched north, and defeated Osman Pasha in a battle near Homs. He then returned for the final assault on Acre, which was captured on 27 May. 'The garrison was 2,000 strong. The assailants were 6,000, commanded by Ibrahim Pasha in person. The loss on the part of the besiegers was probably 2,000–3,000 men. . . . It would seem that the Sultan's policy has been to look on with complacency while the rebels were reciprocally exhausting their strength. At several periods during Abdallah's protracted and brave defence messages from the Porte gave him solemn promises of immediate succour which were never fulfilled'.[23] Abdallah, who was bitter about his treatment by the Porte, surrendered with all the honours of war and, on arriving in Egypt, was granted a pension by Mohamed Ali and assigned one of the old Mamluk palaces on Roda Island as a residence.

After the capture of Acre Mohamed Ali sent an emissary to Constantinople with proposals for peace. Professing himself 'a faithful and humble servant of the Sultan', he asked for a Firman restoring him in the Pashalik of Egypt and granting him the Pashaliks of Acre and Tripoli 'which extend from al-Arish to Lattaqia'. He agreed to waive his original claim to the Pashalik of Damascus and, 'as a proof of his submission', ordered Ibrahim Pasha not to take possession of that city until he had had a reply from the Sultan. But, just after the emissary had set off, the Viceroy received news from Constantinople that the Sultan had declared him and Ibrahim to be outlaws, announced that the coasts of Egypt and Syria were in a state of blockade, and asked the Powers to stop trading with all territories under Egyptian control. Mohamed Ali thereupon appointed a governor for Damascus and ordered Ibrahim to occupy the city, which he did without meeting any resistance.

In the opinion of Acerbi, the Austrian Consul-General in

Egypt, expressed at the time: 'There are now two possible courses before Mohamed Ali. The first is to occupy the whole of Syria, that is to say, the four Pashaliks of Acre, Tripoli, Damascus and Aleppo, and to place himself in a defensive posture north of Aleppo. The second is to go on from Syria and to march on Constantinople. Mohamed Ali prefers the first. The second is too dangerous; it would precipitate European intervention, which is what the Viceroy fears more than anything else'.[24] Ibrahim, as we shall see, preferred the second, more ambitious, alternative. But first, the conquest of Syria had to be completed.

In March Husain Pasha, then at Adrianople, had been appointed by the Sultan as C-in-C of a Turkish force to march against Ibrahim. His progress through Asia Minor was slow and, by July, he had only reached Antioch. Here he sent forward part of his army to join the local forces in north Syria commanded by the Pasha of Aleppo. The combined forces arrived on 7 July at Homs, and were routed there next day by Ibrahim. From Homs Ibrahim marched north, entering Hama on 10 July and Aleppo on 14 July. He then turned west to meet the main body of Husain's army which he defeated on 29 July in the pass of Beylan between Antioch and Alexandretta. The Egyptians were now masters of all Syria.

During the campaign Turkish procrastination on land was accompanied by Turkish timidity at sea. In July, Mohamed Ali, notwithstanding the superiority of the Sultan's fleet in the number and class of vessels, ordered his fleet to sail in quest of the enemy. The Egyptian fleet consisted of four line-of-battle ships, five large and two small frigates, and three or four corvettes, against the Ottoman fleet of six line-of-battle ships, seven large and one small frigate, and twenty corvettes. In spite of this superiority the Ottoman fleet never sought action with the Egyptians and confined itself to guarding Cyprus against the possibility of an Egyptian landing. The Egyptian fleet meanwhile escorted reinforcements sent by sea to Syria from Egypt and Candia. With the approach of winter the Ottoman fleet left its Mediterranean base in Marmorice Bay and retired through the Dardanelles.

After the battle of Beylan, there ensued a long controversy, carried on by correspondence, between Mohamed Ali and Ibrahim about the future course of the campaign. Ibrahim tried to persuade his father to a declaration of independence, and to

181

an advance through Asia Minor, rallying the population on the way, and ending up with the deposition of Sultan Mahmud II and his replacement by his son Abdul Mejid, with a government favourable and subservient to Mohamed Ali. The Viceroy, fearful of European and, particularly, British reactions, would not permit anything of the kind. He at first wished Ibrahim to remain on the defensive near Aleppo. Later, in October, he reluctantly agreed to his advancing as far as Konieh in order to command the Taurus passes. In December, he changed his mind and ordered the exasperated Ibrahim to retire from Konieh.[25]

During the correspondence with Ibrahim the Viceroy was in negotiation with Constantinople. In the second half of August, through the intermediary of Captain Maunsell of HMS *Alfred*, who had been detailed by the C-in-C Mediterranean to watch British interests on the Levant coast, Mohamed Ali sent a message to the Capitan Pasha offering to open negotiations. The Capitan Pasha forwarded the message to the Sultan. The Sultan agreed that Mohamed Ali could send a delegate to the Capitan Pasha. But, by that time, Mohamed Ali's attitude, probably influenced by that of Ibrahim, had momentarily hardened (he had already been talking in open Divan about marching to Constantinople) and he declined the Sultan's offer on the plea that 'he had no person in whose judgment and discretion he could sufficiently confide'. He expressed his willingness to negotiate in Egypt with anyone whom the Sultan might send for the purpose.

Husain Pasha had been relieved of his command after Beylan and replaced by Rashid Mohamed Pasha. Ibrahim, trammelled by his father's orders, had been advancing slowly westwards and occupied Konieh, which had been evacuated by the Turks, on 18 November. The latest orders from his father were that he should retire from Konieh and withdraw into Syria. But Rashid Pasha was already advancing on Konieh at the head of his army. Ibrahim determined to stand his ground and give battle. Taking up an advantageous position a little east of Konieh, which he evacuated, he met Rashid's attack on 21 December. After a short, sharp battle the Turks were defeated and Rashid taken prisoner. The road to Constantinople was open. But Ibrahim remained in Konieh awaiting his father's orders and recommending, urgently but respectfully, an immediate march on the Ottoman capital. 'We can march on Constantinople and depose the Sultan immediately and without

182

difficulty. But I must know as soon as possible if you really want this done, so that we can take the necessary measures. . . . I tell you frankly that propaganda will get us nowhere. It is necessary to threaten Constantinople and force the Sultan to agree to our conditions. We cannot do that by staying at Konieh which is a long way from Constantinople. They will only make peace with us when we are approaching Constantinople, just as they only made peace with the Russians when they were in the suburbs of Constantinople. That is why we must advance as far as Brusa at least, occupy the Asiatic coast of the Marmora and make arrangements to supply the army by sea. From there we can start to make propaganda which will lead to the Sultan's deposition. Even if we don't succeed in accomplishing that, we can at least make peace on our own terms. If you hadn't kept me back I would have been in Constantinople already. Why all this delay? Is it fear of the Powers, or is it something else?'[26]

Up to the time of the battle of Beylan the reactions of the Powers, and particularly British reactions, had been surprisingly mild. On 10 May Stratford Canning, in the light of the Firman depriving Mohamed Ali of all his Pashaliks, and of the request by the Porte to the Powers that they should cease trading with territories under Egyptian control, informed Barker that the British government continued to recognize Mohamed Ali as Viceroy of Egypt and instructed him simply to convey to British subjects the intimation that, in view of the Turkish blockade, trading with territories under Egyptian control would be at their own risk. These instructions were approved by Palmerston who rebuked Barker for having referred to Mohamed Ali, in one of his despatches, as 'the ex-Viceroy'. (Barker was adopting an extremely hostile attitude towards Mohamed Ali.) He was told: 'Owing to the contest on which Mohamed Ali has unfortunately embarked against the Sultan, it is to the existing authority in Egypt that you and the British merchants must look for protection. . . . In the absence of any commands to the contrary from HM's government it is of importance that you should maintain that kind of amicable intercourse with the Pasha and his Ministers which might enable you to preserve an influence useful both to them and to British interests in Egypt. During the future progress of the dispute between the Sultan and the Viceroy you will, in the absence of any positive instructions to the contrary, abstain from the use of language which may in any way . . . tend to create alarm in the minds of British merchants resident in Egypt.'[27]

Barker was, at this time, extremely *mal vu* by Palmerston, who had little confidence in his judgment, by the Viceroy, by the British residents in Egypt, and by the Royal Navy. Before coming to Egypt, John Barker had spent many years as British Consul in Aleppo, having been appointed by Sir Sidney Smith at the time of the siege of Acre. When, after Salt's death, he had been appointed Consul-General in his place, he was regarded by the British government as performing Consular duties only and not as a Political Agent at all.[28] Consequently, very little notice was taken of his political information and hardly any political instructions were ever sent him.

In the course of his duties Barker had incurred Mohamed Ali's displeasure by reason of various representations he had made on behalf of the trading privileges of certain protected British subjects. By this time Mohamed Ali had formed strong links with a little 'ring' of British merchant houses in Egypt who were in the habit of making him short-term loans against guaranteed allocations of cotton and other produce for export. He had particularly strong links with the house of Briggs and Thurburn, who were his agents in London. With the aid of this 'ring' the Viceroy seems to have created a strong British opposition to Barker and, by means of his 'private line' to London via Samuel Briggs, to have created much prejudice against Barker in official circles in England. Local British feeling against Barker came to a head early in 1832 when he arrested and imprisoned the captain and supercargo of a British ship against which a writ of attachment had been issued in London. He was almost certainly within his rights in doing so, but the incident aroused great feeling among some of the British merchant community in Egypt and among the officers of the two British warships *Madagascar* and *Alfred*—which had been detached for service in Levant waters during the Syrian war.

Most of the British merchant houses in Egypt, whose interests were bound up with those of Mohamed Ali, were strongly in favour of the Viceroy in his war against his Suzerain. Barker, whether because of his deteriorating personal relations with the Viceroy, or because he thought he was carrying out the policy of the British government, or because of personal conviction, was strongly hostile until he received the rebuke from Palmerston which has been quoted. These opposing viewpoints were a further source of friction. Complaints and counter-complaints flowed in to the British government. Barker complained that Captain Maunsell of *Alfred* had exceeded his duties in acting as intermediary between Mohamed Ali and the Capitan Pasha, and wrote that he and Captain Lyons, commanding *Madagascar*, were 'playing Mohamed Ali's game by helping to create in the public mind the impression that HM's government has an amicable bias towards him'.[29] He complained that British merchants in Egypt 'support by all means in their power the cause of a man on the fortunes of whom their own mainly depend'.[30] He vigorously defended his action over the captain and supercargo. Palmerston, who was receiving complaints about Barker from the Admiralty, from Briggs, and possibly from other sources, was unimpressed. He severely reprimanded him for imprisoning the captain and supercargo, telling him that 'if the Consul at Alexandria should have a prison attached to his Consular residence, such place of confinement should not be a dark and damp apartment'. He also told him that the Admiralty considered that Captain Maunsell had 'satisfactorily rebutted the insinuations' made against him.[31]

These dissensions, taken in conjunction with the limited view taken by the British government about Barker's functions and abilities, help to explain the inactivity of British policy during the first part of Ibrahim's campaign. Another, and perhaps more important, reason was a lack of unanimity in the British Cabinet about the policy to be adopted. At all events, the only official British initiative taken before the battle of Beylan was that of Stratford Canning, in his instructions to Barker, which showed a more favourable attitude towards Mohamed Ali than that displayed by most of the other Powers. The Russian, Austrian and Prussian Consuls-General were instructed that all commercial intercourse by their nationals with Egypt and Syria must cease, and in August the Russian Consul-General was recalled by his government. Mohamed Ali 'seemed gratified' at the comparative mildness of the British attitude,[32] but he was under no illusions as to what that attitude would be in the event of his adopting the policy being urged on him by Ibrahim. For some time he had been hardly on speaking terms with Barker[33] and he may in any case have guessed that Barker's opinion carried little weight with the British government. But he maintained fairly close contact with British official circles in London through Samuel Briggs, and understood from Briggs that the British government would not view with favour an advance on Constantinople. This information from Briggs was one of the principal reasons which induced him to enforce moderation on his son.[34]

Stratford Canning, who had been appointed temporarily as Ambassador to settle the Greek question, left Constantinople for England on 12 August 1832. A few days before he left 'direct proposals were made to him, first by the Reis Effendi and later by the Sultan himself, for an alliance between Great Britain and Turkey. The immediate object which the Porte had in view was the submission of Mohamed Ali, and it wished to possess the moral and still more the physical force of England for that purpose. The Porte offered in return to give any reasonable advantages to Great Britain. Sir Stratford Canning agreed to submit these proposals to HM's Government but . . . could not answer for more than generally friendly dispositions towards the Porte.'[35]

Soon after these approaches, the Porte despatched M. Mavrojeni, the Turkish Chargé d'Affaires in Vienna, to London to ask for naval assistance against Mohamed Ali, offering to pay all expenses involved and to grant enlarged privileges and advantages to British subjects in matters of commerce. M. Mavrojeni arrived in London on 3 November and, on 5 December, was requested by Palmerston to tell the Reis Effendi that no definite and immediate answer could be given to the Turkish request, but that the British government would convey to Mohamed Ali the regret which his conduct had caused them and the hope that he would make peace by direct negotiation with the Sultan. Meanwhile, yet another emissary, Namik Pasha, had been despatched from Constantinople to London on a similar mission to that of Mavrojeni. He arrived on 13 December and received the same reply. A formal refusal of the Turkish request was sent in the form of letters to the Sultan and Grand Vizier on 7 March 1833.

This dusty answer to Turkish entreaties was almost certainly due to the differences in the British Cabinet which have been referred to. In a letter written eight years later to Lord Melbourne at the time of England's later, decisive intervention in Syria, Palmerston, who was Foreign Secretary both in 1832-3 and in 1840, indicated that he had been in favour of giving aid to the Sultan when it was asked for in 1832, 'before Mohamed

Ali had made any material progress in Syria', but that he had been 'overruled by the Cabinet'.[36]

French diplomacy was much more active. Mimaud, the French Consul-General in Egypt, unlike Barker, was on good terms with Mohamed Ali and in the confidence of his own government. On 29 May 1832 he recommended an arrangement by which Egypt and Syria would form 'a political establishment effectively separated from Constantinople, but tributary to it, with Mohamed Ali having the same relation to the Sultan as the Dey of Algiers'.[37] In July, M. de Varenne, the French Chargé d'Affaires in Constantinople, tendered his good offices in mediating between the Sultan and Mohamed Ali on the lines recommended by Mimaud, but the Porte declined his offer. After the battle of Beylan Mimaud was instructed to urge moderation on Mohamed Ali and to suggest to him that he should be content to remain master of Syria and concentrate on the administration of that country.[38] This admonition of Mimaud's, together with what he was hearing from Briggs about the British attitude, had their effect on Mohamed Ali and, if the Porte had been prepared for a settlement, might well have brought about the possibility of negotiations on the basis of the French plan. But the Porte ordered Rashid to march against Ibrahim and tried to obtain naval assistance from England.

News of the battle of Konieh reached Constantinople on 27 December, almost simultaneously with the arrival from London of news that the Turkish appeals for British help had been virtually turned down. These two serious and, apparently, unexpected blows threw the Turks into a panic. Before long this panic was to spread to the British and French Embassies. For the prospect of Russian intervention was in the air. On 21 December, a few days before the news from Konieh, the Russian Envoy in Constantinople had formally offered armed Russian assistance against Ibrahim. This offer had neither been refused nor accepted at the time. On 22 December, General Mouraviev arrived in Constantinople from Petersburg, announcing that he was on his way to Egypt with a mission from the Tsar to tell Mohamed Ali that he must immediately submit himself to his Suzerain under pain of incurring severe Russian displeasure. Mouraviev left Constantinople for Alexandria on 4 January 1833. At the same time, Colonel Duhamel, an official at the Russian Embassy, left for Konieh with a similar message for Ibrahim.

The Turks were unwilling to leave everything in Russian hands. They also probably saw some hopeful possibilities in the prospect of Great Power rivalries. So they asked M. de Varenne, the French Chargé d'Affaires, to mediate on the lines which Varenne had suggested, and which the Porte had turned down, six months previously. And, on 7 January, they sent Admiral Rifaat Khalil Pasha to Egypt to negotiate direct with Mohamed Ali.

Mohamed Ali expressed to Mouraviev his willingness to order Ibrahim to halt his advance and to abide by whatever agreement might be arrived at with the Sultan as a result of negotiations with Khalil Pasha. He sent a message to Ibrahim accordingly; but Ibrahim had left Konieh by the time the messenger arrived there and, before the message could catch up with him, had already reached Kutahia, some 150 miles from Constantinople, where he halted in obedience to his father's orders. Before leaving Konieh he had written to the Viceroy that it was impossible to keep his army there throughout the winter because of the cold and lack of provisions. He went on to express his view that any arrangement with Khalil would only be in the nature of a truce and that it was necessary to finish matters once and for all, get the Sultan deposed and install a friendly government in Constantinople. 'If you tell me that Europe would not approve, I say that we would not give Europe any time to intervene. We will present Europe with a *fait accompli*. If they like to take advantage of it by partitioning what is left of the Ottoman Empire between themselves, what is that to us? In any case, it is better for both of us and for Europe to bring matters to a head now.'[39]

Having received his father's message at Kutahia, Ibrahim realized that, as a result of his father's hesitations, events had overtaken them, and that it was now too late to think of deposing the Sultan. Instead, he recommended to his father that he should, in his negotiations with the Porte and the Powers, insist on (a) independence, and (b) the possession of the four Pashaliks of Syria, the Pashalik of Adana, Cyprus and, if possible, Tunis and Tripoli. He told him that Adana was necessary because of its timber, 'on which the existence of our fleet depends, our own country not possessing any timber', and that Cyprus was desirable as a base for the Egyptian fleet and that it was, in any case, necessary to deny it to the Turks who might use it against them for an attack on Syria.[40]

Throughout January 1833 Varenne and Mandeville, the British Chargé d'Affaires, showed anxiety lest the Porte should accept the offer of Russian assistance made during December. The Reis Effendi assured Mandeville that the Russian offer had not been accepted because it was not required, and the Seraskier (Minister of War), Mohamed Ali's old enemy Khosrev Pasha, gave him a similar assurance. But the Kiaya Bey (Minister of the Interior) admitted that acceptance depended on whether or not Ibrahim continued his advance. This was in fact the case and, on 2 February, as soon as it was known in Constantinople that Ibrahim was advancing westwards from Konieh, the Porte formally asked Russia to send them four ships-of-the-line, as many frigates, and 20,000–25,000 troops.

On 4 February Mouraviev returned to Constantinople from Alexandria and informed the Porte and the foreign embassies that he had received solemn assurances from Mohamed Ali of his entire submission to the Sultan, and of his having sent orders to Ibrahim to halt his advance. The Reis Effendi, somewhat reassured, told Mandeville that he had asked the Russian government to suspend the reinforcements asked for pending the result of Khalil Pasha's mission.

Events then began to move swiftly. On 16 February messengers arrived in Constantinople from Khalil Pasha bearing Mohamed Ali's proposals for a settlement. These provided for the cession of the four Syrian Pashaliks plus Adana, under the suzerainty of the Sultan, and with the payment of appropriate tribute in respect of them. The messengers also brought a counter-proposal from Khalil providing for the cession to Mohamed Ali of the four Sanjaks of Acre, Jerusalem, Nablus and Tripoli (comprising the old Pashalik of Acre before the recent creation of the Pashalik of Tripoli). On 17 February, Admiral Roussin, the new French Ambassador, arrived at Constantinople. On 18 February, a Russian naval squadron, the first instalment of the Russian assistance which had been promised and requested, arrived in the Bosphorus. (It is not clear whether the Reis Effendi had really asked for its despatch to be delayed and that his request had reached Sebastopol too late, or whether the Russians had decided to despatch it anyway, whether the Turks wanted it or not.)

On 21 February, Roussin, anxious at all costs to reach a settlement and so prevent the arrival of more Russian forces, agreed on behalf of his government to compel Mohamed Ali's acceptance of the terms proposed by Khalil Pasha. This marked an abrupt reversal of French policy which, up to that time, in accordance with Mimaud's recommendation, had been in favour of Mohamed Ali retaining the whole of Syria. Mohamed Ali had been aware of this and had every reason to suppose that France would support the proposal he had transmitted to Constantinople, with the exception of the demand for Adana.

On 22 February Roussin's ADC, Captain Ollivier, left Constantinople for Alexandria in a French frigate with a despatch for Mimaud from Roussin instructing him to present what was virtually an ultimatum to Mohamed Ali, calling on him to agree to the evacuation of the whole of Asia Minor and Syria, except for the Sanjaks of Acre, Jerusalem, Nablus and Tripoli, failing which French and British squadrons would blockade the coasts of Egypt. (Roussin appears to have had no authority from the French government for making this threat.) The same frigate carried a despatch from Mandeville to Barker which read: 'The Sublime Porte, having agreed to renounce the acceptance of Russian military and naval help which has been offered, and to request the immediate departure of the Russian fleet from the Bosphorus on condition that the French Ambassador guarantees that Mohamed Ali will accept the terms proposed to him by the Sultan, i.e. the possession of the four Pashaliks of Syria, and H.E. having entered into a formal engagement to that effect, he has asked me to use my best efforts to remove any difficulty in the way of Mohamed Ali accepting these proposals. You are therefore instructed to inform the Pasha that I do not hesitate to recommend to him the adoption of the advice given to him by Admiral Roussin, knowing that Mohamed Ali could do nothing more agreeable to HM than to make peace with his Sovereign and knowing that he could not himself get more advantageous terms. If he does not accept, HM's government and the French government will take joint action against him.'[41] Incredible as it may seem, Mandeville appears to have been under the impression that Roussin's proposal referred to the four Pashaliks of Aleppo, Tripoli, Acre and Damascus, and not merely the four Sanjaks of Acre, Jerusalem, Nablus and Tripoli, and to have associated himself with Roussin's threats in this belief.[42]

Since Barker, who had just received news of his impending

replacement as Consul-General, was on holiday (and in high dudgeon) in Rosetta at the time, it fell to Richard Sloane, the Vice-Consul, to deal with Mandeville's instructions. He conveyed Mandeville's message to the Viceroy, who told him caustically that there did not appear to be the least understanding between the British and French on Eastern affairs, since Mandeville was proposing that he should have the four Pashaliks of Aleppo, Damascus, Tripoli and Acre, whereas Roussin had only offered him the four Sanjaks of Acre, Jerusalem, Nablus and Tripoli. He went on to tell Sloane that he had rejected Roussin's demand. Sloane expressed to Mandeville the hope that a settlement could be arrived at on the basis of Mohamed Ali's counter-proposal to Khalil Pasha, providing for the cession of the four Syrian Pashaliks plus Adana.[43]

Meanwhile Mandeville and Roussin, at the request of the Reis Effendi, had, on 23 February, sent a message to Ibrahim requesting him to withdraw his troops from Kutahia, through Asia Minor, and back into Syria. On 1 March Ibrahim replied that he would do so if and when ordered by his father, under whose authority he acted.

Mohamed Ali was furious at what he regarded as the French perfidy displayed in Roussin's ultimatum. On 9 March he replied formally to Roussin, turning down his proposal 'as requiring him to abandon a country of which he had entire possession at the price of the small province comprising the four districts incorrectly designated as Pashaliks', and expressed the hope that Roussin would advice the Porte to accept the proposals made by him to Khalil Pasha.[44] By the same ship Rashid Bey, the Ameji (Ottoman Master of Ceremonies), who had accompanied Khalil Pasha to Egypt, went to Constantinople with a message from Mohamed Ali to the Porte reiterating his demand for the four Syrian Pashaliks plus Adana. The Viceroy also wrote to Ibrahim advising him of what had happened and telling him that, unless he received from the Porte within five days advice that they accepted the demands conveyed to them by the Ameji, he was to advance immediately with his army and not to halt until the Porte had formally accepted them. The reply to Roussin, and the Ameji with his message, arrived at Constantinople together on 23 March.

The Porte, when they heard from the Ameji of the order given by Mohamed Ali to Ibrahim, asked the Russian Ambassador to expedite the despatch of troops. On 26 March,

Roussin, who may have been regretting his abrupt intervention in a situation which he had not given himself time properly to understand, advised the Reis Effendi to accept Mohamed Ali's terms 'rather than expose the country to a conflict between the Russian army and the people'.[45] On the following day Mandeville told the Reis Effendi that 'if the Porte see no prospect of successfully opposing Mohamed Ali, concession would be a lesser evil than risking all by continuing the fight'.[46] The Reis Effendi replied that the Porte might agree to the four Syrian Pashaliks but not to Adana, and asked Mandeville if he and Roussin would try to reach an agreement on this basis. Mandeville agreed on condition that the Russians would be asked to withdraw immediately agreement had been reached.[47]

It was then agreed between the Reis Effendi and Roussin and Mandeville that Varenne should accompany the Ameji to Kutahia and tell Ibrahim that the French government would not agree to the cession of Adana, while the Ameji was to try to get Ibrahim to evacuate Asia Minor on the basis of the Porte's granting to Mohamed Ali the four Syrian Pashaliks. The two men left for Kutahia on 30 March.

On 5 April a second squadron of the Russian fleet arrived in the Bosphorus, convoying 5,000 troops, who were disembarked on the Asiatic side. On the same day, Varenne and the Ameji arrived at Kutahia, to be met with a demand from Ibrahim for the Pashaliks of Urfa and Diabekir, in eastern Asia Minor, as well as Adana and the four Syrian Pashaliks. This being summarily rejected, he insisted on his demand for Adana. (The importance of Adana, apart from the question of timber on which Mohamed Ali and Ibrahim set so much store, was that the possession of the Pashalik by the Egyptians would give them command of the Cilician Gates, the principal invasion route from Asia Minor into Syria, and so secure them against a land invasion of Syria by the Turks or, possibly, by the Russians.) Having received a report from Varenne on 11 April, Roussin, on 12 April, agreed with the Reis Effendi that he should, in the name of his government, guarantee to Ibrahim the cession of the four Syrian Pashaliks, but not Adana, provided that he immediately withdrew from Asia Minor. Roussin asked Mandeville to join with him in giving this guarantee, but Mandeville, presumably still sore about the previous misunderstanding, refused.

On 15 April Varenne and the Ameji returned to Constantinople from Kutahia with the news that the Ameji had signed an agreement with Ibrahim by which the four Syrian Pashaliks plus Adana were ceded to Mohaned Ali and that Ibrahim had agreed to withdraw his army over the Taurus Mountains as soon as this agreement had been ratified by the Sultan. The Reis Effendi declared that the Ameji had exceeded his instructions. When news of this disavowal reached Ibrahim he announced that he had already sent a message to his father saying that the Porte had agreed to cede Adana and that, until the question was settled in his favour, he would remain where he was with his army.

While all this was going on in and around Constantinople, a comedy of errors was being enacted at Alexandria between Mohamed Ali and the Representatives of Great Britain, France and Austria.

At the beginning of 1833 the British government had appointed Lieutenant-Colonel Patrick Campbell as Consul General and Political Agent in Egypt in place of Barker. Before leaving for Egypt, Campbell was given 'special instructions for his guidance' drafted by Palmerston personally.[48] He was told that Ibrahim's victory at Konieh had induced the Porte to seek some arrangement with Mohamed Ali and that negotiations were already on foot in Egypt between the Viceroy and Khalil Pasha. If agreement had already been reached the British government would accept whatever had been agreed. If agreement had not been reached, it would be for Campbell to try to facilitate things. He was then told the story of the Turkish request for help and its rejection. The instructions went on:

'Although HM's Government did not determine to send to the Sultan the naval aid applied for, it was not because they viewed with indifference the events that were passing in the East. HM's Government attach great importance to the maintenance of the integrity of the Ottoman Empire, considering that State to be a material element in the general balance of power in Europe, and they are of opinion that any considerable encroachment on the Sultan's Asiatic territories and any consequent defalcation from the resources which he might bring to bear for the defence of his European dominions must operate in a corresponding degree upon his relative position with respect to neighbouring Powers, and must thereby have injurious bearings upon the general interest of Europe.

HM's Government therefore wish to prevent, not only a dissolution but, even a partial dismemberment of the Turkish Empire. Moreover, the relations between Great Britain and Turkey have, with trifling exceptions, been those of friendship and alliance, and the present Sultan has acquired personal claims upon the good offices of HM's Government by the facilities which have been afforded for the settlement of Greece. . . . The Turkish fleet suffered losses at Navarino which have mainly contributed to deprive the Porte of that maritime superiority over Mohamed Ali which it might otherwise have expected to command.[49] The Pasha of Egypt is only Governor of a Turkish Province appointed during the pleasure of the Sultan, removable at will, and exercises a delegated power in the name and for the benefit of the Sovereign by whom that trust was conferred. He has never alleged any injuries as a justification for his revolt, and the only motive hitherto given for invading the Provinces of the Ottoman Empire has been that he considered that he could govern those Provinces more beneficially for the Sultan than the Sultan himself, and that by wresting from his Sovereign the government of Syria he should increase the strength of that Sovereign to resist external attack. . . . HM's Government is desirous of affording the Sultan, in his negotiations with the Pasha, the assistance of its influence and good offices. . . . You will act according to your judgement and discretion, guiding yourself by your knowledge of the opinion of HM's Government. HM's Government's idea of a solution would be that the Pasha should revert to his former status and condition as Governor of Egypt and that the invaded Provinces should be replaced under the Sultan's authority, so that one party should not have suffered by diminution of his territory from the aggression of another. But, since the Sultan has been compelled to sue for peace, such an arrangement is probably impracticable. The next best arrangement is that Mohamed Ali should receive from the Sultan the Pashaliks of Syria with such obligation in point of tribute and military aid as might leave the revenues and resources of the Porte undiminished, with such limits to extent as might least endanger adjacent Powers. You will probably find at Alexandria agents acting on behalf of

France, Austria and Russia with reference to these negotiations. You will communicate freely and confidentially
with the French and Austrian Consuls, who will also be
instructed to cooperate with you.'

The instructions went on to tell Campbell to 'place himself
on a footing of civility with the Russian Agent' but, in effect,
to keep him at arm's length. 'If negotiations should appear
likely to be broken off, and if the Pasha should threaten to
renew hostilities, you will explain to him without disguise and
will represent to him in the strongest terms the importance
which HM's Government attached to the maintenance of the
integrity of the Turkish Empire as an object of European
interest and you will declare to him that Great Britain could
not see with indifference its dissolution or dismemberment.'[50]

Campbell arrived in Egypt on 26 March. Reporting to
Palmerston on 31 March, he told him of Mohamed Ali's
rejection of Roussin's demands and of the breaking-off of
negotiations with Khalil Pasha who, however, was still in
Egypt and apparently on the best of terms with the Viceroy.
Campbell told Palmerston that he had discussed his instructions
with Mimaud and with Acerbi, the Austrian Consul-General,
that Mimaud's instructions were similar to his own, but that
Acerbi had been instructed to cooperate with the British and
Russian, but not with the French, Representative. He had seen
Mohamed Ali on 28 March. The Viceroy had told him that the
British government was not correctly informed about the cause
of dispute between him and the Sultan, and blamed his old
adversary Khosrev Pasha, the Seraskier, for calling in the
Russians. He denied that he was seeking independence and
said that his only aim was to 'renovate and consolidate the
Empire and to serve the desire of the whole Moslem world,
which was calling on him to free them from the shameful
servitude imposed on them by the Russians. His whole object
was to assist in making the Sultan and his Empire free from the
yoke of Russia.' Campbell went on to tell Palmerston that
Mandeville had urged the Roussin proposals on Mohamed Ali
without realizing that these proposals only gave him the
southern part of Syria, and said that, for that reason, he had
avoided discussing them with the Viceroy. Mimaud believed
that Mohamed Ali was sincere in not seeking independence, but
Acerbi did not. The Austrian Consul-General had told Campbell that Mohamed Ali had really been pleased at the oppor-

195

tunity afforded by the Roussin proposals to break off negotiations with Khalil Pasha, and that what he really wanted was an advance by Ibrahim, and a consequent intervention by Russia, which would bring about a revolution in Constantinople and the formation of a government composed of Mohamed Ali's friends.[51]

On 2 April Prokesch-Osten, who had been in Egypt a few years before in connection with the Greek war, arrived at Alexandria on a special mission from Vienna. In conversation with Campbell he told him that the Austrian government were in agreement with the Russians that Mohamed Ali must submit himself to the Sultan and that they mistrusted French attempts at mediation as being inspired by a desire to obtain a virtual protectorate over Egypt. For that reason, he had been instructed to cooperate with Campbell but not with Mimaud.

On 8 April Campbell had an interview with Boghos Yusef, who interpreted in more practical terms the somewhat cloudy generalizations of his master. He told Campbell that the Viceroy was definitely prepared to settle for Syria and Adana and that, if he got them, he would immediately order Ibrahim to evacuate all Asia Minor west of the Taurus. But, if he did not, he would not yield an inch. It would be six months before the Russians could send effective assistance and, in that time, with the whole Moslem world on his side, he could do as he liked. He said that Mohamed Ali put no faith in French mediation, and spoke bitterly of Roussin's intervention which, he alleged, had not been approved by the Duc de Broglie, the French Foreign Minister. Campbell, commenting to Palmerston on this interview, wrote: 'It appears that the Viceroy will not consent to any other terms than those already laid down by him. The question is, whether it would not be more advantageous to give him those terms than that the war should continue.' He added that Mimaud had been instructed by the Duc de Broglie to tell Mohamed Ali that, if Ibrahim did not start evacuating Asia Minor immediately, a French naval squadron would be sent to blockade Alexandria, but that Prokesch-Osten had recommended to Vienna that Mohamed Ali's conditions should be accepted.[52] From this despatch it is to be noted, first, that while Campbell was aware of Prokesch-Osten's and of Mimaud's instructions, neither Mimaud nor Prokesch-Osten were aware of each other's; and secondly, that the previous close relations between England and France over

Egypt were beginning to dissolve, and were being replaced by an intimacy between England and Austria. This tendency was accentuated later by long conversations in Vienna between Metternich and Sir Frederick Lamb, the British Ambassador. In these conversations Metternich acted as a bridge between the British and Russian governments, who were already in conversation in Petersburg about Egypt. In this way evolved a pattern in which, as the Turco-Egyptian situation developed between 1833 and 1840, Britain, Russia and Austria gradually came together in a common opposition to Mohamed Ali's expansion, while France, alternating between a policy of obtaining predominant influence at Constantinople, and one of encouraging Mohamed Ali, became the odd man out.

On 16 April the Viceroy received a message from Ibrahim telling him of the agreement he had made with the Ameji, ceding to him the four Syrian Pashaliks and Adana. The Viceroy immediately announced that peace had been made on these terms, and there were public rejoicings all over Egypt. Towards the end of April, the Viceroy received a Firman from Constantinople revoking the previous bans and deprivations imposed on him and Ibrahim, and referring to him as the Viceroy of Egypt and Syria. In the usual Bairam list of Pashaliks, that of Adana had been left vacant, but a message was received from Ibrahim saying that the future of Adana was the subject of negotiations and that, pending their outcome, he and his army were remaining at Kutahia.

On 1 May Baron de Boislecomte, a special Envoy from the Duc de Broglie, arrived in Alexandria with instructions to urge on Mohamed Ali the immediate evacuation of Asia Minor. Campbell had received no instructions about this mission and he and Prokesch-Osten were 'both of the opinion that we ought not to urge the Viceroy on this matter'.[53] Mohamed Ali told Campbell that he greatly resented the French trying to come between him and the Sultan in a matter which was already in process of being settled between them direct, and indicated that, if the Sultan did not confirm the grant of Adana agreed by the Ameji, he would renew the war.

In Constantinople, Roussin was still trying to persuade Mandeville to join him in inducing Ibrahim to evacuate Asia Minor and so enable the Turks to get rid of the Russians. Ibrahim refused to do so without being confirmed in the possession of Adana. Roussin was opposed to this and succeeded in getting Mandeville to send the following despatch to Campbell by the hand of Rear-Admiral Briggs, who arrived at Alexandria in a warship on 6 May with instructions from Mandeville to discuss with Campbell the possibility of a blockade of Egypt. 'Impress on the mind of Mohamed Ali that, so long as there is an Egyptian soldier in Asia Minor, the Russian fleet and army will not leave the country, and the Russian government probably desire nothing better than to have a pretext for keeping their troops in Turkey. . . . It is important that all pretexts for their remaining should be removed, and Mohamed Ali cannot do anything more disagreeable to HM's Government than by causing any hindrance to their departure. England and France will soon become tired of his obstinacy and will take the enforcement of the [Turkish] conditions into their own hands.'[54]

Campbell, on receipt of these instructions, saw the Viceroy and told him that 'while it was not the wish of HM's Government to object to any concessions which the Sultan might agree to of his own free will, the question of peace had now become a European one and, so long as the Adana question remained unsettled, the tranquillity of Europe was involved'. 'The Viceroy, in reply, while saying that he would not consent to losing Adana, agreed to order Ibrahim to evacuate his army beyond the Taurus, but not to evacuate Adana.' Campbell, reporting this conversation to Palmerston, told him that 'HH, having conceded the chief point, i.e. the retreat of his army beyond the Taurus, I gave my opinion to the Admiral [Briggs] that no blockade should be attempted, but that I would continue to try to prevail upon Mohamed Ali to give up Adana'. Boislecomte had received no instructions about a blockade, was surprised that the question had been raised, and agreed with Campbell and Prokesch-Osten that the best thing would be for the three Powers to prevail upon the Sultan to give way over Adana. Campbell, however, doubted whether the Sultan would agree.[55]

On 8 May Mimaud and Prokesch-Osten received from their respective Ambassadors in Constantinople instructions similar to those which Campbell had received from Mandeville. Campbell and Prokesch-Osten saw Mohamed Ali together. The Viceroy told them that Khalil Pasha was about to return to Constantinople and that he hoped he would be able to settle the question of Adana with the Porte.

Just as this point had been reached, the ground was cut from under the feet of the European negotiators in Egypt by the arrival of news from Ibrahim that the Sultan had granted him the Pashalik of Adana. What had happened was this. On 23 April a third Russian squadron had arrived in the Bosphorus, convoying another contingent of Russian troops. On 1 May, Lord Ponsonby, the new British Ambassador, arrived in Constantinople. As he wrote to Campbell: 'The request made by Ibrahim for the government of Adana was communicated to me before I had landed and I persuaded Roussin, who had been adverse, to unite with me in counselling the Porte to concede this demand. Count Orloff (a Russian Envoy) arrived almost immediately after the affair was concluded, but happily too late to prevent its execution, although he expressed his disapprobation. He has declared to me that the Russian forces will be withdrawn the moment Ibrahim has returned with his forces within the limits of the Pashaliks assigned to him and his father, including Adana.'[56]

Ponsonby told Palmerston that his reason for advising this course was that 'I thought it necessary to put an end to every pretext the Russians could seize upon to justify their continued occupation of the country'.[57] Palmerston, before he had heard of Ponsonby's initiative, instructed Campbell that HM's Government desired that 'the concessions to be made by the Sultan should not extend beyond the Pashaliks of Syria'.[58] But, after he had heard from Ponsonby, he accepted the position and instructed Campbell that 'it is by no means the wish or the intention of HM's Government to oppose any objection to this arrangement or to attempt to disturb it'.[59]

In retrospect, it seems probable that, if Ibrahim had had his way after the battle of Beylan and marched westward through Asia Minor towards Constantinople, the partition of the Ottoman Empire would have been precipitated. The Russians would have occupied Constantinople, the Austrians Bosnia and Herzegovina and the Dalmatian coast, and most of Turkey in Asia would have fallen to Egypt. This was probably what Ibrahim wanted. He was more of an Arab than a Turk. He had no feeling for the Ottoman Empire and would like to have seen it replaced in the leadership of the Moslem world by an Arab Empire based on Egypt and ruled over by his father and his descendants. He was made in the classic mould of the great conquerors of history—a brilliant General, a good, if harsh, administrator, a leader of men, who preferred actions to words, better at ordering people about than negotiating with them. In some ways—in his dress, in his religious scepticism, in his direct manner of speech—he was more westernized, more up-to-date, than his father. But he had not his father's exaggerated respect for Western methods, nor his exaggerated fear of Western power. He believed that the West could be dealt with on its own terms, by direct action, by the presentation of a *fait accompli*. In the Syrian affair he believed that the way of negotiation was to play into the hands of the West, since it meant surrendering that initiative, that power of surprise, which could have been used to offset the superior resources of the West. For him, Constantinople, and the whole mystique which had grown up round the Ottoman Empire, were expendable in pursuit of an Asiatic Empire for the family of Mohamed Ali.

For Mohamed Ali, in his maturity, Constantinople and the Ottoman Empire were not expendable. In his earlier days he had undoubtedly dreamed of achieving independence of the Porte and had admitted as much to the foreign Consuls. But later, in his continual assertions to the Consuls that he desired, not the destruction but the regeneration of the Ottoman Empire, he was not being entirely hypocritical. In his manners, in his dress, in his speech, he was, in spite of his modernistic outlook, entirely a Turk, and he became more and more so as old age advanced on him. He had friends in Constantinople who regarded him not as a rebel but a patriot who represented Ottoman ideals more truly than the existing Ottoman government. And he commanded armies more powerful, territories richer, and energies more sustained than the existing Sultan. He did not want to precipitate a partition of the Ottoman Empire. Although not a fanatical, nor even a particularly devout, Moslem, he did not want to see the Russians in Constantinople. Since he believed that the achievement of his own independence would almost inevitably bring the Russians to Constantinople, he did not desire that independence. What he really wanted was the direction of the destinies of the Ottoman Empire by himself and his descendants, either as a result of his becoming Sultan himself or, more probably, as a result of him and his descendants ruling, nominally as vassals, but actually as independent Rulers, over a wide area of the Empire, professing nominal allegiance to a *fainéant* Sultanate entirely under his and his descendants' control and subject to their wishes. There was, after all, a precedent for this in Islamic and, specifically, in Egyptian history. In the thirteenth century the Mamluk Sultan Baibars had kidnapped Mustansir, the *fainéant* Abbasid Caliph, from Baghdad, taken him to Cairo, and thereafter acted in the name and under the nominal authority of his prisoner. Such a solution would not only preserve the mystique of the Ottoman Empire and Caliphate, which really meant something important to Mohamed Ali, but might also, if circumspectly approached, be made acceptable to the European Powers.

It was to this circumspect approach that Mohamed Ali devoted all the resources of his diplomacy, both in Constantinople and in Egypt. He realized that Ibrahim could not, by his direct methods, exploit the situation his victories had created in the way Mohamed Ali wanted it exploited. Independence, with its corollary of the partition of the Ottoman Empire, could probably have been won, had almost been won, on the battlefield. But he wanted something more subtle. Like Palmerston, he wanted to see the continuation of the Ottoman Empire, undivided and undiminished, but as a mystical unity presided over by a shadowy Sultan-Caliph, in which he and his descendants would wield the real power.

But his diplomacy, while it preserved the integrity of the Ottoman Empire, which he valued and which Ibrahim did not, failed to obtain for him the reality of power. The Syrian adventure gained him nothing but the acquisition of territory and, with it, the use of a limited amount of what proved to be very refractory manpower, and the opportunity to exploit some comparatively meagre natural resources. Against this, he had earned the bitter and vindictive hostility of Sultan Mahmud II and the lively suspicion of the European Powers.

If the settlement agreed at Kutahia, after so much acrimony, could have been regarded as a permanent one, and if there had been any reason to believe that the rancours of Sultan Mahmud II had been appeased and the ambitions of Mohamed Ali satisfied, it is probable that the European Powers would have been content with the *status quo post* Kutahia, once the Russians had been induced to leave the neighbourhood of Constantinople. But it was clear that the settlement was no more than an uneasy truce, unwillingly agreed to by both sides as a result of pressure from the Powers, and liable to be broken by either

201

side once these pressures were removed. It was almost equally clear that while the Powers, with the possible exception of Russia, would have welcomed as a first choice the stabilization of the *status quo post* Kutahia on a basis of developing amity between the Sultan and Mohamed Ali, their second choice, if it were to be forced upon them by the failure of such amity to develop, would be for supporting the Sultan against any renewed pretensions by Mohamed Ali. For the Kutahia settlement represented the extreme limit of what any of the Powers were prepared to concede to Mohamed Ali. As we have seen, the Porte were only induced to concede Adana as a result of Ponsonby's initiative, which was only reluctantly endorsed by the European, including the British, governments. Any further pretensions would be unanimously opposed by England, France and Austria, if only because their being put forward would precipitate another Russian intervention. This being so, Mohamed Ali could only avert the future enmity of the European Powers by a strict adherence to the terms of the settlement, by a wise administration of his territorial acquisitions, and by a scrupulous avoidance of quarrels with the Porte. The Porte, on the contrary, had every incentive to pick a quarrel with Mohamed Ali in the expectation that they could rely on the diplomatic and, possibly, the military support of the Powers, provided only that the scope of the quarrel was limited sufficiently to avoid the possibility of their having, once more, to request armed intervention from Russia.

CHAPTER EIGHT

THE COLD WAR

Over evacuation the Russians were as good as Orloff's word given to Ponsonby. Orloff told the Porte that 'peace having now been concluded, the Sultan no longer had need of Russian succour and nothing therefore remained but to withdraw the Russian fleet and army, which had been sent with no other object than the personal safety of the Sultan and the preservation of his Empire'.[1] Roussin continued to be very suspicious, and a French naval squadron asked for, and was refused, permission to pass through the Dardanelles. Advising Sir Pulteney Malcolm (who had returned as C-in-C Mediterranean) of this, Ponsonby warned him that he should not try himself to enter. In a subsequent conversation with Roussin, who suggested a joint intervention at Constantinople by British and French squadrons, Ponsonby seems to have convinced him of the unwisdom of such a course, and persuaded him that it would be better to have the squadrons cruising outside the Dardanelles.

In the event, Ibrahim completed his evacuation of Asia Minor by 25 June and the Russians completed their evacuation on 9 July. But the Russians, before they departed, signed a treaty with the Porte, known as the Treaty of Unkiar Skelessi, valid for eight years, by which they agreed to come to Turkey's assistance, if requested, in the event of Turkey being attacked, and by which Turkey, in return, agreed not to let any foreign warships enter the Dardanelles under any pretext whatever. This treaty was signed on 8 July, the day before the Russians left, and was kept secret until its ratification on 28 August, when copies were given to the British, French and Austrian Representatives in Constantinople. (The Reis Effendi had told

203

Ponsonby about it unofficially a few days after it had been signed.)

The British and French governments protested against the treaty both in Constantinople and in Petersburg, and there were long subsequent conversations about it both in Vienna between Metternich and Sir Frederick Lamb, the British Ambassador, and in Petersburg between Count Nesselrode, the Russian Foreign Minister, and Mr Bligh, the British Minister. The effect of these conversations, in which Austria acted as a bridge between the British and Russian views, and from which the French were excluded, was gradually to bring the three Powers closer together in their Near Eastern policies.

The furore created by the treaty was due rather to general suspicion of Russian intentions than to any specific objection to its terms. For example, the clause by which the Turks agreed not to let any foreign warship enter the Dardanelles had already been included in the Treaty of the Dardanelles which England had concluded with Turkey in 1808. What was objected to was, as it were, the penumbra of the treaty, which appeared to give Russia an exclusive protectorate over Turkey (or rather to accentuate and perpetuate the protectorate status which existed by virtue of previous, not dissimilar, treaties), and which implied that the prohibition on the entry of foreign warships to the Dardanelles would not, in practice, apply to Russian warships entering or leaving the Mediterranean, but to other warships seeking to come to Constantinople, thus effectually preventing any foreign intervention against a Russian occupation of Constantinople. (There was no comparable Russian objection to the similar clause in the Anglo-Turkish Treaty of the Dardanelles, since that clause on the one hand did not prevent Russian warships from coming to Constantinople and, on the other hand, did prevent other foreign warships from doing so.)

The British suspicion of Russian intentions was, if not entirely dissipated, substantially reduced, by the conversations in Vienna and Petersburg, during which the British and Austrian governments tended to transfer part of their suspicions against Russia for her designs on Constantinople in the direction of similar suspicions against France for her supposed designs on Egypt.

The immediate effect of the Treaty of Unkiar Skelessi on Ponsonby and Palmerston was to make them so afraid of the immediate prospect of Turkey being drawn into the Russian orbit that they drew closer to Mohamed Ali. While the Russian forces were still in the neighbourhood of Constantinople, and before the treaty had been signed, Ponsonby went so far as to express the view to Campbell that 'if the Russians try to take Constantinople, the power and wisdom of Mohamed Ali may become important to us. By his possession of Syria he is now placed at the head of a language and a distinct race of people; the greatest step for the dismemberment of the Ottoman Empire has now been taken; the bad policy which brought the Russians here has made the treaty (i.e. of Kutahia) necessary; not otherwise could Russia have been deprived of all pretext for militarily occupying the country. . . . It is to be hoped that the strength of Mohamed Ali may be found efficient when it seems certain that it must be in his interest to exert it in driving from Asia and the Ottoman territory a Power which, if allowed to spread its roots there, will be great enough to destroy the Egyptian and Arab peoples. . . . The Sultan is incorrigible; he must hate the Russians, but he wants courage and will-power.'[2]

Something of Ponsonby's sentiments must have been communicated by Campbell to the Viceroy for, in June 1833, referring to the presence of Russian forces near Constantinople, he told the British Consul-General that 'within five or six months he would have an army of 125,000 men to act in any way or in any place when the British government might call upon him to employ them.'[3] Palmerston, commenting on this 'remarkable conversation', instructed Campbell to tell the Viceroy that 'HM's Government were highly gratified by Mohamed Ali's friendly sentiments, which were reciprocated', but went on to say that 'the great object of HM's policy is the maintenance of peace. . . . HM's Government were adverse to any great changes in the relative distribution of political power and attached great importance to the independent existence of a powerful State in those countries which now constitute the Turkish Empire, because the dismemberment of that Empire could not be effected without a contest with the other States of Europe . . . and would alter the balance of power in a manner dangerous to peace. . . . HM's Government received with satisfaction the assurance of HH's fidelity and devotion to the Sultan and his determination to devote his resources to the defence of the Ottoman Empire and to the protection and maintenance of its independence.' The despatch

205

concluded by urging Campbell to cultivate Mohamed Ali's goodwill, 'as it is the wish of HM's Government to be on the best possible footing with the Pasha, always keeping this inter-course with him in due harmony with the duties of HM's Government as an ally of the Porte'.[4]

Soon afterwards, Palmerston told Ponsonby that the British government would 'deprecate any hostile proceedings on the side of the Porte against the Pasha'. He also instructed him to warn the Porte of the 'dangers and inconveniences' of a Russian alliance, which might be avoided if the Porte would look to England, 'which Power has the means and also the disposition effectively to control Mohamed Ali so long as Turkey should continue really independent'. He went on to tell Ponsonby to warn the Porte that 'if the option between the establishment of Mohamed Ali at Constantinople and the subjection of that capital to the power of Russia were to be forced on England, it would be impossible for HM's Government not to prefer the former alternative'.[5]

Palmerston displayed the same benevolence towards Mohamed Ali in other respects. The Viceroy was faced with a rebellion in Arabia of his Albanian troops who, according to him, were trying to displace the Imam of the Yemen and set up an independent administration. He wanted to know whether the British government would have any objection to his sending troops to Arabia to put down the rebels, to occupy Mocha, pacify the Yemen, and attach it to the Hijaz. At the same time he enquired whether the British would have any objection to his cutting a canal from Cairo to Suez so as to facilitate com-munications between Egypt and the Red Sea.[6]

Twelve years before, Mohamed Ali's ambitions in the Yemen, and his expansion in the Red Sea area generally, had been viewed with great suspicion by the British government. The port of Mocha, where a British Resident was established, had been regarded by them more or less as a British protector-ate. But in 1833, in spite of the interest which the Government of Bombay was taking in the navigation of the Red Sea, there was no British Resident in Mocha, and the protectorate claim seems to have lapsed. The idea of a canal from Cairo to Suez— this seems to have been the first mention of the possibility of a Suez Canal by Mohamed Ali to the British government—was partly in order to facilitate the movement of warships between the Mediterranean and the Red Sea. Twenty years before the

British government had been very suspicious about this and had stopped an Egyptian corvette at Capetown on its way to the Red Sea. Campbell seems to have been apprehensive about Palmerston's reaction to these plans of Mohamed Ali and, contrary to his usual habit, made no recommendations. But he was authorized to 'give a favourable answer to the enquiry of Mohamed Ali in respect to the feelings of HM's Government upon both of these points'.[7]

There were no further developments over the canal for some years. In Arabia, during 1833-34, Mohamed Ali conducted a successful campaign against the rebellious Albanian troops under Turkiye Bilmez, who had seized the ports of Yemen from the Imam and practically put a stop to the coffee trade at Mocha. An expeditionary force led by Ahmed Pasha, Mohamed Ali's nephew, captured Hodeida and Mocha and the island of Kameran, off Mocha. But it then came into conflict with the Beduin tribes of Asir and never succeeded in accomplishing Mohamed Ali's main object in Southern Arabia, which was to annex Yemen to the Hijaz. During the same period, Mohamed Ali's friendly relations with the Sultan of Musqat caused some anxiety to the government of Bombay which was at this time establishing a series of what amounted to British protectorates over the Sheikhdoms of the Persian Gulf with a view to putting down piracy, gun-running and the slave trade.

After the Russian forces had left Constantinople, and after the diplomatic conversations in Vienna and Petersburg had assuaged British fears of any immediate Russian return, British diplomacy began to concentrate on weaning the Porte away from exclusive dependence on Russia by assurances that England, with her naval resources, was a safer and more acceptable shield than Russia against Mohamed Ali's ambitions. This inevitably encouraged the Porte to believe that they could rely on British benevolence in any attempt which they might make to claw back some of the concessions they had so reluctantly granted at Kutahia.

Trouble soon arose between the Porte and Mohamed Ali over the payment of tribute. When the Viceroy had been granted the Pashalik of Egypt in 1805 the tribute payable had been fixed at 4,000 purses (two million piastres) a year. In 1811, after he had made himself master of Upper Egypt, and when Alexandria had been added to the Pashalik of Egypt after the Fraser expedition, this had been raised to 12,000 purses (six million piastres) a year. It remained at this figure until 1833, in spite of continual demands by the Porte for its augmentation, which were objected to by Mohamed Ali on the ground of the expenses to which he was being put in fighting the Sultan's wars, first in Arabia and then in Greece and Candia. (He also held the Hijaz on which no tribute was customarily payable, and the Sudan, which was not regarded as part of the Ottoman Empire.) In May 1833, soon after the peace of Kutahia, Edhem Effendi came to Alexandria from Constantinople to negotiate a new basis of tribute to cover the four Pashaliks of Syria, Adana and Candia, in addition to Egypt. It was agreed that, as from May 1833, Mohamed Ali should continue to pay 12,000 purses a year for Egypt, 2,000 purses a year for Candia, and 18,000 purses a year for Syria and Adana, making a total of 32,000 purses or 16 million piastres a year. (In 1833 this was the equivalent of about £250,000.)[8] This arrangement was disapproved of by the Porte, which regarded the amount as insufficient and, in July 1833, the Defterdar (Minister of Finance) went to Alexandria to demand the payment of 90,000 purses as arrears of tribute. This was later waived and the Porte agreed to the arrangement made by Edhem Effendi.

Just before the Defterdar's visit, Ponsonby told Campbell that he suspected the Russians of encouraging the Turks to pick a quarrel over money with Mohamed Ali in order to give them an excuse for intervention, and asked Campbell to try to persuade Mohamed Ali 'to evade rather than to refuse' the Defterdar's demands.[9]

Palmerston, anxious to restrain the Porte, and at the same time not wanting to throw them back into the arms of Russia by refusing anything which might seem like a reasonable request for assistance against Mohamed Ali, sent an agitated despatch to Campbell instructing him to impress upon Mohamed Ali 'the extreme importance of abstaining from proceedings calculated to excite alarm at Constantinople'. He told him that the state of preparation in which the Viceroy's army and navy had been kept 'has been the pretext if not the cause for the state of readiness of the Russian troops and squadrons in the Black Sea, and nothing would more contribute to deprive the Russians of any motive or excuse for their present menacing attitude than such military and naval arrangements by the Pasha as might indicate that he has no aggressive intentions.

. . . The Sultan's subservient attitude to Russia is in a great measure due to his fear of Mohamed Ali', who was advised 'to devote the energies of his mind to the improvement of the territories confided to his administration so as to enable the Porte to reorganize its own means and so be in a position to resist in concert with the Pasha any attempt on the independence of the Turkish Empire'.[10]

But the Sultan was quite determined, as the price of the British alliance which Ponsonby was dangling before him in an attempt to wean him from Russia, to exact from England the means to enable him to revoke the concessions which he had been forced to grant to Mohamed Ali. From the time of the signature of the Peace of Kutahia, he sought ways and means of stirring up trouble for Mohamed Ali. At the beginning of June 1833, Vagoridi, Prince of Samos, a Greek notable living in Constantinople, who was sometimes used by the Porte in a diplomatic capacity, called on Ponsonby to enquire about the British government's reaction in the event of the Porte encouraging the Candiotes to revolt against Mohamed Ali. Ponsonby gave a discouraging reply and Palmerston told Campbell to read Mohamed Ali a lecture about his administration of that island. In a revealing despatch[11] he expressed the British government's interest in the welfare of the Greek population of the island and the hope that 'no reason may arise for recommending to the Sultan any change in the present administration'. He pointed out that the Candiotes had been accustomed to a fair measure of autonomy under the Turks and that Mohamed Ali's direct administration on the Egyptian model, with its land reforms and monopolies, was not suitable to them, as involving 'the transfer to the poor of a portion of the cattle and money of the rich'. 'How', Palmerston protested, 'can any people not complain of such a violation of the rights of property?' Towards the end of 1833 there was a rebellion in Candia against Egyptian rule, which was put down with such severity that Osman Bey, the Egyptian governor, left the Viceroy's service in protest. This severity led to protests both from the British and French governments and Campbell was instructed to suggest to Mohamed Ali that he might be disposed to return the administration of the island to the Sultan. The French refused to join in this suggestion, and it was rejected by Mohamed Ali who, however, took immediate steps to liberalize his administration.

Mohamed Ali and Ibrahim, in their administration of territories outside Egypt, and particularly in Syria and Candia, could never accustom themselves to the fact that the Greeks and Syrians were not docile people like the Egyptians and had been accustomed to a great deal of autonomy. Attempts to submit them to the *dirigiste* Egyptian regime inevitably led to rebellion. Mohamed Ali learnt the lesson in Candia. Ibrahim, who acted as his father's representative in Syria, and established himself there in a palace which he had built at Antioch, never learnt it. Although his administration was much more efficient than that of his predecessors, its very efficiency made it unpopular among a people who have never acquired that respect for government characteristic of the Egyptians.

In May 1834 there was a rebellion in the mountains of Nablus, in southern Syria, as a result of Ibrahim's attempts to impose military conscription. The Sultan wished to take advantage of this by sending the Turkish fleet to the Syrian coast and by getting Rashid Pasha of Urfa (a Pashalik in Asia Minor, north of Aleppo), who had commanded the Turkish army at Konieh and been taken prisoner by Ibrahim, to invade Syria. He also asked the Russians whether they would send troops to assist him in the event of his becoming involved in war against Mohamed Ali. The Russians replied that the Treaty of Unkiar Skelessi provided for assistance in the event of Turkey being attacked but not if Turkey were the aggressor. After this rebuff the Reis Effendi asked Ponsonby whether the British would give naval assistance in a war against Mohamed Ali, adding that such a war would not involve calling for Russian assistance. Ponsonby, who knew about the Russian refusal, and who appears to have been greatly encouraged by this sign of Russian reasonableness, told the Reis Effendi that the Sultan would seriously endanger his throne by a war with Mohamed Ali, and that such a war was quite unnecessary, since Great Britain and France were willing and able to protect the Porte against any aggression from him. The French Ambassador made a similar statement to the Reis Effendi. Palmerston, approving Ponsonby's attitude, instructed him to make it clear to the Porte that 'if the Sultan were the aggressor and be defeated, England and France would not protect him from Mohamed Ali, for these Powers would not assist the aggressor against the party attacked'.[12] At the same time Sir Josias Rowley, C-in-C Mediterranean fleet, was sent orders to the effect that, if the

Turkish fleet were sent to the Syrian coast, he was to try to persuade the Turkish Admiral to suspend operations against the Egyptian fleet. 'If the Turkish Admiral were to persist, Sir Josias was to keep company with him and endeavour to dissuade him. . . . If in spite of his efforts, there should be a conflict, he should remain neutral and take no part whatever'.[13] In the event the Nablus insurrection was put down by the end of August 1834 and the Reis Effendi told Ponsonby that the Turkish fleet would not put to sea.

Very soon after this, the Reis Effendi was complaining to Ponsonby that the Treaty of Kutahia was not being observed by Mohamed Ali, that Ibrahim was making incursions into the Pashalik of Urfa, and that the tribute agreed with Edhem Effendi was not being paid. In view of this the Sultan was no longer prepared to recognize its validity. Instead, he would grant to the Viceroy the Pashalik of Acre as well as that of Egypt and make peace with him on these terms. Would Great Britain and France compel Mohamed Ali to agree to this? Ponsonby replied that Great Britain was morally a party to the Treaty of Kutahia and could not with good faith attack Mohamed Ali without his having given any special cause of offence. They would need more proof than the Reis Effendi had given that Mohamed Ali had violated his engagements and, even if given such proof, they would be more inclined to persuade the Viceroy to honour his engagements than encourage the Porte to denounce theirs. The Reis Effendi then told Ponsonby that Rashid Pasha of Urfa had been instructed to sound the feelings of the populations of Damascus and Aleppo and, if he found that these were in favour of the Sultan, he was to invade Syria. The Reis Effendi wished to know whether, in that event, the British and French governments would oblige Mohamed Ali to submit to his loss and content himself with Egypt and Acre. Ponsonby deprecated this proposal but appears to have indicated to the Reis Effendi that, if the Sultan asked for the presence of a British naval squadron at Constantinople, something might be arranged.[14]

On receipt of Ponsonby's account of his conversation with the Reis Effendi, Palmerston instructed Campbell to advise the Viceroy to evacuate Urfa, and to pay the tribute which he had agreed with Edhem Effendi, and to warn him that, if he did not do so, 'HM's Government could not deny the right of the Sultan to enforce his just demands'.[15]

211

Mohamed Ali had already been complaining to Campbell of Ottoman provocations. He accused the Turks of having provoked the Nablus rising, stated that Rashid Pasha was making demonstrations in Northern Syria, and asked what the British attitude would be if, in face of these provocations, he declared his independence of the Sultan. This produced a furious reaction from Palmerston. Campbell was instructed to express to the Viceroy 'HM's regret and surprise at the Pasha's expressed intention, which was utterly at variance with his former professions of duty and absolutely incompatible with the honour and good faith of HM's Government'. He went on to express his 'unqualified rejection' of Mohamed Ali's suggestion, and added that this rejection was grounded 'on principle and not on expediency'. The Viceroy was exhorted to 'abandon designs which the policy of the European Powers will never allow him to realize, and the attempt to execute which would probably be fatal to himself', and was recommended to 'evacuate the districts beyond the Euphrates (the Euphrates marked the border between the Pashaliks of Aleppo and Urfa) and pay the tribute which he owes to the Sultan'.[16]

The Viceroy was in no conciliatory mood. He had come to the conclusion that he must either overthrow Sultan Mahmud and his other enemies at Constantinople, or be himself overthrown by them. Campbell, describing the efforts which he and Mimaud had been making to induce him to evacuate Urfa and pay the tribute owing, wrote: 'It seems to me quite clear that Mohamed Ali has no intention of doing either. He has recently put forward as a new ground for his claim to Urfa that it is a dependency of the Pashalik of Aleppo, and he objects to paying his tribute in consequence of the Sultan's hostile disposition towards him. . . . The Pasha will not rest until he has achieved his independence of the Porte, when his ambitions might probably tempt him to seek pretexts for taking possession of Baghdad and re-establishing the Arab Caliphate in his own family.'[17]

But Mohamed Ali had already missed the opportunity for any such achievement. After he had written to Ibrahim in August expressing the hope that, in view of the bad faith and provocations of the Porte, the European Powers would raise no objection to their getting rid of the 'chain of servitude hanging about our necks',[18] Ibrahim replied that the time for getting rid of the 'chain of servitude' had been after the battle of Beylan, when it would have been easy, but that now it was too late.[19]

The contents of Palmerston's despatch of 1 November, together with a similar warning addressed to him by the French government, temporarily deflated the Viceroy's belligerence. The process was assisted by simultaneous counsels of moderation which Ponsonby was urging on the Porte. (At this time the British and French governments were working in close cooperation over the Turco-Egyptian problem. The French Foreign Minister was de Rigny, the Admiral who had commanded the French squadron at Navarino, and who had a close acquaintance with the Near East.) Immediately after Palmerston's rebuke had been conveyed to him by Campbell, Mohamed Ali sent orders to evacuate Urfa. This was done by the end of the year. At the same time he paid what was owing on the tribute as agreed with Edhem Effendi. In February 1835 the Viceroy's Kapi Kiaya (Representative) at the Porte went back to Constantinople with '19,302 piastres, consisting of 15,069 piastres *in specie* and 4,233 piastres in 31-day European bills on Constantinople'.[20]

All this led to a detente between Mohamed Ali and the Porte. The Porte agreed to remit the arrears of tribute prior to May 1833 which they had been claiming. In November 1835 Campbell was able to report that 'ever since the cession of Urfa, and the certainty that the four Great Powers would not accede to his declaring himself independent, the Viceroy's conduct towards the Sultan has been much more circumspect and the tribute has been regularly paid'. He added that the Viceroy appeared for the time being to have limited his ambition to 'obtaining from the Sultan an acknowledgement that his son Ibrahim should succeed him in the governments of Egypt and Syria', and had instructed his Kapi Kiaya in Constantinople to sound the Porte and the Russian Ambassador on this point. In any case, as Campbell remarked, 'in the event of Mohamed Ali's death Ibrahim would not give up Egypt or Syria to any other Pasha who might be nominated by the Porte'.[21]

Mohamed Ali was nearly seventy years of age and, in spite of his being in very vigorous health, the question of what was going to happen after his death was exercising his own and other people's minds. His dreams of expansion were over; henceforward he was to concentrate on leaving a secure and defensible heritage for his descendants. The pattern of events over the next five years was shaped on the one hand by this determination and on the other hand by the Sultan's determination to prevent him from founding a dynasty.

Towards the end of 1836 possibilities of an understanding between Mohamed Ali and the Porte seemed to be improved by the removal of Khosrev Pasha, Mohamed Ali's old enemy, from his office of Seraskier. At the beginning of 1837 Sarim Effendi, an emissary from the Porte, came to Egypt, ostensibly to discuss arrears of tribute, but in reality to try to lay the basis of a formal settlement between Mohamed Ali and the Sultan. Both were anxious to avoid giving the impression of having taken the initiative. The Porte let the Ambassadors understand that Mohamed Ali had done so; Mohamed Ali told Campbell that the Mullah of Mecca had approached him on behalf of the Sultan and that he had told him that a prior condition of any negotiation was the recognition of his hereditary title to Egypt and Syria. It was originally intended that the Capitan Pasha should come to Egypt to negotiate but, instead, Sarim Effendi came on an exploratory mission with no definite proposals. Campbell was suspicious of the whole thing, on the ground that Sarim Effendi was regarded as a creature of the Capitan Pasha, who was believed to be under Russian influence.[22]

During his talks with the Viceroy Sarim appears to have suggested a settlement on the basis of the hereditary title to Egypt and southern Syria, including Acre, Saida and, possibly, Damascus. Mohamed Ali indicated that this would not be acceptable and made a counter-proposal demanding the hereditary succession to all the territories under his control against an augmentation of tribute. In making this demand he appears to have overrated the complaisance towards him in Constantinople induced by Khosrev's removal. At all events, Sarim Effendi, after his return to Constantinople, told Mohamed Ali that his counter-proposal had been rejected.

The result of the Sarim mission was that 'so far from any reconciliation having taken place, the obstacles to a good intelligence between the Pasha and the Porte have been rendered more strong and appear now of a nature that can never be overcome'.[23] These obstacles were soon made even more intractable by the return to office of Khosrev as Grand Vizier. It was not long before Mohamed Ali was again sounding

214

the Powers about their reactions in the event of his declaring his independence.

Meanwhile, relations between the British government and Mohamed Ali were rapidly deteriorating, in spite of the Viceroy's complaisance over Urfa and the tribute. This deterioration was hastened rather than caused by a number of incidents in which Mohamed Ali incurred official British displeasure. The real cause lay in that increasing antipathy for Mohamed Ali felt by Palmerston in London and by Ponsonby in Constantinople. The fact that these men were respectively Foreign Secretary (with one short interval) and Ambassador from 1833 to 1841 gave the momentum of continuity to these antipathies. Palmerston's antipathy probably had its roots in the Algerian affair (although this had happened before he took office) which gave rise, not without reason, to the suspicion that there was a latent Franco-Egyptian plot to dismember the Ottoman Empire and to replace Franco-Russian for British influence in the Eastern Mediterranean. (He was also probably impressed by the reports he was receiving of the oppressive nature of Mohamed Ali's rule in Egypt itself, in Syria and Candia, and in the Sudan.) Ponsonby's antipathy, in which Roussin, the French Ambassador, who diverged more and more in this matter from the sentiments of his government, vied with and even surpassed him, was due to the belief that another clash between Mohamed Ali and the Porte was probable and would, inevitably, mean another Russian intervention. He recognized that this clash was quite as likely to come from the Porte's as from Mohamed Ali's aggression, and he constantly urged moderation on the Porte. But the result would still be the same—Russian intervention, which could only be avoided, if at all, by the elimination or diminution of Mohamed Ali. These views, held by the two Englishmen principally responsible for British policy in the Eastern Mediterranean, naturally led them to put the worst construction on all the information which they received about Mohamed Ali's activities. They received such information, not only from Campbell, who was well-disposed towards Mohamed Ali, and whose reports were, on the whole, well-informed and objective, but also from others, such as Colonel Taylor, the East India Company agent in Baghdad, from Farren, the British Consul-General in Damascus, and from Richard Wood, a Secretary to the Embassy in Constantinople, whom Ponsonby sent to report on conditions

215

in Syria. These men were less well-disposed, less well-informed, and not so objective. Campbell described Wood as being 'too apt, I may say eager, to believe without proper investigation any reports to the prejudice of Mohamed Ali or Ibrahim',[24] and alleged that the views of Farren and other British Consuls in Syria were influenced by the fact that Ibrahim's administration had curbed the unjustifiable exemptions and privileges enjoyed by Consuls under the previous regime. Colonel Taylor, in Baghdad, feared lest Mohamed Ali's alleged intrigues there would form an excuse for Russian intervention.

The first of a number of incidents between the British and Mohamed Ali occurred towards the end of 1834, in connection with a British expedition to the Euphrates. The British and Indian governments had long been interested in the Euphrates Valley as a channel of rapid communication between England and India. For the past fifty years despatches had passed more or less regularly by couriers along this route. The advent of steam navigation had increased this interest, and various factors caused the British government to view this route more favourably than the alternative route via Egypt, which was also being developed, mainly under unofficial auspices. In 1832 Captain F. R. Chesney, of the Royal Artillery, had, at the request of the British government and the East India Company, made a reconnaissance of the Euphrates route, during the course of which he had floated down the river from near Aleppo to Basra on a raft. He returned to England full of enthusiasm about its possibilities and, as a result of his favourable report, a Parliamentary Select Committee recommended the organization of an ambitious expedition which involved the transport of the components of two steamers across land from Seleucia, on the Mediterranean near Antioch, to Bir, near Aleppo, the highest navigable point on the Euphrates. Here they were to be assembled, and from here they were to be sailed down the river to Basra. Chesney was promoted to Lieutenant-Colonel and placed in command of the expedition, which left England at the beginning of 1835. At that time the overland route from Seleucia to Bir was within Mohamed Ali's dominions. Campbell was instructed to obtain the Viceroy's help for the transport of the steamer components.

Mohamed Ali was not helpful. He told Campbell that 'in the present state of his relations with the Porte, he did not think it possible to do anything relative to the navigation of the

216

Euphrates without the sanction of the Porte'.[25] This, at a time when the Viceroy was being urged by Palmerston to show submission to the Porte in the matters of Urfa and the tribute, was a clever, but irritating, move. Campbell thought that his reluctance was due partly to annoyance with the British for having forced him to evacuate Urfa and pay his tribute, and partly because he feared lest the result of the Euphrates expedition might prejudice the development of the England-India route through Egypt which he valued both politically and as a source of revenue. In the event Ponsonby succeeded in turning the Viceroy's flank by obtaining a Firman from the Porte directing him and the other Pashas concerned to give all possible assistance to the expedition. Thereafter, Ibrahim received instructions from the Viceroy to give such assistance, and appears to have done so in generous measure. But Palmerston had been intensely irritated by the Viceroy's original reluctance and told Campbell that he had been 'on the point of instructing you to express to Mohamed Ali HM Government's surprise and displeasure at the manner in which, under various pretexts, the Pasha had delayed giving the orders in question and at the impediments which, in the absence of these orders, Colonel Chesney has met with'. He went on to state that, if the Pasha had not given way, 'it would have been my duty to have instructed you to renew your demand in the most peremptory manner and to declare that HM's Government could not allow such an undertaking to be defeated by the Pasha or by his subordinate authorities'. The despatch concluded: 'HM's Government cannot submit to being confined in their choice of a line of communication merely because it may suit the local interests of the Pasha of Egypt.'[26] Even after Palmerston had been assured that full cooperation had been obtained, he was still annoyed with Mohamed Ali and, after his return to office in the autumn, told Campbell to 'remonstrate in the strongest terms should any further difficulty arise. . . . HM's Government cannot be blind to the motives which influence Mohamed Ali, but they are determined that the undertaking shall not fail in consequence of obstacles which parties in any quarter may oppose to it.'[27]

In the event the expedition did fail for quite other causes than any obstacles offered by Mohamed Ali. The two ships, *Tigris* and *Euphrates*, were duly assembled and launched, but soon afterwards, *Tigris* sank in a sandstorm. *Euphrates* eventually reached Basra after a long and difficult voyage, but the expedition was soon afterwards abandoned and with it the attempt to develop the Euphrates river route.

Other dissensions arose between Mohamed Ali and the British as a result of the Egyptian occupation of Syria. Before this occupation Syria had been divided into a number of Pashaliks and governed by a number of Pashas who were mostly inefficient and venal, who seldom held their offices for long, and who were generally quarrelling with one another. Under these conditions there had been little strong centralized administration. Local magnates, and foreign Consuls and merchants, had had things much their own way. Considerable abuses had grown up. The 'protection racket', always endemic under the Capitulations, flourished exceedingly. Unscrupulous Consuls, by granting passports to, or by taking into their service, Rayahs (Christians who were Ottoman subjects) were able to invest them with the trading privileges and legal immunities (which included virtual freedom from direct taxation) enjoyed by Europeans under the Capitulations. Rich Rayahs were naturally prepared to pay considerabls sums for being so invested. Campbell, on a trip made to Syria in 1834, found many examples of these abuses. 'I have had proofs in my hand that foreign Consuls in Syria had sold permits to native merchants to land goods in the name of such Consuls, by which the revenue was defrauded of a great part of the duties payable on these goods. European merchants have also lent their names to such transactions. As there is now more difficulty under a vigilant administration, the government have made enemies of all these people'.[28] 'In former times, when different Pashas in Syria paid but little attention to affairs, the Consuls were all-powerful and, by their constant efforts and by bribes at the Porte, they were often able even to succeed in procuring the removal of an obnoxious Pasha. Hence the former Pashas allowed them to give an almost unlimited number of protections to native subjects and these protections removed them from Turkish jurisdiction. . . . The rich natives were happy to pay large sums to the Consuls for their protection. This is no longer the case and those Consuls who for years had enjoyed this authority think they have been deprived of an official privilege and are consequently hostile to the present government.'[29] This hostility led to continual complaints by the foreign

Consuls, and to incidents between them and the local administration. Mohamed Ali, in an attempt to deal with the matter,
sent Soliman Pasha (ex-Colonel Sève) to Syria and put him in
charge of the supervision of European interests there. (He also
became Chief of Staff of the Egyptian army in Syria.) Soliman
Pasha received the backing of the Consuls-General in Egypt to
whom, as a result of Mohamed Ali's conquest, the Consuls in
Syria had been subordinated, much to the disgust of Farren,
the British Consul-General in Damascus, who was continually
at loggerheads with Campbell and the source of many of
Palmerston's and Ponsonby's complaints against Mohamed Ali
and Ibrahim. As a result of a meeting between Soliman Pasha
and the Consuls-General in Alexandria, 'We [i.e. the Consuls-
General] deemed it necessary to check unnecessary and
indiscriminate pretensions which have no other object but
ridiculous pomp or show or a sordid personal interest. . . . We
drew up some instructions in conformity with the full extent
of the rights, privileges and prerogatives granted to us by
treaty.'[30]

Another, slightly more justifiable, cause of complaints against
the Egyptian administration was the attempted extension to
Syria of the monopolies which Mohamed Ali had introduced
into Egypt. As Salt had pointed out, when British merchants in
Egypt had objected to Mohamed Ali's monopolies fifteen years
before, no breach of the Capitulations would have been
involved if monopolies of local produce had been introduced
under the direct authority of the Porte. The only valid objection
was the legalistic one that they had been imposed by the
administrative acts of a local Pasha instead of by an Imperial
Firman. In Egypt the foreign merchants soon became reconciled
to the monopolies, because they were associated with them and
made a great deal of money out of them. In Syria complaints
were made by Farren and by Moore, the British Consul in
Beirut, about a prohibition introduced by Ibrahim on the
export of silk. Palmerston reacted violently. He told Campbell
that 'HM's Government have learnt with extreme concern that
HH again intends to tamper with an article of produce which
forms an important article of commerce between HM's and
Ottoman subjects. If such a prohibition were established by the
Sultan . . . HM's Government would consider it an unfriendly act, but would not deny the Sultan's right to issue such
an order. But HM's Government have yet to learn by what

219

authority the Pasha of Egypt, who exercises only a delegated power, has taken it upon himself to interfere with the commercial practice of British subjects carried on according to the Capitulations between Great Britain and the Porte. HM's Ambassador in Constantinople has been instructed to ask the Porte whether the Pasha of Egypt has acted with their authority, and you will make the Pasha understand that, if the prohibition should have been his own unauthorized act, he will be held responsible for any prejudice which may have resulted to British subjects.'[31] Ponsonby obtained a Firman addressed to 'HH the Pasha of Egypt and Syria' which, in Ponsonby's words, was 'intended not solely as a remedy for the evils occasioned by the restrictions on the silk trade, but to prohibit those innovations by which the Pasha has deprived British subjects of those advantages for trade which are theirs by right of treaty, which he has no authority to introduce, and which HM's Government deny that he has the right to establish'.[32] There was a little subsequent trouble about the export of gum tragacanth from Damascus, but this was soon settled. Generally, the effect of the British intervention was to prevent the application of the Egyptian monopolies to Syria. This was, perhaps, made easier because Ibrahim, unlike his father, did not approve of monopolies and was not reluctant to have an excuse for abandoning them.

There was other trouble between Mohamed Ali and the British government over monopolies, in each case connected with coffee. In one case Ibrahim the Younger (Mohamed Ali's nephew who was commanding the Egyptian forces in Yemen) imposed a restriction on the export of coffee from Mocha, reserving one half of the crop for himself and the other half for US merchants, who had lately established connections in Mocha, thus cutting out the East India Company altogether. It appears from a British complaint that Ibrahim was also imposing an import duty of $7\frac{1}{2}$ per cent on British imports into Mocha, in defiance both of the Capitulations and the 1821 Treaty, while allowing US merchants to import goods against a duty of 3 per cent. These complaints were satisfactorily settled as a result of Campbell's intervention. The other case concerned the attempted import by a British firm of West Indian coffee into Egypt. This had been forbidden on the ground that there was a government monopoly of such imports. Palmerston, whose language towards Mohamed Ali was becoming more and more peremptory and offensive, told Campbell that 'HM's Government cannot admit that any subordinate officer of the Porte has a right of his own authority to issue orders injuriously affecting the commercial interests of British subjects. . . . HM's Government require from him that he will without delay recall the prohibition which, without order from the Porte, he has taken it upon himself to enforce.'[33] In reply to the British protest, Mohamed Ali stated that the coffee monopoly had been granted to him by the Porte, that he would refer the protest to the Porte, and abide by their decision. In the event this monopoly was abandoned.

Yet another source of dissension between the British government and Mohamed Ali was the latter's supposed designs on the Pashalik of Baghdad which, it was feared, might provoke a Russian intervention, and which had already led Colonel Taylor, the East India Company Representative in Baghdad, to suggest that the British should occupy Baghdad themselves. At the beginning of 1836 Palmerston was advised, through Taylor, that Egyptian forces had occupied Deir-ez-Zor, on the Euphrates. The question as to whether this town forms part of Syria or of Iraq has been a matter of frequent contention; it now forms part of Syria. When Mohamed Ali occupied it in 1836 Palmerston expressed himself as 'doubtful whether it is within the limits of the Pashalik of Syria, of which Mohamed Ali has been appointed Governor by the Porte. HM's Government is convinced that, if this place is beyond the limits of the Syrian Pashalik, such an expedition can only have for its object some temporary purpose and that the detachment will, before this time, have been withdrawn into Syria.' Campbell was instructed to 'impress upon Mohamed Ali's mind the serious consequences which he will infallibly draw upon himself by any attempt to extend his authority beyond the limits assigned to it by the Sultan'.[34] Campbell, after discussing the question with Ibrahim, told Palmerston that, since the Egyptians had had to evacuate Urfa, the possession of Deir-ez-Zor was necessary in order to enable them to control the Beduin tribes in the area and so safeguard the Aleppo-Baghdad and Damascus-Baghdad caravan routes. 'If the tribes are not kept in order by the use of power which the Pasha of Baghdad cannot exert, all the eastern frontiers of Syria would be insecure and our trade by caravan to Baghdad and Persia via Damascus would be materially injured. The caravans do not pass through Deir-ez-

Zor, but follow a line of cisterns between Palmyra and Ana, the whole line of which would be open to the depredations of the Aneiza and Mowali [i.e. Beduin tribes] if Deir-ez-Zor were not occupied.' He added that neither Rashid Pasha of Urfa, nor the Porte, nor anybody else, had complained about the Egyptian occupation of Deir-ez-Zor, and implied that Palmerston was listening to old wives' tales in the shape of complaints from Colonel Taylor.[35]

A few months later there were more protests against Mohamed Ali's alleged advances eastward 'which seem to indicate his intention to extend his authority towards the Persian Gulf and the Pashalik of Baghdad'. Palmerston pointed out that 'HM's Government has invariably, since Kutahia, used its influence at Constantinople to induce the Porte to refrain from any attack on Mohamed Ali in Syria and to persuade the Porte to leave the Pasha alone. But, if the Pasha should show a disposition to encroach on the Pashalik of Baghdad, HM's Government would be at a loss to find any just argument to use with the Sultan in favour of the present state of things, and will moreover think her own interest directly concerned in preventing the authority of the Sultan from being shaken or interfered with in Baghdad.'[36]

Palmerston displayed a similar suspicion towards Mohamed Ali's supposed expansionist tendencies in the direction of the Indian Ocean. This was particularly the case after the British occupation of Aden, early in 1838, and after a victory by the Egyptian General Khurshid Pasha, about a year before that, over the Wahhabi tribes of Asir, which enabled him to occupy the whole of Nejd, including the districts adjacent to the Persian Gulf.

In January 1837 a Madrasi merchant ship flying the British flag was stranded near Aden and pillaged. The government of Bombay sent a Political Officer, Captain Haines, to Aden to demand apology and restitution, which he obtained without difficulty from the Sultan of Aden. He was also charged to make an offer to the Sultan of Aden for the purchase of his Sultanate. The government of Bombay was interested in acquiring Aden as a coaling station for the steam route between Bombay and Suez, which had recently come into operation, and this seemed a good opportunity to do so. The Sultan of Aden, whose position on his landward side was threatened by Egyptian forces in Yemen, agreed to the sale, but subsequently went back on his word. So, in January 1838, Aden was forcibly occupied by an expedition sent by the government of Bombay.

While the negotiations for the acquisition of Aden were going on, Mohamed Ali expressed his uneasiness to Campbell and indicated his view that Aden was part of Yemen. Campbell, reporting this to Palmerston, told him that Mohamed Ali was really nervous lest the British should divert the Yemen coffee trade, which was then largely controlled by Egypt and a source of considerable profit to Mohamed Ali, from Mocha to Aden.[37] In reply Palmerston instructed Campbell to warn Mohamed Ali that 'Great Britain could not view with indifference any attempt made by Mohamed Ali to invade and conquer the country lying at or beyond the mouth of the Red Sea'. He also told Campbell that the British government had no desire that Mohamed Ali's occupation of Yemen should continue and 'would be better pleased by any overt act which would show that the Pasha is engaged in improving the administration of the provinces confided to his government instead of employing the energies of his mind and the resources of the countries under his government in aggressive expeditions against neighbouring districts.'[38] Later, Palmerston told Campbell that any hostile attempt by Egyptian troops against Aden would be treated as an attack on a British possession and dealt with as such. Finally, after Mohamed Ali had reiterated to Campbell that Aden was part of Yemen, and that he had taken possession of Yemen with the Sultan's authority, Palmerston tersely instructed Campbell to request Mohamed Ali to withdraw his forces from Yemen. Mohamed Ali replied that he would not do so but, in the event, owing to the exigencies of the Syrian war, he was soon compelled to withdraw all his forces from Arabia.

Palmerston was also suspicious and hostile about Mohamed Ali's expansion towards the Persian Gulf. Primed by reports from Captain Hemell, the British Resident who, towards the end of 1838, complained that Egyptian forces in Arabia were 'about to cross the peninsula to Lahsa and Katif with the ultimate object of taking possession of Bahrain', he instructed Campbell to tell Mohamed Ali that 'such a scheme could not be viewed with indifference by the British government'.[39] There were more complaints from Captain Hemell about Egyptian penetration and, in May 1839, Campbell was instructed to inform Mohamed Ali that 'HM's Government cannot permit him to establish his naval or military power on the shores of the Persian Gulf and that, if he should persevere in such projects, he must expect that a British force will dispossess him from any naval station at which he may attempt to establish himself in the Persian Gulf.'[40] Khurshid Pasha, the Egyptian Commander in Riadh, had in fact written to the Sheikh of Bahrain calling on him to submit to an Egyptian force which was on its way there. The following month, Mohamed Ali was informed that Sir Frederick Maitland, the British Admiral commanding in the Persian Gulf, had been specifically ordered to prevent the occupation either of Basra or Bahrain by Egyptian forces. In the course of correspondence, Campbell, who was becoming more and more *mal vu* by Palmerston on account of what the Foreign Secretary regarded as his predilections in favour of Mohamed Ali, expressed the view that the Viceroy had no aggressive intentions against Bahrain and Basra and merely intended to occupy all that territory which had previously comprised the Principality of Nejd. In making this point, he mentioned, *inter alia*, that 'Kuwait has always paid tribute to the Chief of the Nejd and has never belonged to Basra', that Bahrain had likewise been conquered by and paid tribute to the Amirs of Nejd, that the Firman given to Mohamed Ali for the subjugation and government of Nejd had never been recalled, and that Mohamed Ali, in his occupation of the territories previously controlled by the Amirs of Nejd, regarded himself as carrying out the commands of the Sultan.[41]

This growing antipathy towards Mohamed Ali was increased by a perennial suspicion that the Viceroy was on intimate terms with the Russian government. Colour was given to this suspicion when, early in 1836, Mohamed Ali, on the demand of Colonel Duhamel, the Russian Consul-General, granted to Russian subjects trading in his dominions the right to import goods from Turkey and other parts of the Ottoman dominions against import duty at the rate of 3 per cent—the same as that laid down in the various Capitulations treaties for the import of goods from European countries. This internal trading privilege had never before been granted to foreigners, but Duhamel had stated, and Boghos Yusef had confirmed, that it had been conferred on Russia by the terms of the Treaty of Adrianople. Palmerston, when he heard about this, instructed Campbell 'to state to Mohamed Ali that, as British subjects are entitled, under the Capitulations treaties, to enjoy the same privileges as the subjects of the most favoured nation, HM's Government cannot admit the right of the Porte or of its Pasha to exclude British subjects from a participation in any benefits to which the Porte may admit the subjects of any other foreign Power.'[42] Palmerston menacingly added that Sir Josias Rowley, C-in-C Mediterranean fleet, had been ordered to support 'the representations you may have occasion to make to the Egyptian authorities regarding the rights and privileges of British subjects within their jurisdiction'.[43] It subsequently turned out that the privilege of internal trade had not been conferred on the Russians by the Treaty of Adrianople, or by any other treaty, and that similar privileges had not been granted to Russians in other parts of the Ottoman Empire. This still further heightened Palmerston's suspicions of Mohamed Ali and, in November 1836, he instructed Campbell to 'give the Pasha to understand that his readiness to grant to the Russians at the mere request of their Consul a privilege to which by treaty it seems that they are not entitled, and his refusal to comply forthwith with HM's Consul's demand to grant British subjects that equality of privilege to which they are by treaty entitled, are actions not well calculated to efface the reports . . . that there is a closer understanding between the Pasha and the Russians than either of the two have acknowledged'.[44] As a result of this protest, the privilege granted to Russian subjects was withdrawn. Mohamed Ali, denying that he had any close relationship with Russia, explained to Campbell that he had been misled by Boghos into believing that the privilege had been conferred on the Russians by the Treaty of Adrianople and that it had been granted in other parts of the Ottoman Empire. This was probably the literal truth.

Although the evacuation of Urfa and the payment of the tribute had been brought about as the result of joint British and French representations to Mohamed Ali, the other British protests about monopolies, Russian privileges, etc. had been made by Great Britain unilaterally, although, as Campbell pointed out, the French always took advantage of the results of these British interventions. Despite Roussin's continued presence in Constantinople, there were signs that the French government's ambivalent policy in the Levant was beginning once more to veer in the direction of a modified support for Mohamed Ali. This veering, which took place simultaneously with a

225

hardening British attitude, began to erode that near-identity of policy on Turco-Egyptian affairs which had subsisted between London and Paris since 1831.

As a result of the policy initiated by Drovetti of encouraging the education of young Egyptians in France and providing French experts for the various works of modernization being carried out by Mohamed Ali, French influence was very powerful in Egypt. In June 1837 Campbell wrote: 'The policy of the French government and of its agents here is strongly directed towards obtaining a preponderance in Egypt.' He went on to point out that Mohamed Ali's naval shipyard at Alexandria had been constructed and was being directed by a Frenchman, M. Cerisy, who had received the Legion d'Honneur from the French government for his services in Egypt, that the French government had been asked for experts to advise the Viceroy on building a graving dock at Alexandria, that all the principal civil and military establishments in Egypt were under the superintendence of Frenchmen, and that the Egyptian army and navy were governed by *ordonnances* on the French model. The Director of the Arsenal was French; the Egyptian navy had a French Vice-Admiral and one of the Egyptian line-of-battle ships was commanded by a French Captain. The tutor of Said, the Viceroy's youngest son, was French, and one of the Rear-Admirals in the navy had been educated in France. Soliman Pasha, the Major-General of the army, was a renegade Frenchman, and most of the Staff officers, and the head of the Cavalry School, were French. Clot Bey, the chief of the Medical Establishment, was French, as was the head of the Veterinary School. The Minister of Public Instruction and most of the members of his Board had been educated in France. Artin Bey, the Viceroy's Chief Interpreter, was French-educated. All the French senior officials engaged Frenchmen as their assistants, and 'do all in their power to prevent any but Frenchmen from becoming employed under the government of the Viceroy; I have no doubt that every port in Egypt will soon be filled with Frenchmen, as the French steamers will now arrive three times a month. The French Government appears to encourage them as much as possible.'[45]

As early as 1833 French financial interests tried to get a footing in Egypt by offering the Viceroy a loan of twenty million francs. M. de Cadalvène, acting on behalf of the Rothschilds, came to try to negotiate the loan. But Mohamed

226

Ali, although perennially in need of money, preferred to rely on his usual, small-scale, short-term loans from the European merchant houses in Alexandria, and turned down the offer.

After Mimaud had left Egypt in the middle of 1836, Ferdinand de Lesseps, son of Mathieu, about whom Misset had been so suspicious at the beginning of the century, and the future maker of the Suez Canal, was Acting Consul-General until the arrival of Cochelet in October 1837. In a conversation with him, Campbell received the impression that France had offered good offices to the Viceroy in trying to arrive at a settlement with the Porte. In fact, Roussin had been instructed to try to arrive at such a settlement. But the Porte, suspecting that the French were more favourably disposed towards Mohamed Ali than the British, were not forthcoming. They gathered from their conversations with Roussin that he was in favour of a more generous settlement than that proposed by Sarim Effendi (i.e. hereditary possession of Egypt and southern Syria) and did not tell Roussin about this proposal, although it was known to, and may have been suggested by, Ponsonby.

The real difference between British and French policy lay, not essentially in differences between the territorial areas which they were prepared to recommend to the Porte as a basis of settlement, but in the desire of the French government to make Mohamed Ali believe that French influence at the Porte could obtain for him better terms than British, Russian or Austrian influence. As usual, their ambivalent policy fell between two stools. The Port would not listen to them because they suspected, rightly, they were trying to curry favour with Mohamed Ali. And Mohamed Ali did not benefit because French recommendations were suspect. The Porte preferred to listen to the British, who were equally resolved with the French to support them against Russia, but who did not desire, and were not suspected of desiring, favour with Mohamed Ali. Metternich, who suspected French designs on Egypt, lent the weight of Austrian influence at Constantinople to Great Britain rather than to France.

During the first half of 1838 Mohamed Ali again raised the question of independence. Campbell reported that the Viceroy had told Laurin, the Austrian Consul-General, of his intention, saying that he did not propose to attack Turkey but, instead, to provoke the Sultan into attacking him. At about the same time the Viceroy made a similar declaration to Cochelet, the new French Consul-General. In reporting this to his government, Cochelet supported Mohamed Ali's views: 'Mohamed Ali, once independent, would be the strongest supporter of Islam and would be an offset to Russian influence at Constantinople. England and France would get commercial advantages which Mohamed Ali would grant them out of gratitude for their support, and Europe as a whole would be relieved of all anxiety about a question which, if left unresolved, would remain a source of trouble in international relations.' He added that he thought the British would accept the necessity for Mohamed Ali's independence as being advantageous for the development of their communications with India.[46]

On 25 May Campbell reported a recent conversation with the Viceroy: 'Mohamed Ali said that he had requested me to call on him in order to communicate to me his fixed resolve, from which nothing could divert him, to declare his independence of the Porte. That he was between two swords, his family and the Great Powers; that the interests of his family and his children imperiously called upon him to fix their future state. . . . He was now an old man of seventy years of age and might soon be carried off by death; he could not any longer delay the settlement of the question. He then requested me to inform my government, as early as possible, of his communication to me and of his fixed determination; he would wait a reasonable time for a reply in the full persuasion and hope that the British government would take such measures as would permit an amicable and satisfactory settlement of this affair, so as to preserve peace at the same time that his independence should be established and recognized.'[47]

Both the French and British reacted strongly to Mohamed Ali's expressed determination. The French government, which received the news first, told Cochelet to inform Mohamed Ali that the French and British would not hesitate to use force to prevent the Viceroy from carrying out his design.[48] Palmerston, informed by Lord Granville, the British Ambassador in Paris, of Mohamed Ali's declaration to Cochelet, told him: 'My own opinion is . . . that we ought to support the Sultan heartily and vigorously, with France if France will act with us, without her if she should decline.' He added, however, that he foresaw difficulty in getting the Cabinet to agree with him.[49] A few days later he told Granville: 'The Cabinet yesterday agreed that it would not do to let Mohamed Ali declare himself independent and separate Egypt and Syria from the Turkish Empire. They see that the consequence of such a declaration on his part must be, either immediately or at no distant time, conflict between him and the Sultan, that in such conflict the Turkish troops would probably be defeated, that the Russians would fly to the aid of the Sultan, and that a Russian garrison would occupy Constantinople and the Dardanelles. Once in possession of these points the Russians would never quit them. We are therefore prepared to give naval aid to the Sultan against Mohamed Ali if necessary and demanded, and we intend to order our Mediterranean fleet immediately to Alexandria in order to give Mohamed Ali an outward and visible sign of our inward resolve. We should like a French squadron to go there too at the same time if the French are willing to send it. . . . What I should like, and what I think I could get the Cabinet to agree to, would be a short Convention between England and France on the one hand and the Sultan on the other by which the two former should bind themselves for a limited time to afford to the latter naval assistance in the event of his demanding it to protect his territory against attack. . . . I am convinced that such a Convention . . . would save Turkey and preserve the peace of Europe by its mere moral effect and without our being called to act upon it. . . . It must not be forgotten that the one great danger to Europe is the possibility of combination between France and Russia . . . and that it would be well to fix the policy of France in the right track with respect to the affairs of the Levant while we have the power to do so.'[50]

By this time all the Foreign Offices of Europe had been agitated by the news of Mohamed Ali's threatened declaration of independence. Metternich, opposed equally to Russian and to Anglo-French intervention, worked to bring about a five-Power Concert—Austria, Russia, Great Britain, France and Prussia— in the affairs of the Levant. As a result largely of his conversations with Sir Frederick Lamb, British Ambassador at Vienna, and of his instructions to Count Esterhazy, Austrian Ambassador in London, Palmerston, who was perennially suspicious of France, came round to his point of view. On 6 July he wrote to Granville: 'The short state of the case appears to be this; if Mohamed Ali finds the least disunion between the Great Powers of Europe, he will endeavour to make himself independent and take advantage of a split which subsequent events may produce among us. But if he does declare himself independent and war ensues between him and the Sultan and the Russians interfere, the chances are that some serious quarrel will ensue between France and England on the one hand and Russia on the other; or else that England and France will be forced to remain passive spectators of things being done by Russia which could not be acquiesced in without discredit to the governments of England and France. The question then is, which is the best way to prevent the evil consequences which that step might produce? Our opinion is . . . that a previous Concert between the five Powers would be most desirable. We think, first, that if we could announce to Mohamed Ali that such a Concert is established and that we are all prepared conjointly to help the Sultan against him, he would abandon his intentions and remain quiet. But next, we think that if, in spite of this warning, he was to move, such a Concert would afford the best security for bringing the matter to an end without any disturbance of the peace of Europe.'[51]

The thinking behind this five-Power policy of Metternich's, which had now been adopted by Palmerston, is set out with great clarity in a letter written by Palmerston to Ponsonby on 13 September 1838. After telling him that he had been trying to dissuade Ahmed Fethi Pasha, the Turkish Ambassador in London, from an Ottoman attack on Mohamed Ali 'because Mohamed Ali's army is now probably better than, or at least as good as, that of the Sultan', Palmerston went on: 'The Sultan ought not to break with Russia, or give Russia any just ground for quarrel; but there is no good reason why the Porte should allow Russia to interfere as she does in all the internal details of the administration of the Turkish Empire, and especially to prevent and defeat every arrangement which has for its object the improvement of any part of the Turkish system. . . . This practice of constant interference on the part of Russia arises out of, and is endeavoured to be justified upon, that article of the Treaty of Unkiar Skelessi by which the Emperor [i.e. the Tsar] and Sultan agree to consult each other confidentially upon their respective affairs. It is most important for the interest and independence of the Porte to get rid of that treaty; but the question is, how to get rid of it before it expires? The only way seems to be to merge it into some more general compact of the same nature. The present threats of Mohamed Ali appear to furnish a good opportunity for such an attempt, and the Porte might found upon those threats an application to

England, France, Austria, Prussia and Russia to enter jointly into arrangements with a view to maintaining the independence of the Turkish Empire. Such a treaty, if it could be obtained, would supersede that of Unkiar Skelessi and place the Porte in a state of comparative independence.'[52]

This, then, became the grand object of British policy in the Levant over the next three years; to use the opportunity created by Mohamed Ali's desire for independence to replace the virtual Russian protectorate over Turkey created by the Treaty of Unkiar Skelessi with a joint protectorate of the five Great Powers of Europe. The object of this policy was achieved, and could only have been achieved, at the expense of Mohamed Ali, since, in order to persuade the Porte to acquiesce in it, it was necessary for the Powers to compel Mohamed Ali to a settlement with the Porte more favourable than anything the Porte could have achieved by their own efforts. France, whose ambivalent policy caused her to try to ally herself simultaneously with the Sultan and with Mohamed Ali—*protéger tout le monde contre tout le monde*, as Boghos Yusef once remarked—found herself, first, excluded from any share in the implementation of this policy by the other four Powers, then brought to the verge of war with those Powers in her attempts to oppose this policy, and finally, after the destitution of Mohamed Ali, readmitted to the guardianship of a settlement which she had no share in bringing about, which involved something like a betrayal of her promises to Mohamed Ali, and which she regarded as inimical to her own interests.

Meanwhile Campbell, in answer to his despatch of 25 May conveying the Viceroy's communication about a declaration of independence, had been instructed to tell Mohamed Ali that the British government hoped he would abandon his intention, 'the attempted execution of which would be disastrous to his own fame and fatal to the interests of his family. Success would be impossible, for all the Powers of Europe would side with the Sultan. HM's Government would support the Sultan in his attempt to obtain redress, and in order to prevent the dismemberment of the Turkish Empire, and the Pasha must not expect that any jealousies among the Powers would prevent action against him.'[53] The French government sent a similar despatch to Cochelet, although King Louis-Philippe told Granville that he thought Mohamed Ali would be more ready to abandon his intention if a hope were held out to him that the good offices of France and England would be employed at Constantinople to assist him in obtaining the reversion of his existing authority to his son. Palmerston's reply to this was that Sebastiani, the French Ambassador in London (the same Sebastiani who had been on a mission to Egypt on Napoleon's behalf thirty years before) agreed with him that it would be inexpedient to endeavour to resume at Constantinople the negotiations previously carried on through Sarim Effendi.

In reply to Palmerston's warning conveyed to him by Campbell, Mohamed Ali declared that he would commit no aggression against the Porte, and would remain within his own frontiers, but would not renounce his intention to declare his independence. He added that he hoped to settle matters amicably with the Sultan on the basis of acknowledgement of the hereditary succession, without insisting on independence. On 15 August Cochelet delivered a similar warning to the Viceroy in Campbell's presence and asked for a written reply. This the Viceroy refused to give, but he declared verbally to the two Consuls that he relied on the good dispositions of France and England, whom he regretted to see opposed to him. He assured them that, if the question of the hereditary succession were satisfactorily settled, he would be content with that. He could not suffer his hands to be tied by the Powers and would rather perish than leave his family in a state of uncertainty. On 4 September he made the same point in a note addressed to the Russian Consul-General, copies of which were circulated to the other Consuls-General.

Having thus made his position clear, the Viceroy, in order to give the Powers time to reflect on the position, departed for the Sudan on a trip which lasted from October 1838 to March 1839.

During these winter months the Powers busied themselves with diplomacy and the Turks with military preparations. Hafiz Pasha, commanding the Turkish forces in Asia Minor, raised and trained an army for the invasion of Syria the following spring. In making these preparations, the Porte appears to have followed the advice given by Palmerston to the Turkish Ambassador when he told him that 'the Sultan ought to employ himself in organizing his army and navy and in improving his revenue, and should thus make himself strong enough to be able to beat Mohamed Ali by his own means'.[54]

In the diplomatic field events were moving but slowly

towards the five-Power Concert desired by Palmerston and Metternich. Russia was reluctant to recede from her preponderant position at Constantinople, and took the view that, since Mohamed Ali had, for the time being, renounced his threat of independence, no formal Concert was necessary. The French government favoured the idea of Anglo-French cooperation aimed at recognizing the hereditary succession without independence of Mohamed Ali's existing territories. Molé, the French Foreign Minister, while dissociating himself from Cochelet's attitude of favouring independence for Mohamed Ali, told Granville that 'some expectation should be held out to Mohamed Ali that the Powers would employ their good offices to obtain for his children the reversion of the territories now governed by him, and that the overthrow of Mohamed Ali was not desired in view of the barrier which he afforded to the ambitions of Russia'.[55] But Molé underrated the extent of Palmerston's hostility to this view, which hostility was grounded in the belief, to some extent justified, that France was using Mohamed Ali to advance her own interests in the Levant.

Metternich, who shared Palmerston's suspicions of France, worked to bring England and Russia closer together. In this, he was a good deal hampered by Ponsonby, who was obsessed with the conviction that the Russians and Mohamed Ali were in secret accord to divide the Ottoman Empire between them. He was even opposed to a proposal that the Sultan should grant the hereditary succession of Egypt to Mohamed Ali, in return for the evacuation of Syria, because it had been suggested to the Porte by Russia. In this attitude, he was joined by Roussin, who showed himself increasingly at variance with the government he was supposed to be representing.

Ponsonby, in conjunction with Roussin, recommended the Porte to avoid any aggressive action, not to send the Turkish fleet to sea, but to prepare to resist any attack by Mohamed Ali. He told Palmerston that the Russians had assured the Porte of their readiness to assist them at any time, and insisted that, in order to forestall Russia, it was necessary for the British government to undertake to use force against Mohamed Ali, 'thereby effecting a conclusive union with the Sultan, who is ready to contract the closest alliance with England'. 'But', he warned, 'if England does not act, the Sultan will throw himself into the hands of Russia, as he would prefer submission to Russia to submission to Mohamed Ali'.[56] As a result of this recommendation the British Government started negotiating a draft treaty in London with Rashid Pasha, the new Turkish Ambassador, which provided for a defensive alliance between England and Turkey by which England undertook to come to Turkey's aid if attacked. But this was not what the Sultan, and possibly not what Ponsonby, wanted. The Sultan, certainly, and Ponsonby possibly, wanted a British undertaking to join Turkey in an attack on Mohamed Ali. The British government, in spite of Palmerston's increasing hostility towards Mohamed Ali, refused to agree to this.

On Ponsonby's initiative negotiations for a commercial treaty were entered into between England and Turkey. One of its principal objects, as far as Ponsonby was concerned, was to make monopolies illegal throughout the Ottoman Empire and so, in effect, (a) raise yet one more cause of dissension between Mohamed Ali and his Suzerain, and (b) provide the British government with one more reason for applying pressure to Mohamed Ali. The Porte appear to have regarded the treaty as a means of creating an Anglo-Turkish unity of interest against Mohamed Ali. Negotiations were placed in the hands of Henry Bulwer, then a Secretary at the Embassy. Under the terms of the Capitulations treaties, British and other European merchants paid a duty of 3 per cent on goods imported into or exported from the Ottoman Empire. In practice, however, all sorts of subsidiary imposts were levied on top of this, with the result that 'our imports were taxed forty, fifty and sixty per cent, and Turkish exports sixty, seventy, one hundred per cent. In fact, commerce had become almost impossible. The Board of Trade did not clearly understand the cause of these abuses; to all complaints the Turkish government answered that the provisions of our treaties were fulfilled. And this was literally the case. The goods on landing paid the stipulated charge; but then they could not be sold without an additional charge, and if they were removed from the place of landing another impost was enacted. So also Turkish produce was shipped when purchased at 3 per cent duty; but it was also charged before it got to a port with various internal duties.'[57] Bulwer agreed to a higher basic duty than the 3 per cent stipulated in the Capitulations treaties in return for the effective cancellation of subsidiary dues and monopolies. By the terms of the treaty, which was signed on 16 August 1838, the Porte agreed to abolish monopolies and subsidiary dues in return for an increase

234

of from 3 per cent to 5 per cent in the import and from 3 per cent to 12 per cent in the export duties. It was provided that these conditions should be applied to any other of the Capitulatory Powers who should signify their adherence to the treaty. All the Capitulatory Powers, including Russia (after a short interval), did so adhere.

Palmerston's delight at the treaty, expressed in a private letter to Bulwer dated 13 September,[58] was due more to the ammunition which it afforded for the Porte and the Powers against Mohamed Ali than to the prospect of any amelioration of trade between England and the Ottoman Empire. He told Bulwer that 'we certainly shall not reject it from any concurrence in the French apprehension that it will be bad for Mohamed Ali and drive him to declare himself independent in order to escape from its obligations. We are quite able and willing to keep his Pashaship in order upon a point like this.' When, a few weeks later, the treaty was ratified, Palmerston told Ponsonby he had heard through the French government that Mohamed Ali did not intend to object, and commented: 'How could he? He would neither have the right nor the might to do so. He says he will evade it; that will not be so easy.'[59]

The British government made it clear that they would insist on Mohamed Ali observing the treaty, and Ponsonby suggested that any attempt by him to evade its provisions should be regarded as a *casus belli*. Campbell reported that the Viceroy had raised no objection to it, observing that his monopolies only brought him in 50,000 purses a year, while the additional duties provided for in the treaty would bring him in a larger sum. In the event, no attempt was made by Mohamed Ali to introduce, nor by any of the Powers to enforce, the terms of the treaty in the territories controlled by Mohamed Ali until after the inauguration of the new regime ushered in by the Hatti Sherif of 1841. Events made it unnecessary to take that particular rod from pickle. In any case, it is doubtful whether, by this time, Mohamed Ali attached as much importance to his monopolies as Palmerston imagined. There had been no determined attempt to introduce monopolies into Syria. And, in May 1838, the Viceroy had told Cochelet that he had created the monopolies in order to raise the money for a standing army and that, if and when a standing army ceased to be necessary as the result of a resolution of his differences with the Porte, the monopolies would also cease to be necessary.

CHAPTER NINE

THE LONDON CONVENTION

All through the winter of 1838-39 preparations for war were proceeding on both sides of the Syrian frontier. During the same period, diplomatic activity was concentrated on Vienna, which became a clearing house for information received from the potential battlefield.

On 8 April 1839 Hammelauer, the Austrian Chargé d'Affaires in London, called Palmerston's attention to some information he had received from his government pointing to the Porte's evident intention to attack Mohamed Ali. 'Notwithstanding the formal assurance given by the Porte a month before, the question of an immediate conflict between Turkish and Egyptian troops was now in agitation. The Turkish Minister had desired the Russian Dragoman to inform M. Bouteneff (the Russian Ambassador in Constantinople) that Hafiz Pasha had reported that, from the movements of Egyptian troops, he was led to apprehend an immediate attack and had requested permission to advance towards the Syrian frontier in order to be in readiness to repel any such attack. The Porte was inclined to approve the plan, but before doing so wished to ascertain what would be the opinion of Europe and whether, if a conflict should ensue, the Sultan would be held responsible. M. Bouteneff told the Porte that he did not believe Mohamed Ali had any immediately aggressive intentions but that the approach of Turkish troops to the Syrian frontier might lead to a collision and to a declaration of independence by Mohamed Ali; that as long as the Porte continued in its present peaceful policy, it might reckon on the support and goodwill of the Powers, but that the matter would be viewed differently if the Porte had recourse to measures which would appear to provoke hostilities; that the sacrifices which the *status quo* imposed on the Porte were trifling compared with the chances of a war; that Russia had had nothing to do with the establishment of the *status quo* and had in fact done everything to prevent it; but, once established, the Powers were resolved to maintain it.' Metternich instructed Hammelauer to tell Palmerston that the Internuncio had been instructed to use language similar to Bouteneff's, and to express the hope that Ponsonby would be similarly instructed.[1]

This message, which was obviously part of Metternich's diplomatic efforts to bring England and Russia together, confirmed information already in Palmerston's possession. Ponsonby had already been instructed to tell the Sultan that, while the British government would assist him to repel any attack by Mohamed Ali, it would be quite a different matter if the Sultan were the aggressor. After receiving Hammelauer's message Palmerston again instructed Ponsonby to cooperate actively with his colleagues in endeavouring by all means to persuade the Sultan to abstain from all hostile proceedings.

On 27 April, in spite of all these warnings, Hafiz Pasha's army crossed the Euphrates into Syria. When news of this reached Paris, the new French government (in which Marshal Soult was Prime Minister and Foreign Minister) immediately took two initiatives. First, two French officers were despatched to Constantinople and Alexandria respectively to proceed to the Headquarters of the two armies and try to prevail on their Commanders to refrain from hostilities. Secondly, having heard from Granville that the British government agreed in principle to the despatch of a combined Anglo-French squadron to the coast of Syria to arrest the progress of hostilities, Soult proposed the despatch of a combined squadron, consisting of twelve sail-of-the-line from each navy, which 'would not only obviate the possibility of resistance on the part of the Turkish and Egyptian fleets, but would also deprive Russia of any pretext for putting her fleet or army in motion. A small Austrian squadron might also be attached to the combined squadron.'[2] By this time British naval preparations had already been made and, on 19 June, a copy of orders being sent to Vice-Admiral Sir Robert Stopford, C-in-C Mediterranean fleet was sent to Granville, the British Ambassador in Paris, for communication to the French government. Sir Robert was ordered 'to proceed to such part of the coast of Syria as might be near to the Turkish and Egyptian armies; if, although hostilities might not have commenced, they were so placed as to render a collision between them likely, he would urge the respective Commanders to widen the distance between the two armies. If, on the other hand, he should find that hostilities had already begun, he would press upon the Commanders to suspend operations, as the final settlement of the differences between them would depend, not on the chances of the campaign in Syria, but on the negotiations between the Powers and the contesting parties. If the Turkish Commander refused to accede, it would be difficult to employ any other means than those of persuasion, for the Sultan was HM's ally and the Sovereign of the territory in dispute; moreover, the operations of the Sultan's army did not depend on communications by sea and it would be difficult for the squadron to force its way to Constantinople to support by its presence the representations of the British Ambassador. On the other hand, if the refusal should proceed from the Egyptian Commander, Sir Robert will prevent all communication by Egyptian vessels, whether of commerce or war, between Egypt and Syria; he would send the former to Malta, to be held in deposit, and turn back the latter. Then, leaving a certain force on the coast of Syria for the above purpose, he would proceed with the rest of his squadron to Alexandria and urge Mohamed Ali to send positive orders for the suspension of hostilities. If Mohamed Ali should refuse, Sir Robert will adopt stronger measures, including preventing the Egyptian fleet from entering or leaving port, and detaining Egyptian merchantmen and, at his discretion, Egyptian ships of war. But if, from the defeat of the Sultan's army, extreme vigour should be necessary to stay the advance of the Egyptian forces and save the Turkish Empire, Sir Robert might resort to any measures of compulsion within his means . . . to induce the Pasha to stop his army and bring it back within the confines of Syria. If however a Russian force, naval or military, should enter the ports of territory of Turkey with the professed object of protecting the Sultan and repelling the Egyptians, it would be extremely desirable that the British squadron should proceed to Constantinople and remain there, or in the Black Sea, until Russian forces had evacuated Turkish territory. The Admiral would communicate with Lord Ponsonby to see how this could be done and would determine, if permission to pass the Dardanelles were not granted, whether his force was strong enough to force the passage. If the Turkish and Egyptian squadrons were at sea, Sir Robert would endeavour to prevent a collision between them by interposing his squadron in a friendly manner and by urging the respective Admirals to return to their own ports. Sir Robert would consult and cooperate with the French Admiral in the execution of his instructions.'[3] This was sent to Stopford on 25 June after having been shown to the French government who, while agreeing generally, disagreed with 'the difference in the manner of dealing with the Turkish and Egyptian forces' and with the discretion given to Stopford to force his way through the Dardanelles. This second objection was on the ground that starting a war should not be left to the discretion of an Ambassador and an Admiral. They also suggested that there would be no objection to accepting the cooperation of a Russian squadron if offered. Orders, embodying these reservations, were sent to the French Admiral; Stopford was sent a copy of the French orders with the intimation that there would be no British objection to the cooperation of a Russian squadron. Ponsonby was advised of the orders given to Stopford and told that 'if the course of events should lead the Porte to ask or to accept naval or military aid from any European Power . . . HM's Government trust that the Porte would address itself to them'.[4] Roussin received similar instructions from his government. A few days later, Ponsonby was instructed, more specifically, that, if the Russian fleet entered the Bosphorus, he was to apply for permission for the British fleet to enter the Dardanelles.[5]

During these exchanges the latent divergence between British and French views was becoming apparent. In February 1839 Molé had raised with Granville the possibility of Anglo-French good offices in arriving at a settlement on the basis of hereditary succession to the territories presently controlled by Mohamed Ali. Granville reported this approach to Palmerston but received no reply. In June, Soult, instructing de Bouquenet, the French Chargé d'Affaires in London, about the proposed Anglo-French naval squadron, expressed the view that the necessity of granting Mohamed Ali hereditary succession to at least a part of his present territories was now generally admitted, except by the Porte. Granville told Soult that Palmerston agreed Egypt should become an hereditary fief in Mohamed Ali's family under the Sultan's suzerainty, but that he would have to give up Syria because, unless he did so, no inducement could be found to persuade the Sultan to give him hereditary possession of Egypt. Soult indicated his dissent but stressed his desire to come to an agreement with England on the subject. A little later Granville stated more definitely to Soult that 'HM's Government thought it indispensable that Syria should be returned to the direct authority of the Sultan but that Mohamed Ali should have secured to his family the hereditary succession to the Pashalik of Egypt'. In reply Soult said that he did not agree that the whole of Syria should be returned to the Sultan and doubted the possibility of Mohamed Ali's acquiescence. He added that he had not formed any opinion on the exact settlement to be adopted.[6]

It is apparent from these exchanges that Soult was still extremely anxious to maintain a common front with England. This anxiety persisted until the advent of the Thiers government in April 1840. It is also apparent that, while Palmerston was thinking in terms of the maximum the Sultan might be prepared to concede, Soult was thinking in terms of the minimum Mohamed Ali might be induced to accept. In other words, Soult wanted to win the alliance of Mohamed Ali by trying to manoeuvre the Powers into coercing the Sultan to give concessions to him, while Palmerston wanted to consolidate the British alliance with the Sultan by trying to manoeuvre the Powers into coercing Mohamed Ali. But, while Palmerston was single-minded in that he made no attempt to retain Mohamed Ali's goodwill (or assumed that he could retain it anyway in so far as he needed it), Soult thought he could maintain the goodwill of both contestants, and carry England with him against the other Powers, by dispensing his good offices to both sides.

Meanwhile, events were moving rapidly in Syria, in Egypt, and at Constantinople. On receiving news of the Turkish army having crossed the Euphrates, Mohamed Ali told Campbell that he was ordering Ibrahim to concentrate his forces at Aleppo and not to make any forward movement until he received sure information of a continued Turkish advance. Later, he agreed with Laurin and Meden, the Austrian and Russian Consuls-General, to withdraw his forces to Damascus if the Turks retreated across the Euphrates, to recall Ibrahim to Egypt if they retreated beyond Malatia, and to recall the bulk of his army from Syria if the Powers would secure for him the hereditary succession to all the territories controlled by him.

On 13 June Capitaine Callier, the officer deputed by the

French government, arrived at Alexandria bearing a despatch dated 28 May in which Cochelet was instructed to call upon Mohamed Ali to cease from hostilities if they had begun and to withdraw into Syria if the frontier had been crossed. He was to inform him that the French and British governments were consulting together as to the manner in which the Anglo-French squadron was to be employed and that measures were being taken by the Powers to settle the dispute on a solid and equitable basis. In this despatch the Porte was referred to as the aggressor. At Cochelet's request the Consuls of the other Powers supported the representations he had been instructed to make. As a result, Mohamed Ali agreed to send by Callier's hand a message to Ibrahim directing him, in effect, to halt where he was at the time of Callier's arrival. At about the same time, the other officer deputed by Soult to intervene with the Turkish army arrived at Constantinople, but was forbidden by the Porte to proceed to the battlefront.

On 26 June the Turkish and Egyptian armies met in battle at Nezib, north of Aleppo, and the Turks were defeated. On 30 June Sultan Mahmud II died and was succeeded by his young son Abdul Mejid. On 9 July a Turkish corvette arrived at Alexandria with a message from the Capitan Pasha, who had left Constantinople on 9 June with orders to proceed with the Turkish fleet to the coast of Syria, asking Mohamed Ali's permission to bring the Turkish fleet to Alexandria and put it at the Viceroy's disposal. This triple disaster reduced the Porte to complete dependence on the Powers in their struggle with Mohamed Ali.

Sultan Mahmud II, who had reigned for more than thirty years, was one of the most outstanding of the later Ottoman Sultans. He was a strange mixture of fanaticism and enlightenment. He had succeeded in abolishing the Janissaries and had started on the formation of a new model Turkish army trained by European officers. He had started to introduce European methods into the civil administration. But he was obstinately determined, in so far as he could manage it, to resist European interference in the affairs of his Empire, and was particularly opposed to any extension of autonomy to his non-Turkish and particularly to his Christian subjects. His obstinacy in this respect had been the principal factor in the prolongation of the Greek war. He had come to the throne shortly after Mohamed Ali had received the Pashalik of Egypt and, over the years, a great personal animosity had grown up between the two men, although they never met. During the Wahhabi and Greek wars considerations of policy had urged upon both Rulers postures of mutual deference. But, even during the Greek war, the influence of Khosrev in high office helped to change their relations from suspicion to open hostility. From the time of the first Syrian war Sultan and Viceroy were at daggers drawn. Although Mohamed Ali continued to express respect for the Sultanate, his openly expressed aim was to procure the deposition of Mahmud and the accession of Abdul Mejid. And Mahmud's principal ambition, after his enforced acquiescence in the terms of Kutahia, was to secure Mohamed Ali's overthrow even, if necessary, at the expense of concessions to the European Powers.

Mahmud's death left Khosrev Pasha, the Grand Vizier and Mohamed Ali's old enemy, as the principal authority in the Empire. By this time he was a very old man, even older than Mohamed Ali, 'a shrewd, bold, illiterate barbarian, rather proud of being shorter and stouter than any other man in office . . . ready to have every man in the Empire drowned, shot, poisoned, or decapitated if necessary'.[7] But he was on the bridge of a rudderless and mastless ship. The only alternative to an accommodation with Mohamed Ali seemed to be an invitation to the Russians which, since the Russians had urged the Porte against an invasion of Syria, might not even be accepted.

On Abdul Mejid's accession, Khosrev sent a message to Mohamed Ali advising him of the fact and offering him, in the name of the new Sultan, the Pashalik of Egypt with hereditary succession. In the circumstances, with the Turkish army defeated and the Turkish fleet defected, this was remarkably cool. The Consuls-General, on instructions from their Ambassadors, 'seriously exhorted Mohamed Ali to an amicable arrangement with his Sovereign who, on his part, had given a striking proof of his magnanimity in granting to him the hereditary government of Egypt', and told him that he should give a proof of his submission by sending back the Turkish fleet. The Viceroy replied that the concession offered was a matter of necessity and not of goodwill and that, so long as Khosrev was at the head of affairs, he could not look for a sincere reconciliation. He told the Consuls that he would send the Grand Vizier's messenger back with a letter of congratulation and submission to the Sultan, and with a letter to the Grand Vizier himself in which he would inform him that the late Sultan had, through Sarim Effendi, offered him terms much more advantageous than those now offered, since they comprised Acre and Saida as well as Egypt, that he now demanded hereditary succession to all the territories under his control and that, on that condition, he would be the Sultan's most faithful vassal. He also told the Consuls that he had no intention of keeping the Turkish fleet and would return it as soon as his demand was accepted, and that, as soon as Khosrev was removed from office, he would proceed to Constantinople in person to present his homage to the new Sultan. He concluded by assuring the Consuls that, even if his demands were rejected, he would not make war, but maintain himself in his present position and wait upon events.[8]

Meanwhile Callier, who had left Alexandria on 20 June, reached Ibrahim's Headquarters on 1 July, after the battle of Nezib. Ibrahim had by that time reached Aintab, well outside the northern boundary of Syria. Callier requested him to stop there, but Ibrahim pleaded that there was not sufficient forage in the district and advanced as far as Marash.

Failing some decisive movement by the Powers, it seemed that the Porte, in their derelict condition, would have no alternative but to make the best terms they could with Mohamed Ali, after the Viceroy had rejected the offer made by the Grand Vizier. Ponsonby reported that 'although the Grand Vizier had given a solemn assurance that the Turkish government would make no concession to Mohamed Ali without consulting the Powers and, moreover, that they would not have recourse to the intervention of Russia alone, yet it appears that the Porte was disposed, after Ahiff Effendi's return from Alexandria [Ahiff was the messenger sent by Khosrev], to treat with Mohamed Ali on the basis of giving the hereditary government of Egypt to him and the government of Syria to Ibrahim, the latter to revert to the Sultan on the death of Mohamed Ali, when Ibrahim would succeed to Egypt.'[9] A message was about to be sent to Mohamed Ali to this effect when there occurred a decisive intervention on the part of Metternich which had the effect of removing control of the whole question from the now nerveless hands of the Porte into those of the European Powers.

Metternich, after he had heard of the defeat of the Turkish

243

army and the defection of the Turkish fleet, told Lord Beauvale (previously Sir Frederick Lamb), British Ambassador at Vienna, that he considered it would be necessary for the five Powers first to agree on terms of a settlement, and then to compel Mohamed Ali, by force if necessary, to accept those terms, which would then be implemented and maintained under the guarantee of the Powers. In pursuance of this, Metternich instructed the Internuncio to try to get the Ambassadors of the other four Powers to make a united request to the Porte not to arrive at any agreement with Mohamed Ali without their previous concurrence. The four Ambassadors, faced with the imminent departure for Alexandria of a messenger from the Porte conveying agreement to the substance of Mohamed Ali's demands, and without consulting their governments, agreed with the Internuncio's proposal. As a result, on 28 July, a joint Note, dated the previous day and signed by the Representatives of the five Powers, was presented to the Porte, informing them that the Powers were agreed among themselves on the Eastern Question, and inviting them to suspend any definite determination of this Question without their concurrence. The Turkish Ministers expressed great satisfaction. Khosrev informed Ponsonby that it would now be unnecessary to send the proposed message to Mohamed Ali and that, instead, he would advise him of the decision of the Powers. He asked Ponsonby to arrange that the Consuls in Egypt were similarly informed.

The other European governments, although not consulted beforehand about Metternich's intervention, accepted it without much demur. From that time on, until the venue was moved to London, a Concert of Powers on the Eastern Question was operated from Vienna, with the Ambassadors of Great Britain, France, Russia and Prussia representing their respective Governments.

Palmerston's first reaction to the news of the Capitan Pasha's defection was to order Stopford to perpetrate another Navarino. These orders were however amended at the instance of the French government before being sent, and the British and French Admirals received more or less identical orders to the effect that they were (a) to try to persuade the Turkish fleet to return to its allegiance and join the British and French squadrons in support of the Sultan's authority, and (b) to warn the Egyptian fleet against any attempt to interfere. In the event, the Turkish and Egyptian fleets entered Alexandria harbour before the Allied Admirals received their orders, and no action was taken.

At about the same time, Soult, still anxious to keep in step with Palmerston, and still trying to maintain the ambivalence of French policy over the Eastern question, expressed his view to Granville that 'Mohamed Ali should obtain the hereditary right of his family to govern Egypt on condition of his abandoning the other Pashaliks now under his dominion, but that some latitude should be given to the Representatives at Vienna to accept within certain limits terms more favourable to the Pasha'.[10] But Palmerston was not ready to consider any concession to Mohamed Ali. He told Soult that the return of the Turkish fleet must be insisted on as an indispensable preliminary to any negotiations whatever, and that a demand for its return should be made collectively by the Consuls, who should be directed to leave Alexandria if the Viceroy refused to comply. He added that Stopford would be instructed to enforce this demand, if Lord Beauvale requested this, with or without the cooperation of the French squadron. Soult disagreed with the proposal to withdraw the Consuls from Alexandria and told Bulwer, the British Chargé d'Affaires, that 'no decided measures of a coercive character would be employed by France for limiting the ambitions of Mohamed Ali or for restoring the fleet to the Sultan'.[11] For the time being, French objections and the withdrawal of the Turkish and Egyptian fleets into harbour prevented any decisive action.

Palmerston's attitude to territorial concessions to Mohamed Ali remained unchanged. He set it out clearly in a despatch to Beauvale: 'HM's Government are still of the opinion that Mohamed Ali ought to be compelled to evacuate Syria in exchange for the hereditary grant of Egypt. Short of this there are but two alternatives; one, the continuation of the *status quo*, rendered more full of danger now than heretofore; the other, the grant of Egypt in hereditary tenure on condition that Ibrahim, on the death of Mohamed Ali, should evacuate Syria, Candia and the Holy Cities, a condition which it could not be expected that Ibrahim would fulfill or that the Powers would be disposed to enforce, and which therefore would amount virtually to giving Mohamed Ali hereditary tenure of all that he now occupies. Preferable to such a dismemberment of the Ottoman Empire would be a change in the dynasty and the substitution of the family of Mohamed Ali for that of the

245

Sultan. As this is out of the question, nothing remains but the hereditary grant of Egypt, and it is absurd seriously to contend that, if the five Powers were united and determined, they could not succeed, after a certain time and probably without any violent means, in obtaining the full submission of the Pasha to the arrangement they were resolved to execute.'[12]

On the same day Palmerston addressed an instruction to Beauvale which marks the beginning of the process by which the Concert of five Powers was, by the exclusion of France, replaced by a Concert of four Powers for the regulation of the Turco-Egyptian dispute. On the issue of whether or not force should be used to compel Mohamed Ali to return the Turkish fleet, Palmerston told Beauvale that, if he could not get the consent of all of the Powers, he was to get the consent of some of them, 'if he should find any reasonable and effectual course of proceeding assented to by such a proportion of the five as might give to that course adequate moral weight and sufficient physical means'.

The first results of Palmerston's strong line were not encouraging. Beauvale told him that he did not think that his ideas of a settlement would be agreeable to the Powers. The Austrians were not convinced that Mohamed Ali should be excluded from all of Syria; the King of France was said to have expressed a determination not to fire a shot against Mohamed Ali and to have stated that Syria, Candia and Arabia, as well as Egypt, should be given to him in hereditary possession; Russia, although agreeing with Palmerston's ideas in theory, was doubtful whether they could be carried into effect. Beauvale summed up the position by stating that 'under the circumstances it seems more than probable that only three Powers could be induced to concur in the propositions HM's Government wished to put before Mohamed Ali, and, of these, two would have no intention of making any sacrifices to enforce it.'[13]

At the same time Ponsonby was reporting that the Russian Ambassador was recommending to the Porte that Mohamed Ali should be offered either (a) Egypt in hereditary tenure and Syria for Ibrahim for life, or (b) the terms previously offered by Sarim Effendi. He also reported that the Russian Ambassador had advised the Porte to settle matters themselves with Mohamed Ali, merely keeping the Powers advised of what they were doing. This was confirmed by Lord Clanricarde, the British Ambassador in Petersburg, who told Palmerston that

Nesselrode, the Russian Foreign Minister, was not happy about the joint Note inspired by Metternich. The Reis Effendi, anxious to see some action from the Powers as a result of the joint Note, addressed a formal Note to the Ambassadors, demanding that their governments, having taken matters into their own hands, should induce Mohamed Ali to return the fleet, give up his pretensions to the hereditary possession of Syria, desist from his demands for Khosrev's dismissal, cease from exciting disorder in Asia Minor, and await with patience the result of conversations between the Porte and the Powers. Beauvale pointed out to Palmerston that it appeared from this Note that the Porte did not object to granting Syria to Mohamed Ali for life, provided that he did not get it in hereditary possession. But Palmerston stuck to his guns. He told Beauvale that his views remained the same and that, considering Turkey's present weakness, there was no reason why the Powers should not obtain for them terms more favourable than those for which they had asked, since the Powers were interfering, not only for the Sultan's benefit, 'but to secure peace and a durable state of possession in the East'.[14]

In support of Palmerston, a new alignment was beginning to emerge among the Powers. Nesselrode, encouraged by Metternich, and irritated by French suspicions of Russian designs on Turkey (which was the sole ostensible and probably the principal real reason for French support of Mohamed Ali), saw in increasing Anglo-French divergencies an opportunity to detach England from France, and was prepared to defer to Palmerston's views about the Turco-Egyptian dispute in order to accomplish this. Clanricarde told Palmerston that Nesselrode agreed with him in regarding Mohamed Ali 'as a refractory rebel whose ambitions should be checked by direct and active interference', and in considering that 'the integrity of the Turkish Empire and the rule and independence of the reigning Sultan must be maintained in order to preserve the peace of Europe'.[15] A few days later he reported that Nesselrode had decided to send Baron Brunnow to London to discuss the question, and added that the Russian desire for closer relations was due to the fact that 'France would not be a party to measures of coercion against Mohamed Ali. The prospect of a separation between England and France is a cause of great satisfaction to the Emperor.'[16]

On his arrival at the beginning of September, Brunnow told

Palmerston that the main object of his mission was to explain his government's views about the Turco-Egyptian dispute. The Tsar was anxious to inspire the British with confidence in the sincerity of Russian views and to draw closer the friendly ties between Russia and England. He concurred in the British view that the hereditary government of Egypt alone should be offered to Mohamed Ali and wished to consult HM's Government as to ways and means of bringing this about. The Tsar approved of the series of coercive measures already proposed by Palmerston, such as cutting off communications by sea between Egypt and Syria, and blockading the Egyptian and Syrian coasts, but it was important to settle beforehand what should be done if Mohamed Ali should carry out his threat of marching on Constantinople. Brunnow suggested that, in such a case, Russia could most easily give assistance to the Sultan, but that this would be given, not by virtue of the Treaty of Unkiar Skelessi but because of an engagement to be entered into between the Sultan and the Powers, thus making the assistance an act of the alliance and not of Russia alone. Any Russian force acting in the name of the alliance would, in the same character, leave Turkey when the purpose for which it came had been fully accomplished. The Tsar was willing that the mode of operation should be settled by means of a Convention between the parties concerned. Brunnow proposed that any military or naval operations which might become necessary in Egypt or Syria should be undertaken by England, Austria and France, and whatever might be required within the Straits or in Asia Minor by Russia. The Tsar was willing that an article should be inserted in the proposed Convention by which, when Turkey was at peace, the Dardanelles and Bosphorus should be closed to warships of all foreign nations. Brunnow further stated that, if England and France should come to an understanding over these matters, and if a Convention on these lines were signed, the Tsar would agree not to renew the Treaty of Unkiar Skelessi, and would be prepared to act without France if France could not be persuaded to concur and if England were also prepared to act without her.

In reply, Palmerston told Brunnow that, with one exception, he agreed with all he had said, and, particularly, was of the opinion that the exclusion of all warships from the Straits would be more conducive to peace than that the Straits should be a thoroughfare for warships of all nations. But if, in a time

248

of emergency, one of the Straits should be open for one party, the other ought at the same time to be open for other parties, and he would expect that, if it should be necessary for a Russian force to enter the Bosphorus, a British force should enter the Dardanelles at the same time. But, in the present emergency, as the bulk of the British naval force would be off the coast of Syria, such a British force would only be a token one, 'showing by its smallness that it was sent to record a principle and not to proclaim distrust or exercise control'. Brunnow then urged that the British should, by themselves, take some preliminary measures which, either as a demonstration or as a commencement of coercion, might influence Mohamed Ali. Palmerston replied that England would not act alone, but if the five Powers, or a sufficient proportion of them, could not unite in a common course of action, they would consider what they could do; but, for the time being, they preferred to await the result of the negotiations being carried on in Vienna.[17]

Soon after this conversation Brunnow returned to Petersburg for consultations, which resulted in Clanricarde informing Palmerston in November that the Tsar had agreed, in the event of the Porte asking for military or naval assistance from Russia, to any other Power sending a naval detachment to cooperate within the Straits in order to demonstrate that they were all concerned in the defence and protection of Constantinople. He added that Brunnow would be returning to London to negotiate a Convention on the lines already discussed.

Brunnow returned to London in December; at about the same time Metternich sent Baron Neumann to London to signify his concurrence in British and Russian views and to join with their Representatives in drawing up the proposed Convention. Prussia, which was at this time virtually a satellite of Austria's, also concurred. France had already become the odd man out.

Although Russia undoubtedly wished to isolate France from the European Concert, Palmerston had no such desire and, throughout the period of the conversations with Brunnow, about which the French government were kept closely informed, made continual efforts to reconcile the British and French points of view. He had a series of discussions with Sebastiani, the French Ambassador. When he indicated to him that a proportion of the Five might have to adopt coercive measures against Mohamed Ali without waiting for France's concurrence, Sebastiani's reaction was that this would lead to a dissolution of the Concert of Powers. Palmerston retorted that French unwillingness to act would not prevent the other Powers from moving towards an object important to the general interests of Europe and that, although England was most anxious to continue to act in concert with France, she was by no means bound to stand by France if France should refuse to move while other Powers were inclined to advance. He went on to tell Sebastiani that 'the Ottoman fleet should be demanded by the Consuls in a collective Note and, if it were refused, the Consuls should withdraw. After the lapse of a few days the allied squadrons should prevent any vessels under the Egyptian flag, either of war or of commerce, from entering or leaving any Egyptian or Syrian port and then might detain all merchant ships under the Egyptian flag. Finally, Candia might be occupied by a Turkish force under the protection of the allied squadrons. If these measures should fail, the Powers would have to consider further steps'. In reply Sebastiani said that he did not think the French government would agree. He doubted whether either the withdrawl of the Consuls or a blockade would be effective, and objected to the Candia proposal because it would probably lead to a rebellion of the Greek population there.[18]

In Paris both Soult and the King made it clear to the British Chargé d'Affaires that they would not agree to the use of force against Mohamed Ali. Louis Philippe put the French position frankly to Bulwer when he told him that 'steps should be taken for ascertaining the least that Mohamed Ali would be contented with, and for urging the Porte at once to give it to him'.[19] At about the same time Soult withdrew Admiral Roussin from the French Embassy at Constantinople, replacing him by M. de Pontoise, ostensibly on the ground that he disapproved of Roussin's having associated himself with the joint Note of 27 July. Roussin's views about the Turco-Egyptian dispute, which approximated to those of Ponsonby, had for some time been at variance with those of his government.

The views of Sebastiani also appear to have been different from those of his government. In September, apparently without Soult's approval, he suggested to Palmerston the possibility of a territorial arrangement by which Mohamed Ali, in addition to receiving Egypt in hereditary possession, would also receive territory in southern Syria 'as far north as a line drawn from

Damascus to Beirut, leaving Damascus to the Sultan and giving Beirut to Mohamed Ali, while evacuating all the other territories held by him outside Egypt'. He indicated that his government might be prepared to use force, if necessary, to compel Mohamed Ali to accept such a settlement but that, owing to the state of French public opinion, which was favourable to Mohamed Ali, it would only be possible to justify the use of force to the Chamber if the government could demonstrate that they had obtained for Mohamed Ali the best terms possible.[20]

At the same time as Sebastiani was making this apparently personal suggestion to Palmerston, Soult was telling Bulwer that French ideas for a settlement involved (a) the abandonment by Mohamed Ali of all pretensions to having Khosrev dismissed; (b) the return of the Turkish fleet; (c) the return of Adana, Marash and Candia; and (d) some arrangement in respect of Syria by which the four separate Pashaliks would be granted to various of Mohamed Ali's sons in hereditary possession, provided that, in case of failure of a direct heir, the Pashalik in question should revert to the Porte. Soult indicated that, if Mohamed Ali should refuse to accept this, he might agree to the use of force. M. de St Aulaire, the French Ambassador in Vienna, was also canvassing the possibility of such a settlement with the Representatives of the Powers there. Palmerston told Sebastiani that this proposal 'would be a virtual dismemberment of the Turkish Empire, would give Mohamed Ali independence in all but name, and would leave him stronger than the Sultan and in uncontrolled possession of the resources of the best parts of the Sultan's dominions'. But, as the French were so anxious to do their best for Mohamed Ali, he would suggest that the boundaries of his possessions should be extended to 'a line drawn from Mount Carmel to the southern extremity of Lake Tiberias, then down the Jordan to the Dead Sea, and from there to the Gulf of Akaba and along the western edge of that Gulf to Cape Ras Mohamed and from there to Suez'. The fortress of Acre and the caravan route from Damascus to the Holy Cities would be excluded from Mohamed Ali's territories. 'This arrangement, although objectionable as not interposing a sufficient barrier between the Sultan and the Pasha, might nevertheless be recommended to the Sultan if all the Powers were prepared to employ whatever measures might be necessary to carry it into execution, but this was the utmost extent to which HM's Government would consent to their modifying their original plan. They had afforded repeated proofs of their willingness to modify their own opinions to obtain French cooperation. They had given up one part of the instructions which they proposed should be sent to the Admirals for the restoration of the Turkish fleet. Afterwards they had consented to waive the proposal that a restoration of the fleet should be enforced without waiting for a general agreement to the terms of a final arrangement, and now they were willing considerably to enlarge the boundaries of the hereditary Pashalik to be conferred on Mohamed Ali.'[21] Sebastiani, having consulted his government, told Palmerston that his proposal was unacceptable and indicated that France would not be a party to any arrangement to which Mohamed Ali could not be induced to agree without coercion. Palmerston, in reply, expressed his regret at losing all prospect of arriving at an understanding with France over the Eastern Question and intimated that, since France had objected to his proposal for the partition of Syria, the British government would revert to their original plan for fixing al-Arish as the boundary of the hereditary Pashalik of Egypt. Soult, advised of the content of Palmerston's communication to Sebastiani, strongly denied that France had constituted herself as the protector of Mohamed Ali, for whom he had no particular partiality, and stated that the great object of French policy was to put an end to the protectorate exercised by Russia over Turkey, while at the same time preserving the integrity of the Ottoman Empire. He considered that the most important object of European policy was 'to save at Constantinople the independence of the Empire, without which its territorial integrity was an empty word.'[22]

In Syria there had been no military operations since the battle of Nezib and Ibrahim's subsequent advance to Marash. At the beginning of September Mohamed Ali told Campbell that, unless there was a settlement with the Porte within a few weeks, Ibrahim would advance as far as Konieh. But, in fact, Ibrahim was disinclined to move. The respective positions of father and son, compared with 1832, had become reversed. In 1832 it was Ibrahim who had wanted to advance on Constantinople and his father who had forbidden it. In 1839 Mohamed Ali wanted to march into Asia Minor and Ibrahim refused to do so. On 25 August, before speaking to Campbell,

Mohamed Ali had ordered Ibrahim to advance on Konieh. But Ibrahim, pleading the inadequacy of his army, the certainty of intervention by the Powers, and the probability of insurrection of Syria, remained where he was.[23]

In Constantinople, the Porte were beginning to get impatient. They were confused by conflicting advice from the Ambassadors of the four Powers on the one hand and from Pontoise, the new French Ambassador, on the other. They urgently wanted a settlement of the dispute with Mohamed Ali. Pontoise was urging them in favour of, the other four Ambassadors were urging them against, direct negotiations. The Reis Effendi addressed a series of Notes to the four, requesting them to get a move on. Towards the end of December the Porte determined to send Kiamil Pasha to Alexandria to deliver to Mohamed Ali a Firman enjoining the observance of the Hatti Sherif (Decree) of Gulhané, promulgated, at the instance of the European Powers, on 3 November, which laid down a standard of civil liberties for all Ottoman subjects. The ostensible object of this was to see how far Mohamed Ali, by the publication and observance of this Hatti Sherif, was prepared to recognize the authority of the Sultan. The real object was probably to resume direct contact with the Viceroy with a view to a settlement. When Kiamil returned to Constantinople he reported Mohamed Ali as having told him that, if he could have Egypt and the whole of Syria, he would be prepared to give up all his other territories. In a letter to the Grand Vizier he wrote that the Firman had been duly published and that the provisions of the Hatti Sherif would be put into execution, although, in his dominions, many of them had been in force for some years in advance of the Ottoman decree.

In December 1839 Colonel Campbell was replaced as British Consul-General in Egypt by Colonel Hodges, who had previously been a Consul in Servia and who, at the time of his appointment to Egypt, was in Vienna. Campbell had always been on good terms with Mohamed Ali and was replaced because Palmerston considered that he was taking too favourable a view of the Viceroy's ambitions. (This is quite clear from contemporary official correspondence. In a despatch dated 13 August Palmerston expressed disapproval of Campbell's support for Mohamed Ali's 'extraordinary and unjustified demand to be allowed to dictate to the Sultan'. On 11 September Campbell was instructed to 'confine your language and your conduct to the opinions and intentions of your government'. And on 26 September he was told that 'the opinion . . . you have formed of the power and influence of Mohamed Ali in Turkey is probably founded upon statements made to you by Mohamed Ali himself, and is extremely incorrect and exaggerated'. This was unusually rude, even for Palmerston.) In his instructions, given to him by Beauvale, Hodges was told to 'undeceive Mohamed Ali as to the existence of any wish on the part of HM's government for his destruction. England was opposed to him in Asia because his presence there was destructive to the power of the Sultan, but in Africa England was friendly to him and it was there only that the establishment of his family would be firmly based.' These instructions were approved by Palmerston with the exception of the sentence which implied that HM's Government viewed with favour any increase in Mohamed Ali's power in Africa 'which could only take place at the expense of the Abyssinians, whom HM would be sorry to see subjected to Moslem conquerors, or by encroachments on the territory of Tripoli, which belonged to the Porte'.[24]

In Hodges' first audience with Mohamed Ali, the Viceroy told him that he intended to defend everything he had got, except Candia. In reply Hodges was instructed to tell him that he had no rights except what the Sultan had granted to him and which the Sultan might, if he chose, deprive him of, and would probably do so if his safety required it. In so depriving him, the Powers might well assist him and, if it should become necessary to use force to coerce him, he might, in the end, not obtain from the Sultan terms as favourable as those which had been proposed to him.

The return of Brunnow and the arrival of Neumann in London at the end of 1839 removed the focal point of the Concert of Powers from Vienna to London, where it remained until the end of the crisis. At the beginning of January Palmerston handed a Note to Sebastiani advising him of the position of affairs. The Russians had agreed that British warships should enter the Dardanelles to cooperate in the defence of Constantinople, and Brunnow had been authorized to negotiate with HM's Government for a permanent settlement of the Turco-Egyptian dispute. Baron Neumann had been sent from Vienna for the same purpose and the Prussian Ambassador in London had been instructed to cooperate. 'The concurrence of France was now alone wanting to complete a European agreement.' Palmerston proposed (1) that the Porte should give to Mohamed Ali the hereditary possession of the Pashalik of Egypt and that the territorial limits of that Pashalik should be defined; (2) that Mohamed Ali and his successors should recognize the Sultan's sovereignty and pay the existing rate of tribute in respect of the Pashalik of Egypt; (3) that Syria, Adana and Candia should be restored immediately to the Porte; (4) that the Turkish fleet should be immediately returned; (5) that the above proposals should be communicated to the Sultan and, when approved by him, carried into execution by the Powers, who would call upon Mohamed Ali to submit to them; (6) that, if Mohamed Ali refused to do so, he should be coerced, for which purpose the British and French squadrons in the Mediterranean should (i) take up a position in the Gulf of Scanderoon and intercept all Ibrahim's communications by sea, (ii) re-establish the Sultan's authority in Candia, and (iii) blockade the coasts of Syria and Egypt.

The Note went on to suggest that it would not be expedient to recall the Consuls from Egypt. If Mohamed Ali should reject the proposed settlement and resume hostilities against the Sultan, the Tsar had agreed, on the Sultan's demand, and in the name of the Powers collectively, to send a fleet and army from the Black Sea to defend Constantinople. The Note proposed that the combined squadrons of the other Powers should operate on the coasts of Egypt and Syria and, at the same time, in order to manifest the unity of the Powers, and at the Sultan's request, send a detachment of two or three vessels from each Power into the Sea of Marmora to cooperate with the Russian fleet. The forces of all the Powers, including Russia, would be withdrawn as soon as the threat to Constantinople had ceased, and the entry of foreign warships into the Bosphorus and Dardanelles made necessary by the crisis should be regarded as exceptional and as not affecting the general principle that 'these Straits should be closed by the Porte, in peace and in war, which principles the Powers solemnly record as part of the public Law of Europe'.[25]

Having been sent a copy of this Note by Sebastiani, Soult replied that the French government 'cannot concur in the proposed territorial arrangements, being satisfied that Mohamed Ali would, even if he did not march on Constantinople, at all events attack Mesopotamia, in which case there would be no other means of stopping him than a Russian force

255

in Asia Minor. Mohamed Ali would not yield and, even supposing there was no fighting, the existing state of affairs was
bad for all, and it would be best to bring it to an end by
means of a prompt reconciliation between the Porte and
Mohamed Ali based on a firm estimate of the resources of the
two parties.'[26]

It was now clear that four of the Powers were very near to
an agreement and that such an agreement would shortly be
reached without the concurrence of France. Palmerston
instructed Ponsonby to request the Porte to authorize Nouri
Effendi, the Turkish Ambassador in London, to sign any
Convention which might be proposed to him by the Plenipotentiaries of the five Powers, or by not less than three of
them, provided that it secured for the Sultan advantages in the
shape of assistance and support from these Powers.

At the beginning of March 1840 the Soult government fell
and was replaced by a government headed by Thiers, who
became Prime Minister and Foreign Minister. At the same time
Sebastiani was replaced as French Ambassador in London by
M. Guizot. Thiers's Egyptian policy was set out clearly in a
private letter which he sent to Cochelet on 18 April. 'I take a
great interest in the Viceroy's cause. In this I share a sentiment
which is very general in France; but the Viceroy should have
no illusions about his position. France can be very useful to him
and can secure him some respite from the exigencies of the
other Powers. But, sooner or later, the four Powers will get
together and will take from him those territories which he now
does not wish to relinquish. England is very hostile to the
Viceroy; Russia will refuse nothing to England in order to
get her to accept Brunnow's proposals. Austria and Prussia will
follow England and Russia. They will try hard to get an agreement with France, but in the end they will sign an agreement
without her and, once committed, one cannot say how far they
will go.' He went on to express a fear lest the four Powers might
incite an insurrection against Ibrahim in Syria and, if this
failed, lest England and Austria might invade Egypt and the
Russians Syria. It was therefore necessary to make the Viceroy
appeciate the dangers of the situation, including the limits of
the extent to which France could assist him. If it came to war,
Thiers pointed out that 'la France, prête à se lever toute
entière pour un intérêt sur le Rhin ou sur les Alpes, ne montrer-
ait pas le même élan pour les événements qui se passeraient

256

sur le Nil; et il ne faudrait pas que le Pacha crut que, pour sa cause, une guerre générale serait entamée.' It was necessary therefore for the Pasha to be realistic. It might be possible to obtain for him hereditary possession of Egypt and Syria if he gave up Adana, Candia and the Holy Cities. A second alternative would be the hereditary possession of Syria and a life tenure of the rest. A third alternative would be the *status quo*, as a result of being able to induce a stalemate in the negotiations. 'In any case, the situation is grave. Tell the Viceroy to prepare himself for any reasonable sacrifice and to put his trust in France. If he is offered Egypt and Syria in hereditary succession and is ordered to give up Adana, Candia and the Holy Cities, he should accept. If he is offered Egypt in hereditary succession and Syria, Adana and Candia for life, he should also accept. If we can get either of these alternatives for him, we shall have done all that can be expected of us. If he refuses to make reasonable concessions we cannot go on supporting him; we are not going to risk our alliance with England in order to uphold unreasonable pretensions. So long as he understands that, he can regard us as faithful, sure and disinterested friends. We will not abandon him so long as he understands his position and adapts his conduct to it.'[27]

It will be seen from this letter that Thiers had few illusions about his ability to prevent the four Powers from coming to an agreement on the lines already indicated to Soult. He seems to have based his hopes, such as they were, on Mohamed Ali being able to maintain himself in Egypt and Syria against allied coercion for long enough to enable France to intervene with her good offices to bring about a settlement.

In the event, agreement between the four Powers took rather longer than might have been expected. At the beginning of April Nouri Effendi returned to London from Constantinople with authority to sign a Convention with the Powers. On arrival he sent a Note to the Representatives of the four Powers inviting them, in pursuance of the joint Note of 27 July 1839, to concert measures for the pacification of the Turkish Empire whose tranquillity was being disturbed by Mohamed Ali. The Note set out details of the Porte's grievances against the Viceroy and ended by stating that the writer was furnished with full authority to conclude and sign a Convention for assisting the Sultan to execute an arrangement which would confer on Mohamed Ali the hereditary government of Egypt in return

257

for his restoration of the Turkish fleet and all the Provinces occupied by him outside the Pashalik of Egypt.

At this point Metternich got cold feet and told Beauvale that force should not be used and that Mohamed Ali should be offered the hereditary possession of Egypt and the four Pashaliks of Syria for life. Upon Mohamed Ali's death these four Pashaliks should revert to such of his descendants as he might designate; Candia and Adana should be returned to the Porte and the fleet sent back. Metternich proposed that these terms should be offered to Mohamed Ali by the Sultan as an ultimatum and that, if he refused, the Sultan should withhold all grant of hereditary rights and the Powers would take upon themselves protection of his dominions. Palmerston pronounced this scheme, which was even more generous to Mohamed Ali than the French proposal, as 'illusory and impracticable', and no more was heard of it. But it delayed the conclusion of an agreement, as did another proposal by Neumann who, primed by Metternich, made yet another attempt to reconcile the British and French viewpoints. Neumann pointed out that the real difference between these viewpoints was that France wanted to give Mohamed Ali Egypt and Syria in hereditary possession, while Great Britain only wanted to give him Egypt in hereditary possession. Palmerston had once proposed to France the partition of Syria between the Sultan and Mohamed Ali. Could he not now repeat this offer with the addition of the fortress of Acre for Mohamed Ali on the understand that southern Syria should be given to him for life only? Palmerston agreed to this, and the proposal was put to Guizot by him and Neumann. Guizot said that he would refer it to his government. Palmerston afterwards heard that it had been referred by Thiers to Mohamed Ali and 'it thus appeared that negotiations were to be carried on with Mohamed Ali and not with France'. Eventually Guizot quoted to Palmerston a private letter from Thiers in which he wrote that he was certain Mohamed Ali would never agree to Neumann's proposal, nor indeed to any arrangement which did not leave him in possession of the whole of Syria, that force would be necessary to impose it, that France did not agree to the use of force, and consequently he could not agree with the proposal. 'This answer,' as Palmerston pointed out to Bulwer, 'put out of the question all hope of France cooperating in the policy of the Powers, who considered themselves bound by the Collective Note of 27 July 1839 to obtain for the Sultan better terms than Mohamed Ali would spontaneously agree to, whereas France had avowed that her policy was founded on the principle of requiring the Sultan to submit to such terms as Mohamed Ali was willing to accept.'[28]

On 15 July 1840 the London Convention was signed by the Representatives of Great Britain, Austria, Russia, Prussia and Turkey, 'with the specific object of effecting a pacification of the Levant.' The terms of the Convention were as follows:

I.   The signatories agree to act in perfect unison with a view to compelling Mohamed Ali to conform with the arrangements detailed hereunder, each cooperating according to the means at their disposal.

II.   If the Pasha of Egypt refuses to agree to the undermentioned arrangement, which will be communicated to him by the Sultan, the signatories undertake, at the request of the Sultan, to concert measures to put this arrangement into force. In the meantime, the Sultan having invited his allies to join him in cutting communications by sea between Egypt and Syria and to prevent the movement of ships or supplies of war between one of these Provinces and the other, the signatories undertake to give immediate orders to this effect to the Commanders of their naval forces in the Mediterranean, and also undertake that the Commanders of these forces will, in the name of the alliance, give all the assistance in their power to those of the Sultan's subjects who show their fidelity and obedience to their Sovereign.

III.   If Mohamed Ali, after having refused to submit to the arrangement detailed below, makes an offensive movement towards Constantinople by land or sea, the signatories, at the Sultan's request conveyed to the signatories' Representatives at Constantinople, are willing to come to his defence, by means of a concerted plan, with the object of defending both the Straits and Constantinople itself from aggression. The signatories' forces so employed will remain in Turkish territories or in Turkish waters for so long as the Sultan requires their presence and will retire into the Mediterranean and Black Sea respectively when HM considers their presence no longer necessary.

IV. It is expressly understood that the presence in the Straits of the warships of the signatories provided for in the preceding article will be considered as an exceptional measure, and will not affect the general rule, recognized by the Sultan and all the signatories, that the Straits are closed at all times to warships of all foreign nations.

    V. This Convention to be ratified by the governments of all the signatories, and the ratifications exchanged in London, in not more than two months.

To the body of the Convention, consisting of these five articles, was annexed an 'Acte Separée' containing the terms to be offered to Mohamed Ali by the Sultan and enforced, if necessary, by the signatories.

    I. HM promises to grant to Mohamed Ali, for him and for his descendants in direct line, the administration of the Pashalik of Egypt, and HM also promises to grant to Mohamed Ali, for life, the title of the Pasha of Acre, including the possession of the fortress of Acre and the administration of the southern part of Syria according to the following boundaries: From Ras-al-Naqura on the Mediterranean, east to the mouth of the river Seisaban at the north end of Lake Tiberias, along the west shore of that lake, along the right bank of the river Jordan and the western shore of the Dead Sea, and from there in a straight line to the Red Sea at the northernmost point of the Gulf of Akaba, and from there will follow the east coast of the Gulf of Akaba and the west coast of the Gulf of Suez to Suez. The Sultan makes this offer on condition that Mohamed Ali accepts it within ten days of its being communicated to him at Alexandria by an emissary from HM, and on condition that Mohamed Ali at the same time gives to this emissary instructions for the Commanders of the Egyptian land and sea forces immediately to evacuate Arabia and the Holy Cities, Candia, Adana, and all those parts of the Ottoman Empire not included in the above-mentioned limits.

    2. If within ten days HH does not accept these conditions the Sultan will withdraw his offer for the life tenure of the Pashalik of Acre, but will maintain his offer of the Pashalik of Egypt, in hereditary descent, provided that this offer is accepted within the following ten days, together with the communication about the evacuation of

the other territories of the Ottoman Empire as specified above.

3. The annual tribute payable by Mohamed Ali to the Sultan will be proportional to the tribute now paid, according to the actual territory granted to him in accordance with the preceding articles.

4. It is expressly understood that Mohamed Ali will in any case return the Turkish fleet with its crews and equipment to whatever Turkish official may be appointed to receive it. The Commanders of the allied squadrons will assist in this. It is further understood that no deduction will be made from the tribute to cover any expenses Mohamed Ali may have incurred on this fleet while it has been in Egyptian hands.

5. All the treaties and laws of the Ottoman Empire will be equally applicable to the Pashaliks of Egypt and Acre as to the rest of the Ottoman Empire but, subject to the payment of tribute, the Sultan agrees that Mohamed Ali and his descendants shall themselves collect taxes in the name of the Sultan in the territories confided to them.

6. All land and sea forces raised in the Pashaliks of Egypt and Acre will be considered as part of the armed forces of the Ottoman Empire.

7. If, after the expiration of twenty days, Mohamed Ali does not accept either of the above-mentioned arrangements and the conditions attaching to them, the Sultan will consider himself at liberty to retract both offers and take such action as his own interests and the counsels of his allies may suggest.

8. This 'Acte Separée' will be considered part and parcel of the main Convention.

The signature of this Convention, which had been hanging fire for so long, was hastened by three factors. First, at the beginning of June, Khosrev Pasha, the Grand Vizier, fell from power. Mohamed Ali seized the occasion to send Sami Bey, his secretary and *homme de confiance*, to Constantinople with an offer to 'trade' the return of the Ottoman fleet for the grant of Egypt and the whole of Syria in hereditary possession and Adana and Candia for the term of his life. As for Arabia, the Viceroy told Hodges that 'the Porte could do what they liked with it, but they could not govern it and it would necessarily

261

fall as much as ever under his authority'.[29] On Sami's arrival, Rashid Pasha, the Reis Effendi, asked Ponsonby's advice about what to do. Ponsonby advised him not to negotiate and to 'send secret confidential agents into Syria to promise the inhabitants of Lebanon the enjoyment of their ancient freedoms under British protection, exemption from conscription altogether and from taxation during a specified period'. He also told him that he would ask the British Admiral to send some warships off Beirut 'so that their presence might encourage the Syrians'.[30] But, in spite of Ponsonby's stiffening, it seemed not unlikely that any further delay by the Powers might well decide the Porte to make the best terms they could with Mohamed Ali themselves, as Pontoise was urging them to do.

The second factor was that Palmerston, who had not been carrying all his Cabinet colleagues with him in his attitude towards Mohamed Ali, managed to secure the support of the Prime Minister, Lord Melbourne, as the result of a letter which he wrote to him on 5 July threatening to resign if his policy were not fully supported by the rest of the Cabinet.[31]

The third factor was the outbreak of a serious insurrection in the Lebanon. This mountainous area of Syria, running parallel to the Mediterranean coast between Saida in the south and Tripoli in the north, was principally inhabited by Maronite (Uniate) Christians and Druzes, an heretical Moslem sect, who were politically united under the semi-autonomous rule of the Emir Beshir Shihab, who had for long been an ally of Mohamed Ali and of great assistance to him in his conquest of Syria in 1832. Because of this, and because Ibrahim's rule had been relatively favourable to Christians and to Moslem heretics, the Maronites and Druzes had at first welcomed the Egyptian occupation. But, accustomed as they had been for centuries to a fairly large measure of autonomy under their own leaders, they soon became tired of the dictatorial nature of Egyptian rule and particularly incensed by Ibrahim's attempts, first to conscribe them into his armies and, later, to disarm them. The attempt to disarm them was the immediate cause of the insurrection which broke out in 1840 against Egyptian rule and against the authority of the Emir Beshir. It was, of course, encouraged by the Turks and also by Ponsonby, who sent his Dragoman, Richard Wood, to fish in troubled waters. Its effect was threefold: (i) from the point of view of European public opinion, it weakened Mohamed Ali's contention, supported by the French government, that a continued Egyptian occupation of Syria was in the interest of the inhabitants; (ii) by making it less likely that Ibrahim would be able to advance into Asia Minor, it minimized the possibility of European intervention against Mohamed Ali developing into a unilateral Russian effort; (iii) by opening up an exposed front on the Syrian coast, it presented the possibility of an effective small-scale allied naval intervention.

Thiers was warning Mohamed Ali against any attempt to invade Asia Minor (a warning which was unnecessary since Ibrahim was refusing to do so), but considered that he would be able to hold Syria unaided against such limited armed force as the allies were likely to employ. He immediately saw the dangers inherent in the Lebanon insurrection and urged Mohamed Ali to make such concessions to the Lebanese as were necessary to conciliate them. He recalled Bourré, the French Consul in Beirut, for having supported the Christian insurgents (of whom France claimed to be the traditional protector). Later, he sent a Lazarist Abbé to Lebanon to try to bring about a reconciliation between the Maronites and Ibrahim. But he was fighting a losing battle. The Turks and the British were keeping the insurrection alive by the promise of succour, and the French, having taken a position against using force to coerce Mohamed Ali, were soon to find themselves having to threaten to use force to support him against Christian Ottoman subjects who, in alliance with the Sultan, were resisting his usurpation of the Sultan's authority.

The news of the London Convention came as no great surprise to Thiers who, as we have seen from his letter to Cochelet, expected it. But it caused great surprise and indignation among the French public, who regarded it as an attempt by the other Powers to isolate France. Throughout the nineteenth and during the first half of the twentieth century French public opinion exercised a considerable effect on French policy in the Levant and made successive governments hypersensitive on the subject of prestige there, particularly in relations with England. The legend of *perfide Albion*, nourished by numerous incidents in which the British clashed with, and usually got the better of, French interests, became an article of faith in popular French mythology.

Thiers's unofficial reaction to the news of the Convention was to tell Bulwer that the Franco-British alliance was at an end and that, if England separated herself from France on the Eastern Question, France would regard such a separation as a general one. His official reaction was to intimate that France's future action in the Levant would be dictated by her own interests, and to send a special emissary to Mohamed Ali to try to persuade him formally to accept French mediation with the Sultan on his behalf. The emissary chosen was Count Walewski, a natural son of Napoleon I by the Polish Countess Walewska. He was a naturalized Frenchman, a budding diplomat and a future Foreign Minister. He arrived at Alexandria on 12 August, almost simultaneously with a mission from the Sultan which was formally to place before Mohamed Ali the terms of the London Convention.

After the signature of the Convention, Hodges was advised by Palmerston of its contents but told not to make any official communication about it to Mohamed Ali until the arrival of the Turkish mission. He was, however, authorized to 'state generally to Mohamed Ali that a treaty had been concluded between the four Powers and the Sultan, that the Powers were determined to carry the stipulated arrangements fully into execution, that resistance would only be injurious to himself and his family, and that French help would not be forthcoming'. He was also authorized to tell the Viceroy that the British government bore no ill-will towards him, and had no wish to destroy him or to press upon him more heavily than was necessary to accomplish the great political object in view. The longer he delayed, the less he would ultimately get. In conclusion Hodges was told to remain in Egypt 'for as long as he should find his personal situation there compatible with the honour and dignity of his country.'[32]

At the same time Stopford was told (a) to cut off all communication in Egyptian vessels between Egypt and Syria; (b) to supply arms and ammunition to the insurgents in Lebanon and to tell them that the allies would recommend to the Sultan to 'grant them such future arrangements as might make them happy and prosperous'; (c) in the event of a Turkish force being sent to the coast of Syria, 'for a time to occupy any point on that coast where he might be able to put a few hundred men in security and under the protection of British ships of war'; (d) to try to persuade Turkish ships of the defected fleet to 'return to their allegiance and hoist the Turkish flag and cruise in company with HM's fleet'; (e) to give encouragement and protection to any of Mohamed Ali's troops 'who might manifest a disposition to return to their allegiance to the Sultan'; (f) to require any Egyptian warships found at sea to return to Alexandria, and any in Syrian ports either to remain there or return to Alexandria, and in no case to allow them to proceed to Candia.[33] Stopford was also told to hold a detachment of his fleet in readiness to proceed through the Dardanelles the moment he should receive from Ponsonby an intimation that the Sultan had asked for it. It was explained to him that 'the principal object of such a detachment would be to watch the coast of Asia Minor from the Dardanelles to near Scutari' and that it should only proceed as far as Continople should Ponsonby state that its presence there was necessary. He was told that 'if a French squadron were to attempt to force its way into the Dardanelles, the British squadron would not interfere'. Arrangements were made for supplying Stopford's vessels with arms and ammunition for the Lebanese insurgents from British stores in the Mediterranean, and for embarking a small detachment of artillery and engineers. British Consuls in Syria were instructed to let it be known that the four Powers had entered into arrangements with the Sultan to restore his authority.

News of the signature of the Convention was received in Constantinople on 3 August and the Sultan immediately announced that he would ratify it. It was decided that a Turkish force should be sent by sea to Syria and that the Grand Vizier should write to the Emir Beshir calling on him to reaffirm his allegiance to the Sultan. On 7 August a mission headed by Rifaat Bey left for Alexandria formally to convey the contents of the Convention to Mohamed Ali.

Rifaat Bey was accompanied by Mr Alison of the British Embassy, who bore a message from Ponsonby to Hodges instructing him to cooperate with Rifaat in trying to induce Mohamed Ali to accept the Sultan's offer, to consult the British and Austrian naval Commanders as to the means to be employed in securing the return of the Turkish fleet, and to use every means of informing the people of Syria of the contents of the Convention. At the same time Ponsonby told Robert Wood, the Embassy Dragoman, who was on a mission to the Lebanon, and Moore, the British Consul in Beirut, to spread the news that a Turkish army was coming to Syria, that the Sultan was ready to pardon any of Mohamed Ali's troops who

265

deserted, and that, if the Emir Beshir should abandon Mohamed Ali, 'the Powers would take care that the Porte would give all possible security for the laws, liberty and good government of the Lebanon under the authority of the Sultan'.[34]

Rifaat Bey and his mission arrived in Alexandria on 11 August—the day before Walewski—but Mohamed Ali was away in Cairo and they did not see him until 16 August, on which day Rifaat formally advised him of the contents of the Convention and made him the Sultan's first offer. Mohamed Ali replied that he would rather perish than accept it. On the following day the Consuls of the four Powers saw the Viceroy and urged him to accept. He gave them the same reply as he had given to Rifaat.

Walewski also saw Mohamed Ali on 16 August, after the Viceroy had seen Rifaat. His object was to try to persuade him officially to request French mediation without appearing to advise him to do so. He was somewhat disconcerted by the Viceroy's bellicosity, warned him against advancing into Asia Minor or sending his fleet to sea, and urged him to do everything he could to settle the insurrection in the Lebanon by concessions to the insurgents.[35] After seeing the Viceroy, Walewski made discreet enquiries about Egyptian military and financial resources and was not highly impressed. He seems to have realized that the basis of Thiers's policy—the belief that Mohamed Ali could maintain himself against such force as the Powers were likely to bring against him, provided that he made no attempt to advance into Asia Minor—was invalid, and that a settlement was urgently necessary in the interests both of France and of Mohamed Ali himself.[36] A few days after his audience with the Viceroy, Walewski received a communication from Boghos Yusef containing a formal request for French mediation.[37]

On 26 August, on the expiry of the ten days' delay provided for in the Convention, Rifaat and the Consuls of the four Powers waited on Mohamed Ali to receive his formal answer. The Viceroy repeated his refusal and indicated that he would refuse the alternative offer at the expiration of the following ten days.

In an audience with the Viceroy on 27 August, Walewski agreed to go to Constantinople and treat directly with the Porte on the basis of their granting Egypt in hereditary succession and the whole of Syria for life, with the relinquishment of

Adana, Arabia and Candia.[38] He left for Constantinople on 30 August. In a despatch to Thiers he gave his impression of Mohamed Ali. 'He is a cool and clever gambler; he does not hold very good cards, but he calculates the odds carefully and will not risk his money recklessly. He behaves with a mixture of finesse and frankness, of decision and indecision, of calculation and spontaneity, of pomp and simplicity. . . . He has much vanity but, in the end, calculation will always get the better of his vanity.'[39]

On 29 August, after having seen Walewski, Mohamed Ali summoned Rifaat and the four Consuls and appeared to be in a more conciliatory mood. He said that he was ready to accept the Sultan's offer of the hereditary government of Egypt and would write officially to HM in that sense, adding a request to be granted the government of Syria. Rifaat and the Consuls remarked that he could not attach conditions to his acceptance, and reminded him that unconditional acceptance must be accompanied by an immediate restoration of the Turkish fleet and the delivery of orders for the evacuation of the territories not included in the offer. Mohamed Ali replied that he would wait for the Sultan's answer to his letter and, if it were favourable, he would carry out these measures without delay. He added, however, that if the Sultan's answer were unfavourable, he would 'trust to the force of arms'. Rifaat and the Consuls told him that that would not do, that measures of coercion would have to take their course and could not be averted by any proceedings inconsistent with the Convention. Mohamed Ali then, returning to his former intransigence, refused to discuss the matter further.

News of Mohamed Ali's rejection of the Sultan's first offer having been received at Constantinople on 31 August, the Porte, on the recommendation of Ponsonby and the Internuncio, decided to appoint new Pashas to the several Pashaliks of Syria and to send a Firman to the Lebanon, to be used in the event of the Emir Beshir refusing to return to his allegiance, by which the Emir Qasim, Beshir's nephew, was to be appointed Prince of the Lebanon in his place.

Palmerston, having learnt of Mohamed Ali's rejection of the Sultan's first offer, ordered Stopford to adopt 'every measure within the spirit of the instructions already sent him which might embarrass the movements of Egyptian troops either in Syria or elsewhere and cripple and paralyse their resources, to

267

encourage and assist the insurgents in Syria, and to prevent any Turkish or Egyptian ships from leaving Alexandria except to submit to the Sultan'. If the Egyptian fleet came out of Alexandria *en masse*, he was to attack it.[40]

On 5 September, the second ten-day interval provided in the Convention having expired, Rifaat and the four Consuls again waited on Mohamed Ali for his formal answer. The Viceroy was indisposed and sent Sami Bey, his secretary, to tell them that he accepted the hereditary Pashalik of Egypt and that, with regard to Syria, he would submit himself to the generosity of the Sultan and the Powers. Rifaat replied that he was not authorized to receive a conditional acceptance unaccompanied by a restoration of the fleet and the despatch of orders for the evacuation of Syria and the other territories, and that the Viceroy's answer could only be construed as a refusal. The Consuls then asked whether the Viceroy would insist on their leaving Alexandria. Sami replied that his master considered that he had accepted the Sultan's offer and, as he was no longer in a state of hostility to the Sultan, saw no reason why the Consuls should not remain. The Consuls replied that they too regarded Mohamed Ali's reply as a refusal.

When the news of Mohamed Ali's refusal of the Sultan's second offer reached Constantinople, the Porte, with Ponsonby's agreement, announced Mohamed Ali's deposition from the Pashalik of Egypt, requested that the Consuls of the four Powers should be withdrawn, and asked that the Powers should cooperate with them in a blockade of the coasts of Egypt and Syria. Ponsonby, advising Palmerston of these measures, told him that they had been unanimously supported by the Representatives of the four Powers, who were 'convinced that any other course would give great advantage to Mohamed Ali and provide an opportunity for the operation of the policy of the French government'.[41] The Sultan's sentence of deposition was conveyed to Hodges by Ponsonby, who instructed him to leave Alexandria. He embarked on 22 September, leaving behind Mr Larking as Acting British Consul.

The 'policy of the French government' was being deployed in Constantinople by Walewski, who arrived there on 7 September. He was warned by Pontoise that little could be expected from any French attempt at mediation. The return of Rifaat Bey with the news of Mohamed Ali's attitude, which was followed by the Viceroy's deposition, bore out this gloomy view. Walewski told Cochelet that there was nothing to be done at Constantinople since the Divan (Sultan's Council) was under the thumb of Rashid Pasha, the Reis Effendi, and that Rashid was under the thumb of Ponsonby. He thought that the only possible place for negotiations was London.

Chances of negotiation in London were little, if at all, brighter than in Constantinople. Anglo-French relations were rapidly deteriorating and, throughout August and September, there was, in both countries, a general feeling that they were on the verge of war. On 21 July, just after the signature of the London Convention, Palmerston had written to Bulwer, the British Chargé d'Affaires, telling him to warn the French government that the allies intended to use force against Mohamed Ali if necessary, even though the French should reinforce their fleet in the Levant, as Guizot had told him they were going to do. 'Be it so. We shall not be daunted by any superiority of naval force which she may choose or be able to send thither. We shall go to work quietly and in our own way, in presence of a superior force, if such there be, just as undisturbed as if it were laid up in ordinary at Toulon. France knows full well that, if that superior force should dare to meddle with ours, it is war; and she would be made to pay dearly for a war so brought on.'[42] In another letter to Bulwer on 23 August Palmerston told him that he was more than ever convinced that, in spite of Thiers's threats, 'the French will remain quiet and that there will be no war . . . the smoke will soon blow away from the eyes of the French people and they will see more clearly the objects which have caused their false alarm. . . . The language of Guizot to me is as pacific as possible. The only thing that can now be done by the French government is to use their influence with Mohamed Ali to [induce him to] yield to the four Powers. We cannot modify the arrangement recorded in the treaty, and we are bound to carry that arrangement into effect, and to use whatever means may be necessary for the purpose. When that is done France might unite with the other Powers in a general treaty to support the Sultan.'[43]

But Thiers was not disposed to take Palmerston's advice. On 18 September Bulwer saw him at Auteuil. Thiers told him of the conditions which Walewski had advised that Mohamed Ali was prepared to accept, said that he regarded these conditions as reasonable and just, and indicated that if England and the other Powers would join France in persuading the Sultan to accept them, 'there is once more an *entente cordiale* between us. If not, after the concessions obtained through our influence with Mohamed Ali, we are bound to support him'. In his account of the interview, Bulwer went on: 'With these words, he fixed his eyes on my countenance and added gravely, "Vous comprenez, mon cher, la gravité de ce que je viens de vous dire." "Perfectly", I said with an intentional air of imperturbability, "you wish me to understand that, if we accept the arrangement made through Walewski, you and we are the best friends in the world; if not, you mean to declare for the Pasha and go to war with us in his favour." ' Thiers, possibly a little taken aback, then stressed to Bulwer that he had been expressing his own individual opinions and not necessarily those of a Prime Minister who had to consult the King and also his colleagues.[44] Palmerston, on receiving from Bulwer the substance of this conversation, still held to his belief that the French would be too wise and too prudent to declare war. But he instructed Bulwer, if Thiers should again use similar language, to tell him, 'in the most friendly and inoffensive manner possible', that 'if France throws down the gauntlet, we shall not refuse to pick it up; and that, if she begins a war, she will to a certainty lose her ships, colonies and commerce before she sees the end of it; that her army in Algeria will cease to give her anxiety and that Mohamed Ali will just be chucked into the Nile. . . . These considerations perhaps might weigh more with Louis Philippe than with Thiers, but I am inclined to think that they will weigh with somebody at Paris. . . . We are going on quietly but steadily with our naval armaments. . . . *Britannia* and *Howe*, each of 120 guns, and an 84 whose name I forget, will sail for the Mediterranean in a fortnight and will make 17 good ships on that station. Three more will immediately be got ready to take their place at home; as to the steamers, we have got 700 of various kinds belonging to the country, and I do not believe that the French have got 100. You will therefore be fully justified . . . in declining civilly to accept the threats which they may try to put upon us.'[45]

These gathering war-clouds had their effect on Metternich. Apparently as a result of the Internuncio's intervention, the Porte, in order not to shut the door on the possibility of an arrangement with Mohamed Ali, deferred the appointment of a new Pasha to Egypt. Metternich also told Beauvale that he disapproved of Mohamed Ali's deposition, thought that war could only be avoided by conciliating France, and suggested that the four Powers should pledge themselves to obtain the restitution of Egypt to Mohamed Ali. A few days later he instructed Stürmer, the Internuncio, not to agree to any proposition put forward in Constantinople which went beyond what was provided for in the London Convention. Prussia, as usual, echoed Austrian views and Werther, the Prussian Foreign Minister, told the British Ambassador that he too disapproved of Mohamed Ali's deposition. Russia also was unenthusiastic.

Even Palmerston seems to have thought that Ponsonby had gone too far in pressing Mohamed Ali's deposition on the Porte. He told Granville that he looked on it as a means of coercion employed by the Sultan in order to obtain Mohamed Ali's acquiescence in the terms proposed to him, and did not regard it as prejudicing any arrangement which the Sultan might be disposed to make in Mohamed Ali's favour 'if the Pasha at an early date should withdraw his refusal and accept the conditions of the treaty'. He also warned Stopford that, in spite of the Porte's request for cooperation in blockading the coasts of Egypt and Syria, he should not enforce a commercial blockade by interfering with any merchant ships flying any flags other than those of Turkey or Egypt.

On 15 October, Palmerston told Ponsonby that the Austrian, Russian and Prussian governments were recommending to the Sultan that, if Mohamed Ali should at an early date make his submission, restore the Turkish fleet and withdraw his troops from the whole of Syria, from Candia, Adana and the Holy Cities, he should not only reinstate him as Pasha of Egypt but also grant him the hereditary tenure of that Pashalik. He instructed Ponsonby also to recommend this to the Sultan as soon as he had ascertained that his three colleagues had received similar instructions.

CHAPTER TEN

THE IMPOSED SETTLEMENT

At the beginning of August, after receiving news of the signature of the London Convention, Stopford, in accordance with his orders, sent Commodore Charles Napier to Beirut in command of six warships—*Powerful*, on which he hoisted his broad pennant, *Ganges*, *Thunderer*, *Edinburgh*, *Castor* and *Gorgon*—to assist the insurrection and to encourage the desertion of any of Mohamed Ali's troops who wished to return to their allegiance to the Sultan. On his arrival, Napier found that the insurrection was over, and formed the opinion that its extent had been deliberately exaggerated by Ponsonby in order to encourage and hasten allied intervention. He also found that there were some 4,000 troops of Ibrahim's army, encamped near Beirut, who wished to return to the Sultan's service. He published the news of the Convention, called on the inhabitants to rise against Egyptian rule, and on Emir Beshir and the troops to return to their proper allegiance. He told Soliman Pasha (ex-Colonel Sève), the Egyptian military commander of Beirut, that he had orders to detain all ships of war and vessels bearing troops or military stores from one part of Egypt or Syria to another, and asked him to give orders not to permit any such vessels to leave the ports under his command. In a courteous exchange of letters, Soliman Pasha refused to do this.

On 27 August, after Mohamed Ali had rejected the Sultan's first offer, Napier was reinforced by three more ships—*Revenge*, *Benbow* and *Magicienne*—and received news that a Turkish force of 6,000 troops had arrived in Cyprus en route for Syria. On 9 September Stopford arrived off Beirut in *Princess Charlotte* and, on the same day, the Turkish force from Cyprus, together with a detachment of British Marines and Austrian artillery,

272

landed without opposition in Junieh Bay, a few miles north of Beirut. As Sir Charles Smith, who was to have commanded this force, was ill, Stopford placed Napier in temporary command of it.

Recording the history of the campaign a few months later, Napier wrote: 'Had the Egyptian troops at Beirut, with the exception of the garrison, marched to the heights of Ornacaguan and the high land over the Nahr-el-Kalb (Dog River), those at Baalbek on Ghazir, Harissa and Antoura, and those at Tripoli pushed along the shore by Jebail the moment we landed, there is little doubt but that we should have been withdrawn, and the troops sent to Cyprus, and Mohamed Ali would have been in possession of Syria, and England in all probability involved in war with France. Even had we remained inactive and contented ourselves with occupying a stronghold only, we should have incurred the same risk.'[1]

The force, under Napier's command, did not remain inactive. He despatched two of his ships north to occupy the fortress of Jebail (Byblos), halfway between Beirut and Tripoli, to block a possible advance by Egyptian troops along the coast from Tripoli. Other British and Austrian ships were watching the coast between Junieh and Beirut to guard against a possible Egyptian advance from the south. The bridgehead at Junieh Bay was fortified and the presence of the allied troops encouraged the mountaineers of Lebanon to renew the insurrection. After a few days, Napier enlarged the bridgehead and pushed inland, until he occupied a line along the peaks of Mount Lebanon. There was still no clash with the enemy and such Egyptian reconnaissance parties as were met withdrew without fighting.

On 11 September, two days after the landing, Stopford invited Soliman Pasha to surrender Beirut, and when Soliman refused, bombarded the town. The bombardment was not followed by a landing. Instead, there was another exchange of the courtesies which marked this very gentlemanly war. 'During the time the cannonading was going on, the Indian mail arrived; our intercepting despatches from Alexandria gave Soliman Pasha a fair excuse for stopping this mail, but, as its detention had nothing to do with hostilities then going on, he hoisted a flag of truce and delivered the mail with a very civil message that all letters to and from India would be religiously forwarded. The Admiral, not to be outdone in civility, wrote a

273

letter of thanks, and sent Soliman a package of wine that had been detained in an Egyptian vessel.'[2]

On 12 September, Jebail was stormed and taken by a detachment of British Marines at a cost of five Marines killed and eighteen wounded. These were the first British casualties of the campaign.

On 26 September Stopford sent Napier with two steamers— *Gorgon* and *Cyclops*, one British line-of-battle ship—*Thunderer*, one Austrian frigate and one Turkish corvette, together with one Turkish infantry battalion and 284 British Marines, to Saida (Sidon), some 40 miles south of Beirut, to occupy that port. After the usual invitation to surrender had been declined, a landing was made under the guns of the ships and the town and fortress, which had a garrison of about 300 men, captured.

Meanwhile, Haifa and Sur (Tyre) had also been captured from the sea by small Anglo-Turkish forces, and an unsuccessful attempt had been made to capture Tortosa, north of Tripoli.

The allied successes led the Emir Qasim, nephew of the Emir Beshir, to join the invaders, and the Emir Beshir himself to open negotiations with them. It seemed to Napier, back from Saida, that the time had come to seek action with the enemy with the object of capturing Beirut and driving the Egyptians out of Lebanon. But Stopford, having distributed arms to the mountaineers and having, as it were, got the insurrection going again, was in favour of evacuating before Ibrahim attacked with a superior force. Napier, fending off Stopford's objections, and cooperating closely with the various local chieftains who had declared for the allies, took up a position on the heights above Junieh and waited for Ibrahim to attack him.

At this point, on 9 October, Soliman Pasha, commanding the Egyptian forces in and around Beirut, which had been closely blockaded from the sea for the past two months, and which was being gradually invested from the land by Napier and his local allies, surrendered to Stopford. On the following day Napier and his force joined battle with an Egyptian force led by Ibrahim in person on the heights above Junieh. It was, as Napier afterwards remarked, 'rather a new occurrence for a British Commodore to be on the top of Mount Lebanon commanding a Turkish army and preparing to fight a battle which would decide the fate of Syria'.[3] The Egyptians were defeated in what became known as the battle of Boharsof and Napier's force captured 600 – 700 prisoners.

Immediately after the battle, Napier, who was on very bad terms with Stopford owing to a tendency to insubordination reminiscent of Sir Sidney Smith under somewhat similar circumstances forty years before, was replaced in command of the land force by Colonel Sir Charles Smith, who had recovered from his indisposition. After vainly urging on Stopford and Smith the desirability of pursing Ibrahim to Zahle, on the eastern slopes of Mount Lebanon, where he had retreated, Napier reembarked in *Powerful*, and the allied force was evacuated from Junieh Bay, being then employed to garrison Beirut, Saida, Sur, and, later, Acre. By this time Ibrahim was withdrawing from the whole of northern Syria and Lebanon and concentrating his forces around Damascus. By the time the allied force had been evacuated from Junieh Bay the whole of the Syrian coastal area to as far south as Acre had been evacuated by the Egyptians. Acre was still strongly held and the capture of this fortress was the next target for the allies.

On 5 October Palmerston had told the Admiralty that Stopford should make himself master of Acre and 'continue to protect that part of the Syrian population which might have declared itself for the allies'.[4] Three British warships—*Revenge, Pique* and *Talbot*—had already been off Acre for some time. On 2 November they were joined by the main allied squadron under Stopford's command consisting of seven line-of-battle ships—*Princess Charlotte* (Stopford's flagship), *Powerful* (flying Napier's broad pennant), *Bellerophon, Thunderer, Edinburgh, Benbow* and *Castor*, three frigates—*Carysfort, Wasp* and *Hazard*, and four steamers—*Gorgon, Stromboli, Phoenix* and *Vesuvius*. After a heavy bombardment, during which the fortress's powder magazine blew up, the town and fortress were evacuated by the Egyptian commander and garrisoned by 3,000 Turkish troops and 250 British Marines under the command of Sir Charles Smith.

After the capture of Acre Stopford decided to return to Marmorice Bay (Rhodes) for the winter with most of the British fleet, leaving *Bellerophon* and *Benbow* at Beirut, *Pique* and *Zebra* at Acre, and other small vessels and steamers at various points on the Syrian coast. Napier, who had had another difference of opinion with Stopford over the tactics employed at Acre, was sent in *Powerful* to take command of the British squadron off Alexandria, consisting of six ships of the line. Before leaving Syria he wrote a letter to Palmerston, with whom he seems to have been on friendly terms, giving him his opinion on the state of affairs there. 'Troops are arriving every day from Constantinople, and we cannot now have less than 12,000 men here. Ibrahim Pasha is two days' march from here [Beirut] and is watched by the mountaineers only; and they are so neglected by Izzet Pasha [the Turk who has been appointed by the Porte as Pasha of Lebanon] that they are sometimes without provisions for three days. Izzet is the worst person that can be, and unless he is removed there will be mischief. . . . Nothing would give England so much influence here as giving Lebanon the same government as Samos. The Grand Prince ought to be a Pasha; Sidon, Tripoli and Beirut ought to be added to his government, and if possible, the Bekaa and anti-Lebanon. This would be a prosperous country; but, agreeable to the present system, they are almost shut out from the sea. God knows how the Sultan is going to govern the other provinces; but if his Pashas are all like the man here, they will be worse off than they were under Mohamed Ali, and I verily believe, should the war last, he will have a party in his favour, the Turks treat them so ill. If Mohamed Ali were a wise man he would do with the mountains what I have stated and he would get a strong party in his favour.' Going on to the general political situation, Napier told Palmerston: 'I believe the best thing to settle this affair would be at once to say to Mohamed Ali, "Withdraw from Syria and give up the Turkish fleet and you shall keep Egypt". If Your Lordship and the allies have any notion of that, try me as a negotiator with six sail of the line, which I am to have, and I dare say I shall succeed. I believe Egypt would be just as well governed by him as it would be by one of the Turkish Pashas; he is an old man and it is hardly worth risking a war to turn him out.'⁵

Napier arrived off Alexandria in *Powerful* on 21 November and took command of the British squadron, consisting of *Rodney*, *Revenge*, *Vanguard*, *Ganges* and *Cambridge*—line of battle ships, *Carysfort*—frigate, and *Medea*—steamer. When he joined the squadron he was given a copy of Palmerston's despatch to Ponsonby of 15 October (see p. 271). On the basis of Palmerston's views, as expressed in that despatch, which chimed with his own, Napier determined to open a negotiation himself with Mohamed Ali on behalf of the British government. Captain Maunsell, commanding *Rodney*, was an old friend of Mohamed Ali (he had been in Egyptian waters during the earlier Syrian crisis seven years before). Napier sent him ashore under a flag of truce with a letter to Boghos Bey in which he wrote: 'HH is no doubt aware of the willingness of the allies to secure to Mohamed Ali the hereditary government of Egypt. Will HH permit an old sailor to suggest to him an easy means of reconciliation to the Sultan and the other Great Powers of Europe? Let HH freely, frankly and unconditionally deliver up the Ottoman fleet and withdraw his troops from Syria. The miseries of war would then cease and HH in his latter years would have ample and satisfactory occupation in cultivating the arts of peace and probably laying a foundation for the restoration of the throne of the Ptolemies. By what has taken place in Syria HH must be aware of what can be accomplished in a country where the inhabitants are disaffected to the government. In one month 6,000 Turks and a handful of Marines took Sidon, Beirut, defeated the Egyptian troops in three actions, possessed themselves of 10,000 prisoners and deserters, and caused the evacuation of all the sea-ports, and the passes of Taurus and Mount Lebanon, and this in face of an army of more than 30,000 men, and in three weeks more Acre, the key to Syria, fell to the combined fleets after a bombardment of three hours. Should HH persist in hostilities, will he permit me to ask if he is safe in Egypt? I am a great admirer of HH and would much rather be his friend than his enemy. In the capacity of the former I take the liberty of pointing out to HH the little hope he can have of preserving Egypt should he refuse to be reconciled to the Sultan. . . . Egypt is not invulnerable. . . . Alexandria itself may be made to share the fate of Acre, and HH, who now has an opportunity of forming a dynasty, may sink into a simple Pasha.'[6]

Maunsell returned next day, accompanied by Larking, the Acting British Consul, with an answer from Boghos which was noncommittal but indicated readiness to talk. There followed some more correspondence; Napier sent the Viceroy a copy of Palmerston's despatch of 15 October and offered his assistance in evacuating the Egyptian army from Syria. Boghos pointed out that a settlement of the dispute was expected within a few days as a result of French mediation. Eventually, on 25 November, Napier entered Alexandria harbour in the steamship *Medea*, passed through the Turco-Egyptian fleet, and anchored off the Palace. He then landed and went to the British Consulate. From there he wrote another letter to Boghos pointing out that he knew nothing about French mediation and giving the following undertaking: 'If HH will give immediate orders for the evacuation of Syria and send transports to receive the troops and get the fleet ready for sea, I will not insist on their [i.e. the Turkish fleet's] departure for Constantinople until the Pasha is guaranteed in the hereditary government of Egypt, and on these conditions I will suspend hostilities.'[7]

On 26 November Napier, accompanied by Larking, Maunsell, and others of his captains, went to wait on Mohamed Ali. 'A battalion of Egyptian troops was drawn up in the courtyard of the Palace and presented arms, the band playing martial airs. On entering the reception room of Mohamed Ali, which is in the old Palace, we were most graciously received. The Pasha, in a short dress, was standing, surrounded by his officers, and free admission seems to have been given to Franks of all descriptions. After a few compliments on both sides, the Pasha walked to a corner of the room and seated himself on his Divan. Pipes and coffee were called for and we smoked away for a considerable time, as if we had been the best friends in the world. The Palace was too crowded to enter into business, and it was arranged I should again see the Pasha in the evening, after communicating with Boghos Bey, and give him in writing the terms I wished him to comply with.'[8]

Napier, in his account, gives a description of Mohamed Ali in his old age: 'The Pasha is a man of low stature, is a good deal marked with the small-pox, his complexion sallow, his eyes quick and penetrating. He wears a fine white beard, and when in good humour has a most fascinating manner, but when out of temper his eyes sparkle, he raises himself up in his corner, and soon convinces you that he is much easier led than driven. He is easy of access and, indeed, fond of gossiping; he seems to be informed of everything that is either said or done in Alexandria. He has many friends among the Franks and, once he takes a liking to a man, his fortune is made. He has built a very handsome palace and furnished it with taste. Opposite the palace is the hareem where his wife resides; but the old gentleman has given up his visits to that establishment.'[9]

After some further negotiation with Boghos, a Convention was drawn up, dated 27 November, and signed by the two men, Napier as 'commanding HBM's naval forces before Alexandria' and Boghos as having been especially authorized by the Viceroy of Egypt. It read as follows:

I.   Commodore Napier, in his above-mentioned capacity, having brought to the knowledge of HH Mohamed Ali that the allied Powers had recommended the Sublime Porte to reinstate him in the hereditary government of Egypt, and HH, seeing in this communication a favourable occasion for putting an end to the calamities of war, engages to order his son Ibrahim Pasha to proceed immediately to the evacuation of Syria. HH engages moreover to return the Ottoman fleet as soon as he shall have received the official notification that the Sublime Porte grants to him the hereditary government of Egypt, which concession is and remains guaranteed by the Powers.

II.   Commodore Napier will place a steamer at the disposal of the Egyptian government which will convey to Syria the officer charged by HH to carry to the C-in-C of the Egyptian army the order to evacuate Syria. The C-in-C of the British forces, Sir Robert Stopford, will on his side appoint an officer to watch the execution of this measure.

III.   In consideration of what precedes Commodore Napier engages to suspend hostilities on the part of the British forces against Alexandria or any other portion of Egyptian territory. He will at the same time authorize the free passage of the vessels appointed for the transport of the wounded, the invalids, and any other portion of the Egyptian army which the government of Egypt might wish to return to that country by sea.

IV.   It is well understood that the Egyptian army shall have the liberty of retiring from Syria with its artillery, arms, horses and baggage and, in general, with everything that constitutes the stores of an army.

A copy of this Convention was sent by Napier to Stopford, still off Beirut, to Ponsonby, in Constantinople, and to Palmerston, in London.

Soon after the signature of the Convention, Napier, in *Powerful*, was driven off the coast of Egypt by a storm and made his way to Marmorice Bay, which he reached on 8 December. Here he found a letter dated 2 December for him from Stopford, who had received his copy of the Convention and was not pleased with it. He told Napier: 'I am sorry to say that I cannot ratify or approve of this measure; setting aside the unauthorized manner and unnecessary haste with which so important a document was executed, with the C-in-C within two days' sail of you, the articles of that Convention, if carried into execution in the present state of Syria, would be productive of much more evil than good, and occasion much embarrassment. You will immediately stop the Egyptian transports from coming to this coast and, should any arrive, I have given orders that they return to Alexandria.'[10]

Napier received a similar, but even ruder, letter from Sir Charles Smith, commanding the Turkish land forces in Syria, and also one from Ponsonby which, after acknowledging receipt of a copy of the Convention, told him: 'I immediately laid that Convention before the Sublime Porte and acquainted my colleagues, the Austrian Internuncio, the Prussian Envoy, and the Russian Chargé d'Affaires, with it. It is my duty to acquaint you that the Sublime Porte has made a formal protest against your acts, declaring that you have no power or authority to justify what you have done and that the Convention is null and void. My above-mentioned colleagues and myself entirely concur with the Sublime Porte and declare that we are ignorant of your having had the least right to assume the powers you have exercised and that we consider the Convention null and void *ab initio*.'[11]

On the same day as he had written to Napier, Stopford sent a letter to Mohamed Ali telling him that Napier had had no authority to sign the Convention and making it clear that he did not recognize it.[12]

Meanwhile, further west, events had been moving. On 23 October the Thiers government resigned as the result of a disagreement with the King, who objected to some bellicose remarks which the Prime Minister wished to insert in the Speech from the Throne at the opening of the Chamber. Thiers was replaced by Marshal Soult, who appointed Guizot, the French Ambassador in London, as Foreign Minister. These changes, together with some realistic counsels from Walewski, who had returned to Alexandria after the failure of his mission in Constantinople, brought about a considerable modification in the French official attitude and, consequently, a reduction of the tension between France and England. The chances of a rapid settlement created by this, by Palmerston's despatch of 15 October, and by the success of allied operations in Syria were, however, impaired by Metternich, whose diplomacy was characterized by alternations between cowardice and bullying according to the presumed strength or weakness of his opponent. Hearing the news of the allied success in Syria, he swung round like a weathercock from his former attitude, in which he had advocated a settlement with Mohamed Ali, and objected to the contents of Palmerston's despatch on the ground that these successes (to which the Austrian contribution had been minimal) made it inexpedient for the Sultan to offer Mohamed Ali the hereditary possession of Syria at the very time when the Viceroy might be on the point of submission. Palmerston, who never needed much of an excuse to retreat from the prospect of any concession to Mohamed Ali, agreed with this change of front and ordered Stopford to despatch an officer to Mohamed Ali informing him that the four Powers would recommend to the Sultan to reinstate him in the Pashalik of Egypt provided that he would (a) make immediate submission to the Sultan; (b) deliver into the hands of the officer so sent a written engagement to restore without delay the Turkish fleet; and (c) cause his troops immediately to evacuate the whole of Syria, the district of Adana, the island of Candia, and the Holy Cities.[13] The point about this communication was that no reference was made to the hereditary possession of Egypt. This was not accidental, and Stopford was informed that the officer sent by him should not refuse to accept Mohamed Ali's submission should it be accompanied by the expression of a desire to be invested with the Pashalik of Egypt in hereditary possession. He was also told not to suspend his operations in Syria until he had heard from Constantinople that an arrangement had been arrived at with Mohamed Ali. The effect of this variation from the language of his despatch to Ponsonby of 15 October, on which Napier had based his Convention, was to throw responsibility for the final solution across from London into the laps of the Porte and the four Ambassadors in Constantinople.

Palmerston received a copy of Napier's Convention about three weeks after the orders to Stopford had been sent off. A few days later he told the Admiralty that 'HM's Government approves the steps taken by Commodore Napier on this occasion, though without any instructions and on his own responsibility, to carry into execution the arrangements contemplated by the treaty of 15 July, and to put an end to the contest in the Levant. In the uncertainty, however, which HM's Government felt as to the course which Sir Robert

281

Stopford would take with reference to what Commodore Napier had done as compared with what Sir Robert was instructed to do in the instruction of 14 November, they were obliged to postpone for a time the final communication of their opinion in respect of Commodore Napier's arrangement. But they thought it necessary to say that Sir Robert should lose no time in apprizing Mohamed Ali that the four Powers were unable to guarantee to him the hereditary possession of Egypt, if that grant were made to him by the Sultan, that HM's Government were unable to guarantee to a subject a grant of administration made to him by his Sovereign within the dominions of that Sovereign, and the Powers could not do so jointly, as the standing interference in the affairs of the Ottoman Empire implied by such a guarantee would be inconsistent with that independence of the Sultan's throne which it had been one of the main objects of the July treaty to ensure. The four Powers would however recommend to the Porte to make the concession specified in the Convention, and Sir Robert is authorized to advise Mohamed Ali to this effect.'[14]

Palmerston also told Ponsonby that the fact of Mohamed Ali having put forward (in the Napier Convention), a condition of the restoration of the Turkish fleet, that the Sultan should grant him the hereditary tenure of the Pashalik of Egypt need not prevent the Porte from making that concession. The Convention amounted substantially to a complete surrender by Mohamed Ali, who had been led to suppose that, in requesting the hereditary tenure of Egypt, he was only seeking what the Porte were willing to give and the Powers to recommend. He went on to state that the Article in the Convention providing for the guarantee of the Powers could not be complied with, and concluded: 'HM's Government hope that the unanimous advice of the Powers would remove the objections which the Porte was reputed to have entertained to revoking the decree depriving Mohamed Ali of the government of Egypt, and would lead the Porte to accept the settlement effected by Commodore Napier.'[15]

As soon as Stopford received Palmerston's instructions of 14 November, which reached him just after he had received a copy of Napier's Convention, he sent Captain Fanshawe RN to Alexandria to convey Palmerston's message. Fanshawe arrived in Alexandria on 8 December and delivered his message. Mohamed Ali told him that he had promised to do all that was required of him if Egypt were granted to him in hereditary possession. Fanshawe replied that he had no guarantee to offer and urged him to return the Turkish fleet immediately. On 11 December he received from the Viceroy a letter to the Grand Vizier in which, after describing the visits of Napier and Fanshawe, he declared that he had always desired at any cost to obtain the goodwill of the Sultan. Being sensible, as a result of the efforts of the Powers, that that goodwill was now restored, he would deliver the fleet over to whomsoever the Sultan might send to receive it. He added that Candia, Adana and the Holy Cities had been, or would be, evacuated, and that his submission was complete. He therefore hoped that the Grand Vizier would intervene with the Sultan in his favour. Fanshawe agreed to deliver this letter to the Grand Vizier and also to deliver en route a letter to the Governor of Candia desiring him to deliver the island to the Ottoman authorities.

Fanshawe arrived in Constantinople on 14 December and delivered Mohamed Ali's letter to the Grand Vizier on 18 December. On 20 December Rashid Pasha, the Reis Effendi, asked the Ambassadors of the four Powers whether they thought that Mohamed Ali, by the terms of his letter to the Grand Vizier, had complied with the spirit of Palmerston's message to Stopford of 14 November and whether his submission should be considered as genuine. Ponsonby replied that it was a matter for the Sultan to decide and refused to give any advice. Stürmer thought that the submission should be accepted and an officer sent to Alexandria to take delivery of the fleet. In the end no decision was arrived at.

On 27 December the Reis Effendi told Ponsonby that the Sultan was disposed to accept Mohamed Ali's submission and that Commissioners would be sent to Alexandria to take over the fleet and ascertain that the specified territories had been evacuated. He asked him to request Stopford to assist in the handing-over of the fleet.

On 3 January 1841 the Commissioners set out for Alexandria with a message to Mohamed Ali stating that the Sultan was disposed to accept his submission, and to pardon him entirely, and that, as soon as the fleet had been returned and the specified territories evacuated, he would reinstate him in the government of Egypt. There was no mention in this message of hereditary tenure. Later in the month it became clear that this omission was intentional. Chekib Effendi, the Turkish Ambassador in

London, told Palmerston that the Porte wished to delay the hereditary grant of Egypt and hoped that the British government approved. Palmerston, who had just been advised by Beauvale that Metternich, swinging round again, had instructed Stürmer to press upon the Porte the desirability of granting Mohamed Ali the hereditary government of Egypt immediately, whether his colleagues agreed with him or not, told Chekib that the Porte should bring matters to a conclusion without further delay by immediately granting to Mohamed Ali the hereditary government of Egypt. At the same time he wrote a curt note to Ponsonby implying that the Ambassador should have taken his despatch of 15 October as authorizing him to advise the Porte to grant Mohamed Ali the hereditary government of Egypt and instructing him categorically to advise the Porte to carry out the arrangements set out in that despatch as soon as the good faith of Mohamed Ali's submission had been proved by facts.

The Turkish Commissioners arrived in Alexandria on 10 January. Napier had arrived there two days earlier. Stopford had ordered him to proceed there after receiving notification that Palmerston had accepted the Convention with the exception of the guarantee. On 11 January the Turkish fleet was handed over to Admiral Walker, a British naval officer in the Turkish service who had been deputed by the Porte to receive it. Difficulty then arose about the hereditary government of Egypt since the Commissioners had no authority to offer this. The matter was being cleared up in Constantinople, but the news took some time to reach Egypt.

A few days after the departure of the Commissioners, Stürmer received the instructions from Metternich already referred to, charging him to press upon the Porte, in collaboration with such of his colleagues as were prepared to join him, the desirability of granting to Mohamed Ali the hereditary government of Egypt. On 9 January he approached the Porte accordingly with the Russian and Prussian Representatives. Ponsonby, who had not yet received Palmerston's instructions on the subject, and who appears to have done all he could to encourage the Porte to withhold the hereditary grant, refused to associate himself with the other three. On the following day, however, he received Palmerston's instructions of 17 December and, in a rather sulky note to Mr Pisani, the Embassy dragoman, instructed him to 'acquaint HE the Minister of Foreign

Affairs that I am ordered to counsel the Sublime Porte in the name of the British government to grant to Mohamed Ali the hereditary government of Egypt.'[16]

On 12 January, as a result of the representations made by the Ambassadors of the four Powers, the Sultan issued a Hatti Sherif (edict) conferring on Mohamed Ali the hereditary government of Egypt, and a copy was sent to the Commissioners in Alexandria. This, however, did not settle the dispute, since the conditions under which the hereditary Pashalik was to be held had still to be worked out in detail.

On 4 February the Reis Effendi presented to the Ambassadors of the four Powers the Sultan's conditions for the grant of the hereditary succession:

I. All laws and treaties to be applied in Egypt as in every other part of the Ottoman Empire.

II. Mohamed Ali's heir to be chosen by the Sultan at his discretion from among the Viceroy's male descendants. Such heir to receive the Sultan's investiture, to receive the title of Pasha and be treated like any other Pasha of the Ottoman Empire. Mohamed Ali himself to be exempted from proceeding to the capital for investiture on account of his age.

III. Money coined in Egypt to have the same value and alloy as money coined by the Sultan.

IV. All appointments, military and civil, and all promotions, to proceed from the Sultan, except for military appointments up to and including the rank of Captain.

V. The rate of annual tribute to be fixed separately.

VI. The distinctive marks of every rank, military and civil, to be ordained by the Sultan.

VII. Military and civil uniforms to be the same as worn by those directly in the Sultan's service.

VIII. The number of troops raised in Egypt to be limited to 25,000.

IX. The conscription to be limited to one man in 200 in Egypt (as compared with one man in 100 in other Provinces).

X. The government of Egypt, in accordance with tradition, to be responsible for the requirements of the Holy Cities of Mecca and Medina.

These conditions were agreed to by three out of the four Ambassadors. Ponsonby remained non-committal, taking the view that Mohamed Ali, having refused the terms offered in the London Convention, and having been compelled to submit by force of arms, should not get conditions which he would have got if he had submitted in the first place.[17]

The conditions were drawn up into a Firman dated 13 February with additional or amended clauses providing (a) that the annual tribute should be fixed at one-fourth of Egypt's total revenue; (b) that the governments of Nubia, Darfur, Kordofan and Sennaar (none of which had ever been regarded as part of the Ottoman Empire) should be conferred on Mohamed Ali for life only; (c) that the Egyptian army should be limited to 20,000 men, of which 2,000 should be stationed permanently in Constantinople; (d) that no new ships of war should be built without the Sultan's permission.[18]

Napier, who was in Alexandria when the Firman arrived, and who appears to have established relations of confidential intimacy with Mohamed Ali, advised him not to accept these very harsh terms. 'I knew that in doing so I was taking a good deal of responsibility on myself, as it was probable that these terms had been suggested to the Porte by some of the Ambassadors, if not all. But, being on the spot, and seeing that should Ibrahim, who was at the head of a large army, resist and be supported in his resistance by the officers of the army, which was pretty certain, the whole country would be thrown into confusion, I knew I should incur censure for not taking upon myself the responsibility of advising the Pasha to adopt what I thought was the safest course. Had the British and other Consuls been at Alexandria, I should have left it entirely to them.'[19] Napier wrote to Palmerston, telling him of the advice he had given Mohamed Ali, and saying: 'After the honourable manner in which the Pasha has behaved about the fleet, it is to be regretted that the Porte should have pressed him so hard, particularly as I do not see how they can enforce their demands, and I do not apprehend that the allies will risk another war to enforce them.'[20]

In Syria, all the muddle and delay had caused much confusion and unnecessary loss of life. It was some time before either Stopford or the Turks had orders to stop fighting and facilitate Ibrahim's evacuation. But, with their limited forces, they made no attempt to advance into the interior to attack

Ibrahim, who was able, in November, to concentrate at Damascus the remains of the Egyptian army, consisting of about 50,000 men, most of whom were ill-equipped and in bad shape. Since the Turks were determined to prevent Ibrahim from regaining the coast and evacuating his army by sea, he was compelled to retire on Egypt by land along the difficult route via the Dead Sea and the Negev, while the Turks concentrated between Gaza and Jerusalem, and encouraged the mountaineers of Nablus and Jebel Ajlun, and the Beduin of the Hauran, to harass Ibrahim's retreat. Ibrahim left Damascus with his army on 29 December 1840 and arrived in the neighbourhood of Gaza at the end of January. During this period there were continual negotiations between the British officers in Syria and the Turks (now commanded by the Austrian General Jochmus, as Sir Charles Smith had again fallen sick) as to whether the Egyptian retreat should be assisted or impeded. The Turkish view, supported by Ponsonby, was that the Egyptian army should be weakened as far as possible by harassment in order to avoid the possibility of its arriving back in Egypt in a condition to resist the terms offered to Mohamed Ali. In particular, the Turks insisted that the Syrian conscripts in Ibrahim's army should be handed over to the Turks in Syria and not taken back to Egypt. The British liaison officers, whose authority was supported only by a small force of Marines stationed at Jaffa, and by a few British warships off the coast, were anxious to honour the terms of Napier's Convention and ensure Ibrahim's ordered evacuation in accordance with the terms of that Convention. The Turkish case was put succinctly to Palmerston by Ponsonby: 'If Ibrahim had taken back his large army unharmed, Mohamed Ali would possess a force which might encourage him to resist and might possibly make him stronger than ever. The energy of General Jochmus has rendered all doubt and delusion on the military question impossible and has shown that under able command the Turkish troops are more than a match for the Egyptian army and General; his energy has taken from Mohamed Ali the best means he could have to support resistance and has therefore afforded the best ground for hoping that he will submit.'[21]

Ponsonby's estimate of Jochmus' prowess was rather optimistic. As a result of an agreement negotiated by the British liaison officers at Gaza between Ibrahim and the Turkish force, the Egyptian army, reduced to some 20,000 infantry,

287

6,500 cavalry, and 175 pieces of artillery,[22] was allowed to return to Egypt without further molestation, taking with it the Syrian conscripts, on whose retention in Syria the Turks were trying to insist. This force was arriving in Egypt at about the same time as the Sultan's Firman was communicated to Mohamed Ali, and was a decisive factor in the subsequent amendment of that Firman.[23]

When Palmerston had heard from Stopford that the Turkish fleet had arrived at Marmorice Bay, and from Napier that Ibrahim had evacuated Syria, he assembled the Plenipotentiaries of the four Powers. On 5 March these Plenipotentiaries drew up and signed a Protocol recording that the terms of the London Convention had been fulfilled, that Mohamed Ali had submitted, and that the Sultan had accepted his submission and announced his intention of conferring upon him and his descendants the hereditary Pashalik of Egypt. In view of this, it was determined by the Plenipotentiaries that the Consuls of the four Powers should return to Alexandria forthwith.

On 11 March Chekib Effendi communicated to Palmerston the contents of the Firman investing Mohamed Ali with the hereditary Pashalik and requested him to communicate it to the other plenipotentiaries. As a result, a further meeting of the four was held on 13 March and a message sent to the Sultan expressing satisfaction at the settlement of the dispute. At the same time Palmerston wrote to Ponsonby expressing his doubts about the restrictive nature of some of the conditions offered to Mohamed Ali, making it clear that he thought the hereditary succession should be offered in direct line of male descent. Nobody should be left in doubt that it was the Sultan's intention that Ibrahim should succeed his father.[24]

Meanwhile, in Constantinople, on 6 March, Mohamed Ali's reply to the Sultan's Firman had been received, objecting to several of the restrictive articles contained in it. The Porte, as usual, consulted the Ambassadors. Ponsonby, as usual, urged the Porte to stand firm. The Russian and Prussian Ambassadors declined to give an opinion, but Stürmer, the Internuncio, recommended amendments to the Firman incorporating the substance of Mohamed Ali's requests.[25]

On 29 March Rashid Pasha was replaced as Reis Effendi by Rifaat Bey, who had been the emissary sent to Mohamed Ali to convey to him the terms of the London Convention.

On 31 March Metternich instructed Stürmer to try to get

his colleagues to recommend some amendment in the more restrictive Articles in the Firman and, if his colleagues did not agree, and if the Porte should refuse to listen, to tell all concerned that 'the Emperor will consider himself restored to entire liberty of position and action'.[26]

On 10 April Palmerston wrote an exasperated despatch to Ponsonby telling him that it was time the dispute was settled and that the Sultan ought without delay to modify the Firman in its objectionable parts and particularly in respect of the direct succession. On 21 April he wrote even more peremptorily, enclosing a copy of Metternich's instructions to Stürmer and telling him that he agreed with Metternich.[27]

On 16 May the Plenipotentiaries in London met and recommended (a) that the succession in Egypt should go in direct line from father to son; (b) that the tribute should be fixed, not as a proportion of the total revenue, but as a fixed sum, subject to periodical revision; and (c) that the restrictions on appointments and promotions contained in the Firman should be relaxed.[28]

At last the Porte gave way. On 25 May the Firman of 13 February was amended by means of (a) a Hatti Sherif fixing the hereditary succession on the oldest living male in direct line from Mohamed Ali; (b) a Firman fixing the annual tribute at 80,000 purses (40 million piastres or about £400,000); and (c) a letter from the Grand Vizier authorizing Mohamed Ali to make military appointments up to and including the rank of Colonel.[29] These documents were conveyed to Alexandria and delivered to Said Mohib Effendi, the bearer of the original Firman, who had been waiting in Egypt since February. The messenger, Kiamil Effendi, arrived in Alexandria on 7 June and, on 10 June, in the morning, Mohamed Ali 'received the two Ottoman envoys in solemn audience in the great hall of Ras-el-Tin Palace, where he received them standing, with the officials of his Court grouped around him. He took from the hands of Said Mohib Effendi the Hatti Sherif, conveyed it to his lips and forehead and passed it to his secretary Sami Bey, who read it out in a loud voice. He then put on the Ottoman decoration with which the Sultan had presented him as a reward for his loyal services. Salvoes of honour were then fired from the neighbouring forts and from the warships in the harbour.'[30]

On 10 July the four Plenipotentiaries had a last meeting at

which the Turco-Egyptian dispute was formally declared to be at an end. On 13 July, Great Britain, France, Austria, Russia, Prussia and Turkey signed a Convention in London in which it was declared that the Sultan had determined and the five Powers were agreed that he would in future maintain 'the principle invariably established as an ancient rule of the Empire by which he has at all times forbidden warships of all foreign Powers from entering the Dardanelles or the Bosphorus, and that, as long as the Porte was at peace, HM would not admit any foreign warships into these Straits.'[31]

So the Turco-Egyptian dispute ended with the re-establishment of that Concert of five Powers in defence of the independence and integrity of the Ottoman Empire, which had been temporarily broken up by the defection of France.

The matter ostensibly in dispute, which was whether Syria should remain in Mohamed Ali's possession, was in fact almost entirely irrelevant, either to the integrity and independence of the Ottoman Empire, or to the objects of Palmerston's diplomacy. These objects were two-fold. First, to substitute the virtual protectorate over the Ottoman Empire which Russia had secured at Unkiar Skelessi by a joint protectorate exercised by the five European Great Powers. Secondly, to counter French designs against British communications with India which, as Palmerston believed, had been nourished by France ever since 1763, which Bonaparte had attempted to implement, and which successive French regimes since Waterloo had never relinquished. These suspicions were clearly and brutally stated by Palmerston in a letter to Granville, the British Ambassador in Paris, at the end of November 1840, during the course of the crisis. Guizot, the new French Foreign Minister, had suggested to Granville that 'the final settlement of the Eastern Question shall not appear to have been concluded without French concurrence'. Granville had apparently suggested to Palmerston that this was a matter of French *amour propre*. Palmerston would have none of it. 'As to the stale pretence of wounded *amour propre* and mortified vanity, the recent debates prove that she acted from much deeper and more rational motives than vanity or *amour propre*, and that she has laid down to herself during the last fifty years a systematic plan of aggrandizement in the Levant, to the intended detriment of England. It is the being baffled in this scheme when close upon its accomplishment that excited the fury which has lately burst forth; and the fury was the more intense and ungovernable because they who felt it would not in decency avow its real cause and were obliged to charge it upon feelings of which any man out of his teens must necessarily be ashamed.'[32]

Palmerston's suspicions were anachronistic. After the Seven Years' War there had certainly been a powerful section of French opinion which had wished to colonize Egypt in recompense for lost French colonies elsewhere, and to use a French position in Egypt to harass the British in India. During the Napoleonic wars the French invaded Egypt with the principal object of embarrassing the British in India, and the possibility of a French reoccupation of Egypt was never entirely lost sight of until 1815. Thereafter, the French policy of building up a strong position in Egypt was not specifically directed against the British. It was due partly to a determination to restore France's old trading preeminence in the Levant, partly in order to stake out a French claim in the event of a dissolution of the Ottoman Empire, and partly to secure a friendly eastern flank for French expansionist designs in North Africa. But the tradition of Anglo-French rivalry in the Levant, created immediately before and during the Napoleonic wars, was nourished afterwards by the suspicions of statesmen on both sides of the Channel and, still more perhaps, by the mutual suspicions of British and French Consuls and merchants on the spot. These suspicions did much to determine the course of British and French policies in the Levant for the next 150 years.

In the 1838-41 crisis, Palmerston, exploiting French suspicions of Russia, Russian suspicions of France, and Austrian suspicions of anything that looked remotely like revolution or upsetting the *status quo*, succeeded in his two main objects of replacing the Russian protectorate over the Ottoman Empire by a protectorate of the five Great Powers, and of inflicting a decisive check on the growth of French influence in the Levant. He was able to do this, because the French over-estimated Mohamed Ali's ability to maintain himself in Syria without their armed assistance, and because British naval supremacy prevented the French from supplying that armed assistance without risking a European war, in which France would have been the loser. Mohamed Ali lost Syria, and all his possessions outside Egypt, because he could not hold them against the Porte and the four Powers without that armed assistance which the French were unable, or unwilling, to give. He retained

291

Egypt because he could have held it against the Porte, who would not have persuaded the four Powers to provide the armed assistance necessary to turn him out of it.

As soon as his objects had been achieved, Palmerston was at pains both to prevent the Porte from over-exploiting the ascendancy which he had enabled them to achieve over Mohamed Ali, and to welcome France back to the Concert of Europe, where their influence was a useful counterpoise to Russia. His acceptance of the Napier Convention, and his subsequent calling of Ponsonby to heel, enabled him to emerge from the crisis as the apparent saviour, not only of the Ottoman Empire, but of Mohamed Ali as well, while France appeared to have encouraged rebellion against the one and betrayed the trust reposed in her by the other.

CHAPTER ELEVEN

A RETROSPECT

During the eighty years covered by this book the countries of
the Levant emerged from the cocoon in which Ottoman rule
and Moslem fanaticism had enshrouded them for nearly three
centuries, straight into the mainstream of European history. This emergence was initially precipitated by Bonaparte's invasion of Egypt in 1798 and proceeded thereafter
under the impulse of the European rivalries set in train by that
invasion. It was accompanied both by a continual increase in
European political interference and by a transformation in
trading relations between Europe and the Levant. The British
Embassy at Constantinople which, at the end of the eighteenth
century, existed mainly for the convenience of the Levant
Company, became one of the most important diplomatic posts
under the Foreign Office. Foreign Consuls and merchants, who
previously had lived under ghetto-like conditions, subject to
the whims and exigencies of local potentates, blossomed forth
into local potentates themselves, protected by the guns of
European warships, and lording it over those who had previously lorded it over them.

This simultaneous process of enlightenment and subordination had its origin, as the course of this narrative makes clear,
in the British acquisition of her Indian possessions in 1763. For
this acquisition, and the Directory's desire to threaten it, was
the principal reason for Bonaparte's invasion of Egypt in 1798.
This invasion was the first move in a long and complicated
struggle, not yet played out, between the numerous heirs and
neighbours of the vast Ottoman estate which, by the end of the
eighteenth century, seemed already ripe for dismemberment.
The Russians were nibbling at its northern marches, on the
Danube, the Black Sea and the Caucasus. The Hapsburgs were

casting covetous eyes on its Adriatic coastline. The various Christian peoples of the Balkan Peninsula were in an endemic state of revolt or near-revolt, preparing themselves for independence. In the Arabian Peninsula, in the Lebanon, in Egypt, and all along the coast of North Africa, local potentates ruled with little more than nominal acknowledgement of Ottoman suzerainty. The French, expelled militarily from Egypt by the British, but intent on staking what they regarded as their traditional claim in the event of the dismemberment of the Ottoman estate, concentrated on developing their religious contacts with the Uniate Christians of the Lebanon and on improving the cultural contacts established in Egypt during their short occupation of the country.

The British interest was, at first, more indirect. Their statesmen saw the Ottoman estate primarily as a vast landed property interposed between the homeland and the British dominions in India. They were concerned lest the dismemberment of the estate might lead to the interposition of some unfriendly European rival. And so their policy concentrated on the preservation of the estate in the hands of its existing owners. Their expulsion of the French from Egypt was motivated, not by any desire to replace French by British influence there, but by a determination, in the short term, to keep the Ottoman Empire from falling under the influence of the French enemy, and, in the long term, to keep the Ottoman estate intact.

The course of the Napoleonic wars, which involved the establishment of a predominant British naval presence in the Mediterranean, encouraged the growth of new British trading interests in Egypt and in the Levant generally. Given a head-start during the war as a result of British naval predominance, these trading interests became firmly established, in Egypt particularly, during the 1820s. Flourishing as they did under Mohamed Ali's modernizing regime, exporting Egyptian cotton, importing British manufactures, and financing Mohamed Ali's monopolies, these trading interests were frequently at odds with the official British policy of subordinating Mohamed Ali to his Ottoman suzerain.

This official British policy of preserving the sovereign independence and territorial integrity of the Ottoman Empire was assisted by the climate of political opinion prevailing in Europe immediately after the Napoleonic wars. It was exemplified by the Holy Alliance, and characterized by Metternich's determination to preserve from any nationalist or revolutionary upsets the *status quo* restored at Vienna after the upheavals of the Napoleonic years. The preservation of this precarious balance depended, *inter alia*, on the observance by the Powers of a self-denying ordinance in respect of the Ottoman estate.

But the pressures operating in favour of dismemberment were tremendous. Five years after the Congress of Vienna the Greek War of Independence broke out. Long before it was over, Mohamed Ali in Egypt had become more powerful than, and openly ambitious to overthrow, his nominal suzerain. The Ottoman Sultan and Sublime Porte were unable, of their own motion, to withstand these pressures. Gradually, unwillingly, but inevitably, they were forced to watch the affairs of the Empire passing into the hands of the Concert of European Powers, who were torn between a common desire to keep the Ottoman estate intact and a determination, on the part of each member of the Concert, to grab for themselves a share of that estate in the likely event of the pressures in favour of dismemberment proving to be uncontrollable. This determination naturally led to an increase in the weight of these pressures.

It is of the essence of Palmerston's achievement (for it was mainly Palmerston's work) that he succeeded in controlling these pressures by means of neutralizing them and so, against all the odds, in achieving his object of keeping the Ottoman estate intact. He invoked the support of France in keeping Russia out of Constantinople, and that of Russia, against France, in driving Mohamed Ali out of Syria. He invoked the support of both in arriving at a settlement of the Greek War of Independence. And above all, he achieved his object without precipitating a European war, and with a minimum expenditure of blood and treasure.

But he incurred one imponderable item of expenditure with which all his successors have had to reckon—the undying suspicion of France towards every manifestation of British policy in the Levant, which, on the principle of 'guilt by association', infected French views of British policy almost everywhere else. This suspicion was, naturally, reciprocated. The British occupation of Egypt in 1882 was seen by the French not as a defensive measure for safeguarding British communications with India, but as the logical conclusion of the policy, inaugurated by Palmerston, of replacing French by British influence in Egypt. And the French sponsorship of the Suez

Canal was seen in England, not as an imaginative piece of French commercial enterprise, but as a deliberate French plot to establish French predominance in Egypt with a view to threatening the British possessions in India.

Eighty years later, after events in Europe had forced the two countries into an alliance *de convenance*, and after the long-delayed dissolution of the Ottoman Empire had been precipitated by the 1914-18 war, British support for the claims of Arab nationalism on the one hand and of Zionism on the other was almost universally regarded in France as yet another perfidious move in the century-old British policy of ousting the French from the Levant. And, during and after the second world war, the process of French extrusion from Syria and Lebanon was attributed by the French, not to the ineluctable pressure of the nationalist *Zeitgeist*, which was soon to drive the British as well from the countries of the Middle East, but to the machinations of their British allies.

It is, no doubt, easy to exaggerate the extent to which this corrosive suspicion of each other's intentions in the Levant has affected the cordiality and, consequently, the effectiveness of the Entente Cordiale. On this the reader must form his own judgement. This book has attempted to relate the origins of this suspicion.

NOTES

CHAPTER ONE

1. James Bruce, *Travels to Discover the Sources of the Nile*, Vol. I p. 8.
2. For full text of treaty see Hurewitz, *Diplomacy in the Near and Middle East*, Vol. I p. 1 et seq.
3. ibid. p. 5.
4. For full text see ibid. pp. 5–7.
5. For full text see ibid. p. 25 et seq.
6. F. Charles-Roux, *L'Angleterre, L'Isthme de Suez et L'Egypte au 18me. Siècle*, p. 17.
7. FO 78/11.
8. Bruce, op. cit. Vol. I p. 26.
9. ibid. p. 30.
10. ibid. p. 36.
11. Bruce, op. cit. Vol. IV pp. 625–32.
12. ibid. pp. 635–37.
13. ibid. p. 633.
14. ibid. pp. 638–44.
15. Tur was a port on the eastern, or Sinai, shore of the Gulf of Suez and was sometimes accessible at seasons of the year when Suez was virtually closed to northbound ships owing to contrary winds.
16. The Ambassador, Murray, was at this time about to be replaced by Sir Robert Ainslie. He seems to have taken this protest with him on his recall, intending to deliver it in London, but he died at Vienna en route.
17. 22.1.77. FO SP Turkey 53.
18. 4.3.77. ibid.
19. Arabic 'afrangi'. A generic term denoting all European Christians.
20. 14.3.77. FO SP Turkey 53.
21. 18.3.77. ibid.
22. The Ottoman warning about the dangers of navigation in the north part of the Red Sea was not without substance. The Arabian coast, which it was usually necessary to hug owing to contrary winds, was full of uncharted reefs. It was unfriendly in more senses than one, the alternatives before shipwrecked sailors often lying between death by thirst or starvation and murder at the hands of Arab bandits. Native pilots were difficult to obtain owing to the opposition of the Sherif of Mecca. In 1776 a British merchant ship, *Aurora*, had been wrecked on the Arabian coast near Yenbo. In 1777 another British merchantman, *Adventure*, was forced by bad weather into the harbour of Yenbo and there seized and detained by the local ruler. There were numerous sailings of Arab dhows up and down the Red Sea between Suez, Jidda and Mocha, and some adventurous travellers to and from India used to sail by this means.
23. 25.5.77. FO SP Turkey 53.
24. 11.7.77. ibid.
25. 17.9.77. ibid.
26. 3.12.77. ibid.
27. 17.12.77. ibid.
28. 3.1.78. FO SP Turkey 54.
29. 21.1.78. ibid.
30. 21.2.78. ibid.

31. 29.4.78. ibid.
32. 20.6.78. ibid.
33. 3.8.78. ibid.
34. 1.11.78. ibid.
35. 4.1.79. ibid.
36. Ainslie – Weymouth 17.12.78. ibid.
37. ibid.
38. 25.2.79. ibid.
39. 8.3.79. ibid.
40. Baldwin – Ainslie 5.8.79. ibid.
41. Brandi – Ainslie 5.8.79. ibid.
42. 30.9.79. ibid.
43. 31.8.79. ibid.
44. Ainslie – Weymouth 17.11.79. ibid.
45. 7.12.79. ibid.
46. See FO 78/1.
47. See FO 78/1.
48. Baldwin – Hillsboro' 3.3.80. FO 78/1.
49. Ainslie – Hillsboro' 3.3.80. ibid.
50. ibid. 12.4.82. FO 78/3.
51. See FO 78/1.
52. Ainslie – Fox 27.6.82. FO 78/3
53. There is in the British archives a letter from an unnamed British trader in Aleppo forwarded to Ainslie by Lee, pro-Consul in Smyrna—Lee – Ainslie 31.12.82. FO 78/4—which discusses arrangements being made in Egypt by Cassis and Rosetti to revive the India trade via Suez. Commenting to Ainslie on this letter, Lee wrote: 'It would seem that too many obstacles are present to put into execution again with safety the trade via Suez, but, as the Customs Master and Rosetti possess unbridled ambition and desperate cunning, it is much to be presumed that they aim at no less than a revival of the India trade by themselves and their party by way of Trieste. A very capital house of business is setting up at Trieste for the purpose of carrying on this trade, and several vessels sailed from that port under Imperial colours for the East Indies and may probably come with cargoes to Suez. . . . The influence of the Porte is so very feeble in Egypt that, with or without their commands, Rosetti and the Customs Master might carry their scheme into execution except the Beys could be so indisposed against them as to endanger their safety and make them fly the country, which perhaps would be the only effectual way of nipping in the bud their grand plan, the success thereof would be highly prejudicial to the interests of England and of the East India Company in particular. The tyranny of the Customs Master occasions his having many enemies in Egypt, so that, by dint of paying money, his and Rosetti's overthrow might be effected. If it could be done for £20,000 the purchase might be esteemed very cheap for the East India Company, which will suffer immensely by the success of Rosetti's plan.' It was probably a coincidence that, within a few months, the Customs Master had fled from Egypt.
54. Ainslie – Carmarthen 10.3.85. FO 78/6.
55. ibid.
56. For text of this Note see *Political Recollections Relative to Egypt* by George Baldwin. London 1801.
57. India Board – Foreign Office 23.4.85. FO 78/6.
58. Carmarthen – Ainslie 19.5.85. ibid.
59. Ainslie – Carmarthen 16.8.85. ibid.
60. India Board – Foreign Office 8.8.85. ibid.
61. Ainslie – Carmarthen 24.9.85. ibid.
62. ibid. 12.10.85. ibid.
63. ibid. 18.10.85. ibid.
64. ibid. 25.11.85. ibid.
65. ibid. 25.1.86. FO 78/7.
66. India Board – Foreign Office 19.5.86. FO 24/1.

67. Carmarthen – Baldwin 20.6.86. FO 24/1.
68. Carmarthen – Ainslie 1.9.86. FO 78/7.
69. Ainslie – Carmarthen 8.3.86. ibid.
70. ibid. 25.4.86. ibid.
71. ibid. 9.9.86. ibid.
72. ibid. 6.10.86. ibid.
73. ibid. 25.10.86. ibid.
74. 5.10.86. ibid.
75. Baldwin – Carmarthen 11.4.87. FO 24/1.
76. Ainslie – Carmarthen 10.7.87. FO 78/8.
77. Baldwin – Carmarthen 4.4.88. FO 24/1.
78. Grenville – Baldwin 8.2.93. FO 24/1. It seems that the curtness of Grenville's note may have been due to the fact that Baldwin, in defiance of the instructions given to him on his appointment, had engaged in trade. In a despatch to Grenville in 1792 he admitted that he was financially interested in a cargo of potash from Wadi Natrun which had just sailed from Alexandria for England, and had the impudence to request that it might be imported into England duty-free. After his dismissal from the Consulate he still remained Agent for the East India Company.
79. Baldwin – Grenville 20.5.94. FO 24/1.
80. ibid. 10.10.94. ibid.
81. FO 78/15 February 1794.
82. Extract from letter Baldwin – Liston in Liston – Grenville 11.6.94. FO 78/15.
83. Liston – Grenville 24.1.95. FO 78/16.
84. ibid. 16.6.95. ibid.
85. Baldwin – Grenville 29.3.96. WO 1/344.
86. England, at this time, due to increase of population and the demands of war, was short of corn. Baldwin's idea of obtaining corn from Egypt was adopted some years later.
87. Baldwin – Governor of Bengal 15.5.96. WO 1/344.
88. Baldwin – Dundas 23.4.98. WO 1/344. Baldwin settled down to retirement in Italy, but returned briefly to Egypt three years later when, at Admiral Keith's invitation, he accepted a post as Political Adviser to the expeditionary force under Abercromby. He returned to London soon after the landing at Abuqir and in 1801 published his *Political Recollections Relative to Egypt*. He then went to Naples where he lived in retirement until 1810, when he reappeared in London with a letter from the Queen of Naples to King George III. He then proceeded to bombard the British government with demands for payment of his Consular emoluments for the years 1793–96 and for compensation for losses incurred as a result of having to leave Egypt in 1798. It appears from the correspondence (see FO 24/3 & 24/4) that, having refused a pension of £300 p.a. for life in full settlement of his claims in 1802, he had, in 1803, accepted a payment of £7,000 'in full settlement of all claims in respect of salary as Consul-General and interest thereon'. This did not satisfy him and, after some years of fruitless correspondence, he published, in November 1812, a forty-five-page Journal of Proceedings regarding his claim. He was by that time seventy years old. Presumably as a result of his importunity he was awarded a pension of £400 p.a. for life starting from January 1813. He then petitioned for the backdating of this pension to 1796 (see FO 24/6). On 10 June 1818 he was informed by Castlereagh, the Foreign Secretary, that his claim had been referred to the Treasury (see FO 78/91). There the record ends.

CHAPTER TWO

1. See F. Charles-Roux op. cit. p. 348.
2. F. Charles-Roux, *Les Origines de l'Expedition de l'Egypte*, p. 327.
3. ibid. p. 333.

4. Shafiq Ghorbal, *The Beginnings of the Egyptian Question and the Rise of Mohamed Ali*, p. 31.
5. F. Charles-Roux, 'L'Angleterre etc.' op. cit. pp. 362–63.
6. As an indication of the lack of liaison between the Admiralty and the Foreign Office, Nelson was under the impression that there was a British Consul at Alexandria and sent an officer on shore to try to get some information from him.
7. See undated copy of Talleyrand – Ruffin in FO 78/21.
8. Note from Reis Effendi to British Chargé d'Affaires 11.9.98. FO 78/20.
9. Spencer Smith – Grenville 23.7.98 & 25.7.98. FO 78/19.
10. ibid. 1.8.98. ibid.
11. ibid. 14.8.98. ibid.
12. Spencer Smith – Grenville 3.9.98. FO 78/20. Detention in the Castle of the Seven Towers was at this time the usual fate of foreign diplomatic representatives to the Porte when war broke out between Turkey and the country they were representing. They were held as hostages against the safe return of the Turkish diplomatic representatives from the hostile capital.
13. Grenville – Spencer Smith 14.9.98. FO 78/20.
14. ibid. 3.10.98. ibid.
15. ibid. 1.10.98. ibid.
16. Spencer Smith – Grenville 30.12.98. FO 78/20.
17. In the event the treaty was abrogated in November 1806, a few months before it was due to expire.
18. A few weeks later a joint Russo-Turkish squadron sailed for Corfu, captured it and secured the French evacuation of all the Ionian Islands.
19. Sidney Smith – Admiral Blankett 30.5.99. WO 1/344.
20. As well as *Tigre* he had one or two frigates and, for part of the time, *Theseus*, which Nelson had detached from the blockade of Egypt.
21. Sidney Smith – Admiral Blankett 30.5.99. WO 1/344.
22. Christopher Herold, *Bonaparte in Egypt*, p. 323.
23. Sidney Smith – Spencer Smith 20.10.99. FO 78/22. *Theseus* which, after the siege of Acre, had joined with *Tigre* in the blockade of Egypt, was slower than *Tigre*.
24. Sidney Smith – Nelson 8.11.99. FO 78/23.
25. Dropmore Papers. Cmd. 2811 of 1906, Vol. V. Spencer – Grenville 9.5.99.
26. Spencer Smith – Grenville 12.11.99. FO 78/22.
27. Elgin – Dundas 11.11.99. WO 1/344.
28. Elgin – Mornington undated ibid.
29. Elgin – Grenville 8.12.99. FO 78/24.
30. There is some obscurity about this Turkish plot and the extent, if any, of British connivance in it. When first reporting it to Grenville on 8.12.99, Elgin wrote that 'no inducement shall make me subscribe to it', but added that it appeared to have been approved by Tamara. On 10 December, again referring to the plot, he told Grenville: 'I should never consent to use HM's authority for a transaction of this kind, but the utmost danger would have attended by dissuading him [i.e. the Reis Effendi] from it, whereas its execution must in its consequences be most beneficial and, if ever such a reprisal can be justified, the French in their conduct towards Turkey have brought it on themselves. In writing to Sir Sidney Smith I have mentioned that the Grand Vizier will communicate with him about a strategem of war which the Turks have in view for rescuing Egypt from the domination of the French.' On 22 December, telling Sidney Smith about sending Morier to the Grand Vizier's camp as his representative, Elgin wrote: 'Mr Morier will explain to you the notion which the Reis Effendi held out; while on the one hand the effects of such a plan are obvious, on the other hand it can only be done with you in the background. As to the plan itself, the invasion of Egypt having been effected without provocation, pretext or warning, and France declaring she is not at war with Turkey, the Porte is at liberty to treat the raiders as banditti.' It is apparent from these despatches that Elgin had (a) left the Reis Effendi with the impression that he had no objection to the Turks carrying out their plan provided that the British were not involved, and (b) in effect instructed Sidney Smith not to interfere. Gren-

ville's reaction was unequivocal. On 18 February 1800 he instructed Elgin 'to express in the strongest terms HM's abhorrence and his resolution to proceed to any extremity rather than suffer such an act to be committed', and expressed regret that Elgin had not dissociated himself from it more clearly when the Reis Effendi had first mentioned it. There is no record of Sidney Smith's reaction, although it may be assumed that he disapproved. It may also probably be assumed that he would have warned Kléber had there been any serious possibility of implementing the plot. In a despatch to Elgin dated 7.4.00. (he was then off Alexandria in *Tigre*) he refers to the theft of Morier's papers, while Morier was on a mission to Egypt, and the failure of attempts to recover them. It seems possible that these papers contained some reference to the Turkish plot, that they fell into French hands, and that this was the real reason for Kléber's resumption of hostilities on 20 March. See also Ghorbal op. cit. App. I. pp. 295–96.

31. Elgin – Grenville 17.11.99. FO 78/24. In fact Sir Sidney was not acting as British representative; he was acting on behalf of the Grand Vizier in negotiations to which Great Britain was not a party.
32. Grenville – Elgin 10.12.99. FO 78/24.
33. ibid. 22.12.99. ibid.
34. Desaix was a General who had commanded a French column in Upper Egypt; Poussielgue was the French Director Finances in Egypt.
35. Sidney Smith – Nelson 31.1.00. FO 78/23.
36. Elgin – Sidney Smith 17.12.99. FO 78/24.
37. ibid. 22.12.99. ibid.
38. Barrow, *Life of Sir Sidney Smith*, Vol. I. pp. 384–85.
39. Elgin – Morier undated FO 78/24.
40. Elgin – Grenville 18.2.00. ibid.
41. Elgin – Nelson ibid.
42. Elgin – Grenville 6.3.00 ibid.
43. ibid. 10.3.00 ibid.
44. Grenville – Elgin 28.3.00 ibid.
45. See, *inter alia*, Kléber – Sidney Smith and Grand Vizier – Sidney Smith 30.3.00. FO 78/23.
46. Herold op. cit. p. 356.

CHAPTER THREE

1. Dundas – Abercromby 31.7.00. WO 1/345.
2. ibid. 6.10.00. ibid.
3. Abercromby – Dundas 15.1.01. WO 1/345.
4. ibid. 21.1.01. ibid.
5. ibid. 16.2.01. ibid.
6. ibid. 16.3.01 & 19.3.01. ibid.
7. Hutchinson – Dundas 3.4.01. ibid.
8. ibid.
9. ibid.
10. ibid.
11. ibid.
12. Dundas – Hutchinson 19.5.01. ibid.
13. Hutchinson – Hobart 2.6.01. ibid. The Pitt government had just fallen, and Addington was Prime Minister, with Lord Hawkesbury as Foreign Secretary and Lord Hobart as Secretary of State for War.
14. ibid.
15. ibid.

16. See WO 1/346. Hutchinson was raised to the peerage as a result of his victorious campaign.
17. Hutchinson – Hobart 2.6.01. WO 1/345.
18. The breach was repaired and the canal restored by British engineers after the French capitulation—see Hutchinson – Hobart 22.7.01. WO 1/345.
19. ibid. 26.6.01. ibid.
20. ibid. 5.9.01. ibid.
21. ibid. 5.9.01. ibid.
22. See Lieutenant-Colonel Anstruther's note in WO 1/346.
23. Hobart – Hutchinson 22.7.01 & 18.9.01. WO 1/345.
24. Elgin – Hawkesbury 12.6.01. FO 78/33.
25. Hobart – Hutchinson 12.10.01. WO 1/345.
26. Hutchinson – Hobart 21.9.01. ibid.
27. ibid. 16.8.01. ibid.
28. ibid 24.12.01. ibid.
29. The Porte wished to be assured that the Ionian Islands would be granted their independence and not occupied by either Russia or France.
30. Hawkesbury – Elgin 3.10.01. FO 78/33.
31. Elgin – Hawkesbury 1.12.01. ibid.
32. Elgin – Straton 12.12.01. ibid.
33. Sebastiani was in Constantinople at the time and taking full advantage of the situation to rub this into the Turks. See Elgin – Hawkesbury 5.1.02. FO 78/35.
34. Elgin does not appear to have had any authority for making this offer, which he suggested to HMG on the day he authorized Straton to make it. See Elgin – Hawkesbury 12.12.01. FO 78/33.
35. Straton – Elgin 20.1.02. FO 78/36.
36. See FO 78/35.
37. Hawkesbury – Elgin 29.1.02. FO 78/35.
38. In WO 1/346.
39. Ibrahim and Bardissy – Stuart 25.12.01. WO 1/346.
40. Hawkesbury – Elgin 10.5.02. FO 78/36.
41. Hobart – Stuart 10.5.02. WO 1/346.
42. Stuart – Hobart 31.7.02. ibid.
43. ibid. 28.8.02. ibid.
44. ibid. 18.10.02. ibid.
45. Instructions to Colonel Sebastiani. Correspondence de Napoleon, No. 6308 of 5.9.02, quoted on pp. 6–7 of G. Douin, *L'Egypte 1802 à 1804*.
46. AE Turquie folio 495 et seq. quoted in Douin op. cit. pp. 11–26.
47. Stuart – Hobart 21.11.02. WO 1/346.
48. ibid. 24.11.02. ibid.
49. Hobart – Stuart 26.11.02. ibid.
50. Stuart – Hobart 28.2.03. ibid.
51. Up to the time of the French invasion European vessels had been restricted to the new, or eastern, port. See Chapter One.
52. Stuart – Hobart 28.2.03. ibid.
53. ibid. 9.3.03. ibid.
54. Stuart – Missett and Stuart – Hayes 8.3.03. ibid.

CHAPTER FOUR

1. From about this time the Turkish Pasha, or Governor, of Egypt is usually referred to in British and French correspondence as Viceroy and this title will normally be used in this account.
2. Hayes – Hobart 20.5.03. WO 1/346.
3. On the evidence of the French archives this suspicion appears to have been quite unfounded and more or less unreciprocated. Mathieu de Lesseps was the father of Ferdinand, of Suez Canal fame.

4. Corres. Consulaire Egypt 26, 21.3.03. quoted in Douin op. cit. pp. 40–2.
5. Lesseps – Talleyrand 20.6.03. quoted in Douin op. cit. oo. 53–4.
6. Hawkesbury – Drummond 18.10.03. FO 78/40.
7. See BM Add. MSS 37268.
8. Drummond – Hawkesbury 20.12.03. FO 78/40.
9. See Miscellaneous Papers at the end of WO 1/346.
10. Missett – Hobart 8.7.03. WO 1/346.
11. ibid. 20.12.03. ibid.
12. ibid. 12.2.04. ibid.
13. Hobart – Missett 7.2.04. ibid.
14. Hawkesbury – Lock 30.1.04. FO 24/2.
15. Lock – Hawkesbury 31.5.04. ibid.
16. Straton – Harrowby 24.7.04. FO 78/43.
17. Lock – Harrowby 6.8.04. FO 24/2.
18. Este – Harrowby 14.9.04. ibid.
19. Hobart – Missett 7.2.04. ibid.
20. See letters in FO 24/2.
21. Arbuthnot – Missett 5.6.06. FO 78/50.
22. Missett – Hobart 26.4.04. FO 24/2.
23. Later in the century a legend, almost certainly propagated by Ferdinand de Lesseps, grew up to the effect that Mathieu de Lesseps had been instrumental in assisting Mohamed Ali to power. This legend is completely refuted by a reading of Mathieu's despatches. He seems to have been a rather ineffective diplomat, who spent much of his time in Egypt petitioning for a transfer. He had no influence whatever on the course of events and neither worked in Mohamed Ali's interests nor recognized his potentialities. His personal contacts with Mohamed Ali appear to have been minimal and confined to representations about the security of French subjects in Cairo.
24. Missett – Hobart 28.5.04. FO 24/2.
25. ibid. 29.7.04. ibid.
26. ibid. 3.9.04. ibid.
27. Arbuthnot – Fox 5.5.06. FO 78/50.
28. ibid. 6.6.06. ibid.
29. See copy of letter dated 6.7.06 enclosed with Missett – Windham 14.8.06. WO 1/346.
30. Missett – Arbuthnot 29.9.06 ibid.
31. Merry – Hawkesbury 8.9.02 FO 27/64.
32. Ghorbal op. cit. p. 206.
33. Arbuthnot – Fox 16.8.06. FO 78/51.
34. ibid. 22.8.06. ibid.
35. Arbuthnot – Howick 26.12.06. FO 78/52.
36. Arbuthnot – Fox 29.9.06. FO 78/51.
37. Howick – Arbuthnot 11.11.06. FO 78/52.
38. ibid. 20.11.06. ibid.
39. Howick – Admiralty 21.11.06. ibid.
40. Arbuthnot – Howick 3.2.07. FO 78/55.
41. Ghorbal op. cit. p. 245.
42. Duckworth – Fox 9.2.07. WO 1/303.
43. Arbuthnot – Howick 14.2.07. FO 78/55.
44. Ghorbal op. cit. p. 247.
45. Fraser – Windham 25.3.07. WO 1/348.
46. ibid. 27.3.07. ibid.
47. Drovetti had come out to Egypt as assistant in Alexandria to Lesseps in 1803 and had stayed on as Consul-General after Lesseps's departure in November 1804. His instructions, drafted by Napoleon himself, were to recognize whatever authority should eventually be established in the country and on no account to leave, whatever disturbances there might be. See Napoleon I. Correspondence. Vol. XI. No. 8976. Napoleon – Hauterive 13.7.05.
48. See E. Driault, *Mehemet Ali et Napoleon*, pp. 65–6.
49. Fraser – Missett 21.4.07. WO 1/348.

50. Missett – Windham 26.4.07. ibid.
51. Missett – Fraser 22.4.07. ibid.
52. Fraser – Windham 1.5.07. ibid.
53. Castlereagh – Fox 14.6.07. BM. Add. MSS 37050 f. 178.
54. In March 1807 the Ministry of All the Talents, as it was known, in which C. J. Fox was Foreign Secretary, fell, and was replaced by a Ministry in which Lord Liverpool was Prime Minister, Canning Foreign Secretary, and Castlereagh Secretary of State for War.
55. See WO 1/348. It is pleasant to record that Fraser sent a letter of thanks to Drovetti.
56. Fraser – Windham 8.5.07. ibid. One difficulty about the exchange of prisoners was that several of the British prisoners had been 'taken away by private individuals and, according to the custom of the country, made slaves'. Fraser cited one case in which he had to ransom an Ensign for 4,000 Turkish piastres, the equivalent of £222 sterling. See Fraser – Fox 14.5.07. ibid.
57. Missett – Castlereagh 18.5.07. ibid.
58. Fraser – Castlereagh 9.9.07. ibid. It was some time before all the British prisoners were traced and released. Small batches of them continued to be repatriated throughout 1808 with the assistance of M. Petrucci, the Swedish Consul. British warships arrived at Alexandria from time to time to collect them.
59. Missett – Castlereagh 21.10.07. ibid.

CHAPTER FIVE

1. Canning – Adair 26.6.08. FO 78/60.
2. For text see Adair, *Negotiations for the Peace of the Dardanelles*, Vol. I. pp. 122–23.
3. FO 24/3.
4. ibid. It is apparent from contemporary French Consular correspondence that this was not so. Drovetti was complaining about Mohamed Ali's subservience to the British.
5. An ardeb is about 5½ bushels.
6. Briggs – Wellesley 30.5.10. FO 24/3.
7. He retained his interest in Egypt and became the senior partner in the firm of Briggs & Thurburn, for many years the most important British house in Egypt. He acted as Mohamed Ali's agent in London both in commercial and in many political matters.
8. Waldegrave – C-in-C Mediterranean 24.1.11. FO 24/4. The Viceroy was making similar approaches to the French through Drovetti, having had an interview with him in the same sense in the summer of 1810. See Drovetti – Ministre 5.6.10. Corres. Consulaire Egypte. 26.
9. Missett – Liverpool 14.7.11. WO 1/349. Shahin Bey had been pleading for British assistance almost up to the end. See his letter, dated August 1809, to C-in-C Mediterranean quoted in Driault, *Mehemet Ali et Napoleon*, p. 43. Although Drovetti suspected that the British were in touch with Shahin, this does not seem to have been so. Drovetti also suspected, wrongly, that the British were encouraging Mohamed Ali to declare his independence. See Driault op. cit. p. 57.
10. Waldegrave reported that the Viceroy had caught Drovetti corresponding with them; this may have been a part of the almost pathological British suspicion of French activities in Egypt, which was reciprocated by a corresponding French suspicion of British activities.
11. Missett – FO 4.7.11. FO 24/4. When he returned to Egypt on his second mission Missett was a cripple in a wheel-chair. See Driault op. cit. pp. 132–3. He was responsible to the FO as Consul-General and to the WO as Resident and corresponded with both until his retirement in 1816. Then the post of Resident was abolished and his successor, Henry Salt, was Consul-General only, reporting to the FO.

12. See Missett – Castlereagh 18.5.07. WO 1/348.
13. Missett – FO 20.6.12. FO 24/4.
14. Bathurst – Missett 3.9.12. ibid.
15. Sabry, *L'Empire Egyptien sous Mohamed Ali*, pp. 36-7, quoting Archives de la Citadelle du Caire.
16. Governor of Bombay – Bruce 26.9.21. FO 78/112.
17. Salt – FO 30.6.20. FO 78/96.
18. ibid. 28.4.17. FO 78/89.
19. FO 24/6 June 1815.
20. Salt – Canning 5.5.25. FO 78/135.
21. Salt – FO 25.5.25. ibid.
22. ibid. 17.9.24. FO 78/126.
23. Missett – Liverpool 20.5.12. WO 1/349. It is sadly characteristic of many British export efforts that it took innumerable reminders from Missett, and about three years' delay, before the engine finally arrived. And, when it did arrive, it didn't work. See Missett – Bathurst 15.8.15. ibid.
24. This corvette, on its way back to Alexandria, was, as some kind of *amende honorable*, coppered and refitted free of charge at the Admiralty shipyard at Deptford. It was in return for this service that the obelisk now known as Cleopatra's Needle was presented to HMG by Mohamed Ali. It was not transported to England and set up on the Embankment until 1877.
25. FO – Salt 21.1.22. FO 78/112.
26. The break in Drovetti's career was owing to his Bonapartist sympathies. He continued to live in Egypt during his temporary retirement, during which time French influence fell to a low ebb, and he was a thorn in the flesh of successive French Consuls-General, who continually protested about his activities. His reinstatement was due to the French government's desire to recover French influence in Egypt.

CHAPTER SIX

1. Salt – FO 3.5.23. FO 78/119.
2. ibid. 4.1.25. FO 78/135.
3. S. Canning – Salt 10.6.26. FO 78/147.
4. Canning – Head of Greek Provisional Government 1.12.24. FO 78/135.
5. Salt – FO 10.10.21. FO 78/103.
6. ibid. 12.9.22. FO 78/112.
7. The island of Candia is now known as Crete. It was referred to as Candia in all contemporary despatches etc. and will be referred to as such in this narrative.
8. Meyer – FO 7.11.24. FO 78/135.
9. Letter from Zante 8.6.25. ibid.
10. For the terms of the Greek appeal, see Driault and Leheritier, *Histoire Diplomatique de la Grèce*, Vol. I. pp. 293-4.
11. Salt – FO 1.11.25. FO 78/135.
12. S. Canning – Salt 10.6.26. FO 78/147.
13. Salt – S. Canning 31.8.26. ibid.
14. ibid. 16.9.26. ibid.
15. For an account of Prokesch-Osten's mission to Egypt, which lasted for about a year, see Sabry op. cit. pp. 119-129.
16. For the full terms of the Treaty of London see Driault and Leheritier op. cit. pp. 365-6.
17. Lane Poole, *Life of Stratford Canning*, Vol. I. p. 449.
18. Salt – S. Canning 21.7.26. FO 78/160.
19. ibid. 12.8.27. ibid.
20. Driault and Leheritier op. cit. pp. 369-70.
21. Salt – Dudley 29.8.27. FO 78/160.
22. Lane Poole op. cit. Vol. I. pp. 395-6.

23. For an account of these conversations see Driault and Leheritier op. cit. pp. 379–80.
24. Lane Poole op. cit. pp. 452–3.
25. Barker – Codrington 28.11.27. FO 78/160.
26. FO – Barker 7.12.27. FO 78/160.
27. Barker – FO 26.12.27. ibid.
28. Barker – S. Canning 19.1.28. FO 78/170.
29. Barker – Adam 21.5.28. ibid.
30. Barker – Dudley 27.5.28. ibid.
31. Lane Poole op. cit. p. 469.
32. ibid. p. 506.

CHAPTER SEVEN

1. Barker – Palmerston 10.4.32. FO 78/213.
2. Barker – Gordon 23.6.29. FO 78/184.
3. Barker – Malcolm 7.7.29. ibid.
4. Barker – Gordon 22.9.29. ibid.
5. ibid. 12.10.29. ibid.
6. ibid. 3.3.30. ibid.
7. ibid. 12.10.29. ibid.
8. Mémoires et Documents. Egypte 19.
9. Douin, *Mohamed Ali et l'Expédition d'Alger*, p. iv.
10. ibid. p. lvii.
11. Sabry op. cit. pp. 174–75.
12. The French government consulted HMG after HMG had heard about it from Constantinople. See Douin op. cit. pp. xl et seq.
13. Aberdeen – 29.1.30. FO 78/192. This despatch, which bears the fussy stigmata of Lord Aberdeen himself, is, in style and content, reminiscent of the Rev. Mr Collins' letters to Mr Bennet.
14. ibid. 3.2.30. ibid.
15. Probably a reference to the Malcolm Treaty concluded at the beginning of the century.
16. Barker – Aberdeen 8.3.30. FO 78/192.
17. ibid. 22.6.30. ibid.
18. Barker – Palmerston 27.5.31. FO 78/202.
19. Barker – Codrington 26.12.27. FO 78/160.
20. Barker – Palmerston 10.8.31. FO 78/202.
21. Barker – Hotham 6.10.31. FO 78/202. Vice-Admiral Sir Henry Hotham had replaced Vice-Admiral Sir Pulteney Malcolm as C-in-C Mediterranean.
22. Syria had previously been divided into three Pashaliks—Aleppo, Damascus and Acre. Now a fourth Pashalik—Tripoli—was carved out of the other three.
23. Barker – Palmerston 4.6.32. FO 78/214.
24. Letter from Acerbi to Metternich in Staats-Archiv Vienna Turkei 1832 quoted by Sabry op. cit. p. 199.
25. For details of this correspondence see Sabry op. cit. pp. 211–15, quoting from Egyptian Archives in Cairo Citadel.
26. Ibrahim – Mohamed Ali 5 Shaaban 1248 AH. Citadel Archives quoted by Sabry op. cit. pp. 218–9.
27. Palmerston – Barker 3.10.32. FO 78/214.
28. 'Mr Barker, in whose person the character of a Political Agent was, in a manner, dropped.' Extract from FO Memo. dated 6.2.33. in FO 78/231.
29. Barker – Palmerston 15.9.32. FO 78/213.
30. ibid. 24.6.32. ibid.
31. Palmerston – Barker 3.10.32. ibid.
32. FO 78/472. Narratives & Extracts.
33. Campbell – Palmerston 5.5.33. FO 78/231.
34. See Sabry op. cit. pp. 206 & 214–5.

35. FO 78/472.
36. Bulwer. *Life of Palmerston*. Vol. II. p. 360.
37. Mimaud – Ministre 29.5.32. Corres. Politique Egypte 2.
38. Ministre – Mimaud 13.9.32. Corres. Politique Egypte 2.
39. Ibrahim – Mohamed Ali 29 Shaaban 1248 AH. Citadel Archives quoted by Sabry op. cit. pp. 224–5.
40. Ibrahim – Mohamed Ali 13 Ramadan 1248 AH. Citadel Archives quoted by Sabry op. cit. pp. 227–8.
41. Mandeville – Barker 23.2.33. FO 78/231.
42. Whether this was due to ignorance of the geography of Syria or to his not having mastered the contents of Roussin's proposal is uncertain. No wonder Palmerston referred to him as 'poor Mandeville' and complained that he had nowhere to send him except Constantinople. See Bulwer op. cit. Vol. II p. 200.
43. Sloane – Mandeville 9.3.33. FO 78/231.
44. FO 78/472.
45. ibid.
46. ibid.
47. ibid.
48. Palmerston – Campbell 4.2.33. FO 78/226.
49. This was nonsense. At least as high a proportion of the Egyptian as of the Turkish fleet had been destroyed at Navarino and, in 1832, the Turkish navy was still slightly superior in ships to that of Mohamed Ali.
50. Palmerston's instructions to Campbell have been quoted at length as being the earliest, and probably the most explicit, statement of the policy which he was to pursue for the next eight years.
51. Campbell – Palmerston 1.4.33. FO 78/227.
52. ibid. 9.4.33. FO 78/472.
53. ibid. 7.5.33. ibid.
54. Mandeville – Campbell 22.4.33. FO 78/231.
55. Campbell – Palmerston 7.5.33. FO 78/472.
56. Ponsonby – Campbell 3.5.33. ibid.
57. Ponsonby – Palmerston 22.5.33. FO 78/223.
58. Palmerston – Campbell 10.5.33. FO 78/226.
59. ibid. 1.6.33. ibid.

CHAPTER EIGHT

1. FO 78/472.
2. Ponsonby – Campbell 3.5.33. FO 78/227.
3. Campbell – Palmerston 25.6.33. ibid.
4. Palmerston – Campbell 2.10.33. FO 78/226.
5. Palmerston – Ponsonby 23.12.33. FO 78/472.
6. Campbell – Palmerston 16.4.33. FO 78/226.
7. Palmerston – Campbell 2.9.33. ibid.
8. Most of these details have been obtained from Sabry op. cit. pp. 274–76. The tribute was paid in 'talaris', or Maria Theresa dollars, which were common currency all over the Ottoman Empire. Payment was made partly in specie, partly by the sale of Egyptian produce, especially rice, at Constantinople, and partly by bills drawn on Alexandria by European merchants on their European correspondents and cashed in Constantinople. Since the value of the talari had increased in terms of piastres from about 5 piastres at the beginning of the century to about 20 piastres in 1833, the burden of the tribute had gradually decreased. See Campbell – Palmerston 13.9.33. FO 78/228.
9. Ponsonby – Campbell 15.7.33. ibid.
10. Palmerston – Campbell 1.11.33. FO 78/226.
11. Palmerston – Campbell 23.11.33. ibid.

12. Palmerston – Ponsonby 23.8.34. FO 78/472.
13. Palmerston – Admiralty 19.9.34. ibid.
14. Ponsonby – Palmerston 15.9.34. ibid. A request from the Sultan for a British squadron at Constantinople would have been a clear repudiation of the Treaty of Unkiar Skelessi. This was what Palmerston and Ponsonby wanted. Ponsonby had had for some months in his possession a despatch from Palmerston, dated 10.3.34, authorizing him, at his discretion, and at the request of the Porte, to order Admiral Rowley to take his ships through the Dardanelles to Constantinople in the event of 'any threatened attack by the Russians'. See Palmerston – Ponsonby 10.3.34. FO 78/234. This discretionary authority was later—in March 1835—cancelled by the Duke of Wellington who, for a few months during that year, headed a Tory government. See Wellington – Ponsonby 5.3.35. FO 78.234.
15. Palmerston – Campbell 1.10.34. FO 78/472.
16. ibid. 1.11.34. ibid.
17. Campbell – Palmerston 18.10.34. ibid.
18. Mohamed Ali – Ibrahim 18 rabi' ath-thani 1250 AH. in Citadel Archives quoted in Sabry op. cit. p. 280.
19. Ibrahim – Mohamed Ali 29 rabi' ath-thani 1250 AH. ibid.
20. Campbell – Palmerston 7.2.35. FO 78/257.
21. ibid. 10.11.35. ibid.
22. ibid. 9.1.37. FO 78/319.
23. ibid. 11.4.37. ibid.
24. ibid. 31.7.36. FO 78/283.
25. ibid. 8.12.34. FO 78/247.
26. Palmerston – Campbell Jan. 1835. FO 78/257.
27. ibid. 2.11.35. ibid.
28. Campbell – Palmerston 1.11.34. FO 78/247.
29. ibid. 18.11.35. FO 78/257.
30. ibid. 22.11.35. ibid.
31. Palmerston – Campbell 5.10.35. FO 78/258.
32. Ponsonby – Campbell 28.12.35. FO 78/282.
33. Palmerston – Campbell 24.2.37. FO 78/318.
34. Palmerston – Campbell 2.3.36. FO 78/281.
35. Campbell – Palmerston 15.7.36 FO 78/282.
36. Palmerston – Campbell 8.12.37. FO 78/318.
37. Campbell had already suggested to Palmerston—see 1.11.37 FO 78/321—that one of the advantages of the British occupation of Aden would be that it would facilitate the diversion of the coffee trade.
38. Palmerston – Campbell 24.5.38. FO 78/342.
39. ibid. 24.11.38. FO 78/343.
40. ibid. 11.5.39. FO 78/372.
41. Campbell – Palmerston 6.4.39. FO 78/373.
42. Palmerston – Campbell 27.6.36. FO 78/281.
43. ibid. 2.7.36. ibid.
44. ibid. 2.11.36. ibid.
45. Campbell – Palmerston 12.6.37. FO 78/319.
46. Cochelet – Ministre 2.5.38. Corres. Politique Egypte 7.
47. Campbell – Palmerston 25.5.38. FO 78/342.
48. Ministre – Cochelet 6.6.38. Corres. Politique Egypte 7.
49. Palmerston – Granville 5.6.38. Bulwer op. cit. Vol. II p. 266.
50. ibid. 8.6.38. ibid. pp. 267–8.
51. ibid. pp. 270–71.
52. ibid. pp. 281–2.
53. Palmerston – Campbell 7.7.38. FO 78/472. Earlier, Campbell had been instructed to warn Mohamed Ali to disabuse himself of any idea that 'the imagined conversations of some unrepresentative British subjects might have given him that HMG would either sanction or acquiesce in his renunciation of his allegiance to the Sultan'. Palmerston – Campbell 9.6.38. FO 78/472.
54. Bulwer op. cit. Vol. II p. 281.

55. FO 78/472.
56. Ponsonby – Palmerston 25.6.38. ibid.
57. Bulwer op. cit. Vol. II pp. 257–8.
58. ibid. pp. 284–5.
59. ibid. p. 288.

CHAPTER NINE

1. FO 78/472.
2. Soult – de Bouquenet (French Chargé d'Affaires in London) 17.6.39. ibid.
3. Palmerston – Admiralty 24.6.39. ibid.
4. Palmerston – Ponsonby 5.7.39. ibid.
5. He was not told what to do if permission were refused and the matter was presumably left to his and Stopford's discretion.
6. Granville – Palmerston 29.6.39. FO 78/472.
7. Bulwer op. cit. Vol. II p. 252.
8. Campbell – Palmerston 17.7.39. FO 78/472.
9. Ponsonby – Palmerston 22.7.39. ibid.
10. Granville – Palmerston 2.8.39. ibid.
11. Bulwer (British Chargé d'Affaires in Paris) – Palmerston 30.8.39. ibid.
12. Palmerston – Beauvale 25.8.39. ibid.
13. Beauvale – Palmerston 8.9.39. ibid.
14. Palmerston – Beauvale 18.9.39. ibid.
15. Clanricarde – Palmerston 22.8.39. ibid.
16. ibid. 27.8.39. ibid.
17. For an account of the conversations between Palmerston and Brunnow, see Palmerston – Clanricarde 25.10.39. ibid.
18. Palmerston – Bulwer 10.9.39. ibid.
19. Bulwer – Palmerston 16.9.39. ibid.
20. Palmerston – Bulwer 23.9.39. ibid.
21. Palmerston – Granville 29.9.39. ibid.
22. Soult – Sebastiani 4.12.39. ibid.
23. Ibrahim – Mohamed Ali 12 gamad ath-thani 1255 AH. (4.9.36) Citadel Archives quoted by Sabry op. cit. pp. 472–3.
24. Palmerston – Hodges 28.11.39. FO 78/472.
25. FO 78/472.
26. Soult – Sebastiani 26.1.40. ibid.
27. F. Charles-Roux, *Thiers et Mehemet Ali*, pp. 47–50.
28. Palmerston – Bulwer 21.7.40. FO 78/472.
29. Hodges – Palmerston 19.6.40. ibid.
30. Ponsonby – Palmerston 23.6.40. ibid. In the event Rear-Admiral Louis, Second-in-Command Mediterranean fleet, told Ponsonby that he could not spare the ships and referred the request to Stopford, then at Malta. Ponsonby – Palmerston 24.6.40. ibid.
31. Bulwer op. cit. Vol. II pp. 356–63.
32. Palmerston – Hodges 18.7.40 FO 78/472.
33. Palmerston – Admiralty 16.7.40. ibid.
34. Ponsonby – Palmerston 9.8.40. ibid.
35. F. Charles-Roux op. cit. pp. 132–36.
36. ibid. pp. 136–41.
37. ibid. p. 145.
38. ibid. p. 151.
39. ibid. p. 152.
40. Palmerston – Admiralty 4.9.40. FO 78/472.
41. Ponsonby – Palmerston 14.9.40. ibid.
42. Bulwer op. cit. Vol. II p. 317.
43. ibid. pp. 320–21.
44. ibid. pp. 324–25.
45. ibid. pp. 327–29.

CHAPTER TEN

1. Napier, *The War in Syria*, Vol. I p. 49.
2. ibid. p. 61. An overland mail service between Baghdad and Beirut had been established in 1836 and was the sole result of the Euphrates Valley expedition under Chesney which has been described.
3. ibid. p. 139.
4. Palmerston – Admiralty 5.10.40. FO 78/472.
5. Napier op. cit. pp. 270–71.
6. ibid. pp. 254–57.
7. ibid. pp. 270–71.
8. ibid. pp. 273–74.
9. ibid. pp. 274–75.
10. ibid. Vol. II pp. 3–4.
11. ibid. p. 7.
12. ibid. p. 11.
13. Palmerston – Admiralty 14.11.40 FO 78/472.
14. ibid. 15.12.40. ibid.
15. Palmerston – Ponsonby 17.12.40. ibid.
16. Ponsonby – Palmerston 10.1.41. ibid.
17. Napier op. cit. Vol. II pp. 218–21.
18. For English text of this Firman see, *inter alia*, Bulwer op. cit. Vol. II App. VIII p. 431.
19. Napier op. cit. Vol. II p. 235.
20. ibid. p. 257.
21. ibid. p. 196.
22. There is a difference of opinion about the exact figures in the reports of the various British officers involved. See ibid p. 183.
23. Most of the Syrian conscripts were, after some delay, repatriated to Syria as a result of negotiations undertaken by Lieutenant-Colonel (not Commodore) Napier. See ibid. pp. 259–66.
24. ibid. p. 247.
25. ibid. pp. 251–53.
26. ibid. p. 255.
27. ibid. p. 256.
28. ibid. pp. 257–58.
29. Sabry op. cit. p. 532 et seq.
30. F. Charles-Roux op. cit. p. 315.
31. For full English text of this Convention see, *inter alia*, Bulwer, op. cit. Vol. II App. IX.
32. Bulwer op. cit. Vol. II p. 366.

SOURCES

I UNPUBLISHED BRITISH STATE PAPERS FROM THE ARCHIVES OF THE PUBLIC RECORD OFFICE

S.P. Turkey. FO 48–58 (1772–79)
Egypt. FO 24/1–6 (1785–1818)
Turkey (1780–1841) and Egypt (1819–1841) FO 78 series
Napoleonic Wars. WO 1 series 344–46 (1798–1803), 347–48 (1803–07), and 349 (1808–15)

II UNPUBLISHED FRENCH STATE PAPERS FROM THE ARCHIVES, QUAI D'ORSAY

Turquie. Correspondence Politique
    „   Correspondence Supplementaire
    „   Memoires et Documents
Le Caire. Correspondence Consulaire
Egypte. Correspondence Politique
    „   Memoires et Documents

III OTHER UNPUBLISHED PAPERS
British Museum—Department of Manuscripts

BM. Add. MS. 35574 (Hardwicke Papers) Correspondence with Sir Robert Ainslie (1776–92)
BM. Add. MSS. 29201 and 29210. (Warren Hastings Papers) Correspondence on Red Sea route
BM. Add. MS. (C. J. Fox Papers) Correspondence on Red Sea route
BM. Add. MSS. 37628 and 37050. Correspondence between Sir Alexander Ball and Mamluk Beys 1801–03
BM. Add. MS. 37050 f. 178. Correspondence between Castlereagh and General Fox reevacuation of Alexandria 1807
BM. Add. MS. 30132 f. 204. Sketch of the Turco-Egyptian Question by Sir Robert Wilson Sep. 1839
BM. Add. MSS. 34080–8. (E. W. Lane Papers) Accounts of Egypt under Mohamed Ali 1805–1828

IV PARLIAMENTARY PAPERS CONCERNING THE LEVANT 1763–1841

Sessions Paper	Date	Volume	Page	Cmd. No.	Subject
172	24.5.30	XXXII (1830)	573	—	Convention of Alexandria 6.8.28
222	7.5.36	L (1836)	635	—	Treaty of Unkiar Skelessi
244	17.8.39	XLVII (1839)	311	549	Copy of Customs tariff agreed between UK and Turkey
248	16.8.38	„	45	155	Papers re French occupation of Algiers in 1830

253	11.2.39	„	289	157	Convention of Commerce and Navigation between HM and Sultan signed 16.8.38
254	23.8.39	„	297	205	Collective Note of Powers to Porte
255	22.8.39	„	299	207	Papers re Arrangement between the Porte and Mohamed Ali in 1833
256	22.8.39	„	313	206	Communications with Mohamed Ali in 1838
263	15.4.40	XCIV (1840)	541	247	Correspondence re monopolies 1839–40
272	21.6.41	XXIX (1841)	1	322	Correspondence re affairs of Levant, Part I (1839)
272A	21.6.41	„	21		Correspondence re affairs of Levant, Part I (1839), continued
272B	21.6.41	„	737	323	Correspondence re affairs of Levant, Part II (1839)
275	26.6.41	XXXI (1841)	119	286	London Convention 15.7.40
283	27.8.41	VIII (2nd series 1841)	1	337	Correspondence re affairs of Levant, Part III
293	3.2.42	XLV (1842)	95	350	Straits Convention signed in London 13.7.41

(For references see 'A Century of Diplomatic Blue Books 1814–1914' edited by Harold Temperley and Lilian Penson. Cass 1966)

V STATE PAPERS RELATING TO LEVANT (From 'British and Foreign State Papers' Vols. 17–30. Edited by Lewis Herslet and published by Messrs. Ridgway & Co.)

Volume	Date	Page	
17	2.8.28	380	Convention between Mohamed Ali and Vice-Admiral Codrington for evacuation of Egyptian troops from Morea
17	1828	371	Correspondence between GB, France and Russia re evacuation of Morea
22	Feb.–May 1833	140	Correspondence re settlement of dispute between Porte and Mohamed Ali
23	24.12.35	1291	Firman re execution in Egypt of Treaty of Commerce between Turkey and GB
26	1838	694	Correspondence re military preparations of Pasha of Egypt

VI OTHER RELEVANT PUBLISHED STATE PAPERS
Dropmore Papers. Vols. IV to XI. Historical Manuscripts Series Commission Napoleon I, Correspondence. Vol. XI

VII PUBLISHED BOOKS
Baldwin, George, *Political Recollections Relative to Egypt*, London 1801
Barrow, J., *The Life and Correspondence of Sir Sidney Smith*, 2 Vols, London 1848
Bruce, James, *Travels to Discover the Sources of the Nile*. 1768–73, 5 Vols, London 1790
Bulwer, H. L., *The Life of Palmerston*, 3 Vols, London 1870–74
Capper, James, *Observations on the Passage to India Across the Great Desert*, London 1794

Charles-Roux, F., *L'Angleterre, l'Isthme de Suez et l'Egypte au dix-huitième Siècle*, Paris 1922
       „   *Les Origines de l'Expédition de l'Egypte*, Paris 1910
       „   *Bonaparte, Gouverneur d'Egypte*, Paris 1910
       „   *Thiers et Mehemet Ali*, Paris 1951.
de Cadalvène & Barrault, E., *Deux Années de l'Histoire d'Orient* 1839–40, 2 Vols, Paris 1840
de Guichen, Vicomte, *Le Crise d'Orient de 1839 à 1841*, Paris 1908
Djarbarti, Abdurrahman, *Merveilles Biographiques et Historiques* (tr) 9 Vols, Cairo 1852
Dodwell, H. H., *The Founder of Modern Egypt*, Cambridge 1931
Douin, G. *La Flotte de Bonaparte sur les Côtes d'Egypte*, Cairo 1922
       „   *La Campagne de Bruix en Mediterranée*, Cairo 1923
       „   *L'Egypte de 1802 à 1804*, Cairo 1925
       „   *Les Premières Frégates de Mohamed Ali*, Cairo 1926
       „   *Navarin*, Cairo 1927
       „   *L'Egypte de 1828 à 1830. Correspondance des Consuls Français en Egypte*, Cairo 1935
       „   *La Mission du Baron de Boislecomte*, Cairo 1927
       „   *La Première Guerre en Syrie*, 2 Vols, Cairo 1931
       „   *Mohamed Ali et l'Expédition d'Alger*, Cairo 1930
       „   (with Mrs Fawtier-Jones) *La Politique Mameluke* 1801–03, Cairo 1929
       „   „   *L'Angleterre et l'Egypte* 1804–1807, Cairo 1930
       „   „   *L'Angleterre et l'Egypte. Le Campagne de 1807*, Cairo 1928
Driault, E., *Mehemet Ali et Napoleon* 1807–1814, Cairo 1925
       „   *L'Egypte et l'Europe: La Crise de 1839–41*, 3 Vols, Cairo 1930–31
       „   & Leheritier, M., *Histoire Diplomatique de la Grèce, Vol I, L'Insurrection et l'Independence* (1821–1830), Paris 1925
Elgood, P. G., *Bonaparte's Adventure in Egypt*, London 1936
Fullarton, W., *A View of the British Interests in India*, London 1788
Ghorbal, Shafiq, *The Beginnings of the Egyptian Question and the Rise of Mohamed Ali*, London 1928
Herold, J. C., *Bonaparte in Egypt*, London 1963
Hoskins, H. L., *British Routes to India*, London 1928
Hurewitz, J. C., *Diplomacy in the Near and Middle East. A Documentary Record, Vol I*, 1553–1914, Princeton 1956
Irwin, Eyles, *A Series of Adventures in the Course of a Voyage up the Red Sea on the Coasts of Arabia and Egypt and of a Route through the Deserts of the Thebaid hitherto Unknown to the European Traveller in the Year 1777*, London 1780
Lane-Poole, S., *The Life of R. H. Stratford Canning*, 2 Vols, London 1888
Mackesy, P., *The War in the Mediterranean, 1803–1810*, London 1957
Mahan, A. T., *The Influence of Sea Power during the Wars of the French Revolution*, 2 Vols, Boston 1892
Masson, Paul, *Histoire du Commerce Français dans le Levant au Dix-Huitième Siècle*, Paris 1911
Mengin, F., *L'Egypte sous Mohamed Ali*, 2 Vols, Paris 1823
Morier, J. P., *Memoir of a Campaign with the Ottoman Army in Egypt*, London 1801
Mouriez, P., *Histoire de Mehemet Ali*, 3 Vols, Paris 1858
Muskau, Prinz Puckler, *Egypt under Mohamed Ali* (tr.), 2 Vols, London 1845
Napier, Charles, *The War in Syria*, 2 Vols, London 1842
Paton, A. A., *History of the Egyptian Revolution*, 2 Vols, London 1863
Planat, Jules, *Histoire de la Régénération de l'Egypte*, Paris 1830
Rooke, Henry, *Travels to the Coast of Arabia Felix and further by the Red Sea and Egypt to Europe*, London 1794
Russell of Liverpool, Lord, *Knight of the Sword* (Life of Sir Sidney Smith), London 1965
Sabry, M., *L'Empire Egyptien sous Mohamed Ali et la Question de l'Orient*, 1811–1849, Paris 1930
Savary, M., *Lettres sur l'Egypte*, 3 Vols, Paris 1787
Shaw, S. J., *Organisation and Development of Ottoman Egypt*, 1517–1798, Princeton 1962

Stapledon, A. G., *The Political Life of the Rt. Hon. George Canning from* 1822 *to* 1831, London 1931

Taylor, J., *Considerations on the Practicability of a New Speedy Communication between Great Britain and India*, London 1788

Temperley, H. W. V., *England and the Near East*, London 1936

Thenedat-Duvent, M., *L'Egypte sous Mehemet Ali*, Paris 1821

Volney, M. C–F., *Voyage en Syrie et en Egypte pendant les Années* 1783, 1784 *et* 1785, 2 Vols, Paris 1787

Walsh, T., *Journal of the Late Campaign in Egypt*, London 1803

Warner, Oliver, *The Battle of the Nile*, London 1960

Webster, Sir Charles, *The Foreign Policy of Lord Palmerston*, 1830–1841, London 1951

Wilson, Sir R., *History of the British Expedition to Egypt*, London 1803

Yates, W. H., *The Modern History and Condition of Egypt*, 2 Vols, London 1843

VIII MISCELLANEOUS PUBLISHED PAPERS

F. S. Rodkey, 'The Efforts of Briggs & Co to Guide British Policy in the Levant, 1821–1841', *Journal of Modern History*, Vol V (1933), p. 324 et seq.

Abdul Hamid el-Batrik, 'Egyptian-Yemeni Relations 1819–1840 and their Implications for British Policy in the Red Sea', *Political and Social Change in Modern Egypt* (ed. P. M. Holt), p. 281, London 1968

INDEX

MAR   2 198